I0127389

A FIELD GUIDE TO CROSS-CULTURAL RESEARCH ON CHILDHOOD LEARNING

A Field Guide to Cross-Cultural Research on Childhood Learning

Theoretical, methodological, practical, and ethical considerations for an interdisciplinary field

Edited by Sheina Lew-Levy and Stephen Asatsa

OpenBook Publishers

https://www.openbookpublishers.com

©2025 Sheina Lew-Levy and Stephen Asatsa (eds)
Copyright of individual chapters is maintained by the chapter's authors

This work is licensed under a Creative Commons Attribution-NonCommercial 4.0 International (CC BY-NC 4.0). This license allows you to share, copy, distribute and transmit the text; to adapt the text for non-commercial purposes of the text providing attribution is made to the author (but not in any way that suggests that they endorse you or your use of the work). Attribution should include the following information:

Sheina Lew-Levy and Stephen Asatsa (eds), *A Field Guide to Cross-Cultural Research on Childhood Learning: Theoretical, Methodological, Practical, and Ethical Considerations for an Interdisciplinary Field*. Cambridge, UK: Open Book Publishers, 2025, https://doi.org/10.11647/OBP.0440

Copyright and permissions for the reuse of the images included in this publication may differ from the above. This information is provided in the captions and in the list of illustrations.

Further details about the CC BY-NC license are available at http://creativecommons.org/licenses/by-nc/4.0/

All external links were active at the time of publication unless otherwise stated and have been archived via the Internet Archive Wayback Machine at https://archive.org/web

Any digital material and resources associated with this volume will be available at https://doi.org/10.11647/OBP.0440#resources

Information about any revised edition of this work will be provided at https://doi.org/10.11647/OBP.0440

ISBN Paperback: 978-1-80511-466-6
ISBN Hardback: 978-1-80511-467-3
ISBN Digital (PDF): 978-1-80511-468-0
ISBN Digital ebook (EPUB): 978-1-80511-469-7
ISBN HTML: 978-1-80511-470-3

DOI: 10.11647/OBP.0440

Cover image: Children playing in front of their home in Kafr Elsheikh, Egypt (2016). Photo by Mona Abo-Abda, https://commons.wikimedia.org/wiki/File:ART_and_KIDS.jpg. Cover design: Jeevanjot Kaur Nagpal

This book is dedicated to Prof. Seth Oppong

Prof Seth Oppong passed on 17th February 2024 at the age of 41 years. In his life as an academic, he had published 79 articles, most of them in high-impact journals, with 896 citations and an h-index of 16 on Google Scholar as of 5 May 2024. He was promoted to full Professor of Work and Cultural Psychology in January 2023. Some of his publications have been used as resources for teaching at other institutions such as the US Institute of Shipboard Education and the University of Botswana, as may be the case with the contributions he wrote for this book.

Seth transcended the confines of academia, as he was a beacon of wisdom and invaluable advice. He was grounded and had emotional intelligence beyond his age, was a mentor, and a visionary. In addition to his unparalleled dedication to his work, he went the extra mile to ensure that everyone who knew him reached their fullest potential (including me), instilling a love for learning. This man had a rare gift for making everyone feel seen and heard and fostering a sense of belonging. While we mourn his untimely departure, let us also celebrate the legacy that he leaves behind and find solace in the memories we shared, the lessons we learned, and the profound impact he had on everyone; his spirit will live on in the countless lives he has touched and the myriad of minds he has shaped. As a testament to the incredible person he was and the numerous lives he enriched, we bid him farewell. RIP, dear Prof Seth Oppong. You will be dearly missed, but never forgotten. Thank you for being part of our lives.

Prof Magen Mutepfa
University of Botswana

Contents

List of contributors

Adam Boyette is a Senior Researcher at the Max Planck Institute for Evolutionary Anthropology, Leipzig, Germany, and leader of the Culture, Cooperation and Child Development research group. He is trained as an evolutionary cultural anthropologist with a specialization in cultural learning, cultural evolution, and the anthropology of childhood. He is particularly interested in the ways that people cooperate in caring for and educating children and the role of culture in shaping norms of cooperation and conceptions of children's development. He has worked with Congo Basin peoples since 2008.

Adi Prasetijo is an adjunct lecturer in the Department of Anthropology, Faculty of Cultural Sciences, Diponegoro University, Indonesia. He is also a member of KKI Warsi, an NGO working for Sumatra Indigenous communities. He received a doctorate in anthropology from the University of Science Malaysia (2014). In 2019, he was a visiting research fellow at Minpaku (National Museum of Ethnology, Japan) in Osaka. He is also a member of the International Societies of Hunting and Gathering (ISHGR).

Akira Takada is Professor in the Graduate School of Asian and African Area Studies at Kyoto University, Japan. He has worked with/among groups of the San of southern Africa (particularly !Xun and ǂAkhoe in Namibia, G|ui and Gǁana in Botswana) since the late 1990s. He has published a number of books and articles, including Hunters Among Farmers: The !Xun of Ekoka (2022), and The Ecology of Playful Childhood: The Diversity and Resilience of Caregiver-Child Interactions among the San of Southern Africa (2020).

Alejandrina Cristia is Research Director at Laboratoire de Sciences Cognitives et Psycholinguistique, Département d'études cognitives, École Normale Supérieure, École des Hautes Études en Sciences Sociales, Centre National de la Recherche Scientifique, PSL University, France. Alejandrina Cristia's long-term aim is to shed light on child language development, both descriptively and mechanistically. To this end, her team draws methods and insights from linguistics, psychology, anthropology, economics, and speech technology. With an interest in cumulative, collaborative, and transparent science, she co-founded the first meta-meta-analysis platform (metalab.stanford.edu) and several international networks, including DAylong Recordings of Children's Language Environment (darcle.org), and the Consortium on Language Variation in Input Environments around the World (LangVIEW), which aims to increase participant and researcher diversity in language development studies.

Alyssa Crittenden is Professor of Anthropology and Human Biology at the University of Nevada, Las Vegas, US. Her work contributes to the broader understanding of the evolution of human life history by exploring the intersection of nutrition, social behavior, reproduction, and child rearing. Her cross-cultural research, particularly with Hadza hunter-gatherers of Tanzania, examines how children acquire knowledge and skill through foraging practices and social learning. She is also the co-founder and co-director of a mutual aid organization, Olanakwe Community Fund, that supports the educational sovereignty of children in the Hadza community.

Ana Maria Gomes is Titular Professor at the Faculty of Education, Federal University of Minas Gerais, Brazil. She holds a PhD in Education from the University of Bologna, Italy (1996). She was a postdoctoral researcher in Social Anthropology at the Museu Nacional-UFRJ, Brazil (2008), and in the Department of Anthropology at the University of St. Andrews, UK (2017). She has carried out field research with children in Brazilian metropolises and Italian Roma children. Since 2000, she has been working with Indigenous Peoples in different Brazilian States as a CNPq (National Research

Council) researcher in the field of Anthropology and Education, mainly on the topics of Indigenous intercultural education, culture and schooling, learning and culture, cosmopolitics, and ecology of practices.

Andrea Taverna holds a PhD in psychology and works as a researcher at the Instituto Rosario de Investigaciones en Ciencias de la Educación (IRICE), Consejo Nacional de Investigaciones Científicas y Técnicas (CONICET), Universidad Nacional de Rosario (UNR), Argentina. Her current interest is the study of the acquisition of Wichi, an Indigenous language spoken in northern Argentina, as a mother tongue. She is currently describing the early grammaticalization process of complex morphology and the socialization context in which this ancestral language emerges. She is a group leader and since 2010 she and her students have been conducting fieldwork in the Wichi communities in collaboration with Indigenous teachers and community leaders.

Andrew D. Coppens is Associate Professor in the Department of Education, University of New Hampshire, US. Andrew Coppens' research focuses on cultural processes of informal learning and development in family and community contexts. He has conducted research on young children's development of collaborative helping with rural, middle-class, and Indigenous-heritage communities in the US, Mexico, Ecuador, Germany, India, and Bhutan. Coppens is founding PI of the Youth Retention Initiative, a research collaborative focused on developing sustainable and strengths-based educational and workforce pathways to address human capital extraction patterns among rural communities.

Annemieke Milks is a Paleolithic archaeologist, and currently holds a British Academy Postdoctoral Fellowship at the University of Reading, UK. Her work explores the intersection between material culture, skill, and learning. She specializes in weaponry, early wooden artefacts, and Pleistocene childhoods. Annemieke's work is interdisciplinary, exploring the archaeological record through macro- and micro-imaging of artefacts, morphometrics, experimental archaeology, and ethnography.

April Nowell is a Paleolithic archaeologist and Professor of Anthropology at the University of Victoria, Canada. She specializes in the origins of art, language and modern cognition, Neanderthal lifeways, and the lives of children and adolescents in the Pleistocene. She is the author of *Growing Up in the Ice Age*, winner of the 2023 European Association of Archaeologists book prize.

Ardain Dzabatou holds a Bachelor's Degree in Psychology at Marien Ngouabi University Brazzaville, Republic of the Congo. Since 2018, he has also worked as a research assistant, supporting studies on child development among BaYaka foragers and Bandongo fisher-farmers.

Athul Sarala Nanu is an Indigenous independent research scholar, filmmaker, and designer. His research focuses on the politics of representation, decolonizing education, and the impact of design on marginalized communities. Through his work, he aims to challenge dominant narratives, empower Indigenous voices, and contribute to social change. His experiences as a filmmaker and designer have informed his understanding of the power of visual culture and the potential of design as a tool for social transformation.

Barnabas Simatende is Lecturer at St. Joseph's Theological Institute, KwaZulu-Natal, South Africa. Barnabas Simatende holds a PhD in Psychology and is a dedicated and passionate educator, researcher, and leader with expertise in psychological and theological education, and community development. With 15 years of experience in academic institutions and faith-based organizations, Barnabas has developed a strong commitment to empowering marginalized communities. Through his work, Barnabas strives to foster inclusive and transformative learning environments, inspiring positive change and growth in individuals and communities.

Barry Hewlett is Professor of Anthropology at Washington State University, US. He has conducted research with children in Central and Eastern Africa since 1973. He is the author of eight books and over 100 journal articles and book chapters.

Blanca Guerrero-Meyer is Associate Professor of Psychology, Fresno Pacific University, US, where she teaches cultural psychology and other subjects related to intercultural studies. She graduated from Harvard Graduate School of Education, with a doctorate in Human Development and Psychology. Her research has focused primarily on Latinx immigrant families in the US. She has also worked with the migrant population in the US and early bilingual language and literacy acquisition in Spanish-speaking families. Presently she is doing research on Hispanic Serving Institutions and first-generation college students.

Bonnie Hewlett is Associate Professor in the Department of Anthropology, Washington State University, US. She has conducted research in Gabon and the Republic of Congo on infectious diseases, in the Central African Republic on women's history and adolescent development, and more recently, in Ethiopia on the health and experiences of Ethiopian orphans, and birth mothers/ fathers' reasons for relinquishment and abandonment.

Bruce Rawlings is a developmental, cross-cultural and comparative psychologist, based at Durham University, UK. He holds a PhD in Evolutionary Anthropology from the same university. His work examines cognitive and cultural influences on innovation, creativity, and tool use in children and great apes. He focuses on children across geographically and culturally diverse populations to understand what makes humans so unique. He also works to improve the validity of cross-cultural experiments.

Bruno Ferreira holds a Bachelor's degree in History, Full Teaching License from the Regional University of the Northwest of the State of Rio Grande do Sul, Brazil (1999), a Master's degree in Education from the Federal University of Rio Grande do Sul (UFRGS) (2014), and a PhD in Education from the Faculty of Education at the same university (2020). He is an Associate Professor at the Faculty of Education, UFRGS, and a researcher in the Peabiru Research Group: Amerindian Education and Interculturality (CNPq/UFRGS). His research focuses on Indigenous Methodologies, Indigenous intellectuals, Indigenous school education, and intercultural education.

Camila Scaff earned her PhD in Cognitive Sciences from the École Normale Supérieure–Paris Diderot University (now Université Paris Cité), France. She holds split-time postdoctoral research fellowships with the Human Ecology Group at the University of Zurich's Institute of Evolutionary Medicine and the Language Acquisition Across Cultures group at the École Normale Supérieure's Laboratoire de Sciences Cognitives et Psycholinguistiques (LSCP) in Paris. Her research explores how socio-ecological environments shape human cognitive and linguistic variation.

Carrie Rothstein-Fisch is a Professor of Educational Psychology at California State University, Northridge, US (PhD, UCLA) and is the co-coordinator of the Master of Arts in Early Childhood Educational Psychology. She teaches courses on Issues and Theories in Early Childhood Education and Research Principles in addition to supervising MA and EdD students. She has researched and written on topics ranging from toddler play through adult learning and is a core researcher on the Bridging Cultures Project.

Chantal Medaets is Associate Professor of Anthropology at the School of Education at the State University of Campinas (Unicamp), Brazil, where she coordinates the Anthropology and Education Research Center (Ceape). She holds a Master's degree in Education (2009) and a PhD in Social Anthropology (2015) both from Paris Descartes University (since 2022, Paris Cité University). She has carried out research on Indigenous and river dweller childhoods and forms of socialization in the Lower Tapajós region in the Brazilian Amazon, analyzing parenting styles, informal education (out of school transmission and learning practices) and its connections to the school. In her current research project, she deals with different aspects of the Indigenous presence in Higher Education in Brazil, combining ethnographic fieldwork at Unicamp with the analysis of intercultural educational politics for Higher Education at a national level.

Cika Aprilia is a graduate in Social Anthropology from Diponegoro University, Indonesia, and is currently pursuing her postgraduate studies at the University of Indonesia. She has experience as an instructional facilitator in high schools and serves as the Head of Program Officer at Indonesia Resilience, a research institute dedicated to empowering marginalized communities. Additionally, Cika is actively involved in developing alternative education programs for street children, emphasizing inclusivity and empowerment.

Claire Hodson is a lecturer in Human Bioarchaeology in the Department of Archaeology at Durham University, UK. Claire's research focuses on early life health and wellbeing, as well as evidence of growth disruption, considering the interaction and implications of both intrinsic and extrinsic factors on fetal and infant development. Claire is currently working to develop new methods for the recording and identification of pathology in fetal-infant individuals and the use of imaging technology to enhance this understanding.

David Lancy is Emeritus Professor of Anthropology at Utah State University, US. He has conducted extensive cross-cultural fieldwork with children in interior Liberia, multiple sites in Papua New Guinea, Trinidad, Madagascar, Uganda, and Yemen, among others. More specifically, David Lancy has contributed to a better understanding of childhood-related topics including delayed personhood, the chore curriculum, children as a reserve labor force, children growing up in a gerontocracy, how children acquire their culture, socio-historical analyses of schooling, and the culture of street kids. He has written a survey of the field—recently published in a third edition—*The Anthropology of Childhood: Cherubs, Chattel, Changelings.* In total, David Lancy has authored nine books and edited three. His most recent work is *Learning Without Lessons: Pedagogy in Indigenous Communities.*

Dorsa Amir received her PhD in Anthropology from Yale University, US. She is currently an Assistant Professor of Psychology and Neuroscience at Duke University and the Director of the Mind & Culture Lab. Dorsa's work focuses on cognitive development across diverse cultures, with a particular focus on judgement and decision-making.

Dustin Eirdosh is a postdoctoral researcher at the Department of Comparative and Cultural Psychology, Max Planck Institute for Evolutionary Anthropology, Germany. He is a co-founder of the OpenEvo educational innovation lab, studying the role of concepts of human behavior as an interdisciplinary theme across K-12 curricula. By understanding human origins, and the complex causes of human behaviors, students can be empowered with metacognitive competencies for advancing a more sustainable and equitable society.

Elena Miu is an evolutionary biologist and anthropologist who uses empirical and theoretical modelling approaches to understand the population-level processes that underlie cultural adaptation, cultural change, and innovation. She is currently a postdoctoral researcher in the Department of Archaeology and Heritage Studies at Aarhus University, working on the effect of children's play and exploration on innovation.

Elise Trumbull is an applied linguist (Ed.D., Boston University, US), who specializes in understanding relationships among language, culture, and schooling. Collaborating with colleagues from multiple disciplines, she has investigated how cultural theory and research can help teachers of Mexican immigrant students in the US teach in a more inclusive and effective way. She has also investigated how educational assessments can be improved to be culturally relevant with students from many ethnolinguistic backgrounds, including American Indian and Alaska Native students, Haitian immigrants, Micronesian students in US-affiliated entities, and immigrant Latino students in California.

Felix Riede is Professor of Archaeology in the Department of Archaeology and Heritage Studies, Aarhus University, Denmark. He works in a broad and inclusive cultural evolutionary framework. Focused on understanding the interactions between social learning, niche construction, and environmental change, he explores the role of children in human cognitive evolution, and the role of object play as a motor for material culture variation, innovation, and adaptation.

Feryl Badiani is a final year PhD candidate at Victoria University of Wellington, New Zealand, and is also affiliated with the Centre for Culture and Evolution at Brunel University of London, UK. Her thesis explores Hinduism and the cultural evolutionary explanations as to why it is a popular polytheistic religion. She focuses on two Indo-linguistic communities: Gujarats and Maharashtrians, as a member of both those communities. Her work looks at expanding theories within cognitive science of religion so that they take into account non-western realities.

Gairan Pamei is a final year PhD candidate in the Department of Psychology, the Chinese University of Hong Kong, researching literacies across educational-linguistic contexts. Her work is informed by developmental science of child learning and methodological advances in psychometrics.

Heejung Park is a cultural and developmental psychologist in the Department of Psychology, Scripps College, US. She studies cultural values, identities, and the lived experiences of children, youth, and families across diverse socio-cultural settings and historical periods. She is particularly interested in identifying the challenges and strengths associated with adaptation experiences following social change and migration in an increasingly interconnected world.

Heidi Keller, Professor Emeritus of Human Sciences at University of Osnabrück, Germany, is currently a Distinguished Fellow of the Paul Baerwald School of Social Work and Social Welfare at the Hebrew University, Jerusalem. Besides cross-cultural development research on early child development, she is interested in the scientific and ethical problems of applying basic research to different fields of practice.

Helen Elizabeth Davis is Assistant Professor at the Institute of Human Origins and the School of Human Evolution and Social Change, Arizona State University. She studies cognition and learning across the lifespan. She is the co-director of the Ecology of Mind Project, which operates in Southern Africa, and she is the co-founder and Vice-President of the non-profit One Pencil Project.

Ilaria Pretelli is an evolutionary biologist and anthropologist based at the Institute for Advanced Study in Toulouse, Toulouse School of Economics & University of Toulouse Capitole, France. She is interested in the evolution of human life history, with a focus on the emergence of childhood, learning, and cooperative breeding. She carried out her doctoral studies at the Max Planck Institute for Evolutionary Anthropology in Leipzig, Germany. She has done fieldwork on the island of Pemba, Zanzibar. Her research combines cross-cultural, statistical, and observational methods to study the evolution of human behavior.

Ivan Kroupin is a postdoctoral researcher in the Department of Psychological and Behavioural Science, London School of Economics and Political Science, UK, and the Department of Human Evolutionary Biology, Harvard University, US. As co-director of the Ecology of Mind project (Kunene region—Namibia/Angola), Ivan focuses on how urbanization and technology are reshaping our minds and wellbeing—and the evolutionary dynamics driving this transformation. This perspective informs and is informed by an interdisciplinary theoretical framework, integrating ideas and data from developmental biology, systems theory, cultural evolution, and cognitive science.

Jing Xu is a Research Scientist at the Department of Anthropology, University of Washington, US. She is a cultural and cognitive anthropologist studying how culture and mind interact to shape child development in diverse geographic regions, historical periods and cross-cultural comparative contexts. She pursues interdisciplinary research, bringing together ethnography, experimental techniques, computational methods, and humanistic perspectives to study how humans become moral persons. She is the author of two monographs: *The Good Child: Moral Development in a Chinese Preschool* (2017) and *"Unruly" Children: Historical Fieldnotes and Learning Morality in a Taiwan Village* (2024).

Joscha Kärtner received his PhD from the Department of Culture and Development at the University of Osnabrück, Germany, and is head of the Developmental Psychology Lab and the Center for Learning, Development and Counseling at the University of Münster, Germany. From a dynamic developmental systems perspective, his main research interests include cultural influences on early social, socio-cognitive and socio-emotional development. Besides basic research in these fields, a second emphasis is on developing culturally informed programs and policies for applied developmental science.

Kara Weisman is the Postdoctoral Project Director of the Developing Belief Network, Department of Psychology, University of California, Riverside, US. She is a cognitive scientist and developmental psychologist with roots in psychology, anthropology, and philosophy. She received her PhD in psychology from Stanford University in 2019, followed by postdoctoral roles on two large-scale, international collaborations in cultural anthropology and developmental science. Her work focuses on folk theories and their role in shaping people's behaviors, relationships, and experiences.

Katja Liebal is the head of the Human Biology and Primate Cognition group at the Faculty of Life Sciences, Institute of Biology, Leipzig University, Germany. She is a comparative psychologist with a background in behavioral biology. She is interested in the development and cross-cultural variability of children's attitudes toward other animals. She cooperates with local collaborators from a variety of communities and uses a mixed-method approach, combining qualitative and quantitative methods from anthropology and psychology, to study human-animal relationships across a range of socio-cultural contexts. She has conducted fieldwork in Namibia, Zambia and Indonesia (including research with nonhuman primates).

Maria Julia Hermida holds a PhD in Psychology, and is Adjunct Professor, at the Universidad Nacional de Hurlingham, and assistant researcher at CONICET, Argentina. She is also an invited professor at ENS-Paris and various Latin American Universities. In 2022 she became an IBRO-IBE/UNESCO Science of Learning Fellow. Her research applies insights and techniques from cognitive science to reduce educational, health, and social inequalities through interventions with children.

Marie Schäfer is a Researcher in Developmental Psychology at Leipzig University, Germany, with a background in cognitive science and anthropology. She completed her PhD and conducted postdoctoral research at the Max Planck Institute for Evolutionary Anthropology. Her research focuses on the psychological foundations and development of the human capacity to cooperate and share resources and knowledge based on social norms. She has conducted fieldwork in different communities in the Central African Republic, Kenya, and Namibia.

Mark Nielsen is a Professor of Developmental Psychology at the University of Queensland, Australia, and a Senior Research Associate at the University of Johannesburg. His research interests lie in a range of inter-related aspects of socio-cognitive development in young human children and non-human primates. His current research is primarily focused on charting the origins and development of human cultural cognition.

Michael Gurven is a Distinguished Professor of Anthropology at The University of California, Santa Barbara, US, where he is Associate Chair of Integrative Anthropological Sciences, and Associate Director of the Broom Demography Center. He is a founder and co-Director of the Tsimane Health and Life History Project, a longitudinal study focused on how aspects of environment and lifestyle affect health and lifespan in subsistence-oriented populations of the Bolivian Amazon. His work addresses how acculturation and market integration impact social behavior and chronic disease risk (including heart disease, diabetes, dementia, depression) among Indigenous populations.

Michelle Kline is a Senior Lecturer of Psychology at Brunel University of London, UK. Her work focuses on social learning, including the evolution of teaching, how people learn to be parents, and the learning and creation of present-day spiritual beliefs. Her fieldwork has included research in the Yasawa Islands, Fiji and in the town of Glastonbury, England.

Miguel Silan is the co-founder and Chief Behavioral Strategist in the Annecy Behavioral Science Lab, France. His work involves evaluating how behavioral science methods work and fail, and how to improve them, especially for vulnerable populations. He is also an Associate Director for the Psychological Science Accelerator, a network of more than 2,000 researchers across 84 countries, and is helping advance new ways of conducting large-scale collaborations in psychology.

Monika Abels is Associate Professor of Child Development at UiT The Arctic University of Norway. As a cross-cultural developmental psychologist, she has extensive fieldwork experience in India, mainly in rural areas in North India and more recently with the Hadza in Tanzania. Her research focuses on infants' and children's everyday experiences and socio-emotional development, as well as their caregivers' behaviors and beliefs. Her approach is eco-cultural and her methods frequently include observations and interviews.

Nachita Rosun is a postdoctoral researcher in Psychology at Oxford Brookes University, UK, and an honorary research fellow at the Centre for Culture and Evolution at Brunel University of London. Nachita is interested in processes of cultural shift through changing social norms and religious beliefs. Her research uses theories from cultural evolution and norm psychology to explain how these changes are interlinked with socioecology and cultural transmission mechanisms.

Natália Dutra is Associate Professor at Federal University of Pará, Brazil, in the Behavior Theory and Research Centre. She holds a PhD in Developmental Psychology from Durham University, UK, and an MSc in Psychobiology from the Federal University of Rio Grande do Norte, Brazil. Her research currently focuses on the psychological mechanisms underlying human social learning and cooperation. Natália is also interested in open science and diversity in science.

Nicole Wen is Lecturer in Psychology at Brunel University of London, UK, in the Centre for Culture and Evolution, and Director of the Culture and Minds Lab. Nicole received her PhD in Developmental Psychology from the University of Texas at Austin, and was a postdoctoral researcher in the Department of Psychology at the University of Michigan. Nicole studies the ontogeny of social learning strategies and cooperative behaviors within and across cultures, with a focus on the development of rituals.

Noa Lavi is a social anthropologist working on childhood, education and adult-child relations among Indigenous and marginalized societies. Her other research interests include the anthropology of aid and development, human-animal relations, storytelling, social-emotional learning, and perceptions of child rearing. Noa holds a PhD in Social Anthropology from the University of Haifa (2019). She is also a Forest School Leader and has worked in Outdoor Education for many years. She is currently an adjunct Lecturer in the Department of Counseling and Human Development, Faculty of Education, University of Haifa.

Nokwanda (Kwanda) Ndlovu is a doctoral candidate in Counseling Psychology at Purdue University and she is from Durban, South Africa. Her passion lies in decolonized community work where she collaborates with community-based organizations particularly in South Africa, and leverages community assets and strengths to address issues faced by vulnerable children and families. Through that lens, Kwanda's past research has looked into Indigenous parenting values, traditions, and mores within the context of South Africa. Most recently, Kwanda has been studying systems of healing as conceptualized by traditional healers within the South African context.

Patricia Kanngiesser is Associate Professor of Psychology at the University of Plymouth. She studies social norms, cooperation and cultural learning from a developmental and cross-cultural perspective. She has conducted fieldwork in Argentina, Bolivia, India, Kenya, and Namibia. She has a multidisciplinary background in natural and social sciences, holds a PhD in psychology from the University of Bristol, and was a visiting researcher at Harvard and Kyoto University, a postdoctoral researcher at the Max Planck Institute for Evolutionary Anthropology, and a research group leader at Freie Universität Berlin.

Patricia Greenfield is Distinguished Professor of Psychology, University of California, Los Angeles, US. She earned her PhD from the interdisciplinary Department of Social Relations at Harvard. Her dissertation focused on a cross-cultural study of culture and cognitive development in Senegal. Collaborating with international researchers, she has published cross-cultural and intergenerational studies on learning, socialization, and human development in Maya communities, Mexico; among Bedouin, Northern Arab, and Ethiopian immigrant populations in Israel; and within dominant majority groups in Burma/Myanmar, Romania, Japan, China, and Turkey. In the United States, she and her collaborators have conducted research on these topics among European Americans, Asian Americans, and immigrant groups from Mexico, Central America, and Korea.

Roman Stengelin completed his PhD in Psychology at Leipzig University, Germany, in 2020, followed by postdoctoral research at the Max Planck Institute for Evolutionary Anthropology, where he now works as a senior scientist. His research focuses on the development of childhood social cognition and learning, with an emphasis on (cross-)cultural perspectives. He has conducted fieldwork among Namibian San communities, including the Khwe and Hai||om.

Sarah Pope-Caldwell is Assistant Professor in the Department of Psychology, Georgia State University, USA. Sarah's research focuses on cognitive flexibility, problem-solving, and decision-making, with a strong emphasis on how these processes are shaped by cultural environments and experiences across the lifespan. She explores these areas through a cross-cultural lens, incorporating research from communities around the world, including the United States, Namibia, Germany, and the Republic of the Congo. Additionally, Sarah studies nonhuman primates like baboons, chimpanzees, rhesus macaques, and capuchin monkeys to understand the evolution of flexible problem-solving.

Seetha Kakkoth completed her PhD in Anthropology at the University of Calicut, Kerala, India, followed by postdoctoral research at London School of Economics, UK. She currently works at Kannur University. Since the 1990s, she has been working with Cholanaickan and Aranadan, historically classified as hunter-gatherers living in the Nilambur Forests of Kerala, South India. She recently published *Lost Lullabies of South India: Tale of Vanishing Indigenous People of Nilambur Valley*. Her research interests include hunter-gatherers, tribal aging, and hunter-gatherer education.

Seth Oppong was Professor of Work and Cultural Psychology at the University of Botswana. During his prolific career, he focused on diverse research areas, including occupational health psychology, traffic psychology, psychological testing, the history of psychology, theoretical and philosophical psychology, meta-science with respect to psychological science, Indigenous and African psychology, and decolonizing early childhood development programming.

Sheina Lew-Levy is Associate Professor of Psychology at Durham University, UK. She holds a PhD in Psychology from the University of Cambridge (2019). Drawing from anthropological and psychological theory, she conducts research in hunter-gatherer societies to understand the cultural diversity in, and evolution of, social learning in childhood. As the co-founder and Co-Director of Forager Child Studies, she also conducts cross-cultural reviews and secondary data analysis on the pasts, presents, and futures of hunter-gatherer children's learning.

Srujana Duggirala is a doctoral student at Simon Fraser University, Canada, working with Tanya MacGillivray in the Culture and Development lab. Srujana graduated from Osmania University, Hyderabad, India, with a Master of Philosophy in Psychology and a Master of Arts. Her research centers around parenting across diverse cultural contexts as well as prosocial development and reasoning in children.

Stephen Asatsa holds a PhD in Counselling Psychology and is Senior Lecturer at the Catholic University of Eastern Africa, Kenya. He researches Indigenous knowledge systems with a focus on decolonization of theory, research, and practice. He has published on traditional mourning rituals, traditional marriage rites, traditional circumcision curriculum and use of taboos in behavior regulation. He contributes to multidisciplinary research collaboration networks globally, specifically on personality psychology, cultural evolution, child development, and trauma and death literacy.

Susan Hanisch is an education researcher at the Research Group for Biology Education, Friedrich Schiller University Jena, Germany, focusing on the role of evolutionary and behavioral science in Education for Sustainable Development and for the metacognitive development of student competencies. She develops and researches novel teaching approaches to help learners gain a deeper and more helpful understanding of themselves and fellow humans.

Tanya MacGillivray is Professor of Psychology at Simon Fraser University, Canada. She is the director of the Culture and Development lab and serves on the Board of Directors for the Child and Family Blog, Inc. which communicates science beyond academia. Tanya's research is in the field of cross-cultural developmental psychology with a focus on small-scale and Indigenous societies. She aims to better understand the first few years of life from a global perspective, examining children and families living in diverse ways to determine which features of the early environment foster healthy development. She has been doing field research in culturally diverse regions of the world since 2001. Her work is currently centered on Tanna, Vanuatu as well as urban/rural communities within Canada.

Tatjana Puschkarsky has worked with hunter-gatherer and other Indigenous communities in Africa and Latin America for more than ten years. In 2015, she co-founded OrigiNations (www.originations.org), an NGO offering social spaces for Indigenous youth to strengthen their own capacities, determine their own priorities, and develop strategies to support their communities. These often include initiatives to safeguard their cultural and natural heritage, promote intergenerational knowledge transmission, and design alternative education models adapted to their own culture.

Vidrige Kandza is a conservation biologist and a native Lingala speaker with extensive experience collecting a wide variety of data from populations living in the Congo Basin tropical forest. His PhD focuses on the dynamics of inter-ethnic cooperation at the Department of Human Behavior, Ecology and Culture at the Max Planck Institute for Evolutionary Anthropology, Germany. His research seeks to understand why BaYaka forest foragers in the Republic of the Congo choose to practice shotgun hunting for hire despite apparently highly asymmetrical benefits accrued by neighboring farming groups (BaYambe) who have exclusive ownership over shotguns and bullets.

Vinod Chellan is currently pursuing his PhD in Economics at Cochin University of Science and Technology (CUSAT), Kerala, India. He holds an MPhil in Applied Economics from the Department of Applied Economics, CUSAT. He was awarded the National Fellowship for Scheduled Tribes from the Ministry of Tribal Affairs, New Delhi in 2020. He actively engages with issues related to the hunter-gatherer communities in Kerala. He has presented his works at the International Workshop on 'Contemporary hunter-gatherers and education in a changing world: towards sustainable futures' at Arctic University, Tromsø, Norway (2023), and at the Cultural Evolution Society conference at Durham University (2024). His research interests include hunter-gatherer livelihood and hunter-gatherer education.

Xiaojie Tian holds a PhD in Area Studies and is currently Associate Professor at the Institute of Health and Sport Sciences at University of Tsukuba, Japan. She has conducted anthropological research on pastoralist Maasai communities in Southern Kenya over the past decade. She integrates research methods from different disciplines focusing on ethnobiological knowledge, child learning and development, childhood play and work, and physical culture.

Her recent publication includes *Maasai Childhood: The Rhythm of Learning in Daily Work and Play Routines.*

Yitong Wang is a doctoral student in the developmental psychology program at Simon Fraser University, Canada. Her research focuses on cultural similarities and differences in child development, and how variation in children's early experience affect their developmental processes, including motor development, social learning, and moral development. Yitong is passionate about building authentic partnerships with communities during the research process with the goal of developing participant driven and community-led research.

Zahra Halavani is a Master of Arts graduate in developmental psychology from Simon Fraser University, Canada. She worked at the Culture and Development Lab under the supervision of Dr. Tanya MacGillivray. Zahra's research focuses on infant-caregiver communications across cultures. She also has a background in educational psychology, mental health knowledge translation, and the sociomoral development of infants.

Acknowledgements

Special thanks are owed to all the children we have worked with. By sharing their lives with us, they helped shape ours. Many thanks as well to all the communities we work with for sharing their needs and making solutions possible.

This book is the product of a workshop funded by the Wenner-Gren Foundation Workshop Grant (Gr. CONF-870). Thanks to Zoe Poirier, research assistant extraordinaire, who helped organize the workshop.

Thanks to Robert Serpell and Daniel Haun, who helped shape the contents of the book.

Ilaria Pretelli thanks several researchers at Toulouse School of Economics who were a source of information for Chapter 9, in particular Kristin Michelitch, Mateo Montenegro, Maximilian Müller, and Jean-Paul Azam. Lauren Honig, at Boston College, and Emmanuel Maliti, who works as a consultant in Dar es Salaam, provided precious insight. Recognition is due to JL, who dedicated substantial amounts of time to educate a very unaware academic on the mechanisms of policymaking. Ilaria Pretelli also acknowledges IAST funding from the French National Research Agency (ANR) under grant ANR-17-EURE-0010 (Investissements de l'Avenir Program).

.

List of figures

List of tables

1. Studying childhood learning across cultures

Coordinated by Helen Elizabeth Davis

Contributors: Helen Elizabeth Davis, Dorsa Amir, Feryl Badiani, Michelle Kline, Nokwanda Ndlovu, Sarah Pope-Caldwell, Bruce Rawlings, Nachita Rosun, and Nicole Wen

This opening chapter outlines this book's agenda: to promote a comprehensive, culturally informed approach to studying childhood, and to critically examine the predominance of western-centric methodologies in developmental research. By integrating insights from evolutionary, anthropological, and psychological viewpoints, this chapter underscores the importance of investigating the cultural factors that influence child development and learning processes during childhood. Emphasizing the significance of incorporating Indigenous and local perspectives, we advocate for a more inclusive and culturally attuned approach. Finally, we support a mixed-methods approach as a means to enhance the credibility and ecological applicability of research outcomes, paving the way for a more comprehensive understanding of childhood in diverse cultural contexts.

1.1. Introduction

This chapter introduces the main themes of this volume. We start by discussing the importance of studying childhood development and learning across cultures by posing questions such as what childhood entails and why a developmental approach is necessary

©2025 Helen Elizabeth Davis et al., CC BY-NC 4.0
https://doi.org/10.11647/OBP.0440.01

to understand it. We then explore the concept of culture, addressing different theoretical perspectives. We emphasize the need for a working definition of culture and highlight that culture need not be far from home. Next, we provide an overview of different disciplinary and theoretical perspectives, ranging from biological and evolutionary anthropology to cultural anthropology and psychology.

We argue that the interdisciplinary study of childhood learning across cultures is essential to understanding human ecological diversity and behavioral flexibility. We go on to explain the significance of studying childhood learning, emphasizing that practitioners, educators, and policymakers need to understand cultural differences to create effective policies and educational practices. Ultimately, we emphasize the need to address epistemological, ethical, and political biases, especially western-centric thinking, in our understanding of child development. We also advocate for interdisciplinary research, incorporating naturalistic and ethnographic research at every stage, and collaborative team science to avoid extractive research.

1.2. Why study childhood?

Human childhood is unique. Unlike our primate cousins, human children continue to depend on caretakers for an extended period of time after weaning, taking nearly twice as long as chimpanzees to reach adulthood (Gibbons, 2008). Fossil records suggest that the elongated period of development we call *childhood* slowly emerged with the rise of our genus *Homo*, fundamentally altering the life histories and social structures of our species. For researchers interested in understanding our species, the study of childhood offers an undeniably important window into the origins of our minds, bodies, and cultures.

But why did childhood emerge at all? A closer look into human evolution may reveal clues. Examinations of fossil remains, such as hominin teeth and pelvises, suggest that *Homo erectus*, our ancestor from nearly 2 million years ago, was already experiencing shifts in its development (Gibbons, 2008). A widening pelvis and a larger skull suggest that *H. erectus* brains were increasing in capacity, accompanied by other shifts in morphology and behavior, such as bipedalism and tool use. Early human culture was emerging. As cultural complexity increased with time, so did skull sizes—and so, too, did indicators of a long childhood. *Homo antecessor*, who lived about 1 million years ago, had dental development on track with, but not identical to, that of modern humans (Bermúdez de Castro et al., 1999). By the time we reach the fossil teeth of *Homo sapiens* from 160,000 years ago, dental development is nearly indistinguishable from that of modern children of the same age (Smith et al., 2007). Concurrent with these developmental changes were other dramatic morphological and behavioral changes, namely: the emergence of a large and metabolically hungry brain, the extension of post-reproductive life, and importantly, the rise of more complex social and cultural products. These features co-evolved in tandem, strengthening and reinforcing each other.

Functionally, many have argued that an extended period of development—scaffolded by increased care from *alloparents*, or non-parents who provide childcare—evolved to support the immense amount of learning human children must engage in. Given that our species speaks thousands of languages, and lives across every habitable environment on the planet in a huge diversity of social and cultural structures, none of which are accessible before birth, an extended period of development evolved to allow children the time, resources, and energy to learn the complex cultural skill set of their society. An influential theory posited by anthropologist Hillard Kaplan and colleagues (2000) suggests that the unique trajectory of human life histories—including an extended period of childhood—is a result of co-evolved responses to a dietary shift toward high-quality, nutrient-dense, and difficult-to-acquire resources. That is, as early hominids began to target foods like meat that required high levels of knowledge, skill, and strength—otherwise known as *embodied capital*—the attainment of those abilities began to require longer and longer periods of investment. This led to an extension not just of early development but also of post-reproductive life and the human lifespan, more generally. Recent analyses of child foraging patterns lend support to this hypothesis, demonstrating that foraging returns increase slowly for more skill-intensive resources, with peak productivity in adulthood, underscoring that long childhoods do indeed allow us time to perfect the extraction of complex resources from the environment (Pretelli et al., 2022).

More recently, psychologist Alison Gopnik (2020) has proposed that the evolution of our life history, with its distinctively long childhood, emerged to allow an early period of broad hypothesis search and exploration. In other words, childhood evolved not just to facilitate the acquisition of existing cultural products, but to encourage the genesis and exploration of novel cultural products, as well. Other hypotheses also exist which do not view childhood as emerging through a direct adaptation, but rather as something like a *spandrel*—or, an evolutionary side effect (Bjorklund, 2009; Remmel, 2008) with enormous consequences for our species (Bjorklund, 2020). Though debates continue regarding the exact evolutionary forces that led to our long childhoods, scholars agree that understanding development is critical for understanding our success as a species.

In addition to its length, human development is also marked by its remarkable degree of *phenotypic plasticity*—the ability of an organism to tailor development to environmental conditions (Frankenhuis & Amir, 2022). As anthropologist Clifford Geertz (1973, p. 45) argued, "we all begin with the natural equipment to live a thousand kinds of life, but end in the end having lived only one." How does this calibration process play out? One school of thought has focused relatively more on the role that individual experiences of various environmental inputs—such as extrinsic mortality—play in shaping later life outcomes—such as time preferences (Frankenhuis & Panchanathan, 2011) and health behaviors (Nettle et al., 2011; Amir & McAuliffe, 2020). Through this lens, childhood serves the important function of providing a 'weather forecast' of environmental conditions, allowing individuals to develop phenotypes that are adaptive for those conditions (Bateson et al., 2004; Nettle & Bateson, 2015). A related but distinct school of thought focuses on cultural learning, as opposed to individual experience. This perspective, stemming from *culture-gene coevolutionary theory* (Richerson & Boyd, 2005), offers a view of development as a time for intense and selective social learning, such as of local cultural norms. Empirical research in this field has largely focused on children's learning biases—toward prestigious members of the group, for instance (Chudek et al., 2012)—and the ways in which social learning interacts with more universal psychological mechanisms to produce divergent phenotypes (House et al., 2020). Studies of human development, and in particular those that take cultural context into account, are invaluable in testing the predictions of current theories and informing the genesis of new ones.

The value of developmental work, more broadly, has long been appreciated in the evolutionary sciences. The study of *ontogeny*—or, the development of an organism—was one of biologist Nikolaas Tinbergen's (1963) famous 'four questions', which sought to explain animal behavior. He argued that a complete understanding of behavior requires understanding its ontogeny, and that developmental experiments are critical for teasing apart the relative weights of influence that 'nature' and 'nurture' exert on human behavior. An ontogenetic perspective, and in particular one that takes culture into account, does indeed enable us to evaluate the degree to which cultural and environmental influence can penetrate aspects of cognition, allowing us to extract valuable information about the stability, flexibility, heritability, and structure of behaviors (Amir & McAuliffe, 2020; Liebal & Haun, 2018; Nielsen & Haun, 2016).

1.3. Why study learning in childhood?

While both human and non-human species engage in learning, humans are unique in the complexity and sophistication of their learning. By examining the interplay between biological, cognitive, and socio-cultural factors, we gain a more complete understanding of why learning in childhood is uniquely human. Humans possess early-developing capacities for language acquisition (Tomasello, 2005), cognitive flexibility (Gopnik et al., 2017), and knowledge transmission (Boyd et al., 2011; Csibra & Gergely, 2011), distinguishing them from other species. Moreover, through the use of cultural tools, such as language, writing schemes, and educational institutions, humans can rapidly acquire and innovate upon knowledge, information, and skill sets across generations (Bjorklund, 2000).

But what does it mean to study learning in childhood? This involves a multidisciplinary examination of the cognitive, social, emotional, and cultural processes underpinning both the acquisition and transmission of information and skills across human development. This interdisciplinary approach is not straightforward as the theoretical frameworks, techniques, and methodologies vary greatly by discipline. Throughout this book, we will explore these factors and advocate for an interdisciplinary study of childhood learning as best practice.

The scope of studying learning in childhood extends beyond studying children alone. Parents are under a lot of pressure to guide children's learning and future outcomes. Particularly, in western society, parents face increasing pressures to carefully cultivate their children's developmental and academic outcomes (Nomaguchi & Milkie, 2020). However, most research on parenting has been conducted exclusively in western contexts. Understanding parenting in non-western contexts is crucial to gaining a comprehensive understanding of childhood learning (Super & Harkness, 1986). Parenting practices and ethnotheories vary across diverse cultural environments, and this shapes child socialization and learning experiences (Keller et al., 2006).

Investing in children is investing in our future. It is imperative to prioritize how children will shape our world—how they will solve its many problems and overcome its greatest challenges. Through a comprehensive understanding of childhood learning processes, practitioners, educators, policymakers, and stakeholders can implement evidence-based practices to optimize children's developmental trajectories. It is also critical for practitioners, educators, and policymakers to incorporate culture into policies and programs that are created, to promote inclusive learning environments and provide culturally informed support for families and children. This approach will ensure that children are equipped with the necessary skill set to thrive in an increasingly complex world.

1.4. Why study children's learning across cultures?

Almost fifteen years ago, researchers powerfully showcased that the vast majority of research in the social sciences is based on affluent, western participants—samples that are unrepresentative of most of humanity today and in the past (Henrich, Heine, et al., 2010). Since then, the volume of global, often multi-population, research has rapidly accelerated. Two central yet somewhat contrasting consequences of this expansion are that (1) studies of cognitive and social development have reached numerous and diverse cultural contexts, but (2) there are increasing conversations surrounding cross-cultural research practices, and what it means for our understanding of how culture shapes development.

On face value, conducting developmental research in all parts of the globe can surely only be a good thing, right? It addresses the overreliance on WEIRD (Western, Educated, Industrialized, Rich, and Democratic) samples and broadens our understanding of human behavior (Henrich, Heine, & Norenzayan, 2010). We now know, for example, that culture influences a wide range of cognitive domains, including social information-use (Broesch et al., 2017; van Leeuwen et al., 2018), imitation (Clegg & Legare, 2016; Stengelin et al., 2020), prosocial behavior (House et al., 2013), tool use (German & Barrett, 2005), fairness (Blake et al., 2015; Henrich, Ensminger, et al., 2010), tool innovation (Lew-Levy et al., 2021; Neldner et al., 2019), numerical and other abstract conceptual reasoning (Haun et al., 2011; Pica et al., 2004; Pitt et al., 2021), executive functioning (de Fockert et al., 2011; Legare et al., 2018), risk-taking (Amir et al., 2020), cognitive flexibility (Pope et al., 2019; Vieira et al., Under review), categorization (Ji et al., 2004), and even perceptual biases (Caparos et al., 2013; Nisbett & Miyamoto, 2005).

Yet, diversifying samples alone does not solve all our problems. One issue surrounds what, exactly, we mean by *culture.* Culture is fluid, it is inherently social, it is multifaceted and multileveled. Membership into one culture does not automatically prevent membership in another. Even within seemingly homogenous groups, subcultures and countercultures thrive. The exact definition of culture has been a topic of controversy (see Minkov, 2012: The Concept of Culture). In psychology, culture is thought of as the cognitive inputs and behavioral outputs of a society, including "the values, beliefs, language, rituals, traditions, and other behaviors that are passed from one generation to another within any social group" (American Psychological Association, 2023). While in anthropology, the concept of culture has focused on the material manifestations of a group's "patterned ways of thinking, feeling and reacting, acquired and transmitted mainly by symbols" (Kluckhohn, 1961, p. 73). Throughout this book, we challenge researchers to consider that culture is not only, or necessarily, a group identifier. It is ubiquitous and multidimensional. As a result, cross-cultural research does not require the comparison of widely differing groups. We need only identify and measure variation along dimensions of culture that are relevant to our research topics, even (and arguably especially) when that variation occurs within communities (Barrett, 2020).

Further, as a result of the drive to conduct research in non-western populations, a new wave of concerns has been raised, concerning epistemological, ethical, and political biases—most of which ultimately result from western-centric approaches to theoretical and methodological development (Burger et al., 2023; Kline et al., 2018; Urassa et al., 2021). At their core, these issues stem from the fact that most international research is conducted by western researchers, based and trained in western institutions, who constitute the vast majority of journal authors, with findings disseminated in English. The problem extends beyond manuscript authorship. Editors of flagship journals, scientific body membership, and award recipients are dominated by western researchers (IJzerman et al., 2021).

The direct result of all of this is that our methodology and subsequent conclusions are likely to be inaccurate. As articulately described by Kline et al. (2018), this model can produce a range of biases and problematic assumptions, which include the tendency to use western populations as the standard benchmark for comparison, and that using identical (typically western-derived) methods across cultures will produce valid and reliable data. These are well-founded concerns, with several researchers documenting such biases empirically and theoretically (Holding et al., 2018; Hruschka et al., 2018; Zuilkowski et al., 2016). These biases impede progress on developing generalizable theories. Children growing up in western environments may have significantly different norms, frames of reference, perceptions, and relationships with others than those in different cultural contexts. If we want to study the development of memory or learning, for example, we need to do so in the context of children's lived experiences (Rogoff et al., 2018). How are we meant to truly understand how culture shapes ontogeny if our theories are grounded in western literature?

Solving this issue is not easy and requires introspection, reflection, and moving away from western-centric theories and methods. Rightly so, the replication crisis has encouraged researchers to produce replicable studies. However, an unintended result of this may be that methods are becoming less diverse, and thus less appropriate for diverse populations (de Oliveira & Baggs, 2023). As we continue to expand our samples, it is critical that we develop culturally grounded and appropriate theory, and design and implement appropriate methodology. It may well mean that in doing so, we cannot always make direct comparisons across populations. If that allows us to draw more accurate conclusions from our research, it is a trade-off we must consider.

1.5. How to study childhood in diverse settings

The study of learning in childhood is expansive, with questions shaped by particular disciplines and varying by age ranges as well. These questions pair with research techniques, which span from highly controlled experimental work in developmental psychology, to quantitative or mixed-method observational research more common in field-based psychology and evolutionary/biological anthropology, to qualitative thick description in social/cultural anthropology. Throughout this book, we do not advocate for a single method or field, but instead argue that mixed methods, selected to fit the research question, are the strongest approach *both* for accurately describing learning in childhood and for robustly testing hypotheses about those phenomena.

There are several reasons we advocate for a mixed-methods approach. First, most if not all the methods that currently dominate the academic study of childhood and learning have been developed by western researchers, in western institutions, studying western children. Acknowledging the role of cultural context in child learning and development means re-evaluating if and when these methods are appropriate when taken out of the western cultural contexts in which they were first minted (Chaudhary & Sriram, 2020; Kline et al., 2018). Otherwise, researchers risk offering a poor description of how childhood learning works by ignoring culturally variable but interesting features (Dahl, 2017) and sometimes asking questions that do not fit the context or way of life being studied (Medin & Bang, 2014). Mixed methods can help researchers to question their assumptions (about their own and others' cultural contexts) in a process that will ultimately improve their research design and methodological choices. As argued by Medin et al. (2010), failing to question these assumptions puts the researcher at a disadvantage.

Broesch et al. (2023) argue that a starting point is to begin with open-ended observational and interview methods to map out contextual and conceptual categories. These methods have low levels of control by the researcher, but provide rich context and high ecological validity—meaning they correspond with participants' real-world experiences. See Figure 1.1 for examples of methods that span this continuum.

These observations can be paired with higher-control experimental or quantitative methods to good effect, and can play a role in improving those methods by raising questions about the culture-bound nature of high control methods, informing ecologically valid measurements, and providing meaningful background for the interpretation of high-control methods. For example, Gervais (2017) demonstrates the important influence of real-world relationship norms on participant interpretation and subsequent behavior in supposedly 'neutral' economic games. This approach is illustrated by a case study of teaching, in which Kline (Section 4.2) combines participant observation, semi-structured interviews, and highly structured quantitative observations to construct and implement different definitions of 'teaching' along with different measurements of each. The conclusion yielded by this combination of methods is that while teaching is rare in the Yasawan context when defined as the type of direct, active instruction found in western classrooms, it is important both in the eyes of Yasawan adults (Kline et al., 2013) and as a more subtle set of behaviors woven into everyday interactions with children (Kline, 2017).

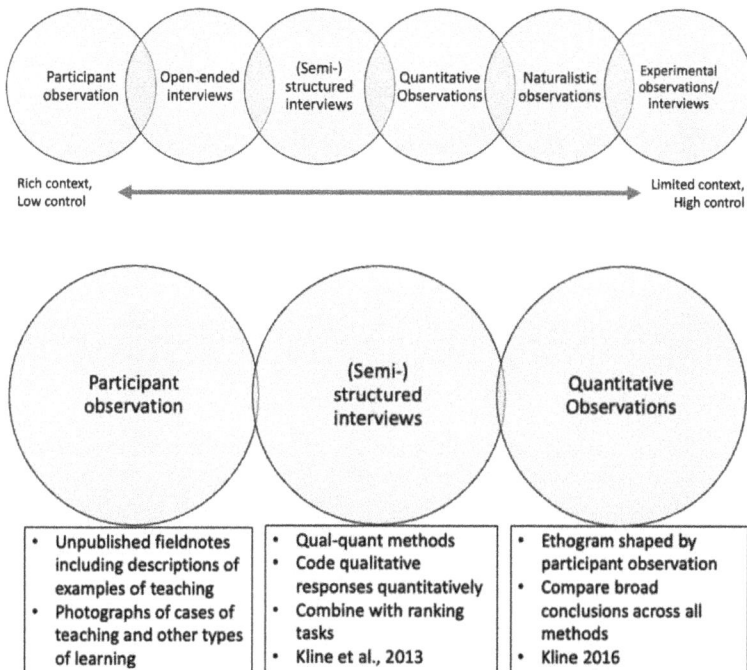

Fig. 1.1 A selection of methods that range from rich context, low control to limited context, high control. These methods can be combined to reconcile the trade-offs between control and ecological validity, improving both the robustness and validity of research.

1.6. Indigenous methodology and prioritizing Indigenous knowledge

Beyond methodology, one key way to address the lack of inclusivity of historically understudied communities in our work is to employ methodologies that prioritize sources of knowledge from historically marginalized communities in ways that also upend power dynamics and produce scholarly work that resonates with understudied communities. Indigenous methodology has been defined as research by and for Indigenous peoples that incorporates Indigenous knowledge(s), cultures, values, and beliefs (Denzin et al., 2008; Ryen, 2019). Indigenous methods are part of broader Indigenous peoples' movements that emphasize decolonization and self-determination through the promotion of Indigenous histories, languages, worldviews, knowledge, value systems, and broader Indigenous experiences in a post-colonial lived experience (Chilisa, 2019; Ryen, 2019). The creation of Indigenous scholarship requires confronting centuries of literature written by outsiders, as well as the need to address the "dominance of Euro-Western languages in the construction of knowledge" (Chilisa, 2019, p. 106). Understanding another culture's worldview is no simple task, and Indigenous scholars face the added hurdles of 'academic imperialism' and 'methodological imperialism', where western methodologies have historically failed to articulate Indigenous ways of knowing in a manner that is meaningful to these communities.

In reflecting on this challenge of prioritizing Indigenous knowledge in the legacy of a western academia, we are reminded of the Audre Lorde (1979) phrase "The master's tools will never dismantle the master's house." The lengthy bodies of literature written by cultural outsiders on Indigenous groups present an uphill battle for Indigenous scholars to infiltrate western academia (master's house) without relying on tools (research processes, ethics, methodologies) that historically have only valued western knowledge production (Chilisa, 2019; Lorde, 1979; Smith, 2021).

Power and perspective

Indigenous research seeks to bring power to historically oppressed perspectives, which is also a common goal of many schools of feminism. For example, Feminist Standpoint Theory (FST) has an overarching goal of challenging historical systems of oppression, prioritizing culturally situated knowledge, and focusing on self-definition and self-valuation (Collins, 1986; Harding, 1991; Intemann, 2019). Forces of oppression influence the lived experiences of marginalized communities, which creates a shared knowledge system across epistemic communities (Harding, 1991; Intemann, 2019). The lived experience and worldview of many Indigenous peoples are bound up in the history of traditions persisting and outliving the systems of oppression that worked to assimilate them with the ultimate goal of destroying and erasing their culture.

When it comes to research on a historically marginalized population, there is an inescapable question of whose reality counts. Western research methodologies often have inherent epistemological imbalances that hold western knowledge systems as more valid than other perspectives (Hayward et al., 2021; Smith, 2021; Wilson, 2008). As researchers we can make efforts to conduct socially and culturally relevant research with local participation, but ultimately the power resides with the researcher to frame and compile their conclusions for publication (Chilisa, 2019). Without further incorporating Indigenous ethics, knowledge, and perspective into our research processes, academic research will continue to be "tainted with a clandestine history of colonialism and neocolonialism" (Hayward et al., 2021, p. 412; Smith, 2021).

Academic imperialism is both an issue of inherited literature and methods as well as a contemporary issue of power, where there is still a challenge regarding whose perspective is prioritized in knowledge production, the researcher, or the researched (Chilisa, 2019). In contemporary research, it becomes critical to position Indigenous communities in a way that gives them a seat at the table because the issue of silencing their perspective is one that's still ongoing in many different parts of the world. For many

Indigenous communities, their lived reality, experience, and history were related on their behalf because of the inherent relationship with power favoring those with resources, while excluding and othering Indigenous peoples' perspectives (Smith, 2021). The history of oppression and subjugation faced by Indigenous and other marginalized communities excluded these communities from accessing education, resulting in many scientific inquiries carried out by those from dominant groups. Subaltern theory offers one way of deconstructing how critical, post-colonial inquiries into marginalized perspectives may continue to fail to allow the marginalized to speak (Spivak, 2023). Many inquiries by cultural outsiders unintentionally speak on behalf of the populations being studied, drawing conclusions built on western knowledge systems for western audiences.

Western methodologies produce knowledge that is valuable to western audiences but has left marginalized and Indigenous cultures othered, so there is a need for both deconstructing the academic systems that have created these misrepresentations and constructing new approaches to research that prioritize and value knowledge and perspectives with consideration for Indigenous cultural values and ethics. There are considerations related to challenging western-centric thinking to be made at every step of the research process, which complicates the question of how to meaningfully tease apart fundamental differences in how the world is perceived. To gain the greatest depth of understanding on topics in dire need of decolonization like child development, Indigenous scholars have drawn from several philosophical approaches, including epistemology (knowledge), ontology (nature of reality), and axiology (values) (Chilisa, 2019).

Epistemology

Indigenous research in child development typically seeks to understand a specific aspect of contemporary Indigenous parenting, which can be described as a window into Indigenous knowledge systems. Epistemology includes belief systems, ways of knowing, or general knowledge systems. Chilisa (2019, p. 105) describes African knowledge systems as relational because we come to understand ourselves and our place in the world through others; our knowledge systems and self-identity are derived through our ties to others. Chilisa (2019, p. 105) defines the relational epistemology found in African cultures as "well-established general beliefs, concepts, and theories of any particular people, which are stored in their language, practices, rituals, proverbs, revered traditions, myths, and folktales."

Epistemology further relates to the formation of ways of knowing, which is important to consider both within the culture and cross-culturally. In considering relational epistemology, knowledge about kinship, parenting practices, and culturally defined developmental milestones needs to be considered as socially constructed, which means that the 'knowers' of Indigenous knowledge come to understand their world through their ties to their family, and the world around them (Chilisa, 2019). When working cross-culturally, western-trained researchers need to consider whether their methods, approach, and positionality have only strengthened their ability to generate western knowledge, and more attention needs to be paid to how Indigenous knowledge is conceived, perceived, and experienced within the culture.

Ontology

One challenge with empirically studying another culture's knowledge system is that many Indigenous knowledge systems are built upon ontological beliefs about the nature of reality that may be shared beyond ethno-linguistic groupings (e.g., Zulu, Nguni, Bantu). In the context of child development, ontological considerations include investigating what kinds of age-sets exist (e.g., developmental age groupings), what cultural traditions and rituals are deemed to be integral to a child's development and their sense of self (e.g., coming of age ceremonies, socialization practices related to an interdependent self), as well as how relationships exist within the broader community (Chilisa, 2019; Mbiti, 1969; Pemunta & Tabenyang, 2021; Wallace, 2015).

Chilisa (2019) describes this as the I/We obligation, relations with the living and non-living, and spirituality, love, and harmony. The I/We obligation relates to the construct of the African self, where one derives personhood through their relations to others, both living and non-living, and this personhood is a process that holds health and illness as contingent on the maintenance of harmony in our interconnected networks (Mkhize, 2004). The ontological concept of an interdependent self in the African cosmos is integral to understanding our culture's conception of family, parenting responsibilities, and developmental milestones from one's worldview. Moreover, concepts like alloparenting and child-headed households need to be understood both within Indigenous values as well as practical socio-economic realities.

Axiology

Often related to ethics, axiology refers to the focus on values and their meaning, characteristics, origins, purpose, and influence on people's choices (Chilisa, 2019). There are axiological considerations regarding how Indigenous knowledge is valued in academic research and whose perspective is prioritized (researcher versus researched). One of the great challenges in Indigenous and decolonized scholarship is the issue of academic and methodological imperialism, which has left Indigenous knowledge systems with long histories of misrepresentation by cultural outsiders. There are axiological considerations in whether the western interpretation of data is valued over the participant's lived experiences, as well as axiological considerations about how a participant perceives their own values while navigating a post-colonial worldview that many contemporary Indigenous cultures find themselves straddling in a post-colonial context.

For instance, Zulu traditions and family values center on traditional African spirituality, which emphasizes honoring the ancestors (Berg, 2003; Viljoen, 1994). Core Zulu family values typically center on respect, obedience, and family connectedness (Ndlovu, 2019; Raum, 1973; Viljoen, 1994). The Zulu concept of *ubuntu* (humanness) sheds light on the ethical principles embedded in what Chilisa (2019, p. 106) calls a "relational axiology." *Ubuntu* is an ontological construct about interconnectedness, which is often paraphrased as 'I am because we are.' In combination with another construct, *hlonipha* (reciprocal respect), *ubuntu* is conceived as a way of prioritizing others, particularly one's family, over the individual, with the ultimate value placed on harmony and community building (Chilisa, 2019). These principles become critical when studying and observing parent-child interactions in child development research and are important to understanding the context of Zulu socialization as well as how a cultural outsider may need to reflexively approach their positionality. It is axiomatic that, when working cross-culturally, researchers need to problematize their power over their participants, while recognizing the innate expertise of their participants' lived experiences.

1.7. What we advocate for

Throughout this book, we strongly advocate for an expanded dialogue on the intricate interplay between childhood development and cultural diversity. Our central thesis argues for a multidimensional approach, integrating various social sciences, other disciplines, and local and/or Indigenous perspectives to enrich our understanding of childhood across diverse cultures. This comprehensive approach is key to understanding the myriad ways in which growing up is experienced and influenced by different social, cultural, and ecological environments. Because the complexities of childhood development cannot be fully comprehended through a single lens, we argue that interdisciplinary work is necessary to further these fields of study.

This work, however, cannot be approached lightly, and researchers focusing on cross-cultural and interdisciplinary investigations into childhood must do so thoughtfully. We argue against extractive research methodologies, which often take more from communities than they give back. Instead, we champion the integration of naturalistic and ethnographic methods at every stage. Such approaches allow for a deeper immersion into the lives of children across cultures, offering a more authentic and respectful portrayal of their experiences. This method not only enriches the quality of our data but also ensures that the research process itself is ethical and sensitive to the cultural contexts being studied.

Furthermore, we strongly oppose 'helicopter research', a term used to describe studies where researchers briefly enter a community, collect data, and leave without any meaningful engagement or lasting impact. Instead, we promote models of research that commit to authentic partnering and support economic, social, and cultural well-being (Norris-Tirrell et al., 2010). Such approaches involve building collaborative research teams that include local researchers, community leaders, and stakeholders. We argue that such an approach better enables our understanding and interpretation of the cultural nuances and ethical considerations unique to each community. This collaborative approach ensures that the research process is not just about data collection but also about building relationships and trust, fostering a deeper understanding of the communities we study.

This book is a call to action for a more ethical, respectful, and holistic approach to studying childhood across cultures. Our hope is that this collection stimulates more research on the evolutionary, developmental, and practical implications associated with studying teaching, learning, and child development among humans. This enriched understanding is not just academically beneficial; it has profound implications for educators, policymakers, and all who work with children, ensuring that their practices are culturally informed and responsive to the diverse needs of children around the world.

1.8. Book structure

This book is structured to take readers through the entire life cycle of cross-cultural developmental research. Each chapter features the perspectives of many contributors from diverse disciplines, continents, career stages, and theoretical orientations.

Theoretical and methodological considerations

Chapter 2 reviews the history of cross-cultural childhood learning by describing the traditions, perspectives, methods, and philosophies from anthropology, psychology, and archaeology, thus helping readers understand the origins and waves of thinking within this interdisciplinary field. Chapter 3 contrasts universalist and culturalist approaches to cross-cultural research, ultimately arguing that, to understand child development, we must navigate a middle course which draws on the best of both viewpoints. Chapter 4 offers a collage of methodologies, in order to demonstrate common practices and explore their theoretical, ethical, and practical implications.

Learning and growing in 'the field'

Chapter 5 discusses the practicalities of preparing for 'the field', emphasizing the development of trusting relationships with the community as critical to ethical research practice and essential for good science. Drawing from the main narrative device of personal storytelling, Chapter 6 offers a personal account of lessons, challenges, and power relations experienced while conducting research with children in diverse cultural contexts.

Making an impact

Chapter 7 outlines the best practices for sharing research on childhood learning in an ethical and impactful way. Chapter 8 offers a series of case studies reflecting on local adaptation to global educational change, ultimately arguing that educational policy must better account for local cultural context, while also more proactively driving participatory means of valued school improvement. Chapter 9 offers a practical guide to engaging policymakers, in order to ensure that our research can ultimately benefit children across the globe. Finally, in Chapter 10, we look to the future of the field by reflecting on the lessons we have learned throughout our careers.

References

American Psychological Association. (2023). Schema. In *APA Dictionary of Psychology.* https://dictionary.apa.org/

Amir, D., Jordan, M. R., McAuliffe, K., Valeggia, C. R., Sugiyama, L. S., Bribiescas, R. G., Snodgrass, J. J., & Dunham, Y. (2020). The developmental origins of risk and time preferences across diverse societies. *Journal of Experimental Psychology: General, 149*(4), 650. http://dx.doi.org/10.1037/xge0000675

Amir, D., & McAuliffe, K. (2020). Cross-cultural, developmental psychology: Integrating approaches and key insights. *Evolution and Human Behavior, 41*(5), 430–444. https://doi.org/10.1016/j.evolhumbehav.2020.06.006

Barrett, H. C. (2020). Towards a cognitive science of the human: Cross-cultural approaches and their urgency. *Trends in Cognitive Sciences, 24*(8), 620–638. https://doi.org/10.1016/j.tics.2020.05.007

Bateson, P., Barker, D., Clutton-Brock, T., Deb, D., D'Udine, B., Foley, R. A., Gluckman, P., Godfrey, K., Kirkwood, T., Lahr, M. M., McNamara, J., Metcalfe, N. B., Monaghan, P., Spencer, H. G., & Sultan, S. E. (2004). Developmental plasticity and human health. *Nature, 430*(6998), Article 6998. https://doi.org/10.1038/nature02725

Berg, A. (2003). Ancestor reverence and mental health in South Africa. *Transcultural Psychiatry, 40*(2), 194–207.

Bermúdez de Castro, J. M., Rosas, A., & Nicolás, M. E. (1999). Dental remains from Atapuerca-TD6 (Gran Dolina site, Burgos, Spain). *Journal of Human Evolution, 37*(3–4), 523–566. https://doi.org/10.1006/jhev.1999.0323

Bjorklund, D. F. (2000). *Children's thinking: Developmental function and individual differences.* Wadsworth/Thomson Learning.

Bjorklund, D. F. (2009). *Why youth is not wasted on the young: Immaturity in human development.* Wiley.

Bjorklund, D. F. (2020). *How children invented humanity: The role of development in human evolution.* Oxford University Press. https://doi.org/10.1093/oso/9780190066864.001.0001

Blake, P. R., McAuliffe, K., Corbit, J., Callaghan, T. C., Barry, O., Bowie, A., Kleutsch, L., Kramer, K., Ross, E., & Vongsachang, H. (2015). The ontogeny of fairness in seven societies. *Nature, 528*(7581), 258–261. https://doi.org/10.1038/nature15703

Boyd, R., Richerson, P. J., & Henrich, J. (2011). The cultural niche: Why social learning is essential for human adaptation. *Proceedings of* the National Academy of Sciences, 108(Supplement_2), 10918–10925. https://doi.org/10.1073/pnas.1100290108

Broesch, T., Itakura, S., & Rochat, P. (2017). Learning from others: Selective requests by 3-year-olds of three cultures. *Journal of Cross-Cultural Psychology, 48*(9), 1432–1441. https://doi.org/10.1177/0022022117731093

Broesch, T., Lew-Levy, S., Kärtner, J., Kanngiesser, P., & Kline, M. (2023). A roadmap to doing culturally grounded developmental science. *Review of Philosophy and Psychology, 14*(2), 587–609. https://doi.org/10.1007/s13164-022-00636-y

Burger, O., Chen, L., Erut, A., Fong, F. T., Rawlings, B., & Legare, C. H. (2023). Developing Cross-Cultural Data Infrastructures (CCDIs) for research in cognitive and behavioral sciences. *Review of Philosophy and Psychology, 14*(2), 565–585. https://doi.org/10.1007/s13164-022-00635-z

Caparos, S., Linnell, K. J., Bremner, A. J., de Fockert, J. W., & Davidoff, J. (2013). Do local and global perceptual biases tell us anything about local and global selective attention? *Psychological Science, 24*(2), 206–212. https://doi.org/10.1177/0956797612452569

Chaudhary, N., & Sriram, S. (2020). Psychology in the "backyards of the world": Experiences from India. *Journal of Cross-Cultural Psychology, 51*(2), 113–133. https://doi.org/10.1177/0022022119896652

Chilisa, B. (2019). *Indigenous research methodologies.* Sage publications.

Chudek, M., Heller, S., Birch, S., & Henrich, J. (2012). Prestige-biased cultural learning: Bystander's differential attention to potential models influences children's learning. *Evolution and Human Behavior, 33*(1), 46–56. https://doi.org/10.1016/j.evolhumbehav.2011.05.005

Clegg, J. M., & Legare, C. H. (2016). A cross-cultural comparison of children's imitative flexibility. *Developmental Psychology, 52*(9), 1435–1444. https://dx.doi.org/10.1037/dev0000131

Collins, P. H. (1986). Learning from the outsider within: The sociological significance of Black feminist thought. *Social Problems, 33*(6), s14–s32. https://doi.org/10.2307/800672

Csibra, G., & Gergely, G. (2011). Natural pedagogy as evolutionary adaptation. *Philosophical Transactions of the Royal Society B: Biological Sciences, 366*(1567), 1149–1157. https://doi.org/10.1098/rstb.2010.0319

Dahl, A. (2017). Ecological commitments: Why developmental science needs naturalistic methods. *Child Development Perspectives, 11*(2), 79–84. https://doi.org/10.1111/cdep.12217

de Fockert, J. W., Caparos, S., Linnell, K. J., & Davidoff, J. (2011). Reduced distractibility in a remote culture. *PLoS One, 6*(10), e26337. https://doi.org/10.1371/journal.pone.0026337

de Oliveira, G. S., & Baggs, E. (2023). *Psychology's WEIRD Problems.* Cambridge University Press. https://doi.org/10.1017/9781009303538

Denzin, N. K., Lincoln, Y. S., & Smith, L. T. (2008). *Handbook of critical and indigenous methodologies.* Sage. https://doi.org/10.4135/9781483385686

Frankenhuis, W. E., & Amir, D. (2022). What is the expected human childhood? Insights from evolutionary anthropology. *Development and Psychopathology, 34*(2), 473–497. https://doi.org/10.1017/S0954579421001401

Frankenhuis, W. E., & Panchanathan, K. (2011). Balancing sampling and specialization: An adaptationist model of incremental development. *Proceedings of the Royal Society B: Biological Sciences, 278*(1724), 3558–3565. https://doi.org/10.1098/rspb.2011.0055

Geertz, C. (1973). *The interpretation of cultures.* Basic Books. https://doi.org/10.15581/009.35.31543

German, T. P., & Barrett, H. C. (2005). Functional fixedness in a technologically sparse culture. *Psychological Science, 16*(1), 1–5. https://doi.org/10.1111/j.0956-7976.2005.00771.x

Gervais, M. M. (2017). RICH economic games for networked relationships and communities: Development and preliminary validation in Yasawa, Fiji. *Field Methods, 29*(2), 113–129. https://doi.org/10.1177/1525822X16643709

Gibbons, A. (2008). The birth of childhood. *Science, 322*(5904), 1040–1043 https://doi.org/10.1126/science.322.5904.1040

Gopnik, A. (2020). Childhood as a solution to explore–exploit tensions. *Philosophical Transactions of the Royal Society B: Biological Sciences, 375*(1803), 20190502. https://doi.org/10.1098/rstb.2019.0502

Gopnik, A., O'Grady, S., Lucas, C. G., Griffiths, T. L., Wente, A., Bridgers, S., Aboody, R., Fung, H., & Dahl, R. E. (2017). Changes in cognitive flexibility and hypothesis search across human life history from childhood to adolescence to adulthood. *Proceedings of the National Academy of Sciences, 114*(30), 7892–7899. https://doi.org/10.1073/pnas.1700811114

Harding, S. (1991). *Whose science? Whose knowledge?: Thinking from women's lives.* Cornell University Press. https://doi.org/10.7591/9781501712951

Haun, D. B., Rapold, C. J., Janzen, G., & Levinson, S. C. (2011). Plasticity of human spatial cognition: Spatial language and cognition covary across cultures. *Cognition, 119*(1), 70–80. https://doi.org/10.1016/j. cognition.2010.12.009

Hayward, A., Wodtke, L., Craft, A., Robin, T., Smylie, J., McConkey, S., Nychuk, A., Healy, C., Star, L., & Cidro, J. (2021). Addressing the need for indigenous and decolonized quantitative research methods in Canada. *SSM-Population Health, 15*, 100899. https://doi.org/10.1016/j. ssmph.2021.100899

Henrich, J., Ensminger, J., McElreath, R., Barr, A., Barrett, C., Bolyanatz, A., Cardenas, J. C., Gurven, M., Gwako, E., & Henrich, N. (2010). Markets, religion, community size, and the evolution of fairness and punishment. *Science, 327*(5972), 1480–1484. https://doi.org/10.1126/ science.1182238

Henrich, J., Heine, S. J., & Norenzayan, A. (2010). The weirdest people in the world? *Behavioral and Brain Sciences, 33*(2–3), 61–83. https://doi. org/10.1017/S0140525X0999152X

Holding, P., Anum, A., van de Vijver, F. J., Vokhiwa, M., Bugase, N., Hossen, T., Makasi, C., Baiden, F., Kimbute, O., & Bangre, O. (2018). Can we measure cognitive constructs consistently within and across cultures? Evidence from a test battery in Bangladesh, Ghana, and Tanzania. *Applied Neuropsychology: Child, 7*(1), 1–13. https://doi.org/10.1080/2162 2965.2016.1206823

House, B. R., Kanngiesser, P., Barrett, H. C., Broesch, T., Cebioglu, S., Crittenden, A. N., Erut, A., Lew-Levy, S., Sebastian-Enesco, C., & Smith, A. M. (2020). Universal norm psychology leads to societal diversity in prosocial behaviour and development. *Nature Human Behaviour, 4*(1), 36–44. https://doi.org/10.1038/s41562-019-0734-z

House, B., Silk, J. B., Henrich, J., Barrett, C., Scelza, B., Boyette, A., Hewlett, B., & Laurence, S. (2013). The Ontogeny of Prosocial Behavior across Diverse Societies. *Proceedings of the National Academy of Sciences of the United States, 110*(36), 14586–14591. https://doi.org/10.1073/ pnas.1221217110

Hruschka, D. J., Munira, S., Jesmin, K., Hackman, J., & Tiokhin, L. (2018). Learning from failures of protocol in cross-cultural research. *Proceedings of the National Academy of Sciences, 115*(45), 11428– 11434. https://doi.org/10.1073/pnas.1721166115

IJzerman, H., Dutra, N., Silan, M., Adetula, A., Brown, D. M. B., & Forscher, P. (2021). Psychological science needs the entire globe, Part 1. *APS Observer, 34.* https://www.psychologicalscience.org/observer/ global-psych-science

Intemann, K. (2019). *Feminist standpoint theory*. Sage. https://doi. org/10.1093/oxfordhb/9780199328581.013.14

Ji, L.-J., Zhang, Z., & Nisbett, R. E. (2004). Is it culture or is it language? Examination of language effects in cross-cultural research on categorization. *Journal of Personality and Social Psychology, 87*(1), 57. https://doi.org/10.1037/0022-3514.87.1.57

Kaplan, H., Hill, K., Lancaster, J., & Hurtado, A. M. (2000). A theory of human life history evolution: Diet, intelligence, and longevity. *Evolutionary Anthropology: Issues, News, and Reviews, 9*(4), 156–185. https://doi.org/10.1002/1520-6505(2000)9:4<156::AID-EVAN5>3.0.CO;2-7

Keller, H., Lamm, B., Abels, M., Yovsi, R., Borke, J., Jensen, H., Papaligoura, Z., Holub, C., Lo, W., & Tomiyama, A. J. (2006). Cultural models, socialization goals, and parenting ethnotheories: A multicultural analysis. *Journal of Cross-Cultural Psychology, 37*(2), 155–172. https://doi.org/10.1177/0022022105284494

Kline, M. A. (2017). TEACH: An ethogram-based method to observe and record teaching behavior. *Field Methods, 29*(3), 205–220. https://doi.org/10.1177/1525822X16669282

Kline, M. A., Boyd, R., & Henrich, J. (2013). Teaching and the Life History of Cultural Transmission in Fijian Villages. *Human Nature, 24*(4), 351–374. https://doi.org/10.1007/s12110-013-9180-1

Kline, M. A., Shamsudheen, R., & Broesch, T. (2018). Variation is the universal: Making cultural evolution work in developmental psychology. *Philosophical Transactions of the Royal Society B: Biological Sciences, 373*(1743), 20170059. https://doi.org/10.1098/rstb.2017.0059

Kluckhohn, C. (1961). Notes on some anthropological aspects of communication. *American Anthropologist, 63*(5), 895–910. https://doi.org/10.1525/aa.1961.63.5.02a00010

Legare, C. H., Dale, M. T., Kim, S. Y., & Deák, G. O. (2018). Cultural variation in cognitive flexibility reveals diversity in the development of executive functions. *Scientific Reports, 8*(1), 1–14. https://doi.org/10.1038/s41598-018-34756-2

Lew-Levy, S., Pope, S. M., Haun, D. B., Kline, M. A., & Broesch, T. (2021). Out of the empirical box: A mixed-methods study of tool innovation among Congolese BaYaka forager and Bondongo fisher–farmer children. *Journal of Experimental Child Psychology, 211*, 105223. https://doi.org/10.1016/j.jecp.2021.105223

Liebal, K., & Haun, D. B. M. (2018). Why cross-cultural psychology is incomplete without comparative and developmental perspectives. *Journal of Cross-Cultural Psychology, 49*(5), 751–763. https://doi.org/10.1177/0022022117738085

Lorde, A. (1979, September 29). Master's Tools Will Never Take Down the Master's House. "The Personal and the Political." Second Sex Conference, New York. https://doi.org/10.1515/9781438488295-034

Mbiti, J. S. (1969). *African traditional religions and philosophy.* Nairobi: East African Educational Publishers.

Medin, D., Bennis, W., & Chandler, M. (2010). Culture and the home-field disadvantage. *Perspectives on Psychological Science, 5*(6), 708–713. https://doi.org/10.1177/1745691610388772

Medin, D. L., & Bang, M. (2014). *Who's asking?: Native science, western science, and science education.* MIT Press. https://doi.org/10.7551/mitpress/9755.001.0001

Minkov, M. (2012). *Cross-cultural analysis: The science and art of comparing the world's modern societies and their cultures.* Sage. https://doi.org/10.4135/9781483384719

Mkhize, N. (2004). Psychology: An African perspective. In D. Hook (Ed.), *Critical psychology* (pp. 24–52). Cape Town, South Africa: University of Cape Town Press..

Ndlovu, N. (2019). *Impact of Urbanization on Indigenous Parenting Values among Parents in KwaZulu-Natal.* Michigan State University.

Neldner, K., Redshaw, J., Murphy, S., Tomaselli, K., Davis, J., Dixson, B., & Nielsen, M. (2019). Creation across culture: Children's tool innovation is influenced by cultural and developmental factors. *Developmental Psychology, 55*(4), 877. http://dx.doi.org/10.1037/dev0000672

Nettle, D., & Bateson, M. (2015). Adaptive developmental plasticity: What is it, how can we recognize it and when can it evolve? *Proc R Soc B, 282*(1812). https://doi.org/10.1098/rspb.2015.1005

Nettle, D., Coall, D. A., & Dickins, T. E. (2011). Early-life conditions and age at first pregnancy in British women. *Proceedings of the Royal Society B: Biological Sciences, 278*(1712), 1721–1727. https://doi.org/10.1098/rspb.2010.1726

Nielsen, M., & Haun, D. (2016). Why developmental psychology is incomplete without comparative and cross-cultural perspectives. *Philosophical Transactions of the Royal Society B: Biological Sciences, 371*(1686), 20150071. https://doi.org/10.1098/rstb.2015.0071

Nisbett, R. E., & Miyamoto, Y. (2005). The influence of culture: Holistic versus analytic perception. *Trends in Cognitive Sciences, 9*(10), 467–473. https://doi.org/10.1016/j.tics.2005.08.004

Nomaguchi, K., & Milkie, M. A. (2020). Parenthood and well-being: A decade in review. *Journal of Marriage and Family, 82*(1), 198–223. https://doi.org/10.1111/jomf.12646

Pemunta, N. V., & Tabenyang, T. C.J. (2021). *Biomedical hegemony and democracy in South Africa.* Brill. https://doi.org/10.1163/9789004436428

Pica, P., Lemer, C., Izard, V., & Dehaene, S. (2004). Exact and approximate arithmetic in an Amazonian indigene group. *Science, 306*(5695), 499–503. https://doi.org/10.1126/science.1102085

Pitt, B., Ferrigno, S., Cantlon, J. F., Casasanto, D., Gibson, E., & Piantadosi, S. T. (2021). Spatial concepts of number, size, and time in an indigenous culture. *Science Advances, 7*(33), eabg4141. https://doi.org/10.1126/sciadv.abg4141

Pope, S. M., Fagot, J., Meguerditchian, A., Washburn, D. A., & Hopkins, W. D. (2019). Enhanced cognitive flexibility in the seminomadic Himba. *Journal of Cross-Cultural Psychology, 50*(1), 47–62. https://doi.org/10.1177/0022022118806581

Pretelli, I., Ringen, E., & Lew-Levy, S. (2022). Foraging complexity and the evolution of childhood. *Science Advances, 8*(41), eabn9889. https://doi.org/10.1126/sciadv.abn9889

Raum, O. F. (1973). *The social functions of avoidances and taboos among the Zulu* (vol. 6). Walter de Gruyter GmbH & Co KG. https://doi.org/10.1515/9783110832884

Remmel, E. (2008). The benefits of a long childhood. *American Scientist, 96*(3), 250–252. https://doi.org/10.1511/2008.71.250

Richerson, P. J., & Boyd, R. (2005). *Not by genes alone: How culture transformed human evolution.* University of Chicago Press. https://doi.org/10.7208/chicago/9780226712130.001.0001

Rogoff, B., Dahl, A., & Callanan, M. (2018). The importance of understanding children's lived experience. *Developmental Review, 50*, 5–15. https://doi.org/10.1016/j.dr.2018.05.006

Ryen, A. (2019). *Indigenous Methods.* Sage. https://doi.org/10.4135/9781526421036854700

Smith, L. T. (2021). *Decolonizing methodologies: Research and indigenous peoples.* Bloomsbury Publishing. https://doi.org/10.5040/9781350225282

Smith, T. M., Tafforeau, P., Reid, D. J., Grün, R., Eggins, S., Boutakiout, M., & Hublin, J.-J. (2007). Earliest evidence of modern human life history in North African early Homo sapiens. *Proceedings of the National Academy of Sciences, 104*(15), 6128–6133. https://doi.org/10.1073/pnas.0700747104

Spivak, G. C. (2023). Can the subaltern speak? In *Imperialism* (pp. 171–219). Routledge. https://doi.org/10.4324/9781003101437-6

Stengelin, R., Hepach, R., & Haun, D. B. (2020). Cultural variation in young children's social motivation for peer collaboration and its relation to the ontogeny of Theory of Mind. *PLoS One, 15*(11), e0242071. https://doi.org/10.1371/journal.pone.0242071

Super, C. M., & Harkness, S. (1986). The developmental niche: A conceptualization at the interface of child and culture. *International Journal of Behavioral Development, 9*(4), 545–569. https://doi.org/10.1177/016502548600900409

Tinbergen, N. (1963). On aims and methods of ethology. *Ethology, 20*(4), 410–433. https://doi.org/10.1111/j.1439-0310.1963.tb01161.x

Tomasello, M. (2005). *Constructing a language: A usage-based theory of language acquisition.* Harvard University Press. https://doi.org/10.2307/j.ctv26070v8

Urassa, M., Lawson, D. W., Wamoyi, J., Gurmu, E., Gibson, M. A., Madhivanan, P., & Placek, C. (2021). Cross-cultural research must prioritize equitable collaboration. *Nature Human Behaviour, 5*(6), 668–671. https://doi.org/10.1038/s41562-021-01076-x

van Leeuwen, E. J., Cohen, E., Collier-Baker, E., Rapold, C. J., Schäfer, M., Schütte, S., & Haun, D. B. (2018). The development of human social learning across seven societies. *Nature Communications, 9*(1), 2076. https://doi.org/10.1038/s41467-018-04468-2

Vieira, W., Pope-Caldwell, S. M., Dzabatou, A., Maurits, L., Padberg, M., & Haun, D. B. M. (Under review). Social learning leads to inflexible strategy use in children across three societies.

Viljoen, S. (1994). *Strengths and weaknesses in the family life of black South Africans. Cooperative Research Programme on Marriage and Family Life.* Pretoria: HSRC.

Wallace, D. (2015). Rethinking religion, magic and witchcraft in South Africa: From colonial coherence to postcolonial conundrum. *Journal for the Study of Religion, 28*(1), 23–51.

Wilson, S. (2008). *Research is ceremony: Indigenous research methods.* Halifax, Winnipeg: Fernwood Publishing.

Zuilkowski, S. S., McCoy, D. C., Serpell, R., Matafwali, B., & Fink, G. (2016). Dimensionality and the development of cognitive assessments for children in Sub-Saharan Africa. *Journal of Cross-Cultural Psychology, 47*(3), 341–354. https://doi.org/10.1177/0022022115624155

2. A history of cross-cultural research on childhood learning

Coordinated by Tanya MacGillivray

This chapter reviews the history of cross-cultural childhood learning by describing the traditions, perspectives, methods, and philosophies that have shaped our field of research. We cover a broad range of topics, from developmental psychology, the history and traditions of different approaches and perspectives, contributions from evolutionary theory and archaeology, as well as noting the narrow framework of the western lens. We highlight the ways in which disciplines have come together to deepen our understanding of the nature of childhood learning. While we recognize the limitations of each approach and method, we focus our chapter on their unique as well as complementary contributions and how they have shaped the field today. This chapter can be construed as a roadmap of research on childhood learning, charting the history of the field.

2.1. Introduction

Tanya MacGillivray

The human developmental period known as 'childhood' is unique in several aspects including the extent to which we learn from others. The study of childhood learning has evolved with different waves of thinking and perspectives over the years and through various discipline traditions, interests, and goals. In this chapter we focus on the unique contributions and limitations of each approach. First, MacGillivray and Halavani provide a brief

©2025 Tanya MacGillivray, et al., CC BY-NC 4.0
https://doi.org/10.11647/OBP.0440.02

overview of the contributions of notable leaders in the field of developmental psychology. Until the early 20th century, there was very little interest in child learning outside of urban life. Then, Kroupin describes the realization within the field that culture matters, leading to an increasing interest in the context of everyday lives of children beyond western societies. Various theories and approaches are described, with Takada articulating the socialization approach to culture, noting the significance of personality theory, and Xu describing Chinese traditions. Oppong and Dutra highlight what is missing with western-biased theories and underscore the need to understand the majority cultures of the world. Hewlett defines and describes cultural evolution theory as an approach to understanding human childhood learning. To better understand our ancestral past and the role of cultural transmission and learning in childhood, Riede and Nowell detail the work of paleoanthropologists focused on the lives of past children. Lastly, Greenfield takes us on a personal journey through historical change within the field.

2.2. Contributions from developmental psychology

Tanya MacGillivray & Zahra Halavani

Since the early 1900s, beginning with the work of Piaget, we have had rich descriptions of the social context in which children learn from others as well as the limitations and remarkable developmental changes that enable children to engage with and learn information and skills from others. Piaget focused on how children engage with and make sense of the world around them by exploring, testing, and exercising their developing abilities. Although Piaget is less well known for his work on social interactions, he argued that children's interest in others drives their ability to engage with and gather information about social interactions (reviewed in Carpendale & Lewis, 2023). In turn, this enables children to learn from others. The primary focus of his work centered on examining how knowledge develops in children and how they progress through different 'stages'. Piaget describes the process of the acquisition of knowledge as 'constructivism', whereby the child constructs or develops expectations about what will occur, based on their experiences. The child is an active engaged agent in the world and this begins at birth with an early developing preference for others (Broesch, 2024).

Since the work of Piaget, research has examined various aspects of social development and learning with a strong focus on the early interest in and preference for human faces, voices, and movements which enable dyadic interaction to develop into more complex forms of human interaction (Goldberg, 1977). Later, infants develop the ability to follow a gaze, and comprehend and produce communicative gestures such as pointing, which allow for complex forms of social learning. Although there are different explanations for this uniquely human ability, there is a consensus that the infant-caregiver system sets the stage for this ability (Broesch, 2024).

Piaget was often misrepresented as focusing on the individual child in isolation (see Carpendale & Lewis, 2004). Following in the steps of Piaget, Lev Vygotsky and his colleagues emphasized the primacy of social and cultural factors in child learning. Vygotsky's emphasis on this systems perspective in human development contrasts with reductionist approaches in science and encompasses both bio-social and bio-psychological aspects of development (Vasileva & Balyasnikova, 2019). Fernyhough (2008) pointed out that specific Vygotskian concepts, including internalization, zone of proximal development, and naïve participation, have become useful for studying the development of social understanding and learning. The concept of the zone of proximal development (ZPD) has become popular in different fields of psychology, including developmental, cognitive, and educational, due to its generalized and applicable nature. Vygotsky (1978) defined the ZPD as the gap between infants' current level of development and the potential level of development they can reach with the assistance of knowledgeable others.

In developmental psychology more recently, much of the work on social learning in early childhood focused on two features of the learning context: (1) the psychological mechanisms that enable social learning (in both infant and caregiver), and (2) the caregiver-infant system that enables social learning. Both of these features focus on the infant or child as well as the knowledgeable other (caregiver) and, interestingly, one is rarely examined without the other but there are few descriptions of the learning mechanisms as dyadic-interactive-systems. Some work describes the dyadic learning system in which both parties are ready for learning and teaching (Csibra & Gergely, 2009). They describe the theory of natural pedagogy, and this has driven more work to examine possible mechanisms that may be supporting this system throughout ontogeny.

Until relatively recently, culture was largely ignored from the study of child development generally and human learning specifically. This reflects the very ethnocentric perspective of family life—many assume family life to reflect urban and western, Eurocentric, heteronormative values, leading to a description of child learning that may be specific to one homogenous cultural context. As a result, we are left with questions of generalizability and an awareness that we may be missing out on a deeper understanding of the range of human diversity (Kline et al., 2018).

2.3. Cross-cultural contributions

Ivan Kroupin

The history of at least one major branch of cross-cultural cognitive research reveals a complex relationship with an apparently opposing school of thought focusing on culture-free laws of cognition and development. In the early 1960s, two parallel trends emerged in developmental psychology. On the one hand, the 'cognitive revolution'—headed by the likes of Chomsky, Simon, and Newell (for a review, see Gardner, 1985)—brought in theories of cognition based in computation and information processing. At the same time, a major wave of cross-cultural psychological research was emerging, spearheaded by researchers such as Michael Cole and Patricia Greenfield (e.g., Gay & Cole, 1967; Greenfield & Bruner, 1966) and soon including a larger group, e.g., Sylvia Scribner, David

Lancy, and Barbara Rogoff (Scribner, 1974; Lancy, 1978; Rogoff, 1981). While the two movements initially shared an interest in exploring general forms of processing in thinking and learning such as memory and formal logic (some of which date back to earlier work by Piaget, e.g., Inhelder & Piaget, 1958), cross-cultural researchers quickly discovered that standardized experiments failed to capture the cognitive processes of populations outside of western, urban, formally schooled groups.

Concretely, the evolution of the cross-cultural school away from cognitivist approaches resulted in influential critiques of standardized experimental methods (e.g., Scribner, 1976; Lave, 1997; Greenfield, 1997). These typically resemble school tests and, consequently, are familiar to schooled participants but may limit the performance of non-schooled groups for whom explicit testing by unfamiliar adults is a strange situation with unfamiliar presuppositions (see Scribner, 1977; Dias et al., 2005 for a case study of differences in assumptions leading to 'failures' in non-schooled groups). Moving away from these standard approaches, cross-cultural researchers developed ethnographically informed experimental paradigms (see, e.g., Greenfield, 1974; Lave, 1977 for important early examples). These methods typically involved constructing experimental contexts in such a way as to avoid removing participants from their familiar cultural contexts.

This divergence culminated in a split between cognitivist and culturalist approaches, exemplified by a large study by Sharp, Cole, and Lave (1979). The authors pursued a multi-year study of the effects of schooling on cognition using standardized experiments, only to conclude, in the words of Cole, that "[D]evelopmental, cognitive research in the United States and other industrialized countries, where years of education and age go hand in glove, has been studying the consequences of education rather than culture-free developmental laws." (p. 85). Rogoff and Chavajay (1995) provide a historical review of this schism and how the culturalist school moved away from domain-general cognitive processing and towards culturally embedded approaches inspired by the Soviet school (e.g., Vygotsky, 1978; Luria, 1976; see also Cole, 1996 for a longer historical and theoretical treatment of this split).

In sum, cross-cultural work on learning and cognitive development and universalist approaches to cognitive science have been historically influenced by each other, but also structured as a reaction to the limitations of the other camp. While the inherent tension between these two camps has often led to a lack of dialogue, a recent wave of work (e.g., Henrich et al., 2010; Medin et al., 2010; Nielsen et al., 2017; Kline et al., 2018; Broesch, Crittenden, et al., 2020; Rad et al., 2018; Barrett, 2020; Kroupin et al., 2024) has once again begun to emphasize the inevitable importance of culture in the study of cognition and learning as a whole.

2.4. A history of socialization approach for cultural research of childhood learning

Akira Takada

The concern that research of childhood learning using standardized tasks reflects (sometimes unconsciously) the western view of development and human nature, and that this may hinder the proper discussion and understanding of childhood learning in non-western communities, is one of the main motivations for anthropologists interested in childhood learning to travel to faraway fields. Anthropologists value cultural diversity in childhood learning and often prefer the concept of socialization, which focuses on enabling children to behave in socially appropriate manners, to the concept of learning, which implies cognitive processes that occur within the individual child.

One of the most important early theoretical frameworks for the study of socialization was 'culture and personality theory'. It attempted to clarify how culturally distinctive personality is formed through the process of socialization. According to Benedict, "identity as a culture depends upon the selection of some segments" from among the potentially infinitely diverse set of segments. As a result, every human society "has made such selection in its cultural institutions" and "each from the point of view of another ignores fundamentals and exploits irrelevancies" (Benedict, 1934/2005, p. 24).

There was a tendency in culture and personality theory to consider individual cultures to be 'personality writ large' (Mead, 1959/2005), with individuals learning to imitate their own cultures through the process of socialization. Reflecting such thinking, analyses of child socialization emphasized the impact of child rearing practices on the formation of personality (e.g., Bateson & Mead, 1942; Mead, 1943; Mead & Wolfenstein, 1955).

The view that culture is the amalgam of segments that cannot be compared is readily linked to the skeptical view that there is no such thing as truth. Culture and personality theory, along with cultural relativism, has generated abundant criticism (e.g., Freeman, 1983; LeVine, 2007). As a response to such criticisms, a research group organized by John and Beatrice Whiting collected data using more standardized procedures and long-term fieldwork. Their 'Six Cultures Project' was an attempt to identify the unique characteristics of child socialization in six cultures (Orchard Town, US; Khalapur, India; Taira, Okinawa; Tarong, the Philippines; Uxtlahuaca, Mexico; Nyansongo, Kenya) (Whiting, 1963; Whiting & Whiting, 1975). According to the Whitings' analysis, social interactions in societies categorized as 'less complex' were more nurturant-responsible (offers help, offers support, suggests responsibly). In contrast, in 'more complex' societies, social interactions were more dependent-dominant (seeks help, seeks attention, seeks dominance). Based on these results, the Whitings proposed a holistic social model as a basis for thinking about the relationship between culture and the mind (Whiting & Whiting 1975, p. xi). In this model, the means of production and mode of subsistence determine the children's learning environment, which, coupled with innate factors, determines the characteristic behavior patterns of a given culture. However, there is likely much room for improvement in the two dimensions for comparing societies (the complexity of socio-economic institutions and household structures), the resulting categorization of societies, and the analyzed behavioral categories.

One promising approach to circumventing the difficulties in setting the standard dimensions of comparison across cultures is to focus on the local activities within which appropriate cultural structures are situated (Goodenough, 1981), and study them thoroughly and empirically. By combining ethnographic methods in studying the local activities with a detailed analysis of face-to-face interactions, we have an opportunity to study language, social organization, and culture from an integrated perspective (Goodwin, 1990, p. 2). This is also a promising approach in that it avoids the aforementioned pitfalls of a relativist view. With this approach, studies of language socialization can examine—through detailed analysis of the use of various semiotic resources, including language—"how children and other cultural novices apprehend and enact the 'context of situation' in relation to the 'context of culture'" (Ochs & Schieffelin, 2012, p. 1).

As an example, Takada (2019) presents a detailed analysis of an emotional word *hazukashii* (lit. shaming, shy, embarrassing, or awkward) in Japanese caregiver-child interactions. After the publication of Benedict's (1946) seminal work, shame became associated with the ethos of East Asian cultures including Japanese culture. According to Takada (2019), a caregiver's *hazukashii* toward the child is likely to occur when the child fails to respond/behave appropriately to the context of the situation and thus caregivers often tease or give a more acceptable account for the inappropriate action performed by the child. His further analysis indicates that sources of *hazukashii* include disorderly appearances (e.g., dressing, eating manner), divergence from expectations in conversation (e.g., greeting to greeting, answer to question), and divergence from role expectations (e.g., as kindergartener, boy/girl, and older brother/sister). As children grow up, caregivers increasingly superimpose the context of culture over the context of the situation, and *hazukashii* is a useful emotional word for promoting this. This leads to the child's understanding of a broader context beyond the 'here and now', and thus to more advanced language socialization. *Hazukashii* thus works as an organizing force as well as a product of socialization practices in Japanese caregiver-child interactions.

2.5. Beyond western theories: Chinese thoughts on childhood learning

Jing Xu

Childhood learning has an important and evolving role in Chinese culture and history. It has assumed a unique significance in Chinese philosophical thoughts for more than 2,000 years (Cline, 2015). It is connected to educational desire, social anxiety, and political governance in larger society across various historical periods and social transitions (Bakken, 2000; Xu, 2022). Chinese traditional theories and thoughts have important insights to inform contemporary cross-cultural research on child development and learning: the relationship between biology and culture—or 'nature' and 'nurture'—remains one of the most important and contested scientific questions today. Instead of imposing a dichotomous and oppositional understanding of 'nature versus nurture', Chinese traditions envision this relationship as dynamic and mutually constitutive in the process of learning. Moreover, the nature of origins of human cooperation and morality is a central issue in the synergetic research across anthropology, psychology, and cognitive science. Since the Axial Age (eighth to third century BCE), Chinese traditions have emphasized the development of morality as the ultimate goal of learning (Li, 2012) and envisioned the process of learning morality as bringing our inborn nature to completion (Jiang, 2021).

Assumptions about human nature and its interaction with the environment constitute the foundations of Chinese thought on learning and human development. Even today, preschool children in metropolitan areas of China still learn to recite this precept from 'Three Character Classic' (*San Zi Jing*), a popular primer during imperial times (Xu, 2017):

> Men at their birth are naturally good.
> Their natures are much the same;
> their habits become widely different.
> If foolishly there is no teaching,
> the nature will deteriorate.[1]

---

1 English translation by Herbert Giles (https://ctext.org/three-character-classic).

Agricultural metaphors, especially those of plant cultivation, abound in Chinese educational culture. The most well-known metaphor was advocated by the ancient Confucian philosopher Mencius (fourth to third century BCE), that humans have innate but incipient tendencies, like sprouts or seeds, toward benevolence, righteousness, wisdom, and propriety, which will develop into full-fledged virtues if given the proper environment. The emphasis on teaching and learning in shaping children's moral personhood, which still finds its resonance in contemporary Chinese communities (Xu, 2017), also originates from classic Chinese philosophy. For example, the Confucian classic *Analects* begins with this sentence: "The Master [Confucius] said, 'Is it not pleasant to learn with a constant perseverance and application?'"[2] Two characters in this sentence constitute a basic theory of learning: First, '學' (*xue)* means 'to learn, to apprehend, to emulate'. The lower part of this character, '子', means 'offspring/child'. Second, '習' (*xi*) means 'to practice; to flap the wings/to flutter [birds practicing flying]'. To early Confucians in the Axial Age, the content of learning refers to repeatedly practicing proper rites and rituals that embody the ideal moral order. But this view of learning also implies and presumes a role of nature: a bird learning to fly is part of 'bird nature', and morality—exemplified in rituals—is part of human nature. The two characters combined together, 學習, became the modern Chinese word for 'learning'.

Building or restoring social order was an existential concern at a time when kingdoms were competing with each other, on the verge of the rise of the first Chinese empire. Intellectuals in early China were pondering fundamental questions about the relationships between self and other, between individual, family, and the larger society or government, formulating thoughts about justice, care, and freedom, and above all, exploring answers to the question of how individuals acquire these virtues—that is, the question of learning (Jiang, 2021). Ever since then, the idea of self-cultivation, or 'becoming human' (*zuoren*), has remained a

---

2   English translation by James Legge (https://ctext.org/analects/xue-er).
    Original text: 子曰：「學而時習之，不亦說乎？」

central concern in Chinese thought and is reflected in educational practices today (Li, 2012; Xu, 2017). Dominant theories of learning and child development today are mostly rooted in western thought, especially moral philosophy. But it is time for researchers to broaden our intellectual horizons and learn from diverse cultural traditions. Classical Chinese philosophy, with its organic view of nature and environment and its longstanding emphasis on moral cultivation, can still inform researchers today to reflect on the meaning and purpose of childhood learning.

2.6. Alternative perspectives on childhood learning – what have we missed with our 'western' lens?

Seth Oppong & Natália Dutra

Child development is a bio-cultural process, with culture playing a major role in defining the shape (developmental pathways and milestones) and content (transmitted skills) of development (Jukes et al., 2021; Keller, 2016, 2017, 2018; Keller et al., 2018; Morelli et al., 2018; Nsamenang, 1992, 2006; Oppong, 2015; Scheidecker et al., 2021, 2023b; Serpell & Nsamenang, 2014; Weisner, 2002). This implies that the context of human development matters as much as the biology of the person. Again, it is the culture that determines the developmental tasks that a person in a particular context must resolve and the types of human capacities that a person develops, in order to become a fully functional person in that particular society. However, the current science and interventions in global early childhood development (ECD) are heavily based on research done in wealthy countries using theories, concepts, methods, and tools informed by their cultural orientations and philosophies (Oppong, 2023a; Scheidecker et al., 2022, 2023).

There are several important human capacities, opportunities for early learning, social partners, and structural barriers that are often missed when western theories and perspectives are applied to persons in the Majority World. For instance, the current western understanding of child stimulation—a very important contributor to cognitive development—is based on the heavily criticized attachment theory (Keller, 2021; Scheidecker et al., 2023a, 2023b). This view enables international bodies such as UNICEF, and proponents of the Nurturing Care Framework (NCF), to frame and measure child stimulation only in the context of primary caregiver/ mother-child play (Scheidecker et al., 2021, 2022, 2023a, 2023b). This has been termed as responsive caregiving in the NCF.

This western bias, therefore, ignores other forms of play such as child-to-child play and adult non-primary caregiver-to-child play that equally provide stimulations for language and socio-emotional development of the child in the Majority World (Scheidecker et al., 2023b). Such focus on child stimulation tends to privilege books and manufactured toys and leads to ignorance of other learning materials such as naturally occurring cultural artifacts in the environment of the child (Scheidecker et al., 2022). Often, the focus on books corresponds to a view that a key desirable developmental outcome is school readiness, with particular emphasis on English Language or the development of other European Languages (adopted or forced upon people in the Majority World as a result of colonization or the global political economy). Though school readiness can be a desirable outcome, it should be seen as only one among varied desirable outcomes, with different contexts emphasizing different outcomes.

This is particularly important as the current educational content/curriculum in the Majority World tends to produce citizens alienated from their own cultures (Oppong, 2013). Given what are considered desirable forms of play, play materials, and the emphasis on certain human capacities, the natural outcome is that childhood assessment tools are also developed with them in mind. For instance, to determine if a child (three to four years) is developmentally on track or delayed, UNICEF (2018) created an Early Childhood Development Index (ECDI) which is used as part of its Multiple Indicator Cluster Surveys (MICS). Within the ECDI, items such as the following are asked: "can a child identify or name at least ten letters of the alphabet?" This question cannot be used to produce comparable data on aspects of literacy among young children across the world. This is because the unintended impact of this question is that children in the Majority World are often not assessed in their native language but in a European Language. This further reinforces the colonial educational curriculum and tends to represent them and their parents as deficient (Scheidecker et al., 2022). The implications are that, when western theories and perspectives are used to understand child development in universalistic ways, there is always a possibility of missing key developmental outcomes in different contexts as well as producing biased evidence that portrays children from the Majority World as deficient and needing interventions (Oppong, 2015, 2019, 2023a). This does not in any way suggest that we should deny help to communities and children in need; rather, by understanding the problems and risks associated with using western theories and perspectives to frame child development in the Majority World, we can improve the basic ECD science that informs ECD policies and interventions. With such improvements in the basic ECD science, we can hope to 'do good' better!

Over the years, calls have been made to develop and present alternative theories and perspectives on child development (Nsamenang, 1992, 2006; Oppong, 2015, 2017, 2019, 2020, 2023a). As a result of these calls, theories and perspectives such as Oppong's (2017, 2023b) bio-cultural theory of becoming a person, Oppong's (2020) model of valued human cognitive abilities, Nsamenang's (1992, 2006) social ontogenesis, and Nwoye's (2017) Africentric theory of human personhood, to mention a few, have been proposed to provide alternative frameworks for understanding an African human person, for instance. Oppong's (2020) model of valued human cognitive abilities holds that cognitive abilities or general intelligence comprise of cognitive competence (demonstrating analytical abilities, good memory, etc.), wisdom (demonstrating thoughtfulness, the intellectual initiative to recognize a problem, and having the skill to solve the problem while displaying concern for one's community), and socio-emotional competence (demonstrating the ability to recognize the needs for social adaptation, obedience, trustworthiness, respectfulness, and cooperation). He shows that the type of cognitive abilities emphasized and their development in each cultural context depend on the currency and values each cognitive ability has in a particular context (Oppong, 2020). Thus, the western models of cognitive abilities tend to emphasize cognitive competence (see how literacy is measured in the ECDI) for its emphasis on school readiness and ignore other cognitive abilities such as wisdom and socio-emotional competence. This implies that if we decide to frame the measurement of cognitive development in Oppong's (2020) model of valued human cognitive abilities, we will obtain different results from African children and may even show that western children are developmentally delayed in terms of wisdom and socio-emotional competence. Indeed, we get exactly what we measure!

2.7. History of cultural evolutionary studies

Barry Hewlett

Evolutionary scholars have been interested in social learning— i.e., learning skills and knowledge from others rather than on your own—for over 100 years. This brief overview and history of evolutionary approaches to the study of child learning examines contributions in the last fifty years. The review focuses on two cultural evolutionary perspectives: cultural transmission theory (CT) and dual transmission theory (DT). Other important evolutionary theories, such as embodied capital theory (Kaplan & Bock, 2001) and cultural attraction theory (Sperber, 1996), have also contributed to the study of childhood learning, but are not covered here because they have generated fewer studies of childhood learning than CT and DT and allocated space was limited.

Cultural Transmission Theory (CT)

Luca Cavalli-Sforza (geneticist) and Marc Feldman (biologist) were hired by Stanford University in the early 1970s and were concerned with racist rhetoric about links between genes and intelligence by Arthur Jensen, a psychologist at UC Berkeley, and

William Shockley, a Stanford faculty member (and Nobel prize winner for his work on semiconductors) who proposed that only intelligent people should have children and that black people were inferior. This motivated Cavalli-Sforza and Feldman to develop sophisticated mathematical models to demonstrate gene-culture coevolution and how modes of cultural transmission influence behavior and evolution. In 1972, they offered a class together, which led to their collaboration. Their first papers on cultural transmission were published in 1973 followed by their 1981 classic book, *Cultural Transmission and Evolution*. Their book identifies eleven different modes of transmission, but most scholars today are familiar with the five outlined in Table 2.1. The modes focus on from whom a child learns, e.g., parents or vertical transmission, and the number of transmitters to receivers. The mathematical models to support the characteristic features of the modes come from genetics (vertical) and disease transmission (horizontal and oblique).

Table 2.1. Modes of cultural transmission (from whom children learn) described by Cavalli-Sforza and Feldman (1981).

Type	**Vertical**	**Horizontal**	**Oblique**	**Many-to-One (Concerted)**	**One-to-Many**
Features	Learn from parents	Learn from members of same generation. Acquisition depends upon frequency of interaction	Learn from non-parental adults. Acquisition depends upon frequency of interaction	Cultural elements that members agree are important to transmit together, e.g., social norms	One individual to group, e.g., formal education, storytelling
Contribution to intracultural variability	High	Varies by frequency of contact	Varies by frequency of contact	Low	Low

Especially adaptive in these social and natural environments	Stable	Changing, parents less available	Changing, parents less available, others with more knowledge	Stable	Changing, high social stratification, population density
General rate of culture change with this transmission mode	Conservative	Can be rapid if frequency of contact is high	Can be rapid if frequency of contact is high	Conservative	Rapid
Age especially important	Infancy, Early Childhood	Middle Childhood	Adolescence	Early Childhood, Adolescence	Any

The first small-scale culture field test of CT models was conducted in the mid-1980s among Aka hunter-gatherers and found that vertical transmission was particularly common, and that transmission often occurred within the same gender (Hewlett & Cavalli-Sforza, 1986). Studies in the 1990s among the Cree (Ohmagari & Berkes, 1997) and other groups (Shennan & Steele, 1999) had similar results, but in the 2000s, observational studies (early studies were based on interviews with parents or children about how they learned particular skills and knowledge) of BaYaka, Tsimane, Hadza, and Baka children demonstrated that other children (horizontal) were regular transmitters in middle childhood and non-parental adults (oblique) were common transmitters in learning more complex skills in adolescence (Lew-Levy et al., 2019). Recent CT research continues to show that vertical transmission is important (Schniter et al., 2022), research methods can influence results (Dira et al., 2016), and that age and gender, skill complexity, size of camp/village, and degree of relatedness impact from whom a child learns. Few studies have been conducted on concerted and one-to-many transmission.

Dual Transmission Theory (DT)

Robert Boyd's (ecologist) and Peter Richerson's (zoologist) interests in cultural transmission developed in a similar way to those of Cavalli-Sforza and Feldman; they were asked to co-teach an introduction to environmental studies course at UC Davis in 1974. Both wanted to understand how culture enabled humans to rapidly adapt to various environments, but they were not impressed with theories of adaptation used by cultural ecologists at the time. They started by making mathematical models found in evolutionary ecology, but then came across the work of Cavalli-Sforza and Feldman and took a class from them at Stanford in 1978. Eventually they published their own classic work on social learning, *Culture and the Evolutionary Process*, in 1985.

DT theorists are interested in identifying psychological mechanisms that influence child learning that have been selected for through natural selection. In their 1985 book, Boyd and Richerson originally used the terms direct and indirect bias to refer to some of the learning biases, but scholars had difficulty with the terminology and their anthropology students Joe Henrich and Richard McElreath (2003) provided alternative and more accessible terms and explanations of content and context biases. Table 2.2 outlines some of the DT biases. Context biases are learning cues that children use and suggest that children are more likely to learn from people who speak the same language or eat similar foods and from people who have more children, wealth, and prestige. Content biases indicate that children are more likely to pay attention to stories or conversations about things like fire, food, and dangerous animals because they could impact their survival. These learning biases generally emerge early in life, and are automatic and unconscious.

Table 2.2. Examples of content and context biases from Dual Transmission theory.

Context Biases	Content Biases
(from whom to learn)	(cultural domains children have evolved to pay attention to)
Model-Based	Dangerous animals
Learn from individuals:	
With more skill, knowledge, competence than others	Fire

That are successful, e.g., greater wealth, high fertility, nice clothes	Explanations for illness
With more prestige, i.e., individuals that receive more attention and deference	Cultural norms
In good health, which is an indicator of adaptation	Social groups
That are older (children or adults) and have accumulated knowledge or skills	Living kinds (classification of animals and plants)
That look and sound like you, e.g., same gender, ethnicity, dialect, dress, foods	Sex
Frequency-Based	Food
Conformist transmission, copy the most common cultural features in the group as they are most likely to be adaptive	Artifacts
Non-conformist transmission, do what everyone else is not doing, e.g., when what most people are doing is not working	

Research in the late 1980s into the 1990s was primarily theoretical (Boyd & Richerson, 2005). In the 2000s, the number of experimental studies with children in western countries and field research in small-scale cultures increased dramatically. Much of the research focused on two major DT contributions: prestige-bias and conformist bias. Experimental studies, field research, and ethnographic descriptions indicate that children are more likely to use prestige bias cues in late, rather than early, childhood because children have easy access to family and friends when they are young but are willing later in life to spend more time to find and learn from successful or prestigious individuals (Henrich & Henrich, 2010). Data to support the assumption that if an individual acquires prestige in one domain, it can lead children to copy that individual across several cultural domains, is limited (Jiménez & Mesoudi, 2019). Cross-cultural data indicate that prestige bias is less common in hunter-gatherers than it is in other modes of production (Garfield et al., 2016).

Conformist transmission—i.e., copying frequently observed behaviors—has now been studied and found in several different species, from fish to chimpanzees, because DT theoretical models indicate that it is favored by natural selection and creates differences between groups. A similar but slightly different evolutionary learning bias is called majority bias, which is "the tendency of an individual to preferentially adopt behaviors *demonstrated* by a majority" (italics added, Sibilsky et al., 2022, p. 1). Experimental studies with children from diverse cultures show that the frequency of copying many demonstrators is relatively low, cultural variability exists in how frequently children copy the demonstrators, and that younger and older children are more likely to copy the majority than middle aged children.

CT and DT approaches to childhood learning have increased substantially in the last fifty years. The approaches have been utilized by researchers in multiple disciplines including anthropology, psychology, economics, and biology, and have led to significant insights into how children learn in diverse cultures.

2.8. Children of the Ice Age: Apprenticeship, communities of practice and embodied cognition in deep-time hunter-gatherer archaeology

Felix Riede & April Nowell

Even before the formulation of the 'grandmothering hypothesis' explaining the extended post-reproductive lifespan that characterizes the *Homo* lineage (Hawkes et al., 1998), paleoanthropologists have been interested in the peculiarities of human life history, including our extended childhood period (Bogin, 1997). Archaeologists, too, had begun to develop an interest in the lives of past children (see Baxter, 2008), although this was most commonly focused on those cases where the fragile bones of children were preserved, and to recent periods. An emphasis on data from burial contexts led to a focus on the deaths of these children rather than on their lived experiences (Nowell, 2021). Over time, however, an interest in the children of deep time—and their relevance for understanding cultural change and adaptation—developed (Nowell & White, 2012; Nowell 2023a).

Detailed studies of material culture (i.e., stone tools), usually conducted at individual sites, have succeeded in making the activities of Stone Age youngsters clearly visible (e.g., Assaf, 2021; Finlay, 1997; Grimm, 2000; Karlin et al., 1993; Stapert, 2007). This catalyzed a greater appreciation for children's role in learning and cultural reproduction, mostly in relation to formal apprenticeships. Most recently, interest in the 'children of the ice age' has intensified. By merging together insights from cognitive archaeology—the notion of historically grounded embodied cognition shaped in interaction with artifacts (Johannsen, 2010; Malafouris, 2013)— with developmental psychology's emphasis on the adaptive importance of play (Gopnik, 2020; Pellegrini et al., 2007), as well as theories of cultural evolution that include the many ways in which humans modify the ontogenetic environs of their young (Laland et al., 2000; Riede, 2019), there now is a vastly improved appreciation of how exploratory play throughout childhood and into adolescence would have contributed to innovation, cultural reproduction, and adaptation (Nowell, 2016; Nowell & French, 2020; Riede et al., 2018). Paleolithic children—approached through their many material culture proxies (see Langley & Litster, 2018; Milks et al., 2021)—are now viewed as integral parts of past communities of practice, playfully acquiring know-how about appropriate technologies, ecologies, and cosmologies (Nowell, 2015, 2023b). Interestingly, play objects clearly recognizable as specifically fashioned for children remain rare until about 40,000 years ago—well after the emergence of *Homo sapiens*—and are also not present in equal measure from then on. While the play objects that are present in the archaeological record of the Paleolithic match those most commonly observed ethnographically (Lew-Levy et al., 2022; Riede et al., 2023), it is possible that play object provisioning with, in particular, functional miniatures was far from universal practice until relatively late in human biocultural evolution. Childhood object play in the domains given by play object provisioning in particular acts as the motor that generates technological variation on which subsequent selection may act. By this token, it is likely that not just the biologically conditioned length of childhood but also the culturally specific ways in which these childhoods were part of wider societal constellations had an impact on the increasing rates of material culture change and innovation at this time (cf. Nowell, 2021; Riede et al., 2021).

Today, the archaeology of childhood is a well-established subfield with handbooks (Crawford et al., 2018) and a bespoke journal backed by a similarly focused scholarly community (https://sscip.org.uk/). The children of the Plio-Pleistocene have now come into quite a clear view (see Nowell, 2021), although much work remains to be done in terms of further qualifying the archaeological evidence for play and learning in relation to past socio-ecological change, and in terms of more robustly integrating changes in life history, early-life learning, and play object provisions into formal models of cultural change in hominin biocultural evolution.

2.9. A personal journey through historical changes

Patricia Greenfield

My contribution to this chapter on the historical development of optimal practices for the study of childhood learning, from a cultural and cross-cultural perspective, will focus on the development of my own research practices from my dissertation research in Senegal in 1963 and 1964 to present. These practices primarily integrate psychology and anthropology.

The first practice that I would like to highlight in comparative research on children's learning is the practice of comparing subgroups within a country rather than comparing child learning in different nations. This is a contribution from the discipline of psychology, which always seeks to isolate single variables as causal factors. When one compares samples in different countries, so many different elements vary that it is impossible to know which element or elements are causing any observed cross-cultural differences.

In line with this principle, my first experiments in cognitive development among the Wolof of Senegal, carried out in 1963 and 1964, compared bush children who went to school with children from the same village who did not attend school (Greenfield, 1966;

Greenfield, Reich, & Olver, 1966). This design enabled me to isolate the effect of schooling on cognitive development because all other potential factors were kept constant in the design. This design led to the discovery that the pattern of cognitive development described by Piaget was as much a function of school learning as it was of chronological age (Greenfield & Bruner, 1966). In other words, it highlighted the role of learning and the specific importance of school-based learning in cognitive development.

However, in my next cross-cultural research, in a Maya community in Mexico, I wanted to correct what I saw as an undesirable practice in my Wolof research—testing children on cognitive tasks that originated in the researcher's culture rather than in the culture of the participants. My Piagetian tasks were adapted in multiple ways to Wolof culture, but they were still cognitive tasks meaningful in Swiss and U.S. culture, not the culture of my Wolof participants who were not exposed to western schooling. An important implication of this design was that there was a fit between the task and the school-based environment in which Swiss, European, or American children received their cognitive socialization; Kroupin et al. (2024) call this the articulation between task and environment. But this was not the case for the Wolof children living in the bush and receiving informal education in very different environments.

Hence, in Nabenchauk—a Zinacantec Maya community in Highland Chiapas, Mexico—I based my learning tasks on the most complex skill acquired by all females and central to Maya culture: weaving on a backstrap loom. We started with a cognitive test of visual pattern representation (Greenfield & Childs, 1977). Since they were all weaving striped patterns at that time, our task required Zinacantec children to create striped patterns, first representing familiar woven patterns by inserting sticks of various colors and widths into a wooden frame, then representing striped patterns started by the researchers in the same wooden frame. The representation of striped patterns involved articulation between the cognitive features of our cognitive tests and the demands of the Zinacantec Maya environment of 1969, essentially a subsistence community. When we compared skilled Zinacantec teenage weavers with U.S. college students, we found that each had their own cognitive style that fit or was articulated with the demands of their respective environments: the Zincantec Maya girls created detailed representations, using narrow sticks as representations of individual threads in the woven patterns. In contrast, the U.S. college students used broad sticks to represent groups of threads, a strategy that eliminated the detail and was therefore more abstract. The former strategy, which we called the thread-by-thread strategy, was adaptive for participants for whom weaving was a culturally central skill—individuals who actually had to weave patterns thread by thread. In other words, there was an articulation between the mode of representation and the cognitive demands of weaving. In contrast, the abstract strategy was adaptive for participants for whom school-based learning was culturally central—and abstraction was part and parcel of this cultural context. Abstract representation articulated with the cognitive demands of university education.

However, after completing the study, I felt that the whole idea of a cognitive test came from my culture and was not familiar to my Zinacantec Maya participants. We therefore progressed methodologically to studying the acquisition of backstrap weaving itself—a skill that was central to their culture, but rare in ours (Childs & Greenfield, 1980). This brings me to an important point relating to the best practices for studying child learning processes across cultures: it is not possible to study the learning process for a skill that the researchers lack. This is one central reason why the use of cognitive tests across cultures usually involves tests that are familiar to the researchers, because they originate in and are central to the researchers' culture. I was therefore very fortunate to have two collaborators, Carla Childs and Ashley Maynard, who were willing to learn how to do backstrap-loom weaving before analyzing our video data on the development of weaving apprenticeship from beginner to skilled weaver. In fact, they were taught how to weave in our study community of Nabenchauk (Maynard & Greenfield, 2005). Their learning how to weave enabled the microanalysis of weaving apprenticeship, allowing us to study how weaving was taught and learned.

Knowing how to weave also enabled a cross-cultural study of Piaget's concrete operations in two contexts—one being the Zinacantec weaving context, the other using the type of objects Piaget had used to study the development of topological concepts (Maynard & Greenfield, 2003). This cross-cultural study of children's learning was carried out in both Los Angeles and Nabenchauk. The prediction was that an understanding of topological concepts in the weaving context would occur earlier in Nabenchauk than in Los Angeles, but that topological concepts using materials similar to Piaget's would develop earlier in Los Angeles where the materials would be more familiar. This type of design and predictions is called the cross-over design. Our prediction of 'cross-over' results was that the learning of topological concepts would occur more precociously in the weaving context in Nabenchauk and more precociously with the Piagetian-style materials in Los Angeles; this hypothesis was in fact confirmed. This method and its results indicate that the same basic patterns of cognitive development are acquired in very different cultural settings and that these settings provide a foundation for particular instantiations of cognitive skills that can subsequently be generalized to new contexts. In other words, culture-general cognitive stages are first learned in culture-specific situations.

The continuity of this research team, their knowledge of weaving as a cultural practice, and the relationships that were made in the study community eventually permitted us to study the cultural evolution of weaving apprenticeship and weaving-related cognition over a period of forty-three years (Greenfield et al., 2003; Maynard et al., 2015; Maynard et al., 2023). This long-term study illustrates my next point about the best research practices: follow a study community over extended periods of chronological time in order to identify historical shifts in cultural learning. Longitudinal study of individuals is central to the discipline of developmental psychology, but longitudinal study is rarely applied at the community level. This design allows the study of cultural evolution over historical time and permits conclusions concerning the relationship between intergenerational shifts in child development and shifts in the ecological surroundings—it is therefore a direct method for articulating child learning with cultural evolution.

However, it takes many years to be able to study cultural evolution directly by testing multiple generations in the same community. Especially for young researchers, a shorter data-collection time window is necessary (but keep your data as a baseline for the long-term study of cultural evolution later in your career!). In order to study the evolution of children's learning processes more quickly, we have developed several research designs that use generation as a stand-in for the passage of time.

One research design is a cross-sectional comparison of three generations (adolescent, parent, and grandparent), where participants in each generation respond to the same scenarios exploring value choices. This technique has been used with the Maya in Chiapas, Mexico (Manago, 2014), and with three ethnocultural groups in Israel: Northern Arabs (Weinstock et al., 2014), Bedouins (El-sana et al., 2023), and Ethiopian immigrants (Rotem et al., in revision).

In another design, Chinese grandmothers who had experienced childhood themselves and subsequently taken care of their children and grandchildren were asked to compare their experience of parenting practices and early childhood behavior in each of three generations (Zhou et al., 2017). In a related design focusing on middle childhood, participating mothers were asked to compare their experiences of being parented and their own child behavior with their own parenting and their children's behavior at the same age (Bian et al., 2022). A valuable methodological feature of these studies was to relate shifting features of the parenting environment to shifting features of child behavior during the sociodemographic evolution of the macroenvironment from the earliest to the most recent generation.

In neither Senegalese nor Maya villages did I find collaborators; that was the case because education was basically at home and in the community, rather than at school. With movement in the world in the WEIRD (Western, Educated, Industrialized, Rich, and Democratic) (Henrich et al., 2010) or Gesellschaft direction (Greenfield, 2009), this situation has changed. In my studies in

China, I was able to collaborate with Chinese PhD students and researchers. This research shows the methodological value of having both an insider and outsider perspective: the insider understands the culture but also takes it for granted. Through contrast with their own culture, the outsider is conscious of cultural features and can make them explicit.

My last point is that an optimal practice for studying children's social learning across cultures is to employ narratives—little stories—as stimuli (Greenfield, 2018). We have been successful in using this method to identify the cultural evolution of values in Mexican and Korean immigrant groups in the United States (Greenfield & Quiroz, 2013; Park et al., 2015; Raeff et al., 2000); Maya adolescents in Mexico (Manago, 2014); Bedouin, Arab, and Ethiopian-origin adolescents in Israel (Abu Aleon et al., 2019; El-sana et al., 2023; Rotem et al., in revision; Weinstock et al., 2014), and adolescents and emerging adults in Romania (Ionescu et al., 2023). Narrative and stories are universal genres. Therefore, they can function as stimuli to compare responses in groups with any level of formal education.

References

Abu Aleon, T., Weinstock, M., Manago, A. M., & Greenfield, P. M. (2019). Social change and intergenerational value differences in a Bedouin community in Israel. *Journal of Cross-Cultural Psychology, 50,* 708–727. https://doi.org/10.1177/0022022119839148

Assaf, E. (2021). Dawn of a new day: The role of children in the assimilation of new technologies throughout the Lower Paleolithic. *L'Anthropologie, 125*(1), 102836. https://doi.org/10.1016/j.anthro.2021.102836

Bakken, B. (2000). *The Exemplary Society: Human Improvement, Social Control, and the Dangers of Modernity.* Oxford University Press.

Barrett, H. C. (2020). Towards a Cognitive Science of the Human: Cross-Cultural Approaches and Their Urgency. *Trends in Cognitive Sciences, 24*(8), 620–638. https://doi.org/10.1016/j.tics.2020.05.007

Bateson, G., & Mead, M. (1942). *Balinese character: A photographic analysis.* The New York Academy of Science.

Baxter, J. E. (2008). The Archaeology of Childhood. *Annual Review of Anthropology, 37*(1), 159–175. https://doi.org/doi:10.1146/annurev.anthro.37.081407.085129

Benedict, R. (2005). *Patterns of culture* (Kindle ed.). Houghton Mifflin. (Original work published 1934)

Benedict, R. (1946). *The chrysanthemum and the sword: Patterns of Japanese culture.* Houghton Mifflin.

Bian, Q., Chen, Y., Greenfield, P. M., & Yuan, Q. (2022). Mothers' experience of social change and individualistic parenting goals over two generations in urban China. *Frontiers in Psychology, 12,* 487039. https://doi.org/10.3389/fpsyg.2021.487039

Bogin, B. (1997). Evolutionary Hypotheses for Human Childhood. *American Journal of Physical Anthropology,* 104(S25), 63–89. https://doi.org/10.1002/(SICI)1096-8644(1997)25+<63::AID-AJPA3>3.0.CO;2-8

Boyd, R., & Richerson, P. J. (1985). *Culture and the evolutionary process.* University of Chicago Press.

Boyd, R., & Richerson, P.J. (2005). *The origin and evolution of cultures.* Oxford University Press.

Boyd, R., Richerson, P. J., & Henrich, J. (2011). The cultural niche: Why social learning is essential for human adaptation. *Proceedings of the National Academy of Sciences, 108,* 10918–10925 https://doi.org/10.1073/pnas.1100290108

Broesch, T., Crittenden, A. N., Beheim, B., Blackwell, A. D., Bunce, J., Colleran, H., Hagel, K., Kline, M., McElreath, R., Nelson, R. G., Pisor, A. C., Prall, S., Pretelli, I., Purzycki, B., Quinn, E. A., Ross, C.; Scelza, B., Starkweather, K., Stieglitz, J., & Borgerhoff Mulder, M. (2020). Navigating cross-cultural research: methodological and ethical considerations. *Proceedings of the Royal Society B,* 287(1935). https://doi:10.1098/rspb.2020.1245

Broesch, T. (2024). Mutual joy and social development. In *WAIMH Handbook of Infant and Early Childhood Mental Health: Biopsychosocial Factors* (vol. 1, pp. 407–420). Springer.

Carpendale, J. I., & Lewis, C. (2004). Constructing an understanding of mind: The development of children's social understanding within social interaction. *Behavioral and Brain Sciences, 27*(01), 79–96. https://doi.org/10.1017/s0140525x04000032

Carpendale, J., & Lewis, C. (2023). Piaget's Theory and Stages of Development: A Foundation for Current Understanding of Children. *Child and Family Blog.* https://childandfamilyblog.com/piaget-stages-cognitive-development/

Cavalli Sforza, L. L., & Feldman, M. (1981). *Cultural transmission and evolution: a quantitative approach*. Princeton University Press.

Childs, C. P., & Greenfield, P. M. (1980). Informal modes of learning and teaching: The case of Zinacanteco weaving. In N. Warren (Ed.). *Studies in cross-cultural psychology* (vol. 2, pp. 269–316). Academic Press.

Cline, E. M. (2015). *Families of Virtue: Confucian and Western Views on Childhood Development*. Columbia University Press.

Cole, M. (1996). *Cultural psychology: A once and future discipline*. Harvard University Press.

Crawford, S., Hadley, D. M., & Shepherd, G. (2018). *The Oxford Handbook of the Archaeology of Childhood*. Oxford University Press. https://doi.org/10.1093/oxfordhb/9780199670697.001.0001

Csibra, G., & Gergely, G. (2009). Natural pedagogy. *Trends in Cognitive Sciences, 13*(4), 148–153. https://doi.org/10.1016/j.tics.2009.01.005

Dias, M., Roazzi, A., & Harris, P. L. (2005). Reasoning From Unfamiliar Premises: A Study With Unschooled Adults. *Psychological Science, 16*(7), 550–554. https://doi.org/10.1111/j.0956-7976.2005.01573.x

Dira, S. J., & Hewlett, B.S. (2016). Learning to spear hunt among Chabu adolescent hunter-gatherers. In H. Terashima & B. Hewlett (Eds). *Social learning and innovation among contemporary hunter-gatherers* (pp. 71–82). Springer.

El-sana, S., Greenfield, P. M., & Weinstock, M. (2023). Ecological change, psychological mindedness, and attitudes toward school psychology: a three-generation study of Bedouin women in Israel. *Applied Developmental Science*, 1–17. https://doi.org/10.1080/10888691.2023.2192498

Fernyhough, C. (2008). Getting Vygotskian about theory of mind: Mediation, dialogue, and the development of social understanding. *Developmental Review, 28*(2), 225–262. https://doi.org/10.1016/j.dr.2007.03.001

Finlay, N. (1997). Kid knapping: The missing children in lithic analysis. In J. Moore & E. Scott (Eds). *Invisible People and Processes: Writing Gender and Childhood into European Archaeology* (pp. 203–213). Leicester University Press.

Freeman, D. (1983). *Margaret Mead and Samoa: The making and unmaking of an anthropological myth*. Harvard University Press.

Gardner, H. (1985). *The mind's new science: A history of the cognitive revolution* (Paperback ed.). Basic Books.

Garfield, Z. H., Garfield, M. J., & Hewlett, B. S. (2016). In H. Terashima & B. Hewlett (Eds). *Social learning and innovation among contemporary hunter-gatherers* (pp. 19–34). Springer.

Gay, J., & Cole, M. (1967). *The new mathematics and an old culture: A study of learning among the Kpelle of Liberia.* Holt, Rinehart and Winston.

Gergely, G., & Csibra, G. (2020). Sylvia's recipe: The role of imitation and pedagogy in the transmission of cultural knowledge. In *Roots of human sociality* (pp. 229–255). Routledge.

Goldberg, S. (1977). Social competence in infancy: A model of parent-infant interaction. *Merrill-Palmer Quarterly of Behavior and Development, 23*(3), 163–177. https://www.jstor.org/stable/23084549

Goodenough, W. (1981). *Culture, language and society.* Benjamin Cummings.

Goodwin, M. H. (1990). *He-said-she-said: Talk as social organization among Black Children.* Indiana University Press.

Gopnik, A. (2020). Childhood as a solution to explore–exploit tensions. *Philosophical Transactions of the Royal Society B: Biological Sciences,* 375(1803), 20190502. https://doi.org/10.1098/rstb.2019.0502

Greenfield, P. M. (1966). On culture and conservation. In J. S. Bruner, R. R. Olver, & P. M. Greenfield. *Studies in cognitive growth* (pp. 225–256). Wiley.

Greenfield, P. M., Reich, L. C., & Olver, R. R. (1966). On culture and equivalence-II. In J. S. Bruner, R. R. Olver, & P. M. Greenfield. *Studies in cognitive growth* (pp. 270–318). Wiley.

Greenfield, P. M., & Bruner, J. S. (1971). Language and learning. *Psychology Today, 5,* 40–43, 74–79. (Original work published 1966).

Greenfield, P. M. (1974). Comparing Dimensional Categorization in Natural and Artificial Contexts: A Developmental Study among the Zinacantecos of Mexico. *The Journal of Social Psychology, 93*(2), 157–171. https://doi.org/10/chz4s2

Greenfield, P. M., & Childs, C. P. (1977). Weaving, color terms and pattern representation: Cultural influences and cognitive development among the Zinacantecos of Southern Mexico. *Inter-American Journal of Psychology, 11,* 23–48. http://dx.doi.org/10.1016/j.cogdev.2003.09.004

Greenfield, P. M. (1997). You can't take it with you: Why ability assessments don't cross cultures. American Psychologist, 52(10), 1115–1124. https://doi.org/10.1037/0003-066X.52.10.1115

Greenfield, P. M., Quiroz, B., & Raeff, C. (2000). Cross-cultural conflict and harmony in the social construction of the child. In S. Harkness,

C. Raeff, & C. M. Super (Eds). *New Directions for Child and Adolescent Development, 87,* 93–108.

Greenfield, P. M., Maynard, A. E., & Childs, C. P. (2003). Historical change, cultural learning, and cognitive representation in Zinacantec Maya children. *Cognitive Development*, 18, 455–487. https://doi.org/10.1016/j.cogdev.2003.09.004

Greenfield, P. M. (2009). Linking social change and developmental change: Shifting pathways of human development. *Developmental Psychology, 45,* 401–418. https://doi.org/10.1037/a0014726

Greenfield, P. M., & Quiroz, B. (2013). Context and culture in the socialization and development of personal achievement values: Comparing Latino immigrant families, European American families, and elementary school teachers. *Journal of Applied Developmental Psychology, 34,* 108–118. http://dx.doi.org/10.1016/j.appdev.2012.11.002

Greenfield, P. M. (2018). Studying social change, culture, and human development: A theoretical framework and methodological guidelines. *Developmental Review, 50A,* 16–30. http://dx.doi.org/10.1016/j.dr.2018.05.003

Grimm, L. (2000). Apprentice flintknapping. Relating material culture and social practice in the Upper Palaeolithic. In J. S. Derevenski (Ed.). *Children and Material Culture* (pp. 53–71). Routledge.

Hawkes, K., O'Connell, J. F., Jones, N. G., Alvarez, H., & Charnov, E. L. (1998). Grandmothering, menopause, and the evolution of human life histories. *Proceedings of the National Academy of Sciences*, 95(3), 1336–1339. https://doi.org/10.1073/pnas.95.3.1336

Henrich, J., & McElreath, R. (2003). The evolution of cultural evolution. *Evolutionary Anthropology*, 12, 123–135. doi.org/10.1002/evan.10110

Henrich, J., Heine, S. J., & Norenzayan, A. (2010). The weirdest people in the world? *Behavioral and Brain Sciences*, 33, 61–135. https://doi.org/10.1017/s0140525x0999152x

Henrich, J., & Henrich, N. (2010). The evolution of cultural adaptations: Fijian food taboos protect against dangerous marine toxins. *Proceedings of the Royal Society B: Biological Sciences*, 277(1701), 3715–3724. https://doi.org/10.1098/rspb.2010.1191

Henrich, J. (2016). *The secret of our success.* Princeton.

Hewlett, B. S., & Cavalli Sforza, L. L. (1986). Cultural transmission among Aka pygmies. *American Anthropologist, 88*, 922–934. doi.org/10.1525/aa.1986.88.4.02a00100

Inhelder, B., & Piaget, J. (1958). An essay on the construction of formal operational structures. The growth of logical thinking: From childhood to adolescence (A. Parsons & S. Milgram, Trans.). Basic Books.

Ionescu, A., Ferdui, R., Gavreliuc, A., Greenfield, P. M., & Weinstock, M. (2023). The effects of social changes on epistemic thinking across three generations in Romania. *PLoS ONE, 18*(3), e0281785. https://doi.org/10.1371/journal.pone.0281785

Jiang, T. (2021). *Origins of Moral-Political Philosophy in Early China: Contestation of Humaneness, Justice, and Personal Freedom.* Oxford University Press.

Jiménez, A., & Mesoudi, A. (2019). Prestige-biased social learning: current evidence and outstanding questions. *Palgrave Communications, 5,* 1–12. doi.org/10.1057/s41599-019-0228-7

Johannsen, N. N. (2010). Technological Conceptualization: Cognition on the Shoulders of History. In L. Malafouris & C. Renfrew (Eds). *The Cognitive Life of Things* (pp. 59–69). McDondald Institute for Archaeological Research.

Jukes, M. C. H., Sitabkhan, Y., & Tibenda, J. J. (2021). *Adapting pedagogy to cultural context.* RTI Press. https://doi.org/10.3768/rtipress.2021.op.0070.2109

Karlin, C., Ploux, S., Bodu, P., & Pigeot, N. (1993). Some socio-economic aspects of the knapping process among groups of hunter-gatherers in the Paris Basin area. In A. Berthelet & J. Chavaillon (Eds). *The Use of Tools by Human and Non-human Primates* (pp. 318–340). Blackwell.

Kaplan, H., & Bock J. A. (2001). Fertility theory: The embodied capital theory of human life history evolution. In N. J. Smelser & P. B. Baltes (Eds). *The international encyclopedia of the social and behavior sciences* (pp. 5561–68). Pergamon.

Keller, H. (2016). Psychological autonomy and hierarchical relatedness as organizers of developmental pathways. *Philosophical Transactions of the Royal Society of London. Series B, Biological Sciences, 371*(1686), 20150070. https://doi.org/10.1098/rstb.2015.0070

Keller, H. (2017). Culture and development: A systematic relationship. *Perspectives on Psychological Science, 12*(5), 833–840. https://doi.org/10.1177/1745691617704097

Keller, H. (2018). Universality claim of attachment theory: Children's socioemotional development across cultures. *Proceedings of the National Academy of Sciences of USA, 115,* 11414–11419. https://doi.org/10.1073/pnas.1720325115

Keller, H., Bard, K., Morelli, G., Chaudhary, N., Vicedo, M., Rosabal-Coto, M., Scheidecker, G., Murray, M., & Gottlieb, A. (2018). The myth of universal sensitive responsiveness: Comment on Mesman et al.

(2017). *Child Development, 89*(5), 1921–1928. https://doi.org/10.1111/cdev.13031

Keller, H. (2021). *The Myth of Attachment Theory*. Routledge

Kline, M. A., Shamsudheen, R., & Broesch, T. (2018). Variation is the universal: Making cultural evolution work in developmental psychology. *Philosophical Transactions of the Royal Society of London. Series B, Biological Sciences, 373*(1743), 20170059. https://doi.org/10.1098/rstb.2017.0059

Kroupin, I., Davis, H. E., & Henrich, J. (2024). Beyond Newton: Why Assumptions of Universality are Critical to Cognitive Science, and How to Finally Move Past Them. *Psychological Review*.

Laland, K. N., Odling-Smee, J. F., & Feldman, M. W. (2000). Niche construction, biological evolution, and cultural change. *Behavioral and Brain Sciences, 23*, 131–175. DOI: 10.1017/s0140525x00002417

Langley, M. C., & Litster, M. (2018). Is It Ritual? Or Is It Children?: Distinguishing Consequences of Play from Ritual Actions in the Prehistoric Archaeological Record. *Current Anthropology*, 59(5), 616–643. https://doi.org/10.1086/699837

Lancy, D. F. (1978). Cognitive testing in the indigenous mathematics project. *Papua New Guinea Journal of Education, 14*, 114–142. https://doi.org/10.1007/BF00308142

Lave, J. (1977). Tailor-made experiments and evaluating the intellectual consequences of apprenticeship training. *The Quarterly Newsletter of the Institute for Comparative Human Development, 1*(2), 1–3.

Lave, J. (1997). What's special about experiments as contexts for thinking? In *Mind, culture, and activity: Seminal papers from the Laboratory of Comparative Human Cognition* (pp. 57–69).

Lew-Levy, S., Kissler, S. M., Boyette, A.H., Crittenden, A. N., Mabulla, I. A., & Hewlett, B. S. (2019). Who teaches children to forage? Exploring the primacy of child-to-child teaching among Hadza and BaYaka hunter-gatherers of Tanzania and Congo. Evolution and Human Behavior 41(1), 12–22. doi.org/10.1016/j.evolhumbehav.2019.07.003

Lew-Levy, S., Andersen, M. M., Lavi, N., & Riede, F. (2022). Hunter-Gatherer Children's Object Play and Tool Use: An Ethnohistorical Analysis. *Frontiers in Psychology, 13*. https://doi.org/10.3389/fpsyg.2022.824983

LeVine R. A. (2007). Ethnographic studies of childhood: A historical overview. *American Anthropologist, 109*(2), 247–260. https://doi.org/10.1525/aa.2007.109.2.247

Li, J. (2012). *Cultural Foundations of Learning: East and West* (1st ed.). Cambridge University Press.

Luria, A. R. (1976). *Cognitive development: Its cultural and social foundations*. Harvard University Press.

Malafouris, L. (2013). *How Things Shape the Mind*. MIT Press.

Manago, A. M. (2014). Connecting Societal Change to Value Differences Across Generations: Adolescents, Mothers, and Grandmothers in a Maya Community in Southern Mexico. *Journal of Cross-Cultural Psychology, 45*(6), 868–887. https://doi.org/10.1177/0022022114527346

Maynard, A. E., & Greenfield, P. M. (2003). Implicit cognitive development in cultural tools and children. *Cognitive Development, 18*, 489-510. https://doi.org/10.1016/j.cogdev.2003.09.005

Maynard, A. E., & Greenfield, P. M. (2005). An ethnomodel of teaching and learning: Apprenticeship of Maya women's tasks. In A. E. Maynard & M. I. Martini (Eds). *Cultural models of learning in context: Families, peers, and schools* (pp. 75–103). Kluwer Academic/Plenum Press.

Maynard, A. E., Greenfield, P. M., & Childs, C. P. (2015). Developmental effects of economic and educational change: Cognitive representation across 43 years in a Maya community. *International Journal of Psychology, 50*, 12–19. https://doi.org/10.1002/ijop.12129

Maynard, A. E., Greenfield, P. M., Childs, C. P., & Weinstock, M. (2023). Social change, cultural evolution, weaving apprenticeship, and development: informal education across three generations and 42 years in a Maya community. *Applied Developmental Science.* https://doi.org/10.1080/10888691.2022.2151445

Mead, M. (1943). *Coming of age in Samoa: A study of adolescence and sex in primitive societies*. Penguin.

Mead, M., & Wolfenstein, M. (1955). *Childhood in contemporary cultures*. University of Chicago Press.Mead, M. (2005). Preface. In R. Benedict. *Patterns of culture*. Houghton Mifflin. (Original work published 1959)

Medin, D., Bennis, W., & Chandler, M. (2010). Culture and the Home-Field Disadvantage. *Perspectives on Psychological Science: A Journal of the Association for Psychological Science, 5*(6), 708–713. https://doi.org/10.1177/1745691610388772

Milks, A., Lew-Levy, S., Lavi, N., Friesem, D. E., & Reckin, R. (2021). Hunter-gatherer children in the past: An archaeological review. *Journal of Anthropological Archaeology, 64*, 101369. https://doi.org/10.1016/j.jaa.2021.101369

Morelli, G., Bard, K., Chaudhary, N., Gottlieb, A., Keller, H., Murray, M., Quinn, N., Rosabal-Coto, M., Scheidecker, G., Takada, A., & Vicedo, M. (2018). Bringing the real world into developmental science: A commentary on Weber, Fernald, and Diop (2017). *Child Development, 89*(6), e594–e603. https://doi.org/10.1111/cdev.13115

Nielsen, M., Haun, D., Kärtner, J., & Legare, C. H. (2017). The persistent sampling bias in developmental psychology: A call to action. *Journal of Experimental Child Psychology, 162*, 31–38. https://doi.org/10.1016/j.jecp.2017.04.017

Nowell, A., & White, M. J. (2012). Growing up in the Middle Pleistocene: Life history strategies and their relationship to Acheulian Industries. In A. Nowell & I. Davidson (Eds). *Stone tools and the evolution of human cognition* (pp. 67–82). University Press of Colorado.

Nowell, A. (2015). Learning to See and Seeing to Learn: Children, Communities of Practice and Pleistocene Visual Cultures. *Cambridge Archaeological Journal, 25*(04), 889–899. https://doi.org/doi:10.1017/S0959774315000360

Nowell, A. (2016). Childhood, Play and the Evolution of Cultural Capacity in Neanderthals and Modern Humans. In M. N. Haidle, N. J. Conard, & M. Bolus (Eds). *The Nature of Culture: Based on an Interdisciplinary Symposium 'The Nature of Culture'*, Tübingen, Germany (pp. 87–97). Springer.

Nowell, A., & French, J. C. (2020). Adolescence and innovation in the European Upper Palaeolithic. *Evolutionary Human Sciences, 2*, e36. https://doi.org/10.1017/ehs.2020.37

Nowell, A. (2021). *Growing Up in the Ice Age: Fossil and Archaeological Evidence of the Lived Lives of Plio-Pleistocene Children.* Oxbow Books.

Nowell, A. (2023a). Paleolithic children come of age. *Childhood in the Past, 16*(1): 3-12. https://doi.org/10.1080/17585716.2023.2191483

Nowell, A. (2023b). Oral Storytelling and Knowledge Transmission in Upper Paleolithic Children and Adolescents. *Journal of Archaeological Method and Theory, 30*(1), 9–31. https://doi.org/10.1007/s10816-022-09591-5

Nsamenang, A. B. (1992). *Human development in a cultural context: A third world perspective.* Sage Publications.

Nsamenang, A. B. (2006). Human ontogenesis: An indigenous African view on development and intelligence. *International Journal of Psychology, 41*(4), 293–297. https://doi.org/10.1080/00207590544000077

Nwoye, A. (2017). An Africentric theory of human personhood. *Psychology in Society, 54*, 42–66. http://dx.doi.org/10.17159/2309-8708/2017/n54a4

Ohmagari, K., & Berkes, F. (1997). Transmission of indigenous knowledge and bush skills among the western James Bay Cree women of subarctic Canada. *Human Ecology, 25*, 197–222. http://dx.doi.org/10.1023/A:1021922105740

Oppong, S. (2013). Indigenizing knowledge for development: Epistemological and pedagogical approaches. *Africanus, 4*(2), 34–50. https://doi.org/10.25159/0304-615X/2300

Oppong, S. (2015). A critique of early childhood development research and practice in Africa. *Africanus, 45*(1), 23–41. https://doi.org/10.25159/0304-615X/252

Oppong, S. (2017). History of psychology in Ghana since 989AD. *Psychological Thought, 10*(1), 7–48. https://psyct.swu.bg/index.php/psyct/article/view/195/htm

Oppong, S. (2019). Overcoming obstacles to a truly global psychological theory, research and praxis in Africa. *Journal of Psychology in Africa, 29*(4), 292–300. https://doi.org/10.1080/14330237.2019.1647497

Oppong, S. (2020). Towards a model of valued human cognitive abilities: An African perspective based on a systematic review. *Frontiers in Psychology, 11*, 538072. https://doi.org/10.3389/fpsyg.2020.538072

Oppong, S. (2023a). Promoting global ECD top-down and bottom-up. *Ethos*, 1–5. https://doi.org/10.1111/etho.12393

Oppong, S. (2023b). An indigenous representation of personhood for citizenship behaviours. In J. Osafo & C. S. Akotia (Eds.), *Personhood, Community and the Human Condition: Reflections and Applications in the African Experience* (pp. 27–47). Ayebia Clarke Publishing Limited.

Park, H., Joo, J., Quiroz, B., & Greenfield, P. M. (2015). Sociodemographic factors influence cultural values: Comparing European American with Korean mothers and children in three settings - Rural Korea, urban Korea, and Los Angeles. *Journal of Cross-Cultural Psychology, 46*, 1131–1149. https://doi.org/10.1177/0022022115600258

Pellegrini, A. D., Dupuis, D., & Smith, P. K. (2007). Play in evolution and development. *Developmental Review*, 27(2), 261–276. http://dx.doi.org/10.1016/j.dr.2006.09.001

Rad, M. S., Martingano, A. J., & Ginges, J. (2018). Toward a psychology of Homo sapiens: Making psychological science more representative of the human population. *Proceedings of the National Academy of Sciences*, 115(45), 11401–11405. https://doi.org/10/gfnv94

Raeff, C., Greenfield, P. M., & B. Quiroz (2000). Developing interpersonal relationships in the cultural contexts of individualism and collectivism. In S. Harkness, C. Raeff, & C.R. Super (Eds). *Variability in the social construction of the child, New Directions in Child and Adolescent Development* (pp. 59–74). Jossey-Bass.

Richerson, P. J., & Boyd, R. (2005). *Not by genes alone: how culture transformed human evolution.* University of Chicago Press.

Riede, F. (2019). Niche Construction Theory and Human Biocultural Evolution. In A. M. Prentiss (Ed.). *Handbook of Evolutionary Research in Archaeology* (pp. 337–358). Springer. https://doi.org/10.1007/978-3-030-11117-5_17

Riede, F., Johannsen, N. N., Högberg, A., Nowell, A., & Lombard, M. (2018). The role of play objects and object play in human cognitive evolution and innovation. *Evolutionary Anthropology: Issues, News, and Reviews, 27*(1), 46–59. https://doi.org/10.1002/evan.21555

Riede, F., Lew-Levy, S., Johannsen, N. N., Lavi, N., & Andersen, M. M. (2023). Toys as Teachers: A Cross-Cultural Analysis of Object Use and Enskillment in Hunter–Gatherer Societies. *Journal of Archaeological Method and Theory, 30*(1), 32–63. https://doi.org/10.1007/s10816-022-09593-3

Riede, F., Walsh, M. J., Nowell, A., Langley, M. C., & Johannsen, N. N. (2021). Children and innovation: Play, play objects and object play in cultural evolution. *Evolutionary Human Sciences, 3*, e11. https://doi.org/10.1017/ehs.2021.7

Rogoff, B. (1981). Schooling's Influence on Memory Test Performance. *Child Development, 52*(1), 260–267. https://doi.org/10.2307/1129239

Rogoff, B., & Chavajay, P. (1995). What's Become of Research on the Cultural Basis of Cognitive Development? *American Psychologist, 50*(10), 859–877. https://doi.org/10.1037/0003-066X.50.10.859

Rotem, O. S., Greenfield, P. M., & Weinstock (in revision). Changes in values and ways of knowing among three generations of Israeli women of Ethiopian origin. *Applied Developmental Science.*

Scheidecker, G., Nandita C., Heidi K., Francesca M., & Lancy, D. F. (2023a). 'Poor Brain Development' in the Global South? Challenging the Science of Early Childhood Interventions. *Ethos, 51*(1), 1–24. https://doi.org/10.1111/etho.12379.

Scheidecker, G., Boyette, A., Chaudhary, N., Fay, F., Keller, H., Lancy, D., Mezzenzana, F., Ng'asike, J. T., Oppong, S., Serpell, R., Spray, J., Takada, A. S., & Weisner, T. (2023). Parents, Caregivers, and Peers: Patterns of Complementarity in the Social World of Children in Rural Madagascar. *Current Anthropology, 64*(3), 286–320. https://www.journals.uchicago.edu/doi/10.1086/725037

Scheidecker, G., Chaudhary, N., Oppong, S., Röttger-Rössler, B., & Keller, H. (2022). Different is not deficient: Respecting diversity in early childhood development. *The Lancet. Child & Adolescent Health, 6*(12), e24–e25. https://doi.org/10.1016/S2352-4642(22)00277-2

Scheidecker, G., Oppong, S., Chaudhary, N., & Keller, H. (2021). How overstated scientific claims undermine ethical principles in parenting interventions. *BMJ Global Health, 6*(9). http://dx.doi.org/10.1136/bmjgh-2021-007323

Schniter, E., Kaplan, H. S., & Gurven, M. (2022). Cultural transmission vectors of essential knowledge and skills among Tsimane forager-farmers. *Evolution and Human Behavior*. doi.org/10.1016/j.evolhumbehav.2022.08.00

Scribner, S. (1974). Developmental aspects of categorized recall in a West African Society. *Cognitive Psychology, 6*(4), 475–494. https://doi.org/10/d5c9kq

Scribner, S. (Ed.). (1976). Situating the experiment in cross-cultural research. In K. F. Riegel & J. A. Meacham (Eds). *The developing individual in a changing world* (pp. 310–345). Routledge.

Scribner, S. (1977). Modes of Thinking and Ways of Speaking. In P. N. Johnson-Laird & P. C. Wason (Eds.), *Thinking: Readings in Cognitive Science* (pp. 483–500). Cambridge University Press.

Serpell, R., & Nsamenang. A. B. (2014). *Locally relevant and quality ECCE programmes: Implications of research on indigenous African child development and socialization.* Early Childhood Care and Education Working Papers Series, 3. United Nations Educational, Scientific and Cultural Organization (UNESCO).

Sharp, D., Cole, M., Lave, C., Ginsburg, H. P., Brown, A. L., & French, L. A. (1979). Education and Cognitive Development: The Evidence from Experimental Research. *Monographs of the Society for Research in Child Development, 44*(1/2), 1–112. https://doi.org/10.2307/3181586

Shennan, S. J., & Steele, J. (1999). Cultural learning in hominids: a behavioural ecological approach. In H. O. Box & K. R. Gibson (Eds). *Mammalian social learning: comparative and ecological perspectives* (pp. 367–388). Cambridge University Press.

Sibilsky, A., Colleran, H., McElreath, R., & Haun, D. B. M. (2022). Expanding the understanding of majority-bias in children's social learning. *Scientific Reports, 12*, 6723. doi.org/10.1038/s41598-022-10576-3

Stapert, D. (2007). Youngsters knapping flint near the campfire: An alternative view of Site K at Maastricht-Belvédère (the Netherlands). *Archäologisches Korrespondenzblatt, 37*(1), 19–35.

Sperber, D. (1996). *Explaining culture: a naturalistic approach.* Wiley.

Takada, A. (2019). Socialization practices regarding shame in Japanese caregiver-child interactions. *Frontiers in Psychology, 10*, 1545. https://doi.org/10.3389/fpsyg.2019.01545

UNICEF (2018). *Multiple Indicator Cluster Surveys 6 (MICS6) questionnaires and indicators.* http://mics.unicef.org/

Vasileva, O., & Balyasnikova, N. (2019). (Re) Introducing Vygotsky's thought: from historical overview to contemporary psychology. *Frontiers in psychology*, *10*, 1515. https://doi.org/10.3389/fpsyg.2019.01515

Vygotsky, L. S. (1978). *Mind in society: The development of higher psychological processes* (M. Cole, V. John-Steiner, S. Scribner, & E. Souberman, Eds). Harvard University Press.

Whiting, B. B. (Ed.). (1963). *Six cultures: Studies of child rearing.* Wiley.

Whiting, B. B., & Whiting, J. W. M. (1975). *Children of six cultures: A psycho-cultural analysis.* Harvard University Press.

Weinstock, M., Ganayiem, M., Igbaryia, R., Manago, A. M., & Greenfield, P. M. (2015). Societal Change and Values in Arab Communities in Israel: Intergenerational and Rural–Urban Comparisons. *Journal of Cross-Cultural Psychology*, *46*(1), 19–38. https://doi.org/10.1177/0022022114551792

Weisner, T. S. (2002). Ecocultural understanding of children's developmental pathways. *Human Development, 45*(4), 275–281. https://www.jstor.org/stable/2676368

Xu, J. (2017). *The Good Child: Moral Development in a Chinese Preschool.* Stanford University Press. http://ww.sup.org/books/title/?id=26737

Xu, J. (2022). "The Moral Child": Anthropological Perspectives on Moral Development in China. In R. Nichols (Ed.). *The Routledge International Handbook of Morality, Cognition, and Emotion in China* (pp. 193–214). Routledge.

Zhou, C., Yiu, W. Y. V., Wu, M. S., & Greenfield, P. M. (2017). Perception of cross-generational differences in child behavior and parent socialization: A mixed-method interview study with grandmothers in China. *Journal of Cross-Cultural Psychology, 49*, 62–81.https://doi.org/10.1177/0022022117736029

3. Charting a middle course: Theory and methods in the practice of cross-cultural research

Coordinated by Ivan Kroupin, Felix Riede, April Nowell, and Chantal Medaets

Recent years have seen a resurgence in work arguing for the importance of cross-cultural research. Yet, there are few guides and worked examples of how theory in cognitive science and anthropology can actually be instantiated in a productive research program. This chapter collects contributions on this topic, with several background essays on the practice of cross-cultural research and six concrete examples of research programs. Across these contributions, the recurring theme is balancing the need for generating generalizable science with attention to local cultural contexts. Instead of converging on a single solution, these contributions provide a lay of the land, demonstrating the various ways in which researchers have found a pragmatic balance between the universal and the specific in studying our cultural species.

3.1. Notes on a difficult terrain

Ivan Kroupin, Felix Riede, April Nowell, and Chantal Medaets

The challenge of this book in general, and this chapter in particular, is to outline a study of childhood learning across cultures. This work would, in some sense, be much easier if we were instead interested in studying only the universal features of the human mind, or only

©2025 Ivan Kroupin, et al., CC BY-NC 4.0

https://doi.org/10.11647/OBP.0440.03

the patterns of thought and behavior of a specific group. Each of these charts a clear path in terms of the desired level of analysis (universal v. local) and methodological approach (standard experiments v. rich ethnography). However, neither can lead to general understanding of human learning. After all, universal patterns alone cannot be the whole science of human cognition in any meaningful sense, because we are inherently cultural beings (e.g., Geertz, 1973; Cole, 1996; Levinson, 2012; Kroupin et al., 2024). Moreover, even if we are interested only in universals, failing to account for culture means that we cannot identify when we may be using methods that do not measure what we intend them to (e.g.,Greenfield, 1997; Hruschka et al., 2018). Similarly, studying exclusively culturally specific phenomena means the scholarship we engage in, while certainly legitimate in and of itself, is no longer part of a generalizable science (D'Andrade, 2000; Bakhurst, 2009).

The study of learning across cultures, then, must chart a middle course. The present chapter provides perspectives from researchers working in this difficult terrain—a series of notes on the territory and sketches of existing routes. Nielsen details the importance and feasibility of cross-cultural work, debunking persistent myths that have prevented the field, and especially universally oriented researchers, from engaging with culture to a greater extent. Moving to concrete methodology, Medaets and Gomez provide an introduction to ethnography, a key tool to bring cultural detail into our research programs. Some of the earliest and most successful integrations of ethnography and experimental psychology, in turn, come from the first wave of cross-cultural research (e.g., Cole et al., 1971; Greenfield & Childs, 1977; Lancy, 1981), which relied on a theoretical framework developed by Vygotsky and his students (e.g.,Vygotsky, 1978; Luria, 1976) to organize their work (see Rogoff & Chavajay, 1995; Cole, 1996 for historical reviews of how this framework came to be adopted). Pamei introduces this framework and Greenfield places it in dialogue with the more universalist approach of Piaget, as well as her own broader theoretical framework. Taverna & Coppens raise a separate set of theoretical issues concerning the epistemologies from which western cognitive science is conducted. In addressing these limitations, they propose a theoretical and methodological approach augmented with insights from the epistemology of the Wichi, a small-scale ethno-linguistic group residing in Argentina and Bolivia. Takada, Silan, Keller and Wiseman further outline their own paths in combining generalizable and culturally salient frameworks, highlighting a range of theoretical and methodological approaches. Finally, Ferreira provides an Indigenous perspective, highlighting the cultural specificity of our assumptions about 'childhood' and sources of knowledge which may not be immediately apparent to outside researchers.

As will become obvious throughout this chapter, there is currently no agreed-upon approach to theorizing or studying learning across cultures. Our goal is to highlight that this challenge is both worthwhile and tractable. The perspectives we offer here are aimed to give a sense of the range of approaches in this domain, any and all of which may serve as models for researchers developing their own cross-cultural program. With that in mind, we close this introduction by directly addressing readers coming from universalist and culturalist backgrounds. Given the typical difference between these camps, it may benefit those coming from each to focus on particular aspects of the perspectives below.

To those coming from a universalist perspective, the following pieces can help illustrate conceptual and methodological steps that can be taken to introduce a greater attention to culture within your research program. Nielsen is a perfect starting point, outlining both the motivation for and practical approach to cross-cultural work. After this, it is perhaps easier to begin by reading those perspectives that more explicitly discuss conventional experimental psychological methods in cultural context (Wiseman, Keller, Greenfield) and work your way towards more cultural approaches in order to understand the relevant methods (Medaets & Gomez, Takada, Silan), frameworks (Pamei, Taverna & Coppens) and perspectives (Ferreira).

Those coming from a culturalist perspective may benefit from focusing on the ways in which more standardized methods can be developed and implemented in conjunction with close attention to culture. Greenfield and Keller provide historically successful integrations between ethnographic and experimental approaches, while Taverna & Coppens review a more recent set of efforts. Wiseman illustrates a contemporary program that has produced ethnographically informed generalizable measures. Pamei, Takada, and Silan likewise focus on the interface of experiment and cultural context in various ways, while Ferreira provides rich material for considering how generalizable methods may be integrated with local knowledge.

3.2. Debunking myths in cross-cultural developmental psychology

Mark Nielsen

Scrutiny persists over the legitimacy of psychology as a science. Criticisms include a reliance on suspect statistical techniques, lack of experimental reproducibility, and failure to consider the potential historical situatedness of research endeavors (e.g., Bakker & Wicherts, 2011; Collaboration, 2015; Muthukrishna et al., 2021). Among these critiques are questions about the cultural specificity of data collection and findings that lack verifiable generalizability (Henrich et al., 2010). An analysis of prominent developmental journals noted that the vast majority of studies were undertaken with WEIRD (Western, Educated, Industrialized, Rich, and Democratic) populations (Nielsen et al., 2017). Despite this, and other attempts at drawing attention to the problem (Amir & McAuliffe, 2020; Draper et al., 2022), it appears little has changed. Taking the latest issue of one of the peak developmental psychology outlets as a guide, 12 of the 18 articles featured only WEIRD data and two articles included minority populations but placed the data in WEIRD contexts. Statements alluding to generalizability remain common (e.g., "This study demonstrates that children ...") even though most data lacks appropriate foundations (Peters et al., 2022). This continued lack of priority afforded to the collection of heterogeneous data is indicative of a majority approach that devalues cross-cultural research and treats it as unnecessary or impractical. This approach rests on the perpetuation of a series of myths that warrant debunking.

Myth #1: Research is generalizable without heterogenous data

If research outcomes are being written as if they speak to general features of human cognition, universality cannot be assumed until evidence demonstrates so. Findings are specific to the population from which data is collected. This is not a necessary consideration if the topic is population-specific, but, if broad claims are to be made, data collection must be extended to contrasting populations. It should no longer be acceptable to make generalized statements about findings without the data to back them up.

Myth #2: Extending data to a different population requires theoretical foundations

For some, the correct approach is to develop theoretically motivated reasons for contrasting disparate populations. With *a priori* predictions, appropriate communities can be targeted and if differences are found there can be some certitude in attributing test outcomes to the variables of interest. However, where research enterprises bear on issues of universality, similar outcomes should arise regardless of where their hypotheses are tested, and differences may not be expected. Where generalizability is a stated aim, greater explanatory power comes from testing among most contrasting populations—but this might not always be feasible. In which case, extending to populations that differ on any dimension, however small, will be better than no comparison at all.

Myth #3: Limited access to different populations

Setting up test sites that represent polarities is not always straightforward—and can be highly resource-intensive. However, it might not be necessary to travel vast distances to novel places that demand considerable investment of time establishing appropriate relationships and understanding necessary local customs. Most populations will have sub-populations that identify in ways that sit outside the mainstream. And these can exist in places not far from well-tried data sources. Targeting such groups might not permit broad generalizations to be drawn, but it is a step in the right direction.

Myth #4: Not having time to establish appropriate relationships

Extending data to make it more meaningful may require a lot of work. When entering other communities, you need to establish relationships and understand local procedures, to know how to ask for things and where to find them. Most importantly, you need to build trust, especially when children and families are involved. This all takes time, and most of us are not blessed with much to spare. Forming collaborative partnerships with those who have already laid the necessary groundwork becomes key. Approaching established field researchers or community liaison representatives may be all that is required. And don't give up—persist until you find that person who says 'yes'; you never know how fruitful it might be.

There remains a real and genuine need for psychology in general, and developmental psychology specifically, to meet head-on the numerous criticisms that have been leveled at it. Failure to do so risks our discipline being slowly treated as a dominion of limited relevance and profligate waste. It is time for change and time for excuses to stop.

3.3. The ethnographic study of learning in childhood

Chantal Medaets & Ana Maria R. Gomes

Originally developed in anthropology, ethnography aims to approach as closely as possible the logics, sensitivities, and ways of perceiving the world of specific groups. In ethnographic studies of learning during childhood, what is expected is a detailed description of interactions, in a natural setting, among children themselves and between children and adults, as well as with the objects, animals, plants, and other non-human entities of their environment, thereby revealing the intricate web of relationships within which learning takes place. Beyond these immediately observable interactions, it is equally important in ethnography to consider the historical and social factors that influence them, such as the political context of the studied group and norms and laws related to childhood.

Some ethnographic studies of childhood place the primary focus on the interaction among children, examining children's peer cultures (Arleo & Delalande, 2010; Corsaro, 2003). Ethnographers in these cases may actively engage with children's groups as 'different adults' (Corsaro, 2003) or assume a more observational role (Arleo & Delalande, 2010). Others adopt a 'generational approach' (Pires & Ribeiro, 2015), investing similar time in observing and analyzing children's actions and the actions of the adults with whom they interact (Lignier, 2019; Medaets, 2016; Morelli, 2023; Sarcinelli, 2021, among others). Still other ethnographers compare learning processes within the community and in institutional settings, like schools (Heath, 1983; Gomes, 1998).

In any case, once the observation focus is determined, ethnography involves the researcher's immersion in the field as they follow interlocutors' movements. This clearly distinguishes ethnography from the dominant approach in childhood learning studies: experimental protocols. In experimental studies, researchers direct the situation, starting with predefined hypotheses and proposing activities (such as exercises or tests) consistent with their goals. In contrast, ethnographers let themselves be guided by their interlocutors, trying to align with their rhythms and grasp their concerns. They integrate into their interlocutors' network for an extended period and seek to describe it, along with detailing the interactions of these individuals with themselves, reflecting on the effects of their presence in the field.

This doesn't mean ethnographers enter the field without a research problem or guiding questions; instead, their questions should: (i) align with the general principle of embracing local practices and (ii) necessarily evolve through their interactions in the field. It also doesn't imply that ethnographers engage in entirely 'natural' situations, in contrast to a total 'artificiality' of experimental settings (Hammersley & Atkinson, 2007). Much has been written about the non-neutrality of the researcher and, on the contrary, the analytical potential in considering the ethnographic encounter (Bensa, 1995). The crucial point is not the illusion of accessing an interference-free reality, but rather the direction and guidance of the activities.

This overall research stance does not prevent proposing certain activities to interlocutors. In ethnographic studies involving children, it is common to suggest activities such as drawing or writing short pieces (Mead, 1932; Toren, 2011; Cohn, 2017). However, as Toren emphasizes, in ethnography these activities must be subordinated to a broader research logic. This means that any device gains its full meaning when considered alongside what is learned from unguided, long-term coexistence that all ethnography involves.

And how long should this 'long duration' in the field be? For this frequently asked question, there is no predetermined answer. As Rockwell reminds us, it depends on the specific research conditions (such as bond intensity or data analysis progress, in dialogue with relevant literature). Sufficient time is needed to witness recurring situations, in order to "be able to anticipate, from what has already been experienced, what might happen" (Rockwell, 2009, p. 41).

Each methodological approach has strengths and limitations. Ethnography is particularly suitable for capturing the cultural specificities of knowledge production and circulation within a particular group. What kind of knowledge and which skills are considered important to be passed on to new generations? Who are the individuals recognized as bearers of this knowledge? Are there any restrictions or rules governing access to it? What are the learning modalities practiced (which may vary depending on different skills)? To what extent do these processes change over time, and what are the historical and social factors that influence them? Ethnographic research, endorsed in interdisciplinary projects since the 1970s (cf. LeVine, 2010), is a valuable way to address these points. It can also be used to address more general questions (e.g., "how do toddlers learn to take things," Lignier, 2019; "the implications of social change for cognitive development," Greenfield, 2004). But in such cases, insights are based on long-term relations with a specific group; not only do researchers take these cultural specificities into account, as well as internal differences in the group, but they lean on them to arrive at more general conclusions.

To understand features of the mind that have been shaped by cultural contexts, or even to identify recurrent cross-contextual features, we cannot settle for superficial descriptions of such contexts. Situated and deeper descriptions are needed. Ethnography provides a crucial tool with which to fill the current gap in cognitive science and other disciplines when it comes to a rich understanding of cultural contexts and how these may shape (and be shaped by) human minds.

3.4. Vygotskian theory: Examining causal relations in learning across contexts

Gairan Pamei

Modern psychological research and the contemporary cognitive science of child development tends to overlook the influence of culture. Partially, this oversight could be attributed to the erroneous reading, interpretation and application of Piagetian scholarship (see Burman, 2020, 2022 for details) in the early history of the discipline. However, in recent years, the loud call to expand the scientific discourse with culture as an essential (e.g.,Henrich et al., 2010; Nielsen & Haun, 2016; D. Medin et al., 2017; Nielsen et al., 2017; Rad et al., 2018) has received more attention. As an overarching framework, the body of work by Lev Vygotsky can be an interdisciplinary inspiration.

The cultural-historical approach to psychological research proposed by Vygotsky (1998, 2012) is a compelling theoretical framework for culturally situated research on learning in childhood. Broadly, it is based on three principles: emphasis on the analysis of process, examining causal relations, and tracing the historical development of an attribute (Vygotsky, 1981). This framework is valuable in examining children's learning in spaces of formal education, as well as in the context of other institutions, such as the family, where unorganized and unsupervised play is a common form of socialization. This is made possible by making explicit the relation and distinction between '*life*' and formal education (Esteban-Guitart, 2018) and acknowledging that both contribute to children's socialization and cognitive development in distinctive ways.

The developmental or genetic method of analysis by Vygotsky involves capturing the structure of the environment and how this environment becomes internalized by the learner. This approach can be used for a wide range of studies, from learning mathematical skills to memory and concept formation (see Vygotsky, 1998). Importantly, the term 'genetic' refers to both ontogenesis and the historical development of cultural contexts within which children learn (Doria & Simão, 2018). A concrete example of this cultural-historical dynamic is the study of word-meaning acquisition in children from northeast India, where most of them use neither their first nor their second language in the school curriculum. In this case, defining the learning environment requires integrating information regarding the political history of the modern Indian nation state, since this historical trajectory characterizes the distinctive socio-cultural and linguistic contexts of this frontier region (Jolad & Agarwal, 2021). Some approaches (e.g., constructivism; Kirschner et al., 2006) assert that if an enriched environment is provided, students inevitably and inadvertently learn the fundamental abstract concepts.

Given the complex patterns of interactions between the learner and various cultural factors (e.g., institutions, languages etc.), hypotheses within a Vygotskian framework can be effectively expressed in a causal inference model which maps multiple causal relationships (Deffner et al., 2022). Specifically, Directed Acyclic Graphs (DAGs) provide a useful formal tool for mapping out the learning context. The major merit of DAGs is that they are able to capture kinds of interactions and relationships without having to specify specific cultural institutions or practices (Rohrer, 2018) that may vary across sites of study. The goal is the transparent and explicit linkage of causal assumptions to subsequent data analysis.

The following is a hypothetical illustration of how the commonalities and specificities of learning can be examined to identify causal relations using DAGs (see also Section 4.3). For example, a study can be designed with (1) the theoretical estimand–reading comprehension variation, (2) a causal model of how the observed data is generated, (3) a generative model of how populations may differ in language backgrounds, educational experiences, and (4) the empirical estimand—an estimation strategy that tells us how to interpret data. In Figure 3.1, the causal assumptions denoted by the arrows are that formal schooling has a causal effect on L1 vocabulary which in turn affects L2 vocabulary. U is the unobserved factor that affects both formal schooling and L2 vocabulary.

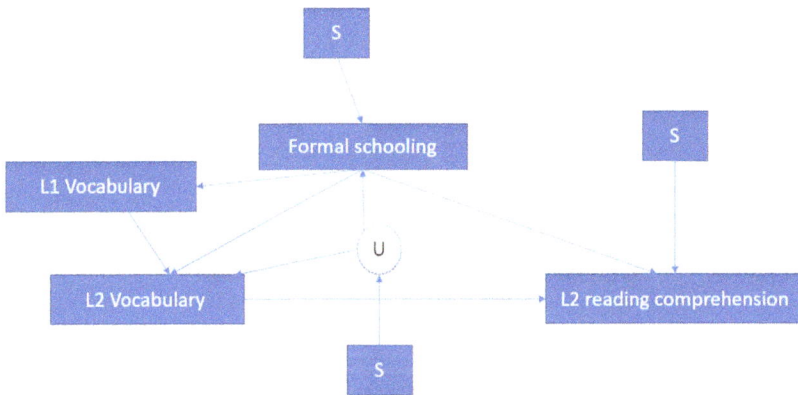

Fig. 3.1 A selection diagram where nodes S represent the assumption that locations differ in their effects on formal schooling and U on L2 reading comprehension.

For exploratory research, it is advisable to draw different DAGs for different field sites to check for hypotheses regarding different mechanisms. If two populations of English L2 students in India, say, from the states of New Delhi and Nagaland, differ in the unobserved cultural variable, U, which affects both formal schooling and L2 reading comprehension, then it can confound the effect. An identification strategy should list or simulate and model the covariation of similar unobserved confounds. Here, L1–L2 distance can be a suitable proxy to control. In this example, the L1 of both the groups are tonal, so fine-grained comparisons can be made.

To conclude, if we are interested in capturing learning in cultural contexts, a Vygotskian framework allows us to systematically capture both the historically located cultural environment and the environmentally located individual learner. The emphasis on causal interactions can be methodologically estimated with a graphical framework (e.g., DAGs) that allows formalization of different functions of the expected variations. A comparative approach can address the inevitability of variability and stability without compromising the eventual scientific goal of generalization.

3.5. Using Piagetian and Vygotskian theory in the study of children's learning across cultures

Patricia M. Greenfield

I went to Senegal in 1963, a graduate student with the explicit mission of testing Piaget's theory of cognitive development in a very different culture. The specific intention of my graduate mentor, Jerome Bruner, was that I would test Wolof children's development of conservation of quantity, the concept that a liquid quantity poured into a container of a different shape still was the same amount, i.e., conserved its quantity. Whereas Piaget and collaborators had concluded from their studies in Switzerland that this cognitive achievement was a matter of age, that is, chronological development, my discovery was that this cognitive milestone did not take place without the environmental influence of formal schooling. My initial conclusion was that this result invalidated Piaget's theory (Greenfield, 1966; Greenfield & Bruner, 1966). However, that conclusion was much too simplistic. I later found that Piagetian theory could be very useful in understanding how children learned central facets of their own culture—even though their culture was very different from Piaget's Switzerland. My two examples are weaving (see Section 2.9, and Maynard & Greenfield, 2003) and Tzotzil sibling terminology (Greenfield & Childs, 1977), to which I now turn.

My first realization of the usefulness of Piagetian theory for the cross-cultural study of children's learning occurred when I compared the ability of Piaget's (1928) theory to predict children's development of Tzotzil kinship terms in a Tzotzil-speaking Maya community in Chiapas, Mexico with theories from anthropology (Greenfield & Childs, 1977). The first theoretical idea from anthropology was that kinship terms for culturally important family relations would be learned before less culturally central terms. The second theoretical idea—componential analysis—came from anthropological linguistics and predicted that less relationally complex terms would be learned more quickly (e.g., 'brother' over 'second cousin' in English). However, neither cultural importance nor terminological complexity predicted the order in which Tzotzil sibling terms were learned. In sharp contrast, all predictions from Piagetian theory were confirmed. Here is the Piagetian developmental sequence that emerged:

Age 4–5: Egocentrism.
   Can answer ego-centered questions
   (e.g., "What is the name of your older sister?")

Age 8–10: Reciprocity
   Can answer other-centered questions about sibling relations external to self, including reciprocal pairs
   (e.g., The oldest sibling Petu is being questioned about a sibling relationship that does not include her: "As for your younger sister, Shunka, what is the name of her younger brother?" Answer: "Shun."
   Reciprocal question: "As for your younger brother, Shun, what is the name of his older sister?" Answer: "Shunka."

Age 13–18: Reversibility
   (e.g., The oldest sibling Petu is still being questioned: "As for your younger sister, Shunka, what is the name of her older brother?" Answer: "Petu."
   This is called reversibility because it is necessary to see the relationship to self from another person's perspective.

This sequence involved exactly the same steps that Piaget (1928) had uncovered in Switzerland, asking similar questions about siblings in Swiss families. Hence, this study illustrates how Piagetian theory can be useful to researchers studying the acquisition of specific cultural knowledge in settings that are very different from Piaget's Switzerland.

Whereas Piagetian theory could provide a framework for understanding the order in which Zinacantec children acquired knowledge of Tzotzil sibling terms, the theory had nothing to offer about how the learning took place. For the study of learning processes, I found Vygotskian theory (Vygotsky, 1998) useful, especially the Vygotsky-derived concept of scaffolding introduced by Wood, Bruner, & Ross (1976).

In the same Maya community, we applied Vygotskian theory to a different kind of learning study; a study of how Zinacantec girls learn how to weave on a backstrap loom. In contrast to the study of kinship terms, which focused on the learner's cognitive development, the emphasis here was on the process of social transmission. The central Vygotskian concept was the Zone of Proximal Development—the theoretical idea that the most useful teaching takes the learner just a small step beyond what they already know. Our video microanalysis of girls of various ages working at the backstrap loom showed this to be an accurate description of the way in which the Zinacantec weaving teacher— almost always a close relative—structures the process by which girls learn how to weave. Wood and Bruner's concept of scaffolding describes the help that teachers give to learners when the learner is not quite able to take the next learning step on their own. Help at such points indicates that the teacher is working in the learner's Zone of Proximal Development. According to Vygotskian theory, the learner is acquiring how-to knowledge with the teacher's help, so that, in the near future, the learner will be able to take that next learning step on their own, without help from the teacher.

Piagetian theory is useful to identify the developmental steps that children pass through with age in mastering a cognitive task, and Vygotskian theory is useful in identifying certain environmental conditions that facilitate this mastery—specifically, fruitful teaching techniques that are applicable both in school and out of school. So Piagetian theory focuses on the maturational variable—the child; and Vygotskian theory focuses on variables in the microenvironment—the adult teacher. However, neither theory incorporates variables in the macroenvironment—the influence of socio-ecological change. This is the contribution of my theory of social change, cultural evolution (see also Section 2.7), and human development, to which I now turn (Greenfield, 2009, 2016, 2018).

Social and ecological change has accelerated globally. My interdisciplinary and multilevel theory provides a unified framework to explore the implications of these changes for cultural values, learning environment and/or socialization processes, and human development and/or human behavior (Greenfield, 2016). Figure 3.2 summarizes important socio-ecological changes and their implications for shifts in values, learning environments/socialization, and development/behavior.

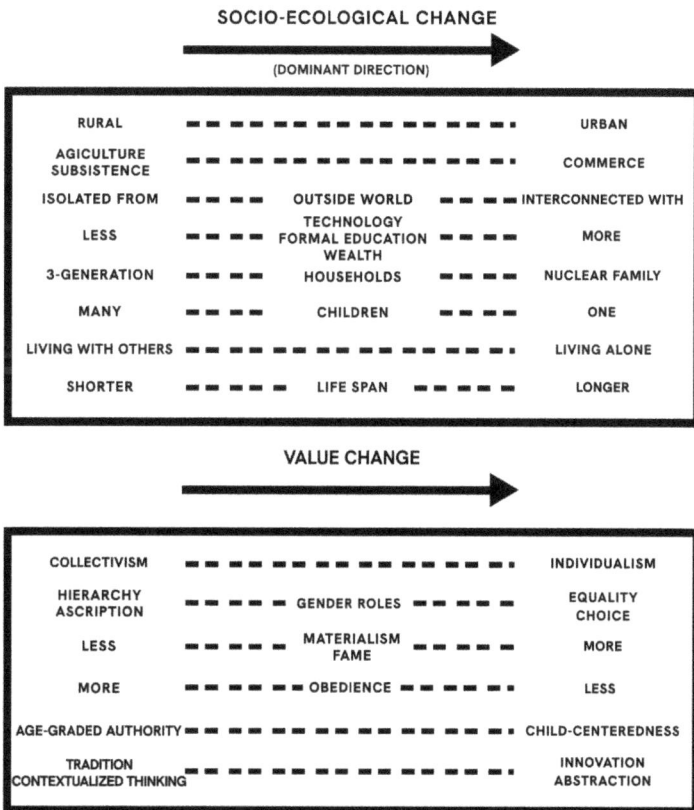

SOCIO-ECOLOGICAL CHANGE

(DOMINANT DIRECTION)

RURAL	URBAN
AGICULTURE SUBSISTENCE	COMMERCE
ISOLATED FROM	OUTSIDE WORLD TECHNOLOGY	INTERCONNECTED WITH
LESS	FORMAL EDUCATION WEALTH	MORE
3-GENERATION	HOUSEHOLDS	NUCLEAR FAMILY
MANY	CHILDREN	ONE
LIVING WITH OTHERS		LIVING ALONE
SHORTER	LIFE SPAN	LONGER

VALUE CHANGE

COLLECTIVISM	INDIVIDUALISM
HIERARCHY ASCRIPTION	GENDER ROLES	EQUALITY CHOICE
LESS	MATERIALISM FAME	MORE
MORE	OBEDIENCE	LESS
AGE-GRADED AUTHORITY		CHILD-CENTEREDNESS
TRADITION CONTEXTUALIZED THINKING		INNOVATION ABSTRACTION

LEARNING ENVIRONMENT/SOCIALIZATION CHANGE

MORE	MOTHER-INFANT BODILY CONTACT	LESS
INTERDEPENDENCE SOCIAL GUIDANCE		INDEPENDENCE
CRITICISM		PRAISE SUPPORT WARMTH
FAMILY OBLIGATION	EXPECTATIONS	INDIVIDUAL DEVELOPMENT
HOUSEHOLD ASSISTANCE	CHILDREN'S TASKS	SCHOOL ACHIEVEMENT
IN-PERSON	INTERACTION	TECHNOLOGICAL

DEVELOPMENTAL/BEHAVIORAL CHANGE

RESPECT OBEDIENCE		SELF-EXPRESSION CURIOSITY INDEPENDENCE
SHYNESS		EXTRAVERSION
DETAILED TRADITION-BASED ABSOLUTISM	COGNITION	ABSTRACT NOVEL MULTIPLE PERSPECTIVES
SOCIAL	SKILLS	TECHNOLOGICAL
MORE	SOCIAL BONDING	LESS
ASCRIBED	GENDER ROLES	CHOSEN
OTHER	FOCUS	SELF
EMPATHY FOR OTHERS		INTERNAL FEELING STATES
LESS	SELF-ESTEEM	MORE
FITTING IN		STANDING OUT UNIQUENESS
SUBSISTENCE	ACTIVITIES	COMMERCIAL
COOPERATION		COMPETITION

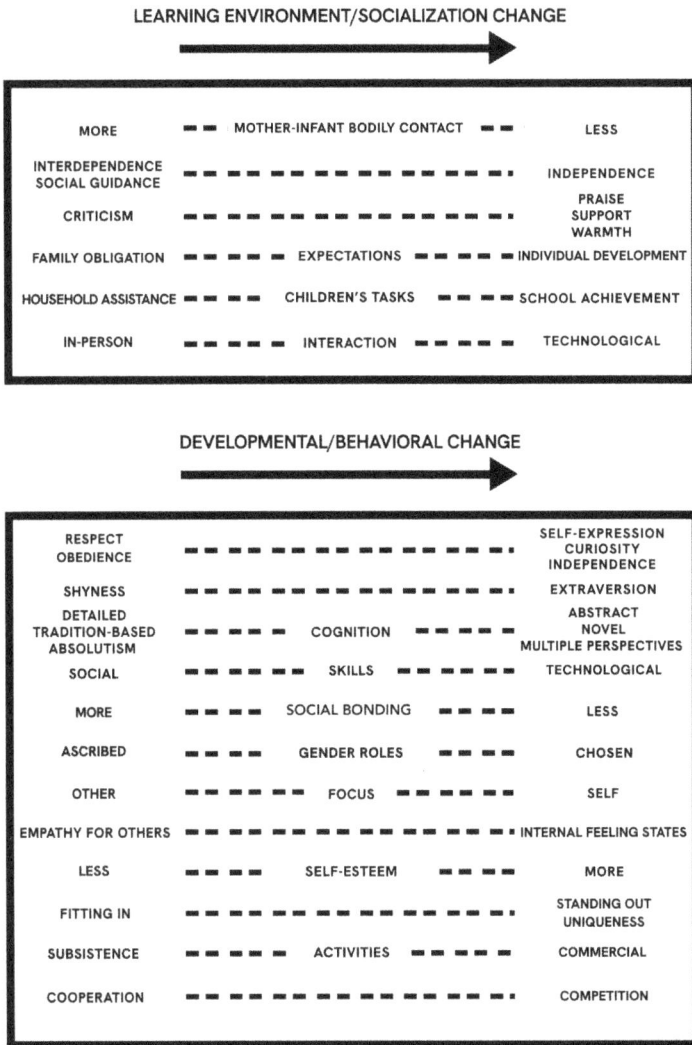

Fig. 3.2 Model of social change, cultural evolution, and human development. Relationships for which there is empirical evidence have been selected for inclusion. While the horizontal arrows represent the dominant direction of social change in the world, socio-ecological change can go in the opposite direction. In that case all the horizontal arrows would be reversed. Adapted from Greenfield (2016).

Note that although there is a dominant direction of socio-ecological change, change also happens in the other direction, leading to opposite shifts on the lower levels (Evers et al., 2021, 2024; Greenfield et al., 2021; Park et al., 2014, 2017). To summarize evidence concerning the dominant direction of social change, socio-ecological shifts in that direction lead to both cultural losses (e.g., interdependence, collectivism, respect, tradition, contextualized thinking, subsistence skills) and cultural gains (e.g., independence, individualism, social equality, innovation, and abstraction). The citations in the next paragraph provide the references for this summary.

Methodologically, the relationships shown in the diagram have been documented through longitudinal study of a single community or country (Mexico: García et al., 2015, 2017, 2020; U.S. Maynard et al., 2015, 2023; China: Zeng & Greenfield, 2015) and by comparing multiple generations at a single point in time (China: Bian et al., 2022; Zhou et al., 2017; Mexico: Manago, 2014; Rotem et al., 2024; Israel: Abu Aleon et al., 2019; El-sana et al., 2023; Weinstock et al., 2015; Weinstock, 2015; Romania: Ionescu et al., 2023). All of this research has documented the effects of socio-ecological shifts that have occurred in place. However, other research has documented the effects of socio-ecological shifts that have occurred through international migration (Mexican immigrants in the US.: Greenfield & Quiroz, 2013; Raeff et al., 2000; Ethiopian immigrants in Israel: Rotem et al., 2024). The conclusion of my theory is that developmental trajectories and learning environments, such as those described by Piaget and Vygotsky, are not constant, but are affected by shifts in the macroenvironment.

3.6. A brief critique of 'factor epistemology' in cultural/cross-cultural research

Andrea Taverna & Andrew Coppens

It is challenging—logistically, ethically, and politically—to gather research samples with sufficient diversity to make generalizable claims about children's learning and development (Henrich et al., 2010; Nielsen et al., 2017). Yet, diverse sampling cannot fully address the challenges and promises of cultural research. Much of what makes cultural research epistemologically challenging comes from the need to make comparisons across cultural boundaries. Conventionally, supporting claims about cultural group differences has relied on factor epistemology, which involves:

- Ontological assumptions that learning and development consist of separable processes and features that can be appropriately operationalized as factor- or variable-based measurements (cf. Rogoff, 2003).

- Analytic assumptions that understanding learning and development entails conceptually reconnecting these measurements via unidirectional causal relations, often in ways that attempt to isolate a narrow set of 'active ingredients' (cf. Taverna et al., 2022).

Factor epistemology has origins in European intellectual heritage—the Cartesian worldview (Lakatos, 1978) —that sharply separates 'internal-to-mind' processes from the 'external' world. A fundamental reason that factor epistemology creates problems for cultural research is that the meaning of objects of measurement or observation cannot be assumed to be consistent from one cultural group to another. Extensive critical discussions of this problem span decades, in cross-cultural cognitive psychology (Cole et al., 1978), language acquisition research (Avineri et al., 2015; Miller & Sperry, 2012), and attachment parenting (Keller & Bard, 2017). These critiques typically present an alternative epistemology of relationality (among many others, see: Cole, 1996; Di Paolo & De Jaegher, 2016; Overton, 2013a, 2013b; Overton & Lerner, 2012; Rogoff, 2003; Szokolszky & Read, 2018; Valsiner, 1998). This relational-ecological paradigm understands learning and development in terms of the organism-environment econiche, encouraging attention to system-level dynamics rather than focusing on components in isolation.

Insights via a relational epistemology from the Wichi

Taverna and colleagues' research, for example, has focused on an alternative scientific-relational epistemological orientation to cross-cultural developmental research, drawn from ontologies common among the Wichi, an Indigenous community living in the Chaco Forest of Northern Argentina (Taverna et al., 2022).

Extending relational perspectives on conceptual development (Medin et al., 2013, 2015; Taverna & Waxman, 2020), this work focuses on how Wichi children and adults conceptualize and reason about *hunhat lheley* (Inhabitants of the Earth). All *hunhat lheley* are perceived by the Wichi in the frame of a relational epistemology that is organized around the notion of *husek* (goodwill) as an agent of vitality and socialization. For example, human beings, non-human animals and spirits, are considered inhabitants with social *husek* because they relate to the world with intentionality and pro-social behavior and are animate beings. They are also considered inhabitants with vital *husek* because they have vital properties, like blood, which are lacking in other entities (metal, stones, soil, etc.). Plants that do not have social *husek* are still considered to have vital *husek* due to their greenness (a sign of life). Thus, entities are understood in terms of the properties of how they relate to the world—either socially or vitally.

These two relational perspectives shape the Wichi's conceptual representations about living (*iloy*) and animate things, since only the inhabitants with social *husek* (animals, humans, spirits) are classified as living, while plants, which have vital *husek*, can die but are not alive. In addition, this relationality also shapes animal concepts, as the *tshotoy* (animals of the forest) are divided into pre-socially aggressive *tshotoy* (cats, snakes) and social and peaceful ones (rats, armadillos, etc., Baiocchi et al., 2019). Finally, relationality is also evident in the causes that the Wichi use to explain the behavior of ecosystem inhabitants, as the Wichi tend to attribute individual causes (e.g., mood) to world inhabitants with social *husek*, but causes related to the annual climate cycle (e.g., rain) to world inhabitants and entities without social *husek* (Fernández Ruiz & Taverna, 2023).

Similarly, children's acquisition of grammatical knowledge in the first language—Wichi *lhomtes*—occurs in the context of native cultural knowledge, values, socialization, and linguistic practices. As in other communities, Wichi language acquisition shows qualitative changes in the child's language—from a pre-grammatical period toward first morphosyntactic combinations—and is also similar in certain aspects of the socialization process (e.g., maternal speech or 'motherese', Taverna & Waxman, 2020; Taverna, 2021). However, this linguistic transition takes place in a social environment that is distinct in important ways from the western environments typically studied in cognitive science. Specifically, in Wichi households, mothers and other caregivers coordinate child attention to create 'lateral joint attention' rather than engaging children solely in joint attention as is common in western populations. Moreover, they use non-verbal channels—gaze, posture, facial expression—to direct their own attention from a lateral (non-focal) position to a central point (the child and the object). They turn to their children with penetrating attention without explicitly intervening and, above all, without being addressed by the child (Taverna et al., 2024).

In the relational perspective considered here, these varying environments of cultural knowledge, values, socialization and linguistic practices are not seen as independent variables, but as stabilized 'cultural cues' that might work as 'cultural affordances' (Ramstead et al., 2016) and support different (linguistic or social) patterns of behavior. At the level of the language-learning system, it is the recursive interaction between the system in question, the learning mechanisms and the role of cultural affordances in any human econiche (practices, values, cultural knowledge, etc.) that synergistically drives changes to the representational resources within the learning system.

These findings leverage insights from relational epistemologies, specifically three organizing ideas: affordances, ecological niches, and representational emergence. Within the cognitive-ecological approach (Medin et al., 2015), it is believed that, like species in an ecosystem, certain ideas may grow better in certain ecologies. These relatively stabilized 'ideas-habitats' work as cultural affordances (Gibson, 1979), a fundamentally relational concept (Ramstead et al., 2016). The ecological niche is, then, a system of interrelated cultural affordances which synergistically drive changes to representational resources within the learning system.

Within the Wichi ecological niche, the *hunhat lheley, tshotoy,* spiritual inhabitants, and the Wichi itself coexist fully integrated with the Chaco Forest. It is precisely the Wichi cognitive, linguistic, and social competencies as stabilized relational patterns that contribute to building and sustaining the econiche.

An important caveat to this brief Wichi case illustration is that learning and development among the Wichi are not 'more relational' than for other cultural groups. Seeing the advantages of a relational epistemology, here in terms of its ability to make visible the explicitly socialized and culturally normative relational values and practices of the Wichi community, can be instructive as both an empirical and epistemological challenge to cultural perspectives (including research approaches) where factor epistemology is an unexamined common sense. This leads to a more general closing point: cultural and cross-cultural research is well positioned to engage in politically equitable inquiry with Indigenous communities, positioning their varied ways of life not only as sources of empirical insight but also as models of relational epistemological inquiry.

3.7. A language socialization approach for studying (social) learning in childhood

Akira Takada

One of the most important theoretical frameworks for analyzing and better understanding the acts of meaning (Bruner, 1990) that constitute and color our social reality is the language socialization approach, which has developed and gained attention in the intersecting fields of anthropology, sociology, linguistics, and psychology (e.g., Duranti et al., 2012; Takada, 2012). According to Ochs and Schieffelin (2012, p. 1), who have led the language socialization approach, "language socialization research examines how children and other cultural novices apprehend and enact the 'context of situation' in relation to the 'context of culture'." The author sympathizes with the language socialization approach and has also promoted it.

This perspective facilitates reconsideration of the concept of learning. I wish to consider individual and social learning separately and independently (Takada, 2016). Social learning is defined as learning that occurs in a social situation; namely, "an environment of mutual monitoring possibilities, anywhere within which an individual will find himself accessible to the naked senses of all others who are present, and similarly find them accessible to him" (Goffman, 1964, p. 135). In contrast, individual learning is defined as a learning process that occurs within each individual. Individual learning is supposed to be observable as changes in behavioral, cognitive, and neural structures. The language socialization approach mainly studies social learning. It analytically examines how cultural novices, including children, learn to behave appropriately in a particular 'context of situation' and 'context of culture'.

Methodologically, the language socialization approach emphasizes observation in natural settings and integrates ethnographic methods with studies of face-to-face interactions to link 'socialization to use language' with 'socialization through language use' (Duranti et al., 2012; Takada, 2019). This is also the case when focusing on social learning.

In ethnographic research, participant observation through fieldwork is the primary method. It requires the researcher to become familiar with the institutions, customs, languages, and practices of a particular group of people through long-term contact with them, and to communicate this familiarity to readers in the society to which the researcher originally belonged in terms they can understand. In order to observe the institutions, customs, languages, and practices of the people in the study area, the researcher must avoid distorting them as much as possible. However, in order to participate in people's lives, the researcher cannot be invisible or even claim to have acted like an invisible person. There is no doubt that it is a difficult task to achieve both participation and observation, and how to reconcile them will differ from researcher to researcher.

In order to analyze face-to-face interactions in detail, data (video and audio) of face-to-face interactions are first collected using video cameras and other equipment. The obtained data are transcribed, and systematic and empirical analysis is conducted. In transcribing conversations, we first identify the speaker of every utterance that is heard by repeatedly viewing the video and audio, and then carefully transcribe the content in a manner that follows the conventions of previous research. In addition, non-verbal features such as eye gaze, gestures, and posture may be also transcribed.

It is theoretically important to point out that the language socialization approach does not presuppose human universals. Rather, it is a theoretical construct that can only be considered after the analysis of the properties of culture. The language socialization approach devotes its energies to showing how cultural practices, customs, and social institutions are integrally organized in concrete and everyday interactions. In most studies of culture, these have often been treated as if they were entities at different levels, categorized relatively from the 'micro' to the 'macro' realm. However, analysis of face-to-face interactions can reveal the function of the actors' agency that link them.

That is to say, in social situations, participants, who often have different stances toward taking part in the situation, engage in interaction for the purpose of mutual understanding. These actions are interrelated and constitute a characteristic sequence of actions. The accumulation of these actions results in the creation of a community that shares various patterns of semiotic resources that have become conventionalized and structured. In this respect, there is no community that does not change, and communities can be born anywhere. Children born into a community or novices to a community gradually become familiar with these patterns as they become involved in the interactions that are taking place there. Social learning occurs in the process. Moreover, all communities continue to be constituted, maintained, and transformed by such dynamics. Attempts to solve local interactional tasks may result in the reproduction or alteration of long-established cultural practices, customs, and social institutions.

3.8. The cross-indigenous approach to multi-site studies

Miguel Silan

The theoretical framework designated as the 'cross-indigenous approach' is a simultaneous multi-emic approach to studying psychological and social phenomena across cultures. While the standard cross-cultural enterprise is to "test the generality of existing [theories] by comparing the responses of different cultural groups on standardized measures of psychological processes" (Ellis & Stam, 2015, p. 298) the cross-indigenous enterprise is to converge (or fail to converge) on psychological universals through multiple independent explorations among source cultures (Silan, 2023). This framework aims to mitigate the vulnerabilities of cross-cultural approaches, such as the methodological artifacts from subjecting non-WEIRD populations to experiments with WEIRD assumptions (Baumard & Sperber, 2010; Feldman-Barrett, 2017) and the strong assumption of measurement equivalence in cross-cultural studies; both of which are difficult to detect in standard cross-cultural studies.

The methods of data collection imply (1) qualitative, ethnographic or mixed-methods data gathering simultaneously across multiple defined target populations, and/or (2) using culturally appropriate scales developed either collaboratively with community representatives to create culturally 'fair' materials ('weak assembly'; van de Vijver & Poortinga, 2016), or by creating separate, culturally-specific scales for each population that measure similar constructs or mechanisms ('strong assembly') (Silan, 2023; van de Vijver & Poortinga, 2016).

The data collection aims to capture behaviors, thoughts, and emotions as they naturally occur in participants' daily lives, also taking into account their specific cultural contexts and social realities. Researchers aim to triangulate data collection, that is, to use multiple methods and data sources to see whether inferences converge or fail to converge (Thurmond, 2001). The establishment of rigorous exploration, description and validation per site is needed before comparability across cultures is warranted.

Here, culture is taken as a "heterogeneously distributed collective system of pragmatic knowledge" (Kronenfeld, 2017, p. 2). And so, we enquire into children's learning in context, taking into account the culture-bearers' social, cultural and ecological realities, which frame the empirical regularities observed in children's learning. While common cross-cultural approaches treat culture as an external variable that causes variability in behavior, when using the cross-indigenous approach, culture is treated as co-constitutive of the individual, or in some important manner 'within' an individual. The cross-indigenous approach is a multi-site approach that has no *a priori* expectation of comparability across sites and populations except in the broadest sense.

The cross-indigenous approach is a principled way of making comparisons across cultures, aiming to stake out what is unique, what is shared, and what is universal across populations, to explain psychological and social processes through culture-sensitive and naturalistic methods (Silan, 2023).

3.9. An ecocultural perspective on children's development and learning

Heidi Keller

Humans start learning at birth and even before, and continue learning throughout the entire lifespan. Learning is the major mechanism of information acquisition and processing, and thus the basis for behavioral and symbolic changes. Put simply, learning is the human way of adaptation. However, learning is not random. On the one hand, there are biological predispositions to acquire specific information at particular points of time during the lifespan (informed hypotheses, Keller, 2002); on the other hand, there are individual preferences that emerge over time and social and/or cultural biases that lead us to focus on specific information that is available from the environment. Cultural norms and values function like a lens through which the environment is perceived. There are universal tasks, ones which every individual in every cultural environment has to solve. Yet, these generally have no fixed solutions. Rather, their solutions show contextual variations with respect to timing, interpatterning with other developmental domains, and phenotypic appearance.

Cultures can be described as contextual representations of norms, values, and behavioral conventions that have proven to be adaptive in particular environments. Nevertheless, culture is not a static term but a dynamic process. Although there is substantial variability in cultural orientations, two general emphases have been reliably differentiated (Keller & Kartner, 2013). One emphasis reflects the western urban middle-class lifestyle with nuclear families, few children in the household, rather late first-parent parenthood and high levels of formal education (WEIRD, Henrich et al., 2010). We have labeled this cultural orientation as psychological autonomy, expressing an individualistic worldview of self-contained mental agents. Of course, relatedness is also important to psychologically autonomous individuals, yet it is conceived of as a set of voluntarily negotiable social bonds between separate individuals. Prototypes of this model have been identified, yet also multiple variations.

The second emphasis characterizes the rural small-scale farmers' life in many sub-Saharan African, South-East Asian, and South American villages. Life is organized in multigenerational households with many children, earlier first parenthood, and lower degrees of formal education. The cultural model representing this lifestyle can be conceived of as hierarchical relatedness, denoting 'we-ness' or interrelatedness as default conception of the self. Typically, the relationships are organized hierarchically, mainly according to age and gender, associated with particular responsibilities for maintaining the social system.

However, autonomy is also needed to master life in these environments, especially in terms of actions, i.e., self-responsible (*eigenverantwortlich)* and independent mastery of behavioral tasks and challenges which are relevant and beneficial to the community more broadly. Hierarchical relatedness can also appear in multiple variations, as can the combinations between psychological autonomy and hierarchical relatedness. These cultural models are related to socialization goals, parenting strategies, and ultimately children's development.

In any context, children grow up in environments structured by cultural scripts; children learn to express these scripts in their behavior and mental representations. However, the available evidence is not evenly distributed across different cultures: there is plenty of research for some cultural environments, especially WEIRD families, but there is much more limited work on other cultural environments such as rural farmers in non-western contexts who live traditional lifestyles, or urban middle-class families in non-western contexts. Strikingly, learning and development in traditional contexts, as among foragers, pastoralists or fishing communities, has received relatively scant attention by cognitive researchers (Keller, 2007, 2022). What is urgently needed, then, is more research in and from different cultural communities.

Doing so requires a research strategy involving a multi-method design, based in preliminary ethnographic field research. This preliminary research must be exploratory, i.e., not guided by hypotheses, and qualitative in nature. Ethnographic work involves assessing practices through observational methods. Equally important is the assessment of local meaning systems in open interviews with multiple actors such as adult and child caregivers, and local cultural informants who are particularly knowledgeable in the requested content domains. Finally, focus groups are a different and complementary approach to assess meaning systems. These different datasets must be triangulated and checked by members of the particular cultural groups for their validity (as an example of this methodological approach, see Schmidt et al., 2021).

This kind of preliminary ethnographic work is key to successful cross-cultural research. After all, taking assessment tools that have been developed in one cultural community, mainly in WEIRD environments by WEIRD researchers with WEIRD participants, and applying them in other cultural communities poses scientific problems. Locally relevant meaning systems may be completely missed, and behavioral data may be misinterpreted. It also poses tremendous ethical challenges, since it may mean that local voices are ignored and superimposed by foreign meaning systems—systems that are often evaluative and judgmental in that the WEIRD pattern is defined as the universal standard (Scheidecker et al., 2023).

Overcoming biased research strategies is necessary to achieve a global understanding of children's learning and development, and it requires a change of perspective in our research. Since there is no universal theory of cognitive development to derive hypotheses, curiosity must be the starting point, especially when working across cultures. Ethnographic qualitative research methodology is crucial to formalize this curiosity, as is local knowledge which allows us to explore and acknowledge local practices and meaning systems. Supporting local researchers and fully integrating them into international research teams is a necessity within such work. As our global database of such curiosity and culture-driven work grows, this will in turn allow us to more confidently posit and test general principles of human development.

3.10. Deeply similar, deeply different: Collaborative and interdisciplinary studies of culture and cognition

Kara Weisman

I begin with two basic theoretical assumptions. First, I assume that, across cultural settings, human minds are similar in deep and important ways. There are many reasons for this: our shared evolutionary history; our shared physiology (brains, sense organs, the general size and shape of our bodies); our experiences of basic biological and psychological sensations, needs, and drives; our existence in this particular world with its laws and regularities.

My second assumption is that, across cultural settings, human minds differ in deep, important, and systematic ways. There may well be parts of human psychology and development that are encapsulated, completely cordoned off from social-cultural influences, but I use specific proposals about innateness as tools for theorizing and not as ground truths. Instead, I take seriously the possibility that cultural forces can shape phenomena as basic as sensory experiences (see, for example, Luhrmann, Weisman, et al., 2021), in addition to concepts as rich as those of emotion and mental life (Weisman et al., 2021).

In designing studies and in interpreting results, then, I seek to describe both what participants have in common and how they vary, and to characterize the nature of these similarities and differences. I rarely find myself describing similarities in the absence of differences, or differences in the absence of similarities; my 'prior,' so to speak, is that both similarities and differences will be present in a dataset.

In the case of children's learning, I take the primary task of the child to be learning how to fit into the places and communities they occupy—in other words, learning to think like, feel like, act like, and interact with the people around them. Following Piaget, I posit that biological forces shape but do not fully determine cognitive development, which proceeds via the child's active exploration in a particular social world. Following Vygotsky and subsequent developments in cultural psychology, I consider 'cognition' and 'culture' to be co-constructed, with children's learning providing critical insights into this ongoing social-cognitive process. Taken together, this means that we should sometimes expect to see that children in diverse cultural settings construct similar construals about the world (though perhaps for different reasons); in other cases, children will come to very different ways of being and understanding (though these ways of being might serve similar purposes).

This framework implies that theories of cognitive development must be rooted in careful comparisons across cultural settings. Large-scale, multi-site, collaborative research networks—like the Mind & Spirit Project (Luhrmann, Weisman, et al., 2021) and the Developing Belief Network (Richert et al., 2022; Weisman et al., in press)—are one critically important tool for producing these kinds of datasets. The best versions of this that I have witnessed so far all involve collaborators with diverse cultural expertise, diverse research skills, and diverse background assumptions coming from differences in their training, their theoretical orientations, and their lived experiences. The combination of cultural anthropologists and cognitive-developmental psychologists has been an especially fruitful one in my experience (see Weisman &

Luhrmann, 2020). The biggest take-away from this combination of theory and methodology is that we must disentangle observations of similarities vs. differences across cultures from conclusions about human universals vs. cultural specificity.

Observed similarities across cultural settings are often taken as evidence for human universals (and, by extension, as evidence for the influence of evolutionary forces, biological constraints, and so forth), especially when these similarities are quantified using experimental or otherwise quantitative, 'empirical' methods. But holding in mind the two theoretical assumptions I laid out above— that we are all deeply similar, while we are all deeply different— forces us to entertain alternative explanations. In some cases, similarities emerge due to similar needs and motivations, or similar constraints in the environment. In some cases, similarities might even emerge from very different pathways, driven by different needs and motivations. For example, people in one setting might construct a category of EMOTION because expressing emotions is understood to be an important part of being one's true self, while people in another setting might construct a similar category of EMOTION because tracking others' emotions is critical for fitting into a more interdependent society (Weisman et al., 2021). Understanding the learning trajectories that converge in similar adult 'endpoints'—i.e., studying conceptual development across cultural settings—is one critical step forward to making meaning from cultural comparisons.

Likewise, cultural specificity need not imply 'culture' alone. When I observe differences across cultural settings, I strive to recognize the higher-order commonalities that might provide a common explanation for observed differences. Are people in two settings trying to solve the same problem? Are there certain clusters of cultural settings that converge on similar solutions, or certain dimensions of cultural variability that might provide some explanation of the observed differences? As I understand it, this is common wisdom in the history of cultural anthropology: the problems are universal, the solutions are variable, and yet there is also likely structure to the variability in solutions.

3.11. Methodological perspectives for the study of Indigenous children

Bruno Ferreira

An appropriate methodology for research with Indigenous children requires us to be open to learning. I write from my experience as a Kaingang Indigenous person and researcher in the field of education, but other research shows that much of what is valid for the Kaingang is also valid for other Indigenous peoples in Brazil (Bergamaschi, 2008; Cohn, 2000; Tassinari, 2007). Therefore, I argue that one of the main devices that must be adopted by researchers who want to understand how Indigenous children learn is to live with them, listen to them, and seek to understand their experience. Most Indigenous peoples regard children as beings who are entitled to autonomy and freedom. We consider that they can learn if they want to, but will not be forced to do so. It is uncommon to see Indigenous parents shouting at or being violent to a child, for if the child is not willing to carry out an activity, she or he is not forced to do so (on the absence of physical punishment among Indigenous peoples in Brazil, see Tassinari, 2007).

From this understanding, it becomes important to resort to the practices of participant observation and the conversation circle. This last methodological tool leads participants to bring their experiences to the circle, allowing them to form reflective opinions and access deeper thoughts about themselves and others, in order to go beyond practical experiences and emotions and bring important details that are hidden or not necessarily conscious in daily life to the research. Both in the conversation circle and in observation and coexistence, the Indigenous mother tongue must be the vehicle of communication. Furthermore, the logic of oral traditions (as opposed to written, school-based ones) must be respected as a guide for reflections relevant to the work.

Living in the community helps the researcher to realize that Indigenous children live within the traditional educational processes of their people's families. They are present in most activities in their community: children are the ones who serve the elders; they are the immediate helpers. They help with planting, producing handicrafts, and looking after other children. There are not many restrictions and separations and children follow most of the adults' activities. When participating in these activities, children also play and talk to each other and older people. In these moments they learn about practical functions within the people's tradition. This also shows that, among Indigenous peoples, the western differentiation between what a child is and what an adult is does not always make sense, or at least not in the same way. Among Indigenous people, there are many moments in which children participate in activities as much as adults; they are not segregated. It is important to remember that the idea of childhood is a western construction, not an Indigenous one.

Furthermore, the researcher's coexistence in the community allows her or him to experience other forms of learning, such as, in the case of the Kaingang people, singing, a way of transmitting the ancestral knowledge and emotional skills that requires the children's concentration. It is also important to mention that the telling of stories—myths—performed by the elderly is fundamental for children to learn their cultural practices rooted in ancestry. In mythical narratives, the present is explained by the action of past events, whose current effects have not been and will never be erased by time. This is demonstrated in the narratives of the Kaingang people, as they bring into their narrated words the relationships between humans, animals, and nature. These narratives are references and have a dimension that produces and guides everyday life, establishing points of reference connected to the past and the present.

References

Abu Aleon, T., Weinstock, M., Manago, A. M., & Greenfield, P. M. (2019). Social change and intergenerational value differences in a Bedouin community in Israel. *Journal of Cross-Cultural Psychology, 50*, 708–727. https://doi.org/10.1177/0022022119839148

Amir, D., & McAuliffe, K. (2020). Cross-cultural, developmental psychology: Integrating approaches and key insights. Evolution and Human Behavior, 41(5), 430–444. https://doi.org/10.1016/j.evolhumbehav.2020.06.006

Arleo, A., & Delalande, J. (2010). *Cultures enfantines: Universalité et diversité*. Presses universitaires de Rennes. https://doi.org/10.4000/books.pur.10732

Avineri, N., Johnson, E., Brice-Heath, S., McCarty, T., Ochs, E., Kremer-Sadlik, T., Blum, S., Zentella, A. C., Rosa, J., Flores, N., Alim, H. S., & Paris, D. (2015). Invited forum: Bridging the "language gap". *Journal of Linguistic Anthropology, 25*(1). https://doi.org/10.1111/jola.12071

Baiocchi, M., Waxman, S., Pérez, E., Pérez, A., & Taverna, A. (2019). Social-ecological relations among animals serve as a conceptual framework among the Wichi. *Cognitive Development, 52*. https://doi.org/10.1016/j.cogdev.2019.100807.

Bakhurst, D. (2009). Reflections on activity theory. *Educational Review, 61*(2), 197–210. https://doi.org/10.1080/00131910902846916

Bakker, M., & Wicherts, J. M. (2011). The (mis)reporting of statistical results in psychology journals. *Behavior Research Methods, 43*(3), 666–678. https://doi.org/10.3758/s13428-011-0089-5

Baumard, N., & Sperber, D. (2010). Weird people, yes, but also weird experiments. *Behavioral and Brain Sciences, 33*(2–3). https://doi.org/10.1017/S0140525X10000038

Bensa, A. (1995). De la relation ethnographique. *Enquête, 1,* 131–140. https://doi.org/10.4000/enquete.268

Bergamaschi, M. A. (2008). *Povos Indígenas & Educação*. Mediação.

Bian, Q., Chen, Y., Greenfield, P. M., & Yuan, Q. (2022). Mothers' Experience of Social Change and Individualistic Parenting Goals Over Two Generations in Urban China. *Frontiers in Psychology, 12*. https://doi.org/10.3389/fpsyg.2021.487039

Bruner, J. (1990). Culture and Human Development: A New Look. *Human Development, 33*(6), 344–355. https://doi.org/10/fk2tqp

Burman, J. T. (2020). On Kuhn's case, and Piaget's: A critical two-sited hauntology (or, On impact without reference. *History of the Human Sciences, 33*(3–4), 129–159. https://doi.org/10.1177/0952695120911576

Burman, J. T. (2022). Meaning-change through the mistaken mirror: On the indeterminacy of "Wundt" and "Piaget (in Translation., Trans.). *Review of General Psychology, 26*(1), 22–48. https://doi.org/10.1177/10892680211017521

Cohn, C. (2000). *A criança indígena: A concepção Xikrin de infância e aprendizado*. University of São Paulo. https://doi.org/10.11606/D.8.2000.tde-15042024-142639

Cohn, C. (2017). Les dessins d'enfants et l'anthropologie: Une étude chez les Xicrin (Pará, Brésil. In A. Pierrot, I. M. Carvalho & C. Medaets (Eds). *Domination et apprentissage. Anthropologie des formes de la transmission culturelle*. Hermann. https://doi.org/10.4000/rfp.6745

Cole, M. (1996). Cultural psychology: A once and future discipline (pp. xvi, 400). Harvard University Press.

Cole, M., Gay, J., Glick, J., & Sharp, D. W. (1971). *The Cultural context of learning and thinking: An exploration in experimental anthropology.* Basic Books.

Cole, M., Hood, L., & McDermott, R. (1978). Ecological niche picking: Ecological invalidity as an axiom of experimental cognitive psychology. LCHC and ICHD, Rockefeller University. https://doi.org/10.13140/2.1.4727.1204

Collaboration, O. S. (2015). Estimating the reproducibility of psychological science. *Science (New York, N.Y.), 349*(6251), 4716. https://doi.org/10.1126/science.aac4716

Corsaro, W. A. (2003). *We're friends, right?: Inside kids' culture.* Joseph Henry Press.

D'Andrade, R. (2000). The Sad Story of Anthropology 1950-1999. *Cross-Cultural Research, 34*(3), 219–232. https://doi.org/10.1177/106939710003400301

Deffner, D., Rohrer, J. M., & McElreath, R. (2022). A Causal Framework for Cross-Cultural Generalizability. *Advances in Methods and Practices in Psychological Science, 5*(3), 25152459221106366. https://doi.org/10.1177/25152459221106366

Di Paolo, E., & De Jaegher, H. (2016). Neither individualistic, nor interactionist. In C. Durt, T. Fuchs, C. Tewes, & enaction (Eds). *Embodiment, enaction, and culture: Investigating the constitution of the shared world* (pp. 87–105). MIT Press.

Doria, N. G., & Simão, L. M. (2018). Differing times and differing measures: Dimensions of historical time in Vygotsky's work. *Theory & Psychology, 28*(6), 757–779. https://doi.org/10.1177/0959354318787345

Draper, C. E., Barnett, L. M., Cook, C. J., Cuartas, J. A., Howard, S. J., McCoy, D. C., & Yousafzai, A. K. (2022). Publishing child development research from around the world: An unfair playing field resulting in most of the world's child population under-represented in research. *Infant and Child Development*, e2375. https://doi.org/10.1002/icd.2375

Duranti, A., Ochs, E., & Schieffelin, B. B. (2012). *The handbook of language socialization.* Wiley-Blackwell. https://doi.org/10.1002/9781444342901

Ellis, B. D., & Stam, H. J. (2015). Crisis? What crisis? Cross-cultural psychology's appropriation of cultural psychology. *Culture & Psychology, 21*(3), 293–317. https://doi.org/10.1177/1354067X15601198

El-sana, S., Greenfield, P., & Weinstock, M. (2023). Ecological change, psychological mindedness, and attitudes toward school psychology: A three-generation study of Bedouin women in Israel. *Applied Developmental Science*, 1–17. https://doi.org/10.1080/10888691.2023.2192498

Esteban-Guitart, M. (2018). The biosocial foundation of the early Vygotsky: Educational psychology before the zone of proximal development. *History of Psychology, 21*(4), 384–401. https://doi.org/10.1037/hop0000092

Evers, N. F. G., Evers, G. W., Greenfield, P. M., Yuan, Q., Gutierrez, F., Halim, G., & Du, H. (2024). COVID-19 increased mortality salience, collectivism, and subsistence activities. *Journal of Cross-Cultural Psychology, 55*(3), 239-259. https://doi.org/10.1177/00220221231226310

Evers, N. F. G., Greenfield, P. M., & Evers, G. W. (2021). COVID-19 shifts mortality salience, activities, and values in the United States: Big data analysis of online adaptation. *Human Behavior and Emerging Technologies*. https://doi.org/10.1002/hbe2.251

Feldman-Barrett, L. (2017). *How emotions are made: The secret life of the brain*. Pan Macmillan.

Fernández Ruiz, M., & Taverna, A. (2023). Native ontological framework guides causal reasoning: Evidence from Wichi people. *Journal of Cognition and Culture, 23*(3–4), 397–419. https://doi.org/10.1163/15685373-12340169

García, C., Greenfield, P., Montiel-Acevedo, D., Vidaña-Rivera, T., & Colorado, J. (2017). Implications of 43 Years of Sociodemographic Change in Mexico for the Socialization of Achievement Behavior: Two Quasi-Experiments. *Journal of Cross-Cultural Psychology, 48*, 002202211769857. https://doi.org/10.1177/0022022117698573

García, C., Greenfield, P., Navarro, A., Colorado-García, J., & Vidaña-Rivera, T. (2020). Cooperative Play and Globalized Social Change: Mexican Children are Less Cooperative in 2017 than in 1967. *Current Research in Ecological and Social Psychology, 2*, 100003. https://doi.org/10.1016/j.cresp.2020.100003

García, C., Rivera, N., & Greenfield, P. M. (2015). The decline of cooperation, the rise of competition: Developmental effects of long-term social change in Mexico. *International Journal of Psychology, 50*(1), 6–11. https://doi.org/10.1002/ijop.12120

Geertz, C. (1973). *The Interpretation of Cultures*. Basic Books.

Gibson, J. J. (1979). *The ecological approach to visual perception.* Houghton Mifflin.

Goffman, E. (1964). The neglected situation. *American Anthropologist, 66*(6), 133–136. https://doi.org/10.1525/aa.1964.66.suppl_3.02a00090

Gomes, A. M. R. (1998). *Vegna che ta fago scriver. Etnografia della scolarizzazione in una comunità di sinti.* CISU.

Greenfield, P. M. (1966). On culture and conservation. In J. S. Bruner, R. R. Olver, & P. M. Greenfield (Eds). *Studies in cognitive growth* (pp. 225–256). Wiley.

Greenfield, P. M. (1997). You can't take it with you: Why ability assessments don't cross cultures. *American Psychologist, 52*(10), 1115–1124. https://doi.org/10.1037/0003-066X.52.10.1115

Greenfield, P. M. (2004). *Weaving generations together: Evolving creativity in the maya of chiapas.* School of American Research Press.

Greenfield, P. M. (2009). Linking social change and developmental change: Shifting pathways of human development. *Developmental Psychology, 45*(2), 401–418. https://doi.org/10.1037/a0014726

Greenfield, P. M. (2016). Social change, cultural evolution, and human development. *Current Opinion in Psychology, 8*, 84–92. https://doi.org/10.1016/j.copsyc.2015.10.012

Greenfield, P. M. (2018). Studying social change, culture, and human development: A theoretical framework and methodological guidelines. *Developmental Review, 50*, 16–30. https://doi.org/10.1016/j.dr.2018.05.003

Greenfield, P. M., Brown, G., & Du, H. (2021). Shifts in ecology, values, behavior, and relationships during the coronavirus pandemic: Survival threat, subsistence activities, conservation of resources, and interdependent families. *Current Research in Ecological Psychology, 2.* https://doi.org/10.1016/j.cresp.2021.100017

Greenfield, P. M., & Bruner, J. S. (1966). Culture and Cognitive Growth. *International Journal of Psychology, 1*(2), 89–107. https://doi.org/10.1080/00207596608247117

Greenfield, P. M., & Childs, C. P. (1977). Weaving, color terms, and pattern representation: Cultural influences and cognitive development among the Zinacantecos of Southern Mexico. *Inter-American Journal of Psychology, 11*, 23–48.

Greenfield, P. M., & Quiroz, B. (2013). Context and culture in the socialization and development of personal achievement values: Comparing Latino immigrant families, European American families, and elementary school teachers. *Journal of Applied*

Developmental Psychology, 34(2), 108–118. https://doi.org/10.1016/j. appdev.2012.11.002

Hammersley, M., & Atkinson, P. (2007). *Ethnography: Principles in practice.* Routledge

Heath, S. B. (1983). *Ways with words: Language, life, and work in communities and classrooms.* Cambridge University Press.

Henrich, J., Heine, S. J., & Norenzayan, A. (2010). The weirdest people in the world? *Behavioral and Brain Sciences, 33*(2–3), 61–83. https://doi. org/10.1017/S0140525X0999152X

Hruschka, D. J., Munira, S., Jesmin, K., Hackman, J., & Tiokhin, L. (2018). Learning from failures of protocol in cross-cultural research. *Proceedings of the National Academy of Sciences, 115*(45), 11428–11434. https://doi.org/10.1073/pnas.1721166115

Ionescu, A., Furdui, R., Gavreliuc, A., Greenfield, P. M., & Weinstock, M. (2023). The effects of sociocultural changes on epistemic thinking across three generations in Romania. *PLOS ONE, 18*(3), e0281785. https://doi.org/10.1371/journal.pone.0281785

Jolad, S., & Agarwal, A. (2021). Mapping india's language and mother tongue diversity and its exclusion in the indian census. https://doi. org/10.31235/osf.io/sjxc6

Keller, H. (2002). Development as the interface between biology and culture: A conceptualization of early ontogenetic experiences. In *Between culture and biology: Perspectives on ontogenetic development* (pp. 215–240). Cambridge University Press. https://doi.org/10.1017/ CBO9780511489853.011

Keller, H. (2007). *Cultures of Infancy*. Erlbaum.

Keller, H. (2022). *Cultures of infancy*. Routledge classis series. Routledge.

Keller, H., & Bard, K. A. (Eds). (2017). *The cultural nature of attachment: Contextualizing relationships and development.* MIT Press. https://doi. org/10.7551/mitpress/9780262036900.001.0001

Keller, H., & Kärtner, J. (2013). Development The Cultural Solution of Universal Developmental Tasks. In M. J. Gelfand, C. Chiu, & Y. Hong (Eds.), Advances in Culture and Psychology (Volume 3. Oxford University Press. https://doi.org/10.1093/acprof: oso/9780199930449.001.0001

Kirschner, P. A., Sweller, J., & Clark, R. E. (2006). Why minimal guidance during instruction does not work: An analysis of the failure of constructivist, discovery, problem-based, experiential, and inquiry-based teaching. *Educational Psychologist, 41*(2), 75-86,. https://doi. org/10.1207/s15326985ep4102_1

Kronenfeld, D. B. (2017). *Culture as a system: How we know the meaning and significance of what we do and say.* Routledge. https://doi.org/10.4324/9781315267326

Kroupin, I., Davis, H. E., & Henrich, J. (2024). Beyond Newton: Why Assumptions of Universality are Critical to Cognitive Science, and How to Finally Move Past Them. *Psychological Review.* https://doi.org/10.1037/rev0000480

Lakatos, I. (1978). *The methodology of scientific research programmes.* Cambridge University Press. https://doi.org/10.1017/CBO9780511621123

Lancy, D. F. (1981). The Indigenous Mathematics Project: An Overview. *Educational Studies in Mathematics, 12*(4), 445–453. https://doi.org/10.1007/BF00308142

LeVine, R. (2010). The six cultures study: Prologue to a history of a landmark project. *Journal of Cross-Cultural Psychology, 41*(4), 513–521. https://doi.org/10.1177/0022022110362567

Levinson, S. C. (2012). The Original Sin of Cognitive Science. *Topics in Cognitive Science, 4*(3), 396–403. https://doi.org/10.1111/j.1756-8765.2012.01195.x

Lignier, W. (2019). The discovery of symbolic violence: How toddlers learn to prevail with words. *Ethnography, 22*(2), 246–266. https://doi.org/10.1177/1466138119872522

Luhrmann, T. M., Weisman, K., Aulino, F., Brahinsky, J. D., Dulin, J. C., Dzokoto, V. A., Legare, C. H., Lifshitz, M., Ng., E., Ross-Zehnder, N., & Smith, R. E. (2021). Sensing the presence of gods and spirits across cultures and faiths. *Proceedings of the National Academy of Sciences, 118*(5), 2016649118. https://doi.org/10.1073/pnas.2016649118

Luria, A. R. (1976). *Cognitive development: Its cultural and social foundations.* Harvard University Press.

Manago, A. M. (2014). Connecting societal change to value differences across generations: Adolescents, mothers, and grandmothers in a Maya community in Southern Mexico. *Journal of Cross-Cultural Psychology, 45*(6), 868–887. https://doi.org/10.1177/0022022114527346

Maynard, A. E., & Greenfield, P. M. (2003). Implicit cognitive development in cultural tools and children. *Cognitive Development, 18*, 489–510. https://doi.org/10.1016/j.cogdev.2003.09.005

Maynard, A. E., Greenfield, P. M., & Childs, C. P. (2015). Developmental effects of economic and educational change: Cognitive representation across 43 years in a Maya community. *International Journal of Psychology, 50*, 12–19. https://doi.org/10.1002/ijop.12129

Maynard, A. E., Greenfield, P. M., Childs, C. P., & Weinstock, M. (2023). Social change, cultural evolution, weaving apprenticeship, and development: Informal education across three generations and 42 years in a Maya community. *Applied Developmental Science*. https://doi.org/10.1080/10888691.2022.2151445

Mead, M. (1932). An investigation of the thought of primitive children, with special reference to animism. *The Journal of the Royal Anthropological Institute of Great Britain and Ireland, 62,* 173–190. https://doi.org/10.2307/2843884

Medaets, C. (2016). Despite adults: Learning experiences on the tapajós river banks. *Ethos (Berkeley, Calif.), 44*(3), 248–268. https://doi.org/10.1111/etho.12134

Medin, D. L., Ojalehto, B., Marin, A., & Bang, M. (2013). Culture and epistemologies: Putting culture back into the ecosystem. In Y. Hong, M. J. Gelfand, & C. Chiu (Eds.), *Advances in culture and psychology* (vol. 4, pp. 177–217). Oxford University Press.

Medin, D. L., Ojalehto, B., Waxman, S. R., & Bang, M. (2015). Relations: Language, epistemologies, categories, and concepts. In E. Margolis & S. Laurence (Eds). *The conceptual mind: New directions in the study of concepts* (pp. 349–378). MIT Press. https://doi.org/10.7551/mitpress/9383.001.0001

Medin, D., Ojalehto, B., Marin, A., & Bang, M. (2017). Systems of (non-) diversity. *Nature Human Behaviour, 1*(5), 1–5. https://doi.org/10.1038/s41562-017-0088

Miller, P. J., & Sperry, D. E. (2012). Déjà Vu: The continuing misrecognition of low-income children's verbal abilities. In S. T. Fiske & H. R. Markus (Eds). *Facing social class How societal rank influences interaction* (1–6, pp. 109–130). Russell Sage Foundation.

Morelli, C. (2023). *Children of the rainforest: Shaping the future in amazonia.* Rutgers University Press.

Muthukrishna, M., Henrich, J., & Slingerland, E. (2021). Psychology as a Historical Science. *Annual Review of Psychology, 72*(1), 717–749. https://doi.org/10.1146/annurev-psych-082820-111436

Nielsen, M., & Haun, D. (2016). Why developmental psychology is incomplete without comparative and cross-cultural perspectives. *Philosophical Transactions of the Royal Society B: Biological Sciences, 371*(1686), 20150071. https://doi.org/10.1098/rstb.2015.0071

Nielsen, M., Haun, D., Kärtner, J., & Legare, C. H. (2017). The persistent sampling bias in developmental psychology: A call to action. *Journal of Experimental Child Psychology, 162,* 31–38. https://doi.org/10.1016/j.jecp.2017.04.017

Ochs, E., & Schieffelin, B. B. (2012). The theory of language socialization. In A. Duranti, E. Ochs, & B. B. Schieffelin (Eds). *The handbook of language socialization* (p. 21). Wiley-Blackwell. https://doi.org/10.1002/9781444342901

Overton, W. F. (2013a). A new paradigm for developmental science: Relationism and relational-developmental-systems. *Applied Developmental Science, 17*(2), 94–107. https://doi.org/10.1080/10888691.2013.778717

Overton, W. F. (2013b). Relationism and relational-developmental systems: A paradigm for developmental science in the post-Cartesian era. *Advances in Child Development and Behavior, 44*, 21–64. https://doi.org/10.1016/b978-0-12-397947-6.00002-7

Overton, W. F., & Lerner, R. M. (2012). Relational developmental systems: A paradigm for developmental science in the postgenomic era. *Behavioral and Brain Sciences, 35*(5), 375–376. https://doi.org/10.1017/S0140525X12001082

Park, H., Twenge, J., & Greenfield, P. M. (2017). American undergraduate students' value development during the Great Recession. *International Journal of Psychology, 52*, 28–39. https://doi.org/10.1002/ijop.12410

Park, H., Twenge, J. M., & Greenfield, P. M. (2014). The Great Recession: Implications for Adolescent Values and Behavior. *Social Psychological and Personality Science, 5*(3), 310–318. https://doi.org/10.1177/1948550613495419

Peters, U., Krauss, A., & Braganza, O. (2022). Generalization Bias in Science. *Cognitive Science, 46*(9), e13188. https://doi.org/10.1111/cogs.13188

Piaget, J. (1928). *Judgment and reasoning in the child.* Harcourt Brace.

Pires, F., & Ribeiro, F. B. (2015). Crianças: Um enfoque geracional. *Política & Trabalho, 43*, 13–17.

Rad, M. S., Martingano, A. J., & Ginges, J. (2018). Toward a psychology of Homo sapiens: Making psychological science more representative of the human population. *Proceedings of the National Academy of Sciences, 115*(45), 11401–11405. https://doi.org/10.1073/pnas.1721165115

Raeff, C., Greenfield, P. M., & Quiroz, B. (2000). Conceptualizing interpersonal relationships in the cultural contexts of individualism and collectivism. *New Directions for Child and Adolescent Development, 2000*(87), 59–74. https://doi.org/10.1002/cd.23220008706

Ramstead, M. J. D., Veissiere, S. P. L., & Kirmayer, L. J. (2016). Cultural affordances: Scaffolding local worlds through shared intentionality and regimes of attention. *Frontiers in Psychology, 7.* https://doi. org/10.3389/fpsyg.2016.01090

Richert, R. A., Weisman, K., Lesage, K. A., Ghossainy, M. E., Reyes-Jaquez, B., & Corriveau, K. H. (2022). Belief, culture, & development: Insights from studying the development of religious beliefs and behaviors. *Advances in Child Development and Behavior, 62*, 127–158. https://doi. org/10.1016/bs.acdb.2021.11.002

Rockwell, E. (2009). *La experiencia etnográfica: Historia y cultura en los procesos educativos.* Paidós.

Rogoff, B. (2003). *The cultural nature of human development.* Oxford University Press.

Rogoff, B., & Chavajay, P. (1995). What's Become of Research on the Cultural Basis of Cognitive Development? *American Psychologist, 19.* https://doi.org/10/ckxthb

Rohrer, J. (2018). Thinking clearly about correlations and causation: Graphical causal models for observational research. *Advances in Methods and Practices in Psychological Science, 1*, 27–42. https://doi. org/10.1177/25152459177456

Rotem, O. S., Weinstock, M., & Greenfield, P. M. (2024). Changes in values and ways of knowing among three generations of Israeli women of Ethiopian origin. *Current Research in Ecological Psychology.* https:// doi.org/10.1016/j.cresp.2024.100186

Sarcinelli, A. S. (2021). Des gamins roms hors-de-l'enfance. Entre protection et exclusion. Éd. des Archives contemporaines. https://doi. org/10.17184/eac.9782813003881

Scheidecker, G., Chaudhary, N., Keller, H., Mezzenzana, F., & Lancy, D. (2023). "Poor brain development" in the global South? Challenging the science of early childhood interventions. *Ethos*, 1–24. https://doi. org/10.1111/etho.12379

Schmidt, W. J., Keller, H., & Rosabal-Coto, M. (2021). Development in context: What we need to know to assess children's attachment relationships. *Developmental Psychology, 57*(12), 2206–2219. https:// doi.org/10.1037/dev0001262

Silan, M. (2023). Rethinking multi-site studies: Can the cross-indigenous approach mitigate common cross-cultural vulnerabilities? In In press social and personality psychology compass. https://doi.org/10.31234/ osf.io/jsyca

Szokolszky, A., & Read, C. (2018). Developmental ecological psychology and a coalition of ecological–relational developmental approaches. *Ecological Psychology, 30*(1), 6–38. https://doi.org/10.1080/10407413.20 18.1410409

Takada, A. (2012). Pre-verbal infant-caregiver interaction. In A. Duranti, E. Ochs, & B. B. Schieffelin (Eds). *The handbook of language socialization* (pp. 56–80). Wiley-Blackwell. https://doi.org/10.1002/9781444342901

Takada, A. (2016). Education and learning during social situations among the Central Kalahari San. In H. Terashima & B. S. Hewlett (Eds). *Social learning and innovation in contemporary hunter-gatherers: Evolutionary and ethnographic perspectives* (pp. 97–111). Springer. https://doi.org/10.1007/978-4-431-55997-9_1

Takada, A. (2019). *Anthropology of interaction: Places where "mind" meets "culture."* Shinyosha.

Tassinari, A. I. (2007). Concepções indígenas de infância no Brasil. *Tellus, 7*(13), 11–25.

Taverna, A. (2021). Motherese in the Wichi Language (El maternés en la lengua wichí. *Journal for the Study of Education and Development, 44*(2), 303–335. https://doi.org/10.1080/02103702.2021.1889290

Taverna, A., Padilla, M., Fernandez Ruiz, M., & Baiocchi, M. C. (2022). Concepts, language, and early socialization in the indigenous wichi perspective: Toward a relational–ecological paradigm. In M. V. Alves, R. Ekuni, M. J. Hermida, & J. Valle-Lisboa (Eds). *Cognitive science and education in non-weird populations: A latin american perspective* (pp. 74–97). Springer. https://doi.org/10.1007/978-3-031-06908-6

Taverna, A., Padilla, M., & Waxman, S. (2024). How pervasive is joint attention? Mother-child dyads from a Wichi community reveal a different form of "togetherness." *Developmental Science.* https://doi.org/10.1111/desc.13471

Taverna, A., & Waxman, S. (2020). Early lexical acquisition in the Wichi language. *Journal of Child Language, 47*(5), 1052–1072. https://doi.org/10.1017/S0305000919000898

Thurmond, V. A. (2001). The point of triangulation. *Journal of Nursing Scholarship, 33*(3), 253–258. https://doi.org/10.1111/j.1547-5069.2001.00253.x

Toren, C. (2011). The stuff of imagination: What we can learn from Fijian children's ideas about their lives as adults. *Social Analysis, 1*, 23. https://doi.org/10.3167/sa.2011.550102

Valsiner, J. (1998). *The guided mind: A sociogenetic approach to personality.* Harvard University Press.

van de Vijver, F. J. R., & Poortinga, Y. H. (2016). On item pools, swimming pools, birds with webbed feet, and the professionalization of multilingual assessment. In *Educational measurement: From foundations to future* (pp. 273–290). The Guilford Press.

Vygotsky, L. S. (1978). *Mind in society: The development of higher psychological processes* (M. Cole, V. John-Steiner, S. Scribner, & E. Souberman, Eds). Harvard University Press.

Vygotsky, L. S. (1981). The genesis of higher mental functions. In J. V. Wertsch (Ed.). *The concept of activity in soviet psychology.* M. F. Sharpe Inc Publisher.

Vygotsky, L. S. (1998). *The collected works of L.S. Vygotsky* (vol. 5, R. W. Rieber Ed.). Springer.

Vygotsky, L. S. (2012). *Thought and Language.* MIT Press.

Weinstock, M. (2015). Changing epistemologies under conditions of social change in two Arab communities in Israel. *International Journal of Psychology, 50*(1), 29–36. https://doi.org/10.1002/ijop.12130

Weinstock, M., Ganayiem, M., Igbaryia, R., Manago, A. M., & Greenfield, P. M. (2015). Societal Change and Values in Arab Communities in Israel: Intergenerational and Rural–Urban Comparisons. *Journal of Cross-Cultural Psychology, 4*6(1), 19–38. https://doi.org/10.1177/0022022114551792

Weisman, K., et al. (2024). The development and diversity of religious cognition and behavior: Protocol for Wave 1 data collection with children and parents by the Developing Belief Network. *Plos one, 19*(3), e0292755. https://doi.org/10.1371/journal.pone.0292755

Weisman, K., Legare, C. H., Smith, R. E., Dzokoto, V. A., Aulino, F., Ng, E., Dulin, J. D., Ross-Zehnder, N., Brahinsky, J. D., & Luhrmann, T. M. (2021). Similarities and differences in concepts of mental life among adults and children in five cultures. *Nature Human Behaviour, 5,* 1358–1368. https://doi.org/10.1038/s41562-021-01184-8

Weisman, K., & Luhrmann, T. M. (2020). What anthropologists can learn from psychologists, and the other way around. *Journal of the Royal Anthropological Institute, 26*(S1), 131–147. https://doi.org/10.1111/1467-9655.13245

Wood, D. J., Bruner, J. S., & Ross, G. (1976). The role of tutoring in problem solving. *Journal of Child Psychiatry and Psychology, 17,* 89–100. https://doi.org/10.1111/j.1469-7610.1976.tb00381.x

Zeng, R., & Greenfield, P. M. (2015). Cultural evolution over the last 40 years in China: Using the Google Ngram Viewer to study implications of social and political change for cultural values. I*nternational Journal of Psychology, 50*(1), 47–55. https://doi.org/10.1002/ijop.12125

Zhou, C., Yiu, W. Y. V., Wu, M. S., & Greenfield, P. M. (2017). Perception of cross-generational differences in child behavior and parent socialization: A mixed-method interview study with grandmothers in China. *Journal of Cross-Cultural Psychology, 49,* 62–81. https://doi.org/10.1177/0022022117736029

4. Research methods: A collage

Coordinated by Elena Miu

This chapter provides a non-comprehensive overview of the research methods used in cross-cultural studies of children. We present a collage of case studies and methods summaries that outline common practices and explore their theoretical, ethical, and practical implications. We first propose guidelines for dealing with issues of theoretical validity by showcasing the benefits of multi-methods perspectives for knowledge triangulation and introducing a design strategy for causal analysis. We cover practical organizational concerns pertinent to large cross-cultural studies. We then touch on ethical concerns and cover the value of long-term cumulative study, revisiting old work from a non-western-centric perspective, intersubjectivity and positionality, and include methods for sustainable and principled anthropology. Finally, we zoom in on methodological approaches used in cross-cultural work on children, summarizing the benefits and limitations of ethno-archaeological approaches, cross-cultural experiments, conversational analysis approaches, and standardized longitudinal assessments.

4.1. Introduction

Elena Miu

This chapter is structured as a collage of case studies and methods summaries, providing an overview of common practices, guidelines, suggestions, and issues pertinent to cross-cultural studies involving children. First, we outline good practices to ensure a successful, valid, and comprehensive study. Kline writes

©2025 Elena Miu, et al., CC BY-NC 4.0   https://doi.org/10.11647/OBP.0440.04

a beautiful demonstration of the investigative power of qualitative and quantitative methods combined, drawing upon her own work on teaching in Fiji. Pretelli lays out a state-of-the-art quantitative workflow for causal inference, complete with causal diagrams, Bayesian statistics, and simulated data. Rawlings reflects on the lessons learned from coordinating a multi-site cross-cultural project, providing a much-needed practical perspective. We then engage with complex and often sensitive aspects of ethnography, providing examples of how to make the most of a study in ethical and appropriate ways. Liebal provides an overview of ways to conduct ethnography at a distance, necessary in a post-pandemic society. Lancy illustrates the benefits of using archival data and casting a wide, curious net. Xu's study is a vivid example of the necessity of revisiting older work, particularly with a non-western perspective. Park shows how a culturally sensitive study and researcher are exactly what is needed when working with vulnerable populations. Finally, we zoom in on specific methodological approaches in more detail. Milks and Riede bring an archaeological perspective to the question of children learning, considering what we can and, importantly, cannot learn about the past. Stengelin examines experimentation in the field and discusses the nuances of what it means for an experiment to be cross-cultural. Takada discusses how conversational analysis can be applied cross-culturally to understand child socialization. Kärtner illustrates how longitudinal standardized assessments can shed light on causal questions regarding mother-infant interaction and socialization.

4.2. Mixed methods in the study of informal teaching in Yasawa, Fiji

Michelle Kline

Often in both anthropological and psychological studies that draw cross-cultural comparisons, a high value is placed on the replication of identical methods across field sites (see Apicella et al., 2020), with the expectation that replicating the same methods means researchers are asking the same questions. Kline et al. (2018) argue that this equivalency assumption is false when comparing across broadly different cultural contexts. Among other problems, issues of language translation, the lack of one-to-one matches among concepts cross-culturally, the mapping of behavioral measures onto existing cultural systems and norms, or general discomfort with experimental/interview methods among participating groups may mean that the results do not mean what the field researcher believes them to mean. In addition, a one-size-fits-all method used cross-culturally may miss out on locally interesting variations.

Beyond questions of the validity of one-size-fits-all methods, a broader concern is that each chosen method necessarily—and by design—constrains the specific conclusions that can be drawn. This is both a strength and a weakness of experimental methods. Broad comparative studies with copy/paste methods across sites are unlikely to uncover novel cross-cultural variation, and are best suited to test specific hypotheses about cross-cultural variation in known variables. However, these methods are often undertaken without any qualitative or observational study to lay the groundwork, with the result that the interesting cultural variation that does exist goes undocumented by researchers, despite being important in the daily lives of participants. We argue that this is not the ideal approach to finding out about how humans live in the world, and even more so it is unlikely to accurately assess the cross-cultural variation in human behavior and human development. Rather, research requires a more varied mix of observational and qualitative methods, suited to a broader set of questions (Broesch et al., 2020). For these reasons, it is useful, if also more labor-intensive, to combine qualitative and quantitative research to study the same phenomenon at the same field site, in a comprehensive mixed-methods approach.

This has been undertaken, for example, in the study of teaching and learning in villages in Yasawa Island, Fiji. In this case study we take each method in turn, beginning with qualitative data collection and analysis, then mixed methods, then quantitative data collection and analysis. The research questions in this case boil down to: who teaches what to whom, when, and how/with what form(s) of teaching?

Qualitative ethnographic methods

Qualitative ethnographic methods can range from reading the existing ethnographic literature of a region, to conducting qualitative ethnographic observations and recording field notes, informal conversations, or qualitative interviews with participants. In the case of Yasawa Island, Fiji, Kline combined existing ethnographic literature with months of on-site field observations and field notes (unpublished) as background to the design of more quantitative methods. This also included photographs and video recordings with consent from parents and assent from children (see Broesch et al., 2020). For researchers in more qualitative fields, such as cultural anthropology, qualitative ethnography and thick description could form the basis of the work. This level of data collection and analysis can provide an in-depth description of participants' lives, contexts, and experiences. In the present case study, these mainly form the basis for qualitative 'field site' descriptions (such as Kline, 2016), for images and descriptive examples in presentations and/or published papers (as in Kline, 2015), and for in-depth background information in order to design feasible quantitative methods that will formally measure types and variations of teaching observed in the Yasawa Islands, Fiji. These qualitative observations and ethnographic literature yielded a general impression that teaching was important and frequent, though less marked than in western formal education, and that teaching happened within the context of everyday activities, not as separate 'lessons' with formal evaluations. These insights are key to understand the variety of results of more structured, quantitative studies of teaching at the same site.

Qualitative interview data, quantitative analysis

Kline et al. (2013) provide a more targeted study of learning and teaching at the same sites in the Yasawa Islands. Using interview data that included open-ended questions with qualitative responses, Kline et al. used quantitative coding of these answers to test hypotheses about who learns from whom, about what, and at what ages. With respect to teaching, participant responses reflect societal norms among adults about teaching: the importance of 'teaching' varied by the domain of learning (e.g., boating, weaving, and other practical concerns), but was lowest when participants were asked about learning in general. When asked if parents must teach their children anything, nearly all participants (42 of 44) highlighted customs or 'ways of the land'—in other words, proper behavior. This and a qualitative review of the uncoded verbal responses reveals that participants treated 'teaching' as shorthand for making someone learn, and not necessarily as a fine-grained behavior such as tutoring, instructing, and so on. Teaching was also most commonly associated with learning from parents, as opposed to other relatives or non-relatives. In combination with the qualitative field data, the results of these interviews help to distinguish the researcher's treatment of 'teaching' as behavior that supports another's learning, versus a responsibility or duty of a parent to ensure that their children have properly learned how to behave in a general sense. Notably, there is some overlap – but these definitions are not the same, and the methods for studying each version of 'teaching' will necessarily differ.

Qualitative observational data, quantitative analysis

Kline et al. (2016) use structured qualitative observations of daily activities, collected between 2003 and 2011, to assess the general frequency of 'teaching' where teaching is defined as a stand-alone or abstract instruction that constitutes its own activity. Through this 'time allocation' method, researchers used a randomized schedule of participants and dates/times, plus instantaneous sampling—recording of who was present and what activities they were doing only at the point they first identified the focal participant—to gain a holistic picture of life in Yasawan villages. Under this method, 'teaching' would include things like: helping a child with homework, instructing a man as to the best way to cultivate yams, demonstrating a new style of weaving to a woman, or formal school sessions. The latter was excluded from analyses since the focus was informal teaching in day-to-day life. This method also excludes subtle forms of observable behavior, such as pointing, telling, showing, correcting, or other behaviors that support another's learning while embedded in another activity. The results of this method show that teaching, when defined as a stand-alone activity, is rare in these villages (only 14 out of 565 observations included teaching). The activities that were labelled as teaching were mostly village or church meetings in which information was being shared with an audience (n=7). Notably, this method and definition of teaching (as an activity) mean that it is rarely observed, in contrast to more frequent qualitative observations of subtle teaching (as a behavior), and the importance of teaching according to Yasawan adults (as a social duty to shape children).

Quantitative ethnographic methods

Finally, as a follow-up to the qualitative and quantitative research above, Kline et al. (2016) used a fine-grained ethogram, or structured list of behaviors, to make quantitative observations of subtle teaching embedded in daily life. In contrast to instantaneous sampling, here teaching is defined as a list of behaviors (the ethogram) which support learning in others rather than as an activity in itself, and the observations were limited to focal individuals six years of age and younger, plus whomever they interacted with during observation sessions. Observations were continuous for fixed time periods, in order to capture these subtle behaviors. This method builds on the earlier qualitative field observations suggesting that teaching behaviors are woven into other daily activities, and the interviews suggesting that parents and grandparents are the most likely to teach (at least for children). In contrast to the time allocation results, this method and definition of teaching show that teaching (as a behavior) is relatively frequent, with teaching present in 484 out of 721 five-minute blocks of observation time (about 67% of observations). It is worth noting that this is a much more heavily constrained and structured method than the qualitative, open-ended field observations or notes. In the case of field notes, interpretation was made and meaning inferred by the researcher in the course of their observations. In the present TEACH (2016) method, interpretation was reserved for after the quantitative analysis of research results and statistically tested patterns.

Conclusion

At first glance, the results of the combination of methods seems a mess: qualitative ethnographic observations provide in-depth examples of teaching in situ but the ethnographic record suggests it is rare; interviews indicate teaching is important but perhaps confined to a few domains and is primarily undertaken by parents or grandparents; time allocation observations indicate teaching is almost never the predominant activity; ethogram-based observations suggest teaching is prevalent (67% of observations) even for very young children (six and under). However, when the interpretation is made with methods and definitions in mind, a more cohesive, holistic picture of what teaching looks like in Yasawan villages is possible:

- Teaching as a stand-alone activity is rare and tends to happen primarily in formal settings, such as village or church meetings, or during formal schooling. In informal settings, teaching does not happen as a stand-alone activity, but is woven in with other daily activities.

- This subtle teaching takes place in the form of behaviors that support learning. For example, demonstration (pointing, slowing down, narrating, and showing while undertaking a task with novices observing) or the providing of abstract information that a novice cannot easily acquire themselves (e.g., what different animals eat or where they sleep, kinship labels, or rules of proper conduct). However, the most frequent form of subtle teaching behavior (for children younger than six years old) is providing additional feedback as to the danger, safety, or desirability of their behaviors.

- From the perspective of Yasawan adults, it is an important social responsibility for parents and elders to have influence by teaching values and proper conduct to children in the village; there are dire consequences if parents fail to teach children how to be proper community members.

Using just one of the above methods would not have yielded such a detailed picture of teaching, nor situated it in cultural context. It is only through the triangulation of methods that such a set of conclusions is possible.

4.3. A framework for quantitative causal analysis

Ilaria Pretelli

Quantitative approaches are often presented in opposition to qualitative ones, but this dichotomy is often forced: as we have seen in the previous section, quantitative analyses require a strong qualitative foundation and 'pragmatic researchers' combining both methodologies have higher potential to address problems in the social sciences (Onwuegbuzie and Leech, 2005). Nonetheless, quantitative work is characterized by certain goals, approaches, and methods, which we review below, with a focus on causal inference.

Quantitative studies are often guided by the objective to identify and test a causal mechanism, provide tools for predictions and/ or offer generalizable explanations by looking for consensus, or trends, in data that are usually manipulated as numbers (Yilmaz, 2013). They stem from hypotheses attached to theories and test them in the real world using a variety of methods and approaches. Here we briefly summarize some important concepts for quantitative analysis, with an emphasis on causality and problem-specific methods for statistical analysis.

Causal inference

A search for causality underlies most quantitative research, even when hidden behind the old mantra of 'correlation does not mean causation' (a warning for researchers that finding an association between two variables does not necessarily imply the causal connection envisioned). In fact, causal analysis is its own field of research and has developed a range of tools, both mathematical and statistical, to identify causation in real world systems (Pearl, 2000). Causal analysis should be included as a first step in the design and considered thoroughly during the development of any quantitative study. In experimental research, causation is usually addressed by randomization: if two samples are randomized to be identical at the start except for the treatment assigned, any difference in the outcome should be attributed only to the effect of the treatment (see the section on causal inference in Chapter 9). However, the situation becomes structurally much more complex in observational studies, and complex experimental set-ups can also encounter serious issues with causal inference. Hence, methods such as causal diagrams—intuitively simple graphs that display causal connections, such as DAGs (Directed Acyclic Graphs)—are a powerful tool that allow researchers to (i) clearly lay out the assumptions and goals of the study and (ii) define identification strategies, i.e., help decide which predictors to include in a statistical model depending on the causal query objective of the study (Pearl, 1995; see also Section 3.4). Contrary to verbal models, i.e., the often imprecise long-form explanations that justify research development and analytical choices, causal diagrams require the researcher to list all of the elements relevant for a certain analysis and to describe their expectations for what causes what. Figure 4.1 shows a DAG describing the factors influencing the development of ecological knowledge in Pemba, Zanzibar (Pretelli et al, 2022)—here we assume that knowledge varies with age, which stands for a proxy of various unmeasured time-varying factors. Moreover, we expect ecological knowledge to differ by sex, not because of innate differences, but rather because of gendered participation in activities and access to schooling. The DAG allows us to schematically represent these assumptions, and guides the analysis (see the supplementary information in Pretelli et al., 2022 for extensive description of the approach).

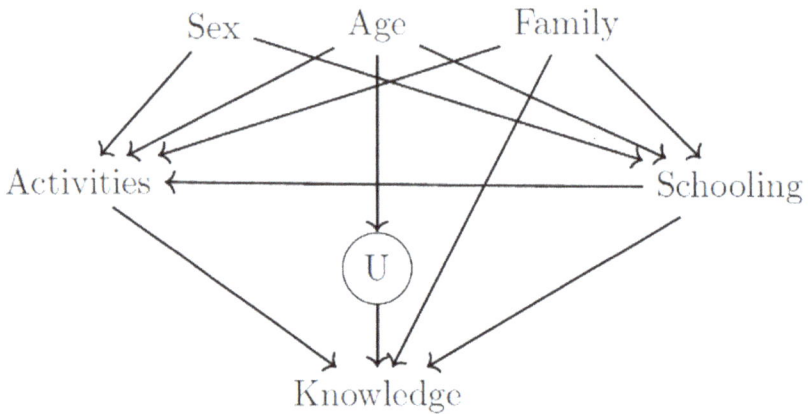

Fig. 4.1 DAG describing the factors influencing the development of ecological knowledge in a part-time foraging population in Pemba, Zanzibar. Originally appears in Pretelli et al. (2022). CC BY-NC-SA.

When used appropriately, the causal diagram should reflect previous knowledge on the subject, draw from theory, and clearly connect hypotheses to the estimand (i.e., the quantity to be estimated as a result of the statistical analysis) to address the issue at hand (Deffner et al., 2022). Moreover, mathematical tools applied to causal diagrams can help define which sets of controls should be included in order to obtain a causal estimate. The common approach in the behavioral sciences of including as many predictors as possible in an analysis does not often achieve its role of inferring not only causality, but any relation at all, because the causal connections between the variables included can either obscure or magnify the relationships. A well-known case is Simpson's paradox: a phenomenon where it is possible to identify a statistical trend when the data is grouped (or when certain controls are included in the analysis), but the trend disappears or reverses when the groups are combined (or if the controls are excluded; see a review of cases in psychology in Kievit et al., 2013). An accessible introduction to the concepts of causal inference can be found in Pearl (2018), and a hands-on approach to causal inference in the behavioral science is illustrated in Chapter 5 of McElreath's *Statistical Rethinking* (2018).

Thinking generatively: Simulations and models

Once the causal structure of the system is laid out, a researcher must choose a statistical approach to address the estimand (the parameter (s) to estimate that will be used to draw our conclusion, see above). A common approach in the behavioral sciences is to choose a statistical model out of several that are commonly used, often named after some statistician (e.g., Pearson, Cox) – this choice is usually driven by the characteristics of the data. This approach disregards the process that generated the data, but rather forces the problem into a mold by applying a statistical tool that implies a certain generative process and a series of assumptions to a set of data that were not necessarily generated by that process or conform to these assumptions. This might lead to erroneous or misleading results. An alternative to this approach is to think generatively: start from defining the process that generates the data, and then reconstruct problem-specific statistical models that can target specific inferences from the model. Statistical models should make minimum assumptions about the data and process, for example considering how a predictor can influence the results as it approaches zero, or if the effect should increase linearly as the predictor increases, rather than tapering off at large values. This approach is within reach of researchers nowadays, thanks to the development of computational and statistical tools that allow reasonably skilled researchers to specify their own statistical models in programming languages such as R or Stan, which use Bayesian inference and allow for very flexible, sophisticated model building (R Core Team, 2023; Stan Development Team, 2021). Bayesian inference offers advantages such as better treatment of small sample sizes, effective management of uncertainty, and easier interpretation of results in terms of predictions and counterfactuals.

Bayesian data analysis implies a workflow that includes (i) model choice and construction (including testing priors), (ii) fitting the model to data (i.e., estimation of the parameters), and (iii) evaluation of the model fit and interpretation of different kinds of results (Gelman et al., 2020). One important step, which can help enormously during the development of a Bayesian workflow, and is incredibly useful for statistical analysis generally, is to produce and use simulated data. Artificial data can be produced through computational simulation according to the causal model proposed by the researcher, and it can then be used to test the statistical model. In particular, simulations allow us to (i) determine whether the statistical model used is able to offer information on the causal model we expect, as certain causal inferences are non-identifiable: multiple causal models can produce similar data and thus make it impossible to identify the generative process, and thus support or reject hypotheses, a phenomenon known as equifinality; (ii) estimate minimum sample sizes, or how much data would be necessary to produce reliable results, depending on effect size and variability in the data—the Bayesian version of a power analysis; (iii) understand the statistical model, evaluate its fit to real data and test the limitations of the model (Gelman et al., 2020).

Of course, at some point during this process, data have to be collected. Thinking with causal and generative models (i.e., simulations) is helpful to determine which kind of data are needed, what they mean and how they will be used in the analysis. Thus it is advisable to plan the analysis and produce a simulation before collecting the data. This can help anticipate issues that might arise later on when, for example, the researcher might realize they have not collected data for a fundamental control variable, or that the data recorded as continuous have no real continuous meaning and ethnographic background is needed to determine cut points.

Results and interpretation

Once the model is fit to the data, researchers must evaluate and interpret the results. Most commonly, researchers interpret and present resulting effect sizes, i.e., the value of a parameter as estimated in the model, and some measure of the confidence in the results, usually a p-value. Bayesian analysis does not rely on p-values, as these are a feature of frequentist statistics, but encourages researchers to carefully interpret the results of the models in terms of counterfactuals and predictions. The results of a Bayesian model based on a causal model can be used to calculate what would happen under certain conditions (i.e., counterfactuals) and to predict outcomes for certain combinations of predictors. This moves away from interpreting results for specific predictors in isolation, and towards interpreting the joint output of the model on the outcome scale. Part of the interpretation of Bayesian model results should include monitoring how the model updates its priors, i.e., whether the model has learned anything from the data, evaluating model fit to check if the sample space was appropriately explored. Detailed instructions on model construction and results recovery are presented in McElreath's *Statistical Rethinking* (2018).

4.4. Lessons from a large-scale cross-cultural project

Bruce Rawlings

Conducting research in multiple populations in a single project is very difficult. Arguably, particularly so when a project is centrally led (i.e., by a PI or group of researchers at one institution), rather than dispersed across a group of researchers or institutions. In these cases, every decision—concerning what data to collect, how much to modify established protocols, who to consult for feedback and when, recruiting research assistants and translators, how to recruit participants, run data collection, handle and organize data, and how to disseminate the work—ultimately fall upon one or a few people.

My postdoctoral research project aimed to examine cognitive and academic development in children in a large-scale cross-cultural project, in which we worked with children and adults in 12 countries. This was my first major incursion into cross-cultural research. I came into the position from a comparative psychology background, with little exposure to studying (human) samples outside of the UK and US. My role was to develop experimental protocols, train local research assistants, help oversee data collection and data quality control, analyze, and disseminate the data—working with international collaborators, my PI, and my other lab members throughout.

Across this project—through things that worked well and not so well—I learned a vast amount about both cross-cultural research and good research practices in general. Here, I reflect on my experiences and present three key points I learned that I want to pass on to researchers engaging in cross-cultural research. These are not exhaustive and may seem obvious for those more experienced, but things I took away with me as someone new to the field. While I hope these reflections will be useful to those of all experience levels, they may be particularly useful for those who are new to cross-cultural research.

Design a thorough and careful workflow protocol

This is one of the most important things I learned. Our project manager was a strong advocate for clear and high-quality workflow protocols, and I cannot emphasize enough how valuable they are. Cross-cultural research provides unique workflow challenges, which may include some or all of the following: designing and refining protocols suitable for one or more populations; ethical approval administration (at central and local levels); training local research assistants; piloting; participant recruitment; collecting data; translations (including back-translations); video coding and/ or audio transcribing; and data storage, handling, and processing. Each of these steps are complex, particularly when multiple samples are involved, and require careful tracking, individually and in unison. Research teams should devote time and energy to developing a system that documents, tracks, and explains these steps in detail, and the decisions made to reach them. This will minimize mistakes, ensure transparency, facilitate replication, and allow identification of any unintended biases that may manifest in our work (Burger et al., 2023). It also helps collaborators from different institutions and/or backgrounds, and those from the wider research community, to understand your project and the decision processes from its inception to completion.

What a workflow looks like depends on the nature of the research, but researchers should document all decisions, modifications, difficulties, and successes throughout their project, to allow the research community to understand and learn from them, to continue to improve our practices. Several authors have described their cross-cultural workflow steps in detail, providing excellent points of departure (Hruska et al., 2018; Holding, 2018; Burger et al., 2023).

Engage with local researchers and stakeholders from the onset

Putting aside the growing (correct, in my opinion) acceptance that many western scientists have for a long time engaged in poor and inequitable research practices by using methods such as helicopter research, failure to engage with local researchers, community members, and other stakeholders from the project onset will almost always make the research quality poorer. I was trained in psychology and anthropology at exclusively western (UK and US) institutions, based on theories and methodology derived almost exclusively from western researchers, based on western samples. Let's say, for argument's sake, I wanted to study cognitive development in Kyoto, or Buenos Aires, or Marrakesh. I have no background or training in child development in these populations. If I were to design a study or experimental protocol, it would be (whether I was aware of it or not) driven by my own experiences, training, and knowledge, which may not be appropriate for these samples. This can generate a range of problems concerning task validity and how participants perceive protocols, which may impact participant performance and lead to erroneous conclusions. Scientists are increasingly calling for researchers (particularly western-based researchers) to work alongside experts in relevant local cultural contexts, to ensure that theoretical frameworks, protocols and materials are culturally informed and appropriate (Hruska et al., 2018; Broesch et al., 2020), and in my experience this is a crucial first step to make.

Factor in sufficient time for protocol and data translations and processing

Often the native language of the researchers conducting the work is different to that of the study population(s). Developing protocols and processing data (regardless of whether it is observational or experimental), including a (rigorous) translation process, takes a lot of time and effort. There are multiple points at which high-quality translations are essential, including recruitment documents, consent or assent information, study protocols, debriefing information, any training information for research assistants, and of course the data itself. Back-translation means a document is translated into the target language and then re-translated into the source language by a translator who does not see the original. This provides an extra step to catch errors than is present in a single translation process. This can, though, be a time-consuming process, requiring diligent and skilled translators, with clear dialogue between them and the research group. If there are many (or complex) protocols, or data with lengthy transcripts requiring translation, months may be needed both before and after data collection. Translators can be expensive, particularly for rarer languages, and researchers often fail to factor in sufficient funds or time to account for this—meaning shortcuts inevitably are taken. To maximize the research quality, translations need skilled translators, careful consideration, and time.

Conclusion

There are multiple resources available (referenced throughout and including this book) to help researchers who are involved in cross-cultural research at any stage. Good research requires ensuring that projects are well-documented, locally informed, appropriate for the study sample(s), and that enough time is factored in.

4.5. Remote ethnographic methods

Katja Liebal

What are ethnographic methods?

Ethnographic methods are qualitative methods, widely used by anthropologists. In addition to participant observation, sometimes referred to as "method par excellence" in anthropology (Sousa, 2022, p. 7), ethnographic methods may include interviews, PhotoVoice, drawings, and diaries (Sullivan et al., 2018), and rely on multiple practices, such as listening, recording, reading, and documenting (Ploder & Hamann, 2021). Conducting such ethnographic research is closely linked with "going to the field" and establishing relations with other people (Sousa, 2022, p. 3).

For ethnographic research with children, there has been a fundamental change from research on children to research with or for children, resulting in the adaptation of existing methods (e.g., questionnaires) and the development of new 'participatory' or multi-method approaches (Fargas-Malet et al., 2010). While earlier work focused on the detailed description of child development within one cultural context (e.g., Dennis, 1940; Leighton & Kluckhohn, 2013), later ethnographic work considered the quantification of observations (Barr et al., 1991) and multi-site comparisons (Amir & McAuliffe, 2020), including some of the few studies specifically dedicated to different learning strategies in childhood (Lancy et al., 2010).

What are distant methods?

Distant approaches in ethnographic research, also known as remote, digital, or virtual ethnography (Bengtsson, 2014), are not a recent development. What is new, however, is the increase in the use of distant methods in research with children, as a result of the COVID-19 pandemic and the corresponding restrictions on travelling and close social contact (Lupton, 2021; Watson & Lupton, 2022). Since the pandemic resulted in the closure of research labs, schools, and kindergartens, the usage of distant methods with children has not been limited to ethnographic and qualitative approaches, but also involves experimental methods (Tsuji et al., 2022). Most of such distant ethnographic studies with children have an educational focus, investigating the effects of online schooling during the COVID-19 pandemic (Aladsani et al., 2022; Ratih et al., 2021).

Distant ethnographic methods used with children include interviews, observations, surveys and drawings, which can be either conducted by the researchers themselves during the online interaction with the child (in real time, but with the researcher and the child being in different locations), or asynchronously as the data are collected by the child and/or their family and then later transferred to the researcher (Watson & Lupton, 2022). For example, Sandberg and colleagues (2022) conducted online ethnographic fieldwork with very young Swedish children (up to three years old) and their families to study their engagement with digital media technologies in their homes. They conducted interviews, observations, and surveys online, while interacting with the children and their families (via Zoom). Sousa (2022) investigated children's representation of COVID-19 in Brazil. Unlike in Sandberg et al. (2022), data were collected offline and asynchronously, as children's parents acted as mediators and collected the data on their children, such as interviews, audio recordings, and drawings, based on the researcher's instructions. New developments, such as adapting the PhotoVoice method through digital diaries (Volpe, 2019), were specifically used in research with young people to take into account the significance of mobile communication in their everyday lives.

Other studies use a mixed-methods approach (Doyle et al., 2009) and combine qualitative ethnographic approaches with quantitative psychological methods. For example, a team of developmental psychologists, biologists, and anthropologists (Children & Nature project) used interviews, PhotoVoice, and drawings in addition to sorting tasks and other experiments to investigate the attitudes of children and adolescents towards other animals in 16 countries, across different socio-cultural contexts (Thajib et al., under review). Because researchers were not allowed to travel during the COVID-19 pandemic, they instead collaborated with members of a range of different communities. During several online meetings, interviews or experimental procedures were translated, and, if necessary, adapted to the corresponding socio-cultural context. Collaborators were then trained online in using these different methods, and, after a piloting phase, they then worked with the children and adolescents of their community to collect the data, always synchronously, but either during online or in-person meetings, depending on the COVID-19 regulations. Thus, local collaborators either used the different methods remotely or during direct interactions with the participants (Thajib et al., under review).

What are the methodological and ethical challenges?

An important challenge is not being able to go into the field, which is considered an integral part of conducting ethnographic research and raises the question whether remote methods enable a relation between the researcher and the researched (Bengtsson, 2014; Sousa, 2022). For example, Sousa (2022, p. 5) concluded that "I produced my first ethnography without being there [...]. For the first time, participant observation was not my main guide, and I did not have a qualified informant." This is particularly the case for asynchronous modes of distant data collection: researchers need to rely on other mediators, e.g., parents or local collaborators, and only receive the data with some delay. Unlike in synchronous interviews, researchers cannot ask for clarification or check whether their interview partners understood their questions (Lupton, 2021). Synchronous online sessions, on the other hand, often come with the challenge of limiting interactions to a tiny screen and the handling of different types of equipment (tablet, mobile phone, laptop) and software (Sandberg et al., 2022).

Ethical issues related to using distant methods mostly concern the challenge of providing safe conditions for collecting, transferring, and storing data (Tsuji et al., 2022), and acknowledging that their use merges participants' homes and researchers' fields in a new way that did not previously exist (Konken & Howlett, 2023). Still, an important benefit overall of using remote methods—ethnographic as well as more quantitative—is that a greater number of often difficult-to-reach communities can be included, resulting in greater samples and increased diversity (Hall et al., 2021).

4.6. Discovery and the ethnographic record

David F. Lancy

The paper entitled 'The Weirdest People in the World?' (Henrich et al., 2010) was an urgent call to take psychology's core theoretical propositions overseas to test their viability outside WEIRD (Western, Educated, Industrialized, Rich, and Democratic) society. Researchers are being exhorted to determine whether a particular pattern of results would also be found in Indigenous communities. If not, any claim of universality would be withdrawn. But Global WEIRDing (Cooperrider 2019) is rapidly shrinking the pool of communities that can serve as unacculturated comparison sites (Kramer, 2021, p. 10; Berl and Hewlett, 2015, p. 3; Maynard et al., 2023). Alternate research strategies must be used to cope with this problem.

One alternative is to adopt a historical perspective and draw on fieldwork undertaken before modern schooling and WEIRD child-rearing practices became entrenched. My approach has been to review the ethnographic record to tease out emergent patterns in child development. Storing, organizing and retrieving ethnographic accounts has become so much faster and more convenient. Studying childhood through the lens of archived accounts is, in a word, cheap, relative to the cost of sending researchers to, say, the South Pacific for three months of fieldwork.

Ethnography has some unique virtues that make ethnographic 'data' particularly valuable. By gathering information as a participant observer, the ethnographer weaves together three strands of information. First, ethnographers describe what they are seeing, compiling an impressive observational log (complemented with photos and audio/video recordings) from which patterns can be detected. Second, by interviewing or engaging their informants in a discussion of what they've witnessed, they may gain an insider's or 'emic' perspective, which often makes intelligible the foreign or exotic practices one has documented. The results of focused investigation (e.g., testing, spot observations and the like) can thus be more readily interpreted. Third, ethnographers record their own or 'etic' perspective. I pay particular attention to the anthropologist's 'aha' moments, when they are surprised or shocked by something that violates their own assumptions about childhood (Lancy, 2016).

Taking an open-ended and inductive approach to archived data allows one to go beyond the evaluation of WEIRD theory into the realm of discovery. The inductive study of archival records constructed from hundreds of ethnographic studies spanning a century or more will be illustrated by a specific case study. In this case study I discovered patterns in child development that were at odds with prevailing ideas about human evolution. Human life history is unique in the great length of the juvenile or immature period. The extended period is attributed to the time required for youth to master the culture, particularly subsistence skills.

However, in my comprehensive surveys—focused on children's learning—of the ethnographic, historical and archaeological records (Lancy, 2008, 2015, 2022), I kept finding case after case of apparent 'precocity'. An increasing number of studies show that children become skilled well before they gain complete independence and the status of adults. The Birds' work on Mer Island in the Torres Straits is representative:

> Four-year-old children [...] have knowledge of appropriate reef prey, but [...] are also extremely slow and tire easily when the substrate is difficult to negotiate [...] The learning process involves little or no direct adult instruction [rather, by foraging] in groups with older children, observing intently their prey choice and processing strategies [...] *by age six, children have become fairly efficient foragers.* (D. W. Bird and R. B. Bird, 2000, p. 291, emphasis added).

> Children begin spearfishing with toddler-sized spears as soon as they begin walking [and those] that choose to invest in spearfishing practice *reach the same efficiency as the most practiced adult by ages ten–fourteen.* (R. B. Bird and D. W. Bird, 2000, p. 262, emphasis added).

The Birds conclude: "How much experience do Meriam children need before they become efficient reef foragers? Evidently very little" (D. W. Bird and R. B. Bird, 2000, p. 291). Similar findings of precocity and initiative have proliferated (Endicott and Endicott, 2008; Hill and Hurtado, 1996; Odden and Rochat, 2004; Table 7.7 in Lancy, 2022 lists 14 examples). Diaries and letters provide a parallel account from history. "Children, in fact [...] labored at a wider variety of tasks than either mothers or fathers. They were [...] the most accomplished and versatile workers of the farming frontier" (West, 1992, p. 30). But the literature makes clear that children usually approach the learning and practice of subsistence skills in a casual and playful manner, which masks their real skill to the casual observer. Nevertheless, these reports cast considerable doubt on the need for a lengthened childhood to learn critical subsistence skills (Blurton-Jones and Marlowe, 2002, p. 199).

The model that best seems to explain this extended period of juvenility is referred to as 'embodied capital' (Bock, 2002). The long period of dependency on others and heightened risk of perishing before passing on one's genes is offset by a longer, healthier, and more fertile adulthood. There is also another aspect of precocity, which I have characterized as children serving as a 'reserve labor force' (Lancy, 2015).

The long, tedious hours spent reviewing archival material is sometimes rewarded by serendipity. Probing the precocity issue further, I found many descriptions of children—especially in historical accounts—throwing off the leisure and frivolity of youth to ratchet up their contributions to subsistence, usually in response to a crisis in the family or community. The arrival of a new baby, death or disability of an adult member (Crittenden et al., 2013), and seasonal demand for labor are among many reasons offered when children assume greater responsibility and more reliably and efficiently practice skills they had earlier mastered. A sample of illustrative cases can be found in Lancy (2022, pp. 290–293). Just recently, two more relevant reports dropped into my lap. At UCLA, a sample of 1137 California residents was surveyed around one month after the beginning of the COVID-19 stay-at-home orders (March 2020). In roughly two thirds of the sample, parents raised their expectations of children's help at home (He et al., 2022). A more dramatic case emerged from a remote area of Amazonia where a plane carrying an Indigenous Huitoto family crashed, killing the adults but leaving four siblings aged 13, nine, four, and 12 months to fend for themselves for five weeks before being rescued. They gathered edible foods, erected a shelter and competently tended the baby, which came as no surprise to their village relatives when interviewed by incredulous reporters (Acosta, 2023).

Like the evidence for 'precocious' learning, the idea that children constitute a reserve corps of workers is not compatible with theory that a lengthy period of juvenility is essential for learning one's culture. However, both of these ideas are compatible with the embodied capital model of human juvenility (Kaplan and Bock, 2001).

In conclusion, I would urge scholars to undertake a broad review of the ethnographic record with as few prior assumptions as possible. The possibility of discovering aspects of child development unanticipated in WEIRD social science are excellent.

4.7. Intersubjectivity and meaning

Jing Xu

The intersubjective nature of social behavior and its implications for meaning interpretation is important in research with children, because children are superb learners and even very young children are developing complex social cognition. When we are studying children, children are also studying us. They try to make sense of their social contexts. They read social cues about the identity, status, and communicative intention of their social interaction partners. Yet these intersubjective and contextual dimensions are easily obscured in our analytical process—especially in studies using standardized methods—but ignoring them can lead to erroneous conclusions. Drawing from my mixed-methods research, I have been introducing such ethnographic reflections into child development research (Xu, 2019). The following study about children's narratives, understanding, and physical aggression in a rural Taiwanese community provides an apt example.

The materials of this study came from what I call the 'Wolf Archive,' a historically significant set of fieldnotes collected by the late anthropologist Arthur P. Wolf in a Hokkien-speaking village near Taipei (1958–1960) at the height of Taiwan's martial-law era. Intended to replicate the Six Cultures Study of Child Socialization

(CSC), a landmark project in the history of anthropology (LeVine, 2010), the Wolfs' project was the first field research of ethnic Han Chinese and Taiwanese children in the world. With the help of excellent local research assistants, Wolf gathered a rich mine of data from multiple methods, such as natural observations, standardized interviews, and projective tests, but he never published systematic analyses from this archive. Decades later, my re-analysis of this archive provides a rare opportunity to reflect on the question of intersubjectivity in knowledge production.

Ethnographic records of close-knit, rural communities in post-war Taiwan, including Wolf's research in this village, noticed a common cultural model in parenting, that is, the prohibition of children from fighting, for the purpose of social harmony among neighbors. Parents readily intervened if they witnessed these conflicts or were called upon to help, and they did not hesitate to scold and beat children who got into fights. Results from a systematic analysis of the 'Mother Interview' with over 40 mothers in the Wolf Archive conformed to this ideology. However, children's audacious responses in the standardized 'Child Interview' (ages 3–10, 74 children) posed a stark contrast to their mothers' beliefs: 75 children (ages 3–10) responded to this first-person, hypothetical question: "Suppose another child (O) your age comes up and hits you: What would you do?" Fifty-seven children (76%) said they would intervene or avenge, contrary to the cultural model of "no fighting back" (Xu, 2020).

Children's narratives in another context, nonetheless, aligned with the cultural model and revealed the opposite pattern of their responses to the 'Child Interview'. Wolf's team conducted a survey called 'School Questionnaire' in local elementary schools. This questionnaire contained a similar hypothetical question about physical assault, but children tended to circle the answer "Do nothing," despite some boys raising their fists ready to fight back. Such a contradiction has to do with whom these two different types of data were collected by and how they were collected. 'Child Interview' was conducted in Taiwanese in a familiar, informal setting by a local research assistant, a Taiwanese teenage girl whom these children trusted, played with, and confided in—the children even called her "older sister Chen." But the survey data were collected by Wolf himself, a foreign, white man whom these children were much less familiar with. Not only might the children have felt less comfortable interacting with Wolf than with "older sister Chen;" the classroom setting itself also mattered. During the martial-law era in Taiwan, schools were a key setting for authoritarian socialization. At the time of Wolf's fieldwork, the Kuomintang (KMT) regime was promoting a Chinese nationalistic language policy: Mandarin was the only language allowed at school and children were punished for not speaking it (Klöter, 2004). Children's cautious responses tell us what they thought would be the 'correct' thing to say.

I also analyzed 'Child Observation' data—over 1,600 episodes of timed observations of children's social interactions in their natural context—also collected by the research assistant, Chen. I found that children's fights appeared in over 20% of observations, and 81% of children were involved in fighting. Many scenarios described in responses in 'Child Interview' appeared in observational episodes. A few examples include "Hit him with a bench," "Hit him with my fist," "Slap him," "Call older brother to hit him," "Take a rock and hit him," "Hit him with a slingshot" (Xu, 2024). Taken together, these narratives and observations not only reveal children's explicit attitudes, but also normative knowledge and actual behavior. This case study alerts us to children's acute sensitivity to communicative contexts, partners and intentions in our research and prompts us to reflect on the nature of our knowledge production.

4.8. Uplifting authentic voices: A qualitative study of North Korean youth's cross-cultural journeys

Heejung Park

The process of socialization entails learning and internalizing cultural values and norms that govern a society, culminating in an individual's integration into their respective context (Gauvain & Parke, 2014; Hill, 2021). This process undergoes transformation when children and youth migrate to societies with divergent cultural values and norms, necessitating adaptation (Portes & Rivas, 2011). This transformation is particularly pronounced among vulnerable migrant populations, such as refugees and persons of concern, necessitating research approaches that are both methodologically robust and ethically responsible (UNHCR, 2023). Here, I delineate best practices for conducting research with vulnerable groups of migrant children and youth, drawing upon insights from my qualitative study (Park, 2019) on the acculturation and identity formation of North Korean defector youth in South Korea (hereafter referred to as NK youth).

Ethnographic research and community partnership

Effective research with vulnerable populations requires a solid foundation in ethnography and community partnership. Prior to data collection, it is imperative to immerse oneself in the community's culture, norms, and history. Collaboration with community stakeholders further ensures that the research reflects participants' lived experiences. In my study, accessing the life stories of NK youth demanded establishing trust with the NK community, which often harbors wariness towards outsiders due to experiences of trauma and confidentiality concerns.

I dedicated significant time at a boarding school for NK youth, initially focusing on ethnography and respecting their privacy. Observing the community offered valuable insights into their social dynamics and cultural nuances. Over time, I transitioned from an outsider to a community member, earning the trust of the students, teachers, and administrators. This trust-building process culminated in a NK defector teacher inviting me to stay in their housing, recognizing my genuine commitment to understanding the community. This opportunity provided unparalleled insight into their lives.

My approach and relationship with the community marked a departure from past methods that lacked care and sensitivity. For instance, one participant disclosed their avoidance of another researcher in the past due to perceptions of a solely research-focused agenda. Furthermore, a teacher expressed dissatisfaction with a biased research article that negatively portrayed the NK community and did not align with their experiences. As my two-month stay concluded, the community expressed appreciation for my presence and urged me to authentically represent their stories and perspectives.

Culturally sensitive and empowering design

The success of my research was also attributable to a participatory design that prioritized participants' agency and cultural sensitivity. The main approach involved life-line drawings and participant-led unstructured interviews, fostering a trauma-sensitive and participant-centric data collection process. Participants created life-line drawings depicting significant life events and predicted future trajectories (Figure 4.2), followed by narratives about their past, present, and future, articulated at their own pace, without external cues. This methodology empowered participants, contrasting with past studies that my participants said they found insensitive, stigmatizing, or irrelevant to their lived experiences.

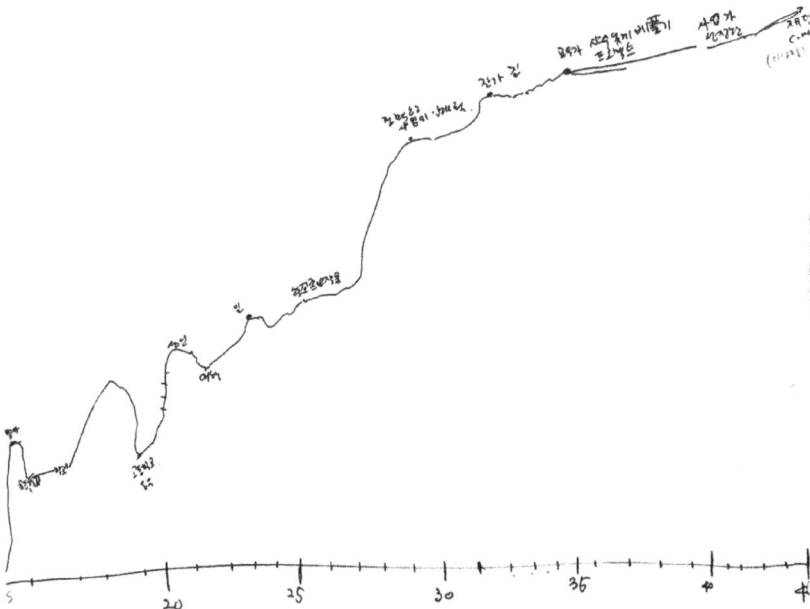

Fig. 4.2 A participant's life-line drawing. First appeared in Park (2019).
©Heejung Park. All rights reserved.

Data analysis and dissemination

In qualitative research with vulnerable populations, it is imperative to preserve the authenticity of participants' stories during analysis, considering cultural, political, and historical contexts. The analysis of NK youth narratives entailed an extensive review of data without preconceived assumptions, utilizing grounded theory, thematic analysis, and situational analysis. This approach revealed participants' multifaceted cultural adaptation and identity development, emphasizing not only their adversities but also their resilience and growth.

The dissemination of findings carries the dual responsibility of contributing to academic discourse while ethically representing the study population. Careful selection of terminology and balanced portrayal were prioritized to respect the dignity and privacy of participants. For instance, the term 'NK youth' was used due to aversions to the official term, 'North Korean defectors,' revealed in my interviews and reported elsewhere (J. E. Lee, 2024). My ongoing efforts to share these findings aim to challenge stigmas and misconceptions about the population.

Researcher bias and positionality

Addressing researcher bias and positionality is critical when working with vulnerable populations. Researchers must continually assess their assumptions, approach communities with humility and compassion, and stay attuned to political discourses. Given the susceptibility of vulnerable populations to marginalization and partisan discourses, understanding the political context is crucial for researchers to avoid being influenced by local, national, or international political agendas or ideologies. For instance, my position as a Korean American researcher with roots in South Korea, familiar with South Korean culture yet somewhat external to it, provided a balanced approach, especially given the politicized nature of narratives about NK communities in South Korea.

Another specific example illustrates my commitment to ethical considerations. I voluntarily withdrew from a highly attractive recruitment site due to internal politics among teachers and administrators, prioritizing the well-being of the study population. Despite the allure of a large student size, I chose to protect student narratives from potential censorship or coercion within the school context. This careful approach is crucial for all research studies but especially imperative when working with vulnerable populations.

Conclusion

This case study imparts crucial lessons for researchers working with vulnerable populations, underscoring the value of compassion, cultural sensitivity, and dedication to understanding and respecting participants' experiences. By prioritizing the voices and agency of NK youth, the study not only advances academic knowledge but also respects and empowers its study population. The lessons learned from this study, conducted with an understudied population that has endured trauma and cultural dislocation, are broadly applicable to research on cultural learning among other vulnerable groups of migrant children and youth.

4.9. Archaeological perspectives

Annemieke Milks & Felix Riede

While the archaeological record is often coarse-grained, the detailed examination of material culture as a proxy for social learning offers the unique opportunity to extend the temporal depth of our investigations. Archaeologists have devised numerous methods to reverse-engineer and hence infer processes of social learning from material proxies. These methods can be applied to contemporary objects, objects found in museum collections, as well as those retrieved from excavations. The strongest research design emerges in the combination of perspectives, as they allow us to connect the detailed observations offered by fieldwork in the present with the temporal depth offered by the archival and archaeological records.

Several recent reviews have surveyed what objects forager children are known to play with ethnographically (Lew-Levy, Andersen, et al., 2022; Riede et al., 2023) and what evidence there is for object play in the archaeological record (Milks et al., 2021). These surveys provide a strong framework for focusing our attention on particular artifacts known to be common play objects and likely to survive the vagaries of preservation at least to some extent. In order to reconstruct social learning dynamics, a given object needs to be deconstructed into the technological elements it consists of, so that the sequence of actions that make up the production and use of the object may be reconstructed. Originally developed in ethnoarchaeological contexts of adult technology, this form of operational chain analysis has been successful deployed to qualitatively and quantitatively infer processes of social learning (Jordan, 2015; Tehrani & Riede, 2008) as well as cognition (Haidle & Stolarczyk, 2020)—and it can be transferred to play-object production and use. Moreover, this approach can be employed both when analyzing objects from ethnographic contexts, from museum collections and archives, and from archaeological excavations, each at different resolution and temporal depth (Table 4.1). Those designing studies that aimed to better understand the production and use contexts of children's material culture thus need to pay close attention to the raw materials used and their provenance, the time spent on manufacture and use, as well as the who and when of production and use. When working with museum or ethnographic objects, the latter information is only available where either direct observation or archival notes or photos provide such contextualization. Detailed recording schemes and photographic documentation are essential for descriptions to be useful, while standardized annotations of technological characteristics facilitate downstream quantitative analyses (Figure 4.3). New fieldwork programs provide fresh opportunities to gather such contextual information about existing and new collections of objects for museums.

Children's contributions towards the archaeological record can be particularly difficult to discern for myriad reasons, including the potential for overlapping engagement with material culture attributed to adults, play with expedient objects, and use of materials that are less likely to preserve over time. Archaeologists frequently make use of existing ethnographic and ethnoarchaeological studies to interpret the material record, including the activities and material culture of children (Arnold, 2012). Ethnoarchaeological fieldwork can also deliberately be designed to capture new information that may leave an ambiguous archaeological signature, contributing to further identification of children's activities in the past. For example, a study of intertidal gathering of shellfish by Meriam children of the Eastern Torres Strait suggests that variability in shell middens in the past may indicate subsistence activities of younger group members (Bird & Bliege Bird, 2000). Similarly, a study of stone alignments made by Dukha reindeer herders sheds light on archaeological examples of constructed play areas (Mackie et al., 2015). Fieldwork designed to understand how spear hunting is learnt amongst BaYaka foragers illustrates how new data can show processes that may be virtually invisible in archaeological contexts (Lew-Levy, Bombjaková, et al., 2022; Lew-Levy et al., 2021). Whether designed to collect more data on objects and materials, or on behaviors and processes, new research projects benefit from interdisciplinary collaborations. These are best established at the outset, and in such a way as to benefit communities alongside a wider array of researchers who together pose different and/or intersecting questions. It is essential that all contributors are sensitive to understanding the pitfalls of the use of ethnographic data for archaeological purposes in both study design and publication (French, 2019; Gosselain, 2016; Warren, 2021).

Table 4.1. Summary of the strengths and weaknesses of different methodological approaches. In some cases, the pros and cons will vary depending on the scale and methods selected within an approach (-/+).

Methodological approach	Strengths & weaknesses		
	Resolution	Time-depth	Generalizability
Ethnographic fieldwork	+++	---	--

Cross-cultural research	--	-	+++
Ethnographic museum and archival research	+/++	+	-/+
Archaeological excavation	--	+++	-/+

Fig. 4.3 Images from a joint ethnographic and ethnoarchaeological study on BaYaka spear hunting led by Sheina Lew-Levy and Annemieke Milks. Clockwise from top left: (1) Research Assistant Francy Kiabiya Ntamboudila using a radar gun to capture throwing velocity of an adult thrower in the spear-throwing experiment. (2) An adolescent taking part in a spear-throwing experiment. (3) High-speed video still frame of a spear hitting a target in the spear-throwing experiment. 4) BaYaka children engaged in pretense hunting. ©Sheina Lew-Levy. All rights reserved.

4.10. Un-natural observation: Experimentation in the cross-cultural study of childhood learning

Roman Stengelin

Cross-cultural research on childhood learning is full of causal assumptions. Culture shapes children's learning, and children's learning is foundational to human cultural diversity. Childhood learning is both a product of and a precondition for culture.

Experimentation is a leading paradigm to study how cultural experience affects children's learning, and vice versa. Assuming participants bring "the preferences and beliefs that they have acquired in the real world into the decision-making situation" (Henrich et al., 2005, p. 813), experiments shed light on cultural variation in childhood learning by testing and falsifying theories on how such variation comes into play. At the same time, experimental research often receives skepticism from cultural psychologists and anthropologists given its emphasis on standardization and related impediments in measurement equivalence (Broesch et al., 2020; Kline et al., 2018). Indeed, cross-cultural experiments are, like any other approach, limited in scope and prone to misinterpretation. However, they also have decisive advantages that make them essential to cross-cultural research on children's learning.

Before showing some of the unique opportunities of experimentation in cross-cultural research on childhood learning, I first want to reduce some of the definitional ambiguity relating to cross-cultural experiments. Experimentation is a scientific method in which a variable of interest (i.e., the independent variable) is manipulated to assess its causal effect on another (i.e., dependent) variable. Participants from a joint population are randomly assigned to one manipulation (or condition) while potential confounds, assessed prior to the experimental manipulation, are controlled for. Rigorously designed experiments ensure that group-level variation in the dependent variable is—by design—caused by the experimental manipulation.

Studies in which children from two or more cultural communities are observed in a somewhat standardized study are often labeled cross-cultural experiments. For example, researchers may test effects of culture on children's learning from instruction by testing participants in two communities varying in a cultural variable of interest to the study (e.g., high and low emphases on child-directed pedagogy). Such research typically tests the effects of culture on a dependent variable, treating experimentation loosely analogous to standardization. An obvious issue with this is that participants cannot be randomly assigned to their complex cultural experience, they are already found nested within cultures. This approach is essentially quasi-experimental.[1] Indeed, cross-cultural quasi-experiments can barely single out variables driving cultural variation, given the immense complexity of human cultural experience. In our example, cultural variation in children's learning might indeed be driven by cultural emphases on pedagogy, or alternatively by variation in the role of adults versus peers as sources of learning more generally, or countless other variables that differ across the sampled communities. To establish causality, such variables could be unpacked iteratively through cultural contrasts, or by priming culture via language or other aspects of cultural experience and thought (see also Ma-Kellams, 2021; Norenzayan & Heine, 2005; Pfundmair, 2017).

In a narrower sense, cross-cultural experiments subsume approaches in which participants from two or more cultural communities are randomly assigned to experimental conditions to investigate how cultural variation modulates the effects of independent on dependent variables of interest. In the example above, researchers may tap into cultural emphases on pedagogy by contrasting participants from the same cultural group in one condition in which children receive instruction, with a second condition relying on uninstructed observational learning. Such paradigms allow for causal inference by focusing on the relative gains in social learning from instruction across cultural communities.

Cross-cultural experiments designed as such can help identify universally or locally efficient variables that affect (i.e., promote or hinder) childhood learning, providing solid grounding for culturally informed learning contexts and pedagogical practices. Randomized assignment of participants to experimental conditions within cultural communities can help control for the

---

1   This is often discussed as a limitation or weakness of this research paradigm. Note that, strictly speaking, any mono-cultural research is just as much quasi-experimental with $n_{cultures} = 1$ whenever research findings are generalized beyond the cultural community from which participants were randomly sampled. This is almost always the case—true experimental research is a rarity in human social sciences.

countless confounds that make rigorous hypothesis testing and falsification so difficult in cross-cultural quasi-experiments and less standardized approaches.

Moving away from culture-level comparisons of children's absolute learning rates (e.g., instructed learning: community A > community B), cross-cultural experiments also enable more nuanced comparisons of learning within cultures (e.g., community A: instructed learning > observational learning; community B: instructed learning = observational learning), which can then be interpreted in context. Standardizing participants' responses within cultures can further prevent often stigmatizing misinterpretations of group-level variation in learning by focusing on relative, rather than absolute, variation in the dependent variable. Cross-cultural experimentation can also promote the reproducibility and replication of research procedures and findings as long as methodological details are communicated transparently. Although generalizability constraints are often discussed for experimentation (Yarkoni, 2022), adequate experimental design ensures that results generalize to the larger populations from which participants were recruited.

At the same time, the standardization inherent in cross-cultural (quasi-)experiments presents substantial challenges, often exacerbated in childhood research. Experimental manipulations (i.e., the communicative intent of child-directed instruction) may be differently interpreted and navigated by participants in different cultural communities (e.g., Hruschka et al., 2018). When this is the case, group-level variation in children's responses may not be driven by variation in cultural experience, but variant interpretations of the experimental manipulation. This threatens the equivalence assumption central to experimentation (Kline et al., 2018). These challenges can be mitigated through culturally informed research designs, and multiple rounds of piloting and revision that incorporate local expertise in cross-cultural research. Extensive piloting involving local researchers, adults, and children above or below the focus age range may help ensure sufficient sample sizes, while fine-tuning procedures to local settings. Testing study protocols in neighboring communities sharing crucial features for cultural fit can further preserve sample sizes. Within-subjects (i.e., repeated measures) research designs and the careful selection of response formats with adequate psychometric properties can bolster experimental research in the face of statistical power issues common to quantitative cross-cultural research.

As a general note, experimental researchers working cross-culturally need to compromise between standardization and cultural adaptation, and to communicate such trade-offs transparently. For example, they may define standardized ways of refining study settings and instructions to local contexts in order to develop a reproducible and standardized protocol for designing culturally grounded sub-experiments, rather than exclusively focusing on rigid procedural outcomes. After all, paradigms that seem objectively similar to the researcher may be interpreted differently, and paradigms thought different may be interpreted much more similarly across cultures. The right decisions can only be made with local perspectives and experience. Finally, mixed-methods research designs can increase the cultural and ecological validity of experiments (see also Lew-Levy et al., 2021).

Cross-cultural experiments are tedious, artificial, and never free of context. To some extent, they need to be just that: by taking children's learning out of the everyday, experimentation provides helpful abstraction to establish causality by research design in the cross-cultural study of childhood learning.

4.11. Conversation analysis approach

Akira Takada

Conversation analysis emerged at the intersection of micro-sociology, linguistic anthropology, pragmatics, and cultural psychology. Although it is generally regarded as a qualitative research method, it is also highly empirical. According to Schegloff (1987), who established conversation analysis with his colleagues, the appropriateness of researcher's characterization (analysis) of interaction can be warranted by providing some evidence that it is also appropriate for the participants to engage in interaction. This idea can be simplified as follows.

Suppose there are two interactants, A and B. Action X is performed with reference to context X and constitutes context X+1. When A and B meet in the morning (context 1), A greets B with a "Good morning" (action 1). In response (context 2), B also greets A with a "Good morning" (action 2). Following this (context 3), A asks, "Have you done the assignments?" (action 3). In response (context 4), B replies, "Not at all" (action 4). Here, the researcher characterizes each of the actions 1, 2, 3, and 4 as greeting, greeting, question, and answer, respectively. By greeting in action 2 and answering in action 4, B displays her understanding of A's actions 1 and 3 as greeting and question, respectively. Responding to greeting with greeting and responding to question with answer is determined by linguistic conventions. The meaning of each action characterized by the researcher here does not depend solely on its semantic basis. Rather, they are proposed, negotiated, and constructed in the course of interaction. And it is this exchange of meanings that shapes our social reality.

In order to analyze interaction in detail, audio or video data are first collected using video cameras and other equipment. The obtained data are transcribed, on which systematic analysis is conducted. In transcribing conversations, we first identify the speaker of every utterance by repeatedly viewing the data, and then carefully transcribe the content in a manner that follows the conventions of previous research. Non-verbal features such as eye gaze, gestures, and posture may be also transcribed (Schegloff, 2007). As discussed below, it is particularly important to consider such non-verbal features in interactions involving children.

Conversation analysis basics

Conversation analysis and related fields have empirically shown that even in our daily interactions, which we tend to take for granted, there are extremely elaborate rules by which social order is maintained (Schegloff, 2007). For example, our daily conversation is considered to be ordered by a turn-taking system as the most basic mechanism. Since spoken language is primarily an auditory medium of communication, having several people speak at the same time about different things interferes with the listener's understanding and is therefore avoided. For this reason, the one-at-a-time rule, in which only one person is basically speaking at a time, is recognized. When a possible completion point is approaching, the speaker often indicates the next speaker explicitly or suggestively. If the next speaker is not indicated by the point at which the utterance can be terminated, any participant in the conversation can be the next speaker.

An adjacency pair is considered to be the smallest unit of speech exchange that constitutes the turn-taking system. Adjacency pairs include greeting–greeting, and question–answer shown above. In other words, each utterance is some kind of social action, and the former action is called the first pair part (FPP) and the latter the second pair part (SPP). The sequence of utterances consisting of FPP and SPP is called the base sequence. The most basic task in analyzing ordinary conversation is to find the base sequence in the conversation. However, base sequences are often developed in a much more complex way than mere adjacency pairs. Additional conversational elements may be added before FPP, between FPP and SPP, and after SPP, collectively called expansion. The turn-taking system, one-at-a-time rule, and adjacency pairs have normative characteristics. In other words, participants in interactions refer to them when selecting and implementing their actions. However, actions do not necessarily follow norms in their practice: situations frequently arise in which an action is misspoken or difficult to hear. For such conversational 'trouble', repair often occurs. The occurrence of repair reveals that the participants in the conversation are oriented toward a common norm.

Incorporating culture and children in conversation analysis

The basic analytical concepts of conversation analysis described above were derived mainly from the analysis of conversations in English-speaking communities, so it is necessary to examine carefully whether these concepts can be applied to interactions in cultures that use languages other than English. Many researchers have expressed doubts about the universality of these analytical concepts (e.g., Gudykunst & Nishida, 1994; Agliati et al., 2005). In this respect, the theory of language socialization promoted by Elinor Ochs and her colleagues expands the scope of conversation analysis. Ochs and her colleagues have accumulated empirical data on language socialization in various societies and cultures around the world (e.g., Ochs, 1988; Duranti et al., 2012). They propose that children do not develop or acquire cognitive abilities during their development (as most psychologists assume) but rather develop appropriate actions in response to socio-cultural contexts. Their language socialization theory explores the reasons why an action is performed by a particular participant, in a particular way, at a particular time of interaction in the society under study. Specifically, they argue that "each community's habitus of communicative codes, practices, and strategies is to be judged in terms of its own socio-cultural logic" (Ochs et al., 2005, p.548). Relatedly, Takada (2021) demonstrated how caregivers of !Xun, Indigenous people of Namibia, socialize the behaviors of young children into socio-culturally constructed actions. This involves reframing, which refers to "a change in what the discussion is about," and often accompanies rekeying, which refers to "a change in the tone or tenor of an interaction" (Tannen 2006, p. 601). Reframing and rekeying mobilize a constellation of multiple semiotic resources. For the !Xun, central among these resources is gymnastic behavior, namely, holding infants upright or moving them up and down (bouncing). Takada (2021) examined how !Xun caregivers reframe and rekey infant behavior from distress to playfulness in the course of multi-modal interactions.

4.12. The emergence of social smiling: Linking ethnotheories to the dynamics of social interaction and child development

Joscha Kärtner

In research on the emergence and further development of infant social smiling, it is a basic assumption—as in many other domains of child development—that caregivers establish interactional routines that organize children's experience and behavior. As time progresses, these interactional routines are internalized and manifest in child development. Importantly, caregivers' interactional routines are informed by specific ethnotheories on good parenting and optimal child development that may differ between cultures, potentially leading to culture-specific developmental pathways.

In order to provide evidence for the cultural differences in maternal ethnotheories and their consequences for social interaction and child development, we combined different methods: (i) standardized assessment of maternal ethnotheories on infant smiling in postnatal week 7; (ii) longitudinal assessments of semi-standardized observations of mother-infant interaction from week 8 to 18; and (iii) standardized assessments of developmental outcomes in week 12 and 18 (see Figure 4.4).

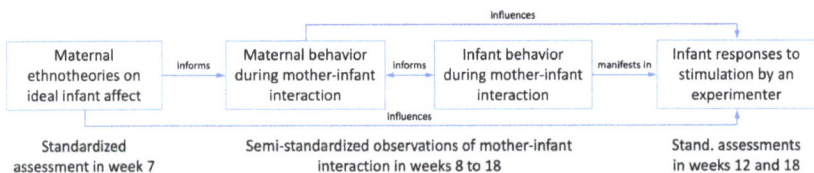

Fig. 4.4 Conceptual model and methods of project on social smiling.

In this project, we contrasted two cultural contexts, namely educated urban middle-class families in Münster, Germany, and Indigenous Kichwa families living in villages around Cotacachi and Otavalo in the Northern Andes in Ecuador. The project was realized in cooperation with the University of Otavalo, mainly planned at the University of Münster and organized by Helen Wefers, who initiated the project and took the main responsibility for its implementation. Although the project was well received by the participating families and local research assistants, future projects would ideally start as joint endeavors from the beginning in order to minimize biases (Wefers, Krüger, et al., 2023).

Assessment of maternal ethnotheories

Maternal ethnotheories are often implicit and difficult to reflect on, so we based our assessment of ethnotheories regarding ideal infant states on a series of short video clips of a Münster and a Kichwa infant with different states of positive affect and activity. Based on these clips, mothers could indicate which of the two states they preferred when presented with a series of pairwise comparisons (see Figure 4.5), and, in a more open format, mothers were invited to comment on how they would react when interacting with an infant after looking at specific video clips again. As expected, mothers in Münster preferred higher levels of positive affect than Kichwa mothers (Wefers et al., 2022).

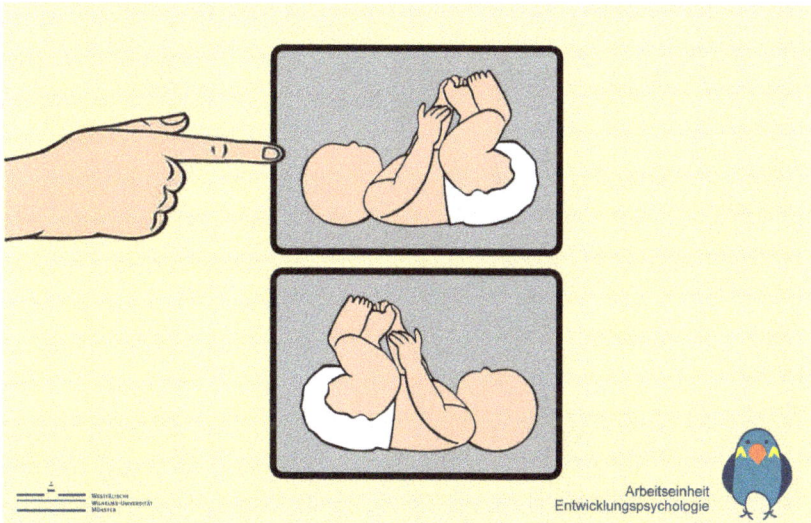

Fig. 4.5 Assessing maternal ethnotheories about ideal infant affect. Figure shows initial tablet screen: mothers were shown stills of clips of one of 10 pairwise comparisons. Originally appears in Wefers et al. (2022).

Longitudinal assessments of mother-infant interaction

While the main analyses of mother-infant interaction are still pending, a mixed-method analysis of a subsample of 10 mother-infant dyads per culture at week 9 and 13 showed that the Münster mothers' accentuated preference for high-intensity infant smiling manifested in their mother-infant interactions. More specifically, a quantitative analysis of infant smiling showed culture-specific developmental pathways, as there was a significant increase in the frequency of Duchenne smiles (i.e., high-intensity infant smiling) from week 9 to 13 in the Münster sample but not the Kichwa sample, resulting in cross-cultural differences in week 13 (Kärtner et al., 2022). The qualitative analyses explored whether interactional preludes to infants' Duchenne smiles were similar across the two cultural contexts, which in fact was the case: mothers used similar means to make their infants laugh, consisting of, first, intense and multimodal stimulation with repetition and theme variation and, second, positively tuned and mutually contingent responsiveness, often in the form of prolonged proto-conversations (see Figure 4.6).

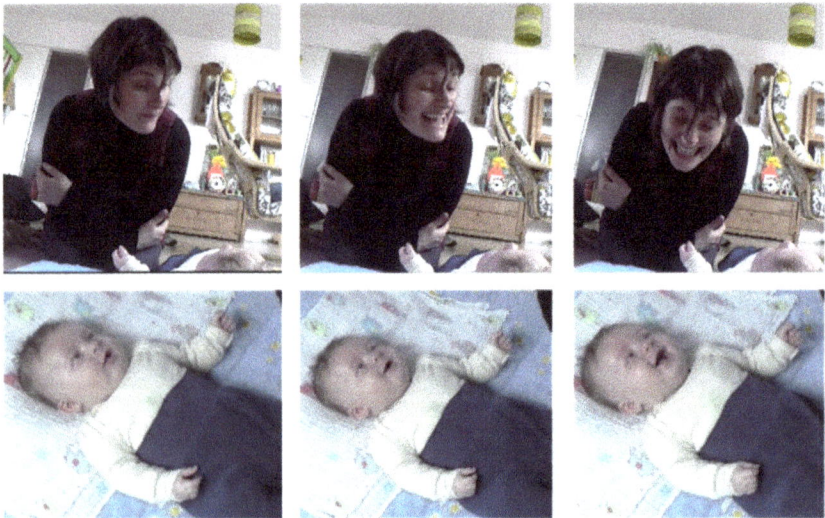

Fig. 4.6 Images taken from a prolonged proto-conversation between mother and infant. The mother acknowledges the infant's second turn by a head nod (left), then she mirrors and intensifies the infant's smile (middle), further exaggerating her smile to a voiceless laugh as the infant peaks.
©Joscha Kärtner. All rights reserved.

Standardized assessments of infants' responsiveness

From the mother-infant observations alone, one cannot determine whether differences in infant behavior are a result of differential input (e.g., frequency with which mothers try to make their infants smile) or differential development (i.e., differences in expectations and habitualized ways of experiencing and responding to specific events). To probe the latter, infants were confronted with a female experimenter who stimulated the infant in a standardized way when they were 12 and 18 weeks old.

In a variant of a still-face paradigm, the experimenter showed a medium and a high level of positive stimulation via gaze, voice and smile for one minute each, before showing a still face. While the infants showed the still-face effect (i.e., decrease in gaze and positive affect and an increase in negative affect) in both cultures and at both ages to similar degrees (Wefers, Schuhmacher, Chacón, et al., 2023), culture-specific patterns appeared in how infants responded to positive stimulation during the first phase. More specifically, while the 12-week-olds in both cultures showed similar smiling responses to medium positive stimulation, Münster infants showed higher smiling intensities in response to more intense positive stimulation (Wefers, Schuhmacher, & Kärtner, 2023). At 18 weeks, in contrast, the infants from both cultures responded with an increase in smiling when there was an increase in positive stimulation, which suggests that, by then, infants from both cultures have had enough interactional experience around high-intensity smiling to engage in highly positive interactions with others.

Summary and conclusion

Combining the strengths of both standardized assessments and more ecological observations of mother-infant interaction, the overall design of this project allowed us to test the different assumptions underlying developmental theories and provided converging evidence for cultural differences in maternal ethnotheories on infant smiling. Further, it helped reveal how these ethnotheories affect both maternal and infant experience and behavior across the first weeks of life and how they resulted in differences as well as similarities in infant smiling development.

References

Acosta, L. J. (2023, June 10). Four Colombian children found alive in jungle weeks after plane crash. *Reuters*. https://www.reuters.com/world/americas/four-missing-colombian-children-found-alive-jungle-sources-2023-06-10/

Aladsani, H., Al-Abdullatif, A., Almuhanna, M., & Gameil, A. (2022). Ethnographic Reflections of K–12 Distance Education in Saudi Arabia: Shaping the Future of Post-Pandemic Digital Education. *Sustainability, 14(16)*, Article 16. https://doi.org/10.3390/su14169931

Agliati, A., Vescovo, A., & Anolli, L. (2005) Conversation patterns in Icelandic and Italian people: Similarities and differences in rhythm and accommodation. In L. Anolli, S. Jr Duncan, M. S. Magnusson, & G. Riva (Eds). The hidden structure of interaction: From neurons to culture patterns (pp. 223–235). IOS Press.

Amir, D., & McAuliffe, K. (2020). Cross-cultural, developmental psychology: Integrating approaches and key insights. *Evolution and Human Behavior, 41*(5), 430–444. https://doi.org/10.1016/j.evolhumbehav.2020.06.006

Apicella, C., Norenzayan, A., & Henrich, J. (2020). Beyond WEIRD: A review of the last decade and a look ahead to the global laboratory of the future. *Evolution and Human Behavior, 41*(5), 319–329. https://doi.org/10.1016/j.evolhumbehav.2020.07.015

Arnold, J. E. (2012). Detecting Apprentices and Innovators in the Archaeological Record: The Shell Bead-Making Industry of the Channel Islands. *Journal of Archaeological Method and Theory, 19(2)*, 269–305. https://doi.org/10.1007/s10816-011-9108-1

Barr, R. G., Konner, M., Bakeman, R., & Adamson, L. (1991). Crying in !kung San Infants: A Test of the Cultural Specificity Hypothesis. *Developmental Medicine & Child Neurology, 33(7)*, 601–610. https://doi.org/10.1111/j.1469-8749.1991.tb14930.x

Bengtsson, S. (2014). Faraway, so close! Proximity and distance in ethnography online. *Media, Culture & Society, 36*(6), 862–877. https://doi.org/10.1177/0163443714531195

Berl, R. E. W., & Hewlett, B. S. (2015). Cultural Variation in the Use of Overimitation by the Aka and Ngandu of the Congo Basin. *PLoS ONE, 10*, e0120180. https://doi.org/10.1371/journal.pone.0120180

Bird, D. W., & Bliege Bird, R. (2000). The Ethnoarchaeology of Juvenile Foragers: Shellfishing Strategies among Meriam Children. *Journal of Anthropological Archaeology, 19(4)*, 461–476. https://doi.org/10.1006/jaar.2000.0367

Blurton-Jones, N. G. & Marlowe, F. W. (2002). Selection for delayed maturity: Does it take 20 years to learn to hunt and gather? *Human Nature, 13(2)*, 199–238. https://doi.org/10.1007/s12110-002-1008-3

Bock, J. (2002). Learning, life history, and productivity: Children's lives in the Okavango Delta of Botswana. *Human Nature, 13(2)*, 161–198. https://doi.org/10.1007/s12110-002-1007-4

Broesch T., Crittenden, A. N., Beheim, B. A., Blackwell, A. D., Bunce, J. A., Colleran, H., Hagel, K., Kline, M., McElreath, R., Nelson, R. G., Pisor, A. C., Prall, S., Pretelli, I., Purzycki, B., Quinn, E. A., Ross, C., Scelza, B., Starkweather, K., Stieglitz, J., & Mulder, M. B. (2020). Navigating cross-cultural research: methodological and ethical considerations. *Proceedings of the Royal Society B, 287*, 20201245. https://doi.org/10.1098/rspb.2020.1245

Broesch, T., Lew-Levy, S., Kärtner, J., Kanngiesser, P., & Kline, M. (2023). A roadmap to doing culturally grounded developmental science. *Review of Philosophy and Psychology, 14(2)*, 587–609. https://doi.org/10.1007/s13164-022-00636-y

Burger, O., Chen, L., Erut, A., Fong, F. T., Rawlings, B., & Legare, C. H. (2023). Developing Cross-Cultural Data Infrastructures (CCDIs) for research in cognitive and behavioral sciences. *Review of Philosophy and Psychology, 14(2)*, 565–585. https://doi.org/10.1007/s13164-022-00635-z

Cooperrider, K. (2019, January 23). What Happens to Cognitive Diversity When Everyone Is More WEIRD? *Aeon*. https://aeon.co/ideas/what-happens-to-cognitive-diversity-when-everyone-is-more-weird

Crittenden, A. N., Conklin-Brittain, N. L., Zes, D. A., Schoeninger, M. J., & Marlowe, F. W. (2013). Juvenile foraging among the Hadza: Implications for human life history. *Evolution and Human Behavior, 34*, 299–304. https://doi.org/10.1016/j.evolhumbehav.2013.04.004

Deffner, D., Rohrer, J. M., & McElreath, R. (2022). A causal framework for cross-cultural generalizability. *Advances in methods and practices in psychological science, 5(3)*, 25152459221106366. https://doi.org/10.1177/25152459221106366

Dennis, W. (1940). *The Hopi child* (pp. xi, 204). Appleton-Century.

Doyle, L., Brady, A.-M., & Byrne, G. (2009). An overview of mixed methods research. *Journal of Research in Nursing, 14(2)*, 175–185. https://doi.org/10.1177/1744987108093962

Duranti, A., Ochs, E., & Schieffelin, B. B. (Eds). (2012). *The handbook of language socialization*. Blackwell.

Endicott, K. M., & Endicott, K. L. (2008). *The Headman was a Woman: The Gender Egalitarian Batek of Malaysia*. Waveland Press, Inc.

Fargas-Malet, M., McSherry, D., Larkin, E., & Robinson, C. (2010). Research with children: Methodological issues and innovative techniques.

Journal of Early Childhood Research, 8(2), 175–192. https://doi.org/10.1177/1476718X09345412

French, J. C. (2019). The use of ethnographic data in Neanderthal archaeological research. *Hunter Gatherer Research, 4(1),* 25–49. https://doi.org/10.3828/hgr.2018.3

Gauvain, M., & Parke, R. D. (2014). Socialization. In *Handbook of cultural developmental science* (pp. 239–258). Psychology Press.

Gelman, A., Vehtari, A., Simpson, D., Margossian, C. C., Carpenter, B., Yao, Y., Kennedy, L., Gabry, J., Bürkner, P.-C., & Modrák, M. (2020). Bayesian workflow. *arXiv preprint arXiv:2011.01808.* https://doi.org/10.48550/arXiv.2011.01808

Gosselain, O. P. (2016). To hell with ethnoarchaeology! *Archaeological Dialogues, 23(2)* https://doi.org/10.1017/S1380203816000234

Gudykunst, W. B., & Nishida, T. (1994) *Bridging Japanese/North American differences.* Sage.

Haidle, M. N., & Stolarczyk, R. (2020). Thinking Tools. With Cognigrams from Reconstructions and Interpretations to Models about Tool Behavior. *Intellectica, 73(2),* 107–132. https://doi.org/10.3406/intel.2020.1967

Hall, J., Gaved, M., & Sargent, J. (2021). Participatory Research Approaches in Times of Covid-19: A Narrative Literature Review. *International Journal of Qualitative Methods, 20,* 16094069211010087. https://doi.org/10.1177/16094069211010087

He, A., Greenfield, P. M., Akiba, A. J., & Brown, G. (2022). Why do many parents expect more help from their children during COVID-19? *Current Research in Ecological and Social Psychology, 3,* 100052. https://doi.org/10.1016/j.cresp.2022.100052.

Henrich, J., Boyd, R., Bowles, S., Camerer, C., Fehr, E., Gintis, H., McElreath, R., Alvard, M., Barr, A., Ensminger, J., Henrich, N. S., Hill, K., Gil-White, F., Gurven, M., Marlowe, F. W., Patton, J. Q., & Tracer, D. (2005). "Economic man" in cross-cultural perspective: Behavioral experiments in 15 small-scale societies. *Behavioral and brain sciences 28,* 795–815. https://doi.org/10.1017/S0140525X05000142

Henrich, J., Heine, S. J., & Norenzayan, A. (2010). The Weirdest People in the World?. *Behavioural and Brain Sciences 33,* 61–81. https://doi.org/10.1017/S0140525X0999152X

Hill, N. E. (2021). In search of the individual embedded in context: Applications of the specificity principle. *Journal of Applied Developmental Psychology, 75,* 101289. https://doi.org/10.1016/j.appdev.2021.101289

Hill, K. & Hurtado, A. M. (1996). *Ache Life History: The Ecology and Demography of a Foraging People.* Aldine de Gruyter.

Holding, P., Anum, A., van de Vijver, F. J. R., Vokhiwa, M., Bugase, N., Hossen, T., Makasi, C., Baiden, F., Kimbute, O., Bangre, O., Hasan, R., Nanga, K., Sefenu, R. P. S., A-Hayat, N., Khan, N., Oduro, A., Rashid, R., Samad, R., Singlovic, J., Faiz, A., & Gomes, M. (2018). Can we measure cognitive constructs consistently within and across cultures? Evidence from a test battery in Bangladesh, Ghana, and Tanzania. *Applied Neuropsychology: Child, 7*(1), 1–13. https://doi.org/10.1080/2162 2965.2016.1206823

Hruschka, D. J., Munira, S., Jesmin, K., Hackman, J., & Tiokhin, L. (2018). Learning from failures of protocol in cross-cultural research. *Proceedings of the National Academy of Sciences, 115,* 11428–11434. https://doi.org/10.1073/pnas.1721166115

Jordan, P. (2015). *Technology as human social tradition: Cultural transmission among hunter-gatherers.* University of California Press.

Kaplan, H. S., & Bock, J. A. (2001). Fertility theory: The embodied capital theory of life history evolution. In J. M. Hoem (Ed.). *International Encyclopedia of the Social and Behavioral Sciences* (3.3, 155, pp. 5561–5568). Elsevier Science.

Kärtner, J., Schwick, M., Wefers, H., & Nomikou, I. (2022). Interactional preludes to infants' affective climax – Mother-infant interaction around infant smiling in two cultures. *Infant Behavior and Development, 67,* 101715. https://doi.org/10.1016/j.infbeh.2022.101715

Kievit, R., Frankenhuis, W. E., Waldorp, L., & Borsboom, D. (2013). Simpson's paradox in psychological science: a practical guide. *Frontiers in psychology, 4,* 54928. https://doi.org/10.3389/fpsyg.2013.00513

Kline, M. A., Boyd, R., & Henrich, J. (2013). Teaching and the life history of cultural transmission in Fijian villages. *Human Nature, 24,* 351–374. https://doi.org/10.1007/s12110-013-9180-1

Kline, M. A. (2015). How to learn about teaching: An evolutionary framework for the study of teaching behavior in humans and other animals. *Behavioral and Brain sciences, 38,* e31. https://doi.org/10.1017/S0140525X14000090

Kline, M. A. (2016). TEACH: An ethogram-based method to observe and record teaching behavior. *Field methods, 29*(3), 205–220. https://doi.org/10.1177/1525822X16669282

Kline, M. A., Shamsudheen, R., & Broesch, T. (2018). Variation is the universal: making cultural evolution work in developmental psychology. *Philosophical Transactions of the Royal Society B: Biological Sciences, 373,* 20170059. https://doi.org/10.1098/rstb.2017.0059

Klöter, H. (2004). Language Policy in the KMT and DPP eras. *China Perspectives, 2004*(6), Article 6. http://journals.openedition.org/chinaperspectives/442

Konken, L. C., & Howlett, M. (2023). When "home" becomes the "field": Ethical considerations in digital and remote fieldwork. *Perspectives on Politics, 21*(3), 849–862. https://doi.org/10.1017/S1537592722002572

Kramer, K. L. (2021). Childhood Teaching and Learning among Savanna Pumé Hunter-Gatherers. *Human Nature, 32*(1), 87–114. https://doi.org/10.1007/s12110-021-09392-x

Lancy, D. F., Bock, J., & Gaskins, S. (2010). *The Anthropology of Learning in Childhood*. Rowman Altamira.

Lancy, D. F. (2008, 2015, 2022). *The Anthropology of Childhood: Cherubs, Chattel, Changelings* (1st, 2nd, and 3rd ed.). Cambridge University Press.

Lancy, D. F. (2015). Children as a reserve labor force. *Current Anthropology, 56*, 545–568. https://doi.org/10.1086/682286

Lancy, D. F. (2016). Playing with knives: The socialization of self-initiated learners. *Child Development, 87*, 654–665. https://doi.org/10.1111/cdev.12498

Lee, J. E. (2024, February 12). More than half of South Koreans reject 'defector' labels for North Korean escapees. *Radio Free Asia*. https://www.rfa.org/english/news/korea/defector-refuegee-escapee-north-korea-south-korea-terminology-07152024154618.html.

Leighton, D., & Kluckhohn, C. (2013). Children of the People: The Navaho Individual and His Development. In *Children of the People*. Harvard University Press. https://doi.org/10.4159/harvard.9780674423558

LeVine, R. A. (2010). The Six Cultures Study: Prologue to a History of a Landmark Project. *Journal of Cross-Cultural Psychology, 41(4),* 513–521. https://doi.org/10.1177/0022022110362567

Lew-Levy, S., Pope, S. M., Haun, D. B. M., Kline, M. A., & Broesch, T. (2021) Out of the empirical box: A mixed-methods study of tool innovation among Congolese BaYaka forager and Bondongo fisher–farmer children. *Journal of Experimental Child Psychology, 211,* 105223. https://doi.org/10.1016/j.jecp.2021.105223

Lew-Levy, S., Andersen, M. M., Lavi, N., & Riede, F. (2022). Hunter-Gatherer Children's Object Play and Tool Use: An Ethnohistorical Analysis. F*rontiers in Psychology, 13*, 824983. https://doi.org/10.3389/fpsyg.2022.824983

Lew-Levy, S., Bombjaková, D., Milks, A., Kiabiya Ntamboudila, F., Kline, M. A., & Broesch, T. (2022). Costly teaching contributes to the acquisition of spear hunting skill among BaYaka forager adolescents. *Proceedings of the Royal Society B: Biological Sciences, 289(1974),* 20220164. https://doi.org/10.1098/rspb.2022.0164

Lew-Levy, S., Milks, A., Kiabiya Ntamboudila, F., Broesch, T., & Kline, M. A. (2021). BaYaka Adolescent Boys Nominate Accessible Adult Men as Preferred Spear Hunting Models. *Current Anthropology, 62(5)*, https://doi.org/10.1086/716853

Lupton, D. (2021). *Doing fieldwork in a pandemic.* https://docs.google.com/document/d/1clGjGABB2h2qbduTgfqribHmog9B6P0NvMgVuiHZCl8/edit#heading=h.ze8ug1cqk5lo

Mackie, M. E., Surovell, T. A., & O'Brien, M. (2015). Identifying Stone Alignments Created by Adults and Children: A Case Study from a Dukha Reindeer Herder Summer Camp, Khövsgöl Aimag, Mongolia. *Sibirica, 14(2)*, https://doi.org/10.3167/sib.2015.140202

Ma-Kellams C. (2021). Using true experiments to study culture: Manipulations, measurement issues, and the question of appropriate control groups. *Methods in Psychology 4*, 100046. https://doi.org/10.1016/j.metip.2021.100046

Maynard, A. E., Greenfield, P. M., Childs, C. P., & Weinstock, M. (2023). "Social change, cultural evolution, weaving apprenticeship, and development": Informal education across three generations and 42 years in a Maya community. *Applied Developmental Science, 28(1)*, 82–105. https://doi.org/10.1080/10888691.2022.2151445

McElreath, R. (2018). *Statistical rethinking: A Bayesian course with examples in R and Stan.* Chapman and Hall/CRC.

Milks, A., Lew-Levy, S., Lavi, N., Friesem, D. E., & Reckin, R. (2021). Hunter-gatherer children in the past: An archaeological review. *Journal of Anthropological Archaeology, 64*, 101369. https://doi.org/10.1016/j.jaa.2021.101369

Norenzayan A., & Heine, S. J. (2005). Psychological Universals: What Are They and How Can We Know? *Psychological Bulletin, 131*, 763–784. https://doi.org/10.1037/0033-2909.131.5.763

Ochs, E. (1988). *Culture and language development: Language acquisition and language socialization in a Samoan village.* Cambridge University Press.

Ochs, E., Solomon, O., & Sterponi, L. (2005). Limitations and transformations of habitus in Child-Directed Communication. *Discourse Studies, 7(4-5)*, 547–583. https://doi.org/10.1177/1461445605054406

Odden, H., & Rochat, P. (2004). Observational learning and enculturation. *Educational and Child Psychology, 21*, 39–50. https://doi.org/10.53841/bpsecp.2004.21.2.39

Onwuegbuzie, A. J., & Leech, N. L. (2005). On becoming a pragmatic researcher: The importance of combining quantitative and qualitative research methodologies. *International journal*

of social research methodology, 8(5), 375–387. https://doi.
org/10.1080/13645570500402447

Park, H. (2019). A model of identity development: Life-course narratives of North Korean youth resettling in South Korea. *Journal of Adolescence, 6,* 162–172. https://doi.org/10.1016/j.adolescence.2019.08.014

Pearl, J. (1995). Causal diagrams for empirical research. *Biometrika, 82(4),* 669–688. https://doi.org/10.1093/biomet/82.4.669

Pearl, J. (2000). *Causality: Models, reasoning, and inference.* Cambridge University Press.

Pearl, J., & Mackenzie, D. (2018). *The book of why: the new science of cause and effect.* Basic Books.

Pfundmair M. (2017). Cross-Cultural Experimental Research. In Y. Y. Kim (Ed.) *The International Encyclopedia of Intercultural Communication* (pp. 1–8). Wiley. https://doi.org/10.1002/9781118783665.ieicc0099

Ploder, A., & Hamann, J. (2021). Practices of Ethnographic Research: Introduction to the Special Issue. *Journal of Contemporary Ethnography*, *50*(1), 3–10. https://doi.org/10.1177/0891241620979100

Portes, A., & Rivas, A. (2011). The adaptation of migrant children. *The Future of Children, 21,* 219–246. https://doi.org/10.1353/foc.2011.0004

Pretelli, I., Borgerhoff Mulder, M., & McElreath, R. (2022). Rates of ecological knowledge learning in Pemba, Tanzania: Implications for childhood evolution. *Evolutionary Human Sciences, 4,* e34. https://doi.org/10.1017/ehs.2022.31

R Core Team. (2023). R: A Language and Environment for Statistical Computing [Computer software]. *R Foundation for Statistical Computing.*

Ratih, K., Syah, M. F. J., Nurhidayat, N., Jarin, S., & Buckworth, J. (2021). Learning Patterns during the Disruptive Situation in Informal Education: Parents' Efforts and Challenges in the Adjustment of Progressive Learning. *Indonesian Journal on Learning and Advanced Education (IJOLAE), 3(3),* Article 3. https://doi.org/10.23917/ijolae.v3i3.15151

Riede, F., Lew-Levy, S., Johannsen, N. N., Lavi, N., & Andersen, M. M. (2023). Toys as Teachers: A Cross-Cultural Analysis of Object Use and Enskillment in Hunter–Gatherer Societies. *Journal of Archaeological Method and Theory, 30(1),* 32–63. https://doi.org/10.1007/s10816-022-09593-3

Sandberg, H., Sundin, E., & Sjöberg, U. (2022). When ethnographic work turns into distant screen visits: A note on flexible inflexibility during the COVID-19 pandemic. *Contemporary Issues in Early Childhood, 23(3),* 361–365. https://doi.org/10.1177/14639491221107361

Schegloff, E. A. (1987). Between micro and macro: Contexts and other connections. In J. C. Alexander, B. Giesen, R. Munch, & N. J. Smelser (Eds). *The micro-macro link* (pp. 207–234). University of California Press.

Schegloff, E. A. (2007). *Sequence organization in interaction : A primer in conversation analysis* (vol. 1). Cambridge University Press.

Sousa, E. L. (2022). Ethnography with children in times of pandemic: An ethical and methodological reflection. *Cadernos de Pesquisa, 52*, e09122. https://doi.org/10.1590/198053149122_en

Stan Development Team. (2021). Stan Modeling Language Users Guide and Reference Manual [Computer software].

Sullivan, A., Brewis, A., & Wutich, A. (2018). Studying Children's Cultural Knowledge and Behaviors Related to Environment, Health, and Food: Methods for Ethnoecological Research with Children. *Journal of Ethnobiology, 38(2)*, 276–294. https://doi.org/10.2993/0278-0771-38.2.276

Takada, A. (2021). Pragmatic reframing from distress to playfulness: !Xun caregiver responses to infant crying. *Journal of Pragmatics, 181*, 180–195. https://doi.org/10.1016/j.pragma.2021.05.021

Tannen, D. (2006). Intertextuality in interaction: Reframing family arguments in public and private. *Text & Talk, 26(4–5)*, 597–617. https://doi.org/10.1515/TEXT.2006.024

Tehrani, J. J., & Riede, F. (2008). Towards an archaeology of pedagogy: Learning, teaching and the generation of material culture traditions. *World Archaeology, 40(3)*, 316–331. https://doi.org/10.1080/00438240802261267

Thajib, F., Stodulka, T., Haun, H., Meng, T., Sun, W., Masaquiza, S., Arroyo Garcia, B., Junker, M., Petrovic, L., Striegler, B., Weyrowitz, J., Sunderarajan, J., Swastyastu, M., Taek, D. J., Abis, A., Tjizao, D., Kanngiesser, P., Shishala, D., & Liebal, K. (under review). No Safe Distance? Reflections on decolonising large-scale, remote collaborative research during and beyond COVID-19. *Ethos.*

Tsuji, S., Amso, D., Cusack, R., Kirkham, N., & Oakes, L. M. (2022). Empirical research at a distance: New methods for developmental science. *Frontiers in Psychology, 13*, 938995. https://doi.org/10.3389/fpsyg.2022.938995

UNHCR. (2023). Figures at a glance. Retrieved October 14, 2023, from UNHCR website: https://www.unhcr.org/figures-at-a-glance.html

Volpe, C. R. (2019). Digital diaries: New uses of PhotoVoice in participatory research with young people. *Children's Geographies, 17(3)*, 361–370. https://doi.org/10.1080/14733285.2018.1543852

Warren, G. (2021). Is There Such a Thing as Hunter-Gatherer Archaeology? *Heritage, 4(2),* 794–810. https://doi.org/10.3390/heritage4020044

Watson, A., & Lupton, D. (2022). Remote Fieldwork in Homes During the COVID-19 Pandemic: Video-Call Ethnography and Map Drawing Methods. *International Journal of Qualitative Methods, 21,* 160940692210783. https://doi.org/10.1177/16094069221078376

Wefers, H., Krüger, V., Iza Simba, N. B., & Guandinango, Y. A. (2023). Ethical challenges of cross-cultural research – The example of a psychological research project in the Andean context. *Journal of Empirical Research on Human Research Ethics, 18*(4), 233-245. https://doi.org/10.1177/15562646231181880

Wefers, H., Schuhmacher, N., Chacón, L. H., & Kärtner, J. (2023). Universality without uniformity – infants' reactions to unresponsive partners in urban Germany and rural Ecuador. *Memory & Cognition, 51(3),* 807–823. https://doi.org/10.3758/s13421-022-01318-x

Wefers, H., Schuhmacher, N., & Kärtner, J. (2023). Developmental changes in infants' affective reactivity across cultures. Manuscript Submitted for Publication.

Wefers, H., Schwarz, C. L., Hernández Chacón, L., & Kärtner, J. (2022). Maternal ethnotheories about infants' ideal states in two cultures. *Journal of Cross-Cultural Psychology, 53(6),* 603–625. https://doi.org/10.1177/00220221221096785

West, E. (1992). Children on the plains frontier. In E. West & P. Petrik (Eds). *Small Worlds: Children and Adolescents in America, 1850–1950* (pp. 26–41). University Press of Kansas.

Xu, J. (2019). Learning "Merit" in a Chinese Preschool: Bringing the Anthropological Perspective to Understanding Moral Development. *American Anthropologist, 121*(3), 655–666. https://doi.org/10.1111/aman.13269

Xu, J. (2020). The Mischievous, the Naughty, and the Violent in a Taiwanese Village: Peer Aggression Narratives in Arthur P. Wolf's "Child Interview" (1959). *Cross-Currents, 9*(1), 180–208. https://doi.org/10.1353/ach.2020.0003

Xu, J. (2024). *"Unruly" Children: Historical Fieldnotes and Learning Morality in a Taiwan Village.* Cambridge University Press.

Yarkoni, T. (2022). The generalizability crisis. *Behav Brain Sci, 45,* e1. https://doi.org/10.1017/S0140525X20001685

Yilmaz, K. (2013). Comparison of quantitative and qualitative research traditions: Epistemological, theoretical, and methodological differences. *European journal of education, 48*(2), 311–325. https://doi.org/10.1111/ejed.12014

5. Preparing for the field

Coordinated by Adam Boyette

Contributors: Dorsa Amir, Adam Boyette, Alejandrina Cristia, Alyssa Crittenden, Ardain Dzabatou, Michael Gurven, Vidrige Kandza, Patricia Kanngiesser, Nokwanda Ndlovu, Sarah Pope-Caldwell, Marie Schäfer, and Andrea Taverna

This chapter aims to help readers prepare for going to 'the field'—the location(s) where data will be collected. We discuss starting a new field site, collaborating at established sites, and practical strategies for building and maintaining ties to the field site longitudinally. Throughout, we emphasize that developing trusting relationships with the community is critical to ethical research practice and essential for good science. Starting from this principle, we review the practical strategies for relationship-building and establishing ethical research practices, especially in regard to work with children and in settings with little to no infrastructure for research oversight. Also, personal experiences and practical aspects of conducting research are presented, including: obtaining permissions to conduct research with 'human subjects', developing rigorous consent procedures, writing codes of conduct for research staff, data storage and access concerns, staying safe and healthy in the field, and designing comprehensive and ethical budgets.

5.1. Introduction

Researchers who study children's learning across cultures come from a diversity of disciplinary and theoretical approaches. The idea of 'the field'—the location(s) where we collect our data—is

©2025 Adam Boyette, et al., CC BY-NC 4.0

https://doi.org/10.11647/OBP.0440.05

central to each of these approaches. We also believe it is useful—if not critical—for researchers from disciplines like experimental psychology to think of the university laboratory as a 'field site'. This is because many of the steps that lead to the encounter between the researcher and study participants are the same no matter where this encounter happens. Moreover, these encounters always involve social dynamics resulting from individual differences among the researcher(s) and participant(s)—in terms of gender, race, class, ethnicity, age, relative power in the situation, and so on. If we are unconscious of these dynamics, they can influence data collection in unexpected ways, especially when doing cross-cultural research. Guided by both senior and more junior researchers and those who have worked both within and far from their home communities, this chapter aims to help prepare the researcher for these encounters 'in the field'.

First, we discuss different field situations that a researcher might encounter, as well as the logistical and relational affordances and challenges each presents. Whether the researcher wishes to develop a new field site or work at an established site, work far from home or in their local community, the choice of where to study children's learning involves balancing convenience, cost, chance, and curiosity. We aim to leverage our varied experiences and those of the broader fields of anthropology and cross-cultural psychology to guide researchers through some of the complexities of these choices.

Then, we discuss the value of the researcher working with as well as in a community. Developing trusting relationships with the community is critical to ethical research practice and essential for good science, even when a researcher may have a single or only a few encounters during their work (e.g., visiting a collaborator's site to run a single study). We will discuss the role of the researcher as part of the community, building local collaborations, working with international and multicultural teams, and planning with the community. Additionally, recruitment of research participants and local assistants will be considered, with an emphasis on the embeddedness of such simple processes within complex community norms and social networks.

Finally, in conducting their work, the researcher is typically representing one or more institutions or organizations that pay their salary and fund their research, and they are therefore accountable to them. As an interface between the community at the field site and these other bodies, the researcher must navigate a range of ethical obligations to all of the parties involved. We will walk through our experiences with such practical aspects of conducting research, including obtaining permissions to conduct research with 'human subjects', developing rigorous consent procedures, writing codes of conduct for research staff, data storage and access concerns, staying safe and healthy in the field, and designing comprehensive and ethical budgets.

We wish to acknowledge that, while efforts are ongoing to diversify academic fields conducting cross-cultural research, including from a geographic perspective (Apicella et al., 2020; Krys et al., 2024), the overwhelming majority of researchers doing fieldwork are foreigners, who do not come from the community of study, nor necessarily from the same country. This is also the case among the contributors, with important exceptions (see especially Boxes 5.1 and 5.2). Given this situation, we hope that the experiences and guidance we share in this chapter will inform the reader of some best practices regardless of their situation vis-à-vis their field site, but also that we can motivate contributions from and collaborations with local researchers to the field of cross-cultural research on children's learning.

5.2. Finding and maintaining a 'field site'

Deciding where to work

Where should you conduct fieldwork? A number of factors should be carefully considered. The first set of factors relate to the scientific fit between the research question and the field site. What is the central question of the research, and how well can that question be answered through fieldwork with the community in question? In other words, what is the relevance of the field site to the question at hand? For example, the motivation to conduct cross-cultural fieldwork is often to test the generalizability of a certain phenomenon outside of the original testing site. While this can be a useful endeavor in its own right (Barrett, 2020), we can increase the depth of our explanatory power by being more thoughtful in our approach. First, we should clearly identify the appropriate cultural community that best fits our research question—be it a nation, a village, a family, or some other unit (Amir & McAuliffe, 2020). Second, we should clearly identify the specific cultural or environmental features of interest and, ideally, pre-register how we expect those features to co-vary with outcome variables (see Nosek et al., 2018 for further detail; though we understand that pre-registration is not always feasible or appropriate). For instance, if our hypothesis concerns the role that subsistence strategy may play in shaping children's sharing behavior (e.g., Rochat et al., 2009), the appropriate cross-cultural sample should tap into a diversity of subsistence strategies.

Of course, not all researchers have equal ability to travel to or access communities of interest. Nor do all communities want to engage in research collaborations. As such, a second set of factors relating to field site choice concern the practical and logistical challenges a certain site may pose. Accessibility, safety, and permission to conduct research are often determinative factors. When possible, however, researchers should seek to strike a balance between feasibility and scientific fit. In some cases, where access plays a greater role in site selection, researchers should consider tailoring and adjusting their research approach to better match the unique features of the site. We also encourage researchers to clearly state the factors that influenced site selection in academic manuscripts, even if it is simply stating that the field site choice was opportunistic. This follows a longstanding tradition in anthropology, where dialogue between place and research questions has been a core, if sometimes conflicted, part of the scientific process (Johnson, 1991; Weisman & Luhrmann, 2020).

Once the researcher finds a field site that fits their scientific objectives, what about personal fit? Ideally, researchers should demonstrate cultural competence, remaining highly aware of the variety of cultural values, norms, and customs inherent to a given site. The ability to communicate in a common language using shared vocabulary is hugely important for success in the field, as is the ability to contextualize the research question within the community's cultural framework. In many cases, the best way to achieve cultural competence is to collaborate with communities that the researcher is a part of, collaborate with local researchers in their communities, and/or spend a significant amount of time learning about and participating in the community's culture prior to conducting any research (Agar, 2008; Broesch et al., 2020). Below, we lay out strategies for working in and with communities to achieve successful and equitable research partnerships.

Setting up a field site

It is daunting to set up a project at a 'new' field site. By new, we mean one unfamiliar at least to the social and life sciences, or that may no longer have active researchers working there. Doing so, however, can be immensely rewarding when other field sites are either crowded or over-studied, or when other sites may be ill-suited for pursuing particular questions or a poor fit to the individual researcher. Given the role of culture and the physical and social environment in shaping many aspects of development, progress in both theory and empiricism will require broadening the range of studied populations (Amir & McAuliffe, 2020; Greenfield et al., 2003; Gurven, 2018).

Where to start in setting up a field site? First, scour prior studies, government and non-governmental reports, news articles, and any other relevant information about the region and local culture (Karasik et al., 2018). This is crucial for providing background information and potential contacts to make direct inquiries. Together, these and contacted sources can provide insights into the history, politics, and ecology of a region, and practical logistical information before your first visit.

A first visit should not be rushed. Give yourself enough time to seek permits (see Section 5.3), make broad contacts and organize meetings with community leaders and other relevant entities. Devote time to meet community members, and to gain their trust.

This could take months, not days, or even weeks, depending on the size of the community(ies). Trust often comes from participating in activities of daily life, eating local foods, trying to learn the local language (even when translators are available), and sharing experiences in ways that are distinct from data collection. Having key informants, reputable go-betweens who function as both translators (if needed) and cultural facilitators, can help accelerate how quickly you are received and welcomed. The difference from doing the same in an established site is that here you can't piggyback on the established trust of other reputable workers.

Cognitive and emotional development, learning, social networks, and other topics involving children can be delicate to study in some communities unless trust is well established. To work with children, trust relationships must be established with parents and teachers. Ongoing commitments to help support schools, with supplies and other materials, and from volunteering your time to help serve educational needs, are two ways both to contribute locally and to establish a public commitment to working with children and adolescents (e.g., Morelli, 2012).

Ensuring you are welcomed back to the same field site, whether for longitudinal study or to conduct additional studies, requires mutual respect and mutual gain (see Box 5.1). Explicit conversations about community needs and interests are vital to see how fulfilling your own project goals can at the same time be a source of pride and commitment for community members. When one of us (MG) was building infrastructure for the Tsimane Health and Life History Project (THLHP) over multiple visits between 1999–2001, community members in multiple villages often complained that rampant sickness and limited healthcare were major obstacles. There were certainly other problems, but addressing health concerns tied directly to the major themes of the THLHP. When the THLHP officially launched in 2002, three Bolivian physicians were hired to serve community primary health care needs, while simultaneously collecting epidemiological information, in sync with anthropological studies. Later initiatives included public health outreach and health promoter training. The desire for health care contributions in a remote region with very limited biomedical surveillance or outreach quickly became a strong motivation for villages to invite the THLHP to work there, and to return year after year.

There is no doubt that setting up a new field site involves major time and financial costs, and can slow one's professional trajectory. A few conditions can help make the burden more bearable. First, going it alone is not just old-fashioned; it is limiting, and not as much fun. So much more can be accomplished with multiple, mixed-gender, ideally international (see Box 5.2) collaborators from the outset. Multiple Principal Investigators (PIs) or co-Directors not only ease the joint burden of organizing and maintaining a field site, but also help increase total productivity. Working together can increase your chances of finding grants to support the management of ongoing projects. In all cases, you can bring in students, postdocs and other collaborators.

Second, even if your designs are for a longitudinal study, few can afford to wait years before publishing. It is therefore helpful to organize a few initial short-term studies. For example, initial self-contained studies employing experimental methods to study effects of market integration on economic cooperation (e.g., Gurven, 2004a, 2004b) helped ensure no major gaps in productivity during the early years of investment in the THLHP. Indeed, every long-term project starts out as a limited, cross-sectional foray. Full disclosure: the THLHP was originally designed as a one-year study. The generous buy-in from local communities, the web of new questions that spun from initial findings, a team of committed researchers, and a reliable, sufficient funding source all helped to slowly extend a one-year study to a three-year study, then five years, and now 22 years and still going (see also Leonard et al., 2015).

Collaborations with established field sites

Often, field researchers work in places where others have worked before them. Even if you intend to branch off to establish a new site, it is typical to follow a path already laid as an entrance to 'the field.' For instance, many of us followed a mentor or other colleague to their site—or at least their first site. There are many advantages to this approach, including the benefits of teamwork mentioned above. Working at an established field site means you can be introduced to the community by someone people know and trust, and your colleague(s) will be able to give you important local information and facilitate access to the interlocutors and research participants your work requires. As noted in the previous section, however, it is essential to fieldwork that researchers have the trust of the local community, and this is especially the case for working with children. Thus, sharing a site—even if for a short stay for a single study—means sharing the burden of making and maintaining positive relations. As part of the same outsider researcher community, the local reputations of you and your collaborators will be entangled.

Even if you will stay at the site for a short while, it will be advantageous to relationship building in the community—and therefore to data collection—that you come to understand local norms and what your role is as a researcher in the community. People are more or less familiar with what researchers do, and this will influence what cultural categories people will ascribe to you, and therefore which norms apply. Some things a new researcher at a field site should ask their more experienced collaborator(s) are:

- What is your role in the community?

- What assumptions do people have about you? (e.g., is there a historical context, such as colonization, that affects how outside people with different identities are perceived?)

- What can I do to build good rapport?

- What is the role of children in the community (e.g., more or less autonomy)? How does this affect consent/assent procedures?

- Who should be approached regarding consent for a particular child participant (both parents, primarily the mother/father, any supervising adult)? How should they be approached?

- What is the appropriate physical, psychological, and emotional distance to keep from people in this community?

Very often cross-cultural researchers work with research assistants who are more familiar with the community and cultural context, perhaps because they are from the community. These people are critical cultural liaisons and can also be important intellectual partners in projects. In the context of field research in small, rural communities, sometimes research assistants are recruited from cities where there might be more people with research-relevant skills and experience. If you bring an assistant from outside the community, you will also need to think through how this person will be viewed by the community. What is the relationship between the urban and rural communities? Are there relevant ethnic, class, or other differences that may impact how your assistant will be perceived? Of course, following the guidance of experienced collaborators at the site will be critical here as well.

We will discuss the ethics from the position of institutions in Section 5.3, but the reality of how you ethically recruit participants in your cross-cultural research project at a field site is often not as simple as asking someone to participate and having them sign a consent form. This is again an area that benefits greatly from the help of experienced collaborators. Anthropologists recognize consent as an ongoing process, where the researcher must be attentive to when those with whom they work feel coerced or do not fully understand what is being asked of them (LeCompte & Schensul, 2015; Spradley, 1979). This is especially the case with children. For instance, some of us have had experiences where parents consented to their children's participation and pushed their children to comply when they did not want to. At other times, both parents gave consent for their child, and their child assented to participate, but eventually expressed discomfort or fear during data collection. In such situations, we ceased working with the child, despite their parents' disappointment. Everyone is different, and there are often differences at the group level as well. The researcher must be sensitive to this. For instance, during a focal-follow observational study (where data is collected with one child at a time, see also Section 4.2), a child who had assented but showed fear later continued their activities alongside the other children and the researcher (AB) and data collection went ahead as planned—the child simply did not like being the focus of attention. As much knowledge as you can gain from collaborators about their process of consent, and experiences they have had with refusals as well as consent or assent, the better prepared you will be to respectfully recruit participants.

Box 5.1 Indigenous perspectives on field research

As researchers, we need to continually reflect on whose perspective and knowledge system is prioritized in a given research project, from how the topic is framed to the choice of methods used. Entering the child development research space as a Zulu scholar who is also from the communities that I (NN) tend to study has often left me feeling a different sense of responsibility than an outsider might feel. Specifically, my approach reflects my role as a community member, and that has meant different things depending on the study but always shapes my research questions. For instance, I am interested in moving away from 'damage-centered' questions that focus on what is wrong from an outsider perspective (Tuck, 2009) and instead towards those that highlight aspects of our cultural values and beliefs, particularly around why these beliefs exist and the purpose that they serve within the culture from an Indigenous perspective.

The end goals of research projects might look different for Indigenous scholars that conduct research in their own communities, where there is an orientation towards rectifying past ills from research (and larger societal misgivings) and, often, an aim to empower and heal the community. My research process is informed by my Zulu cultural values that underscore the relationships and interactions in my home communities in South Africa.

There are a few ways I have worked to attend to the Indigenous worldview and center the community's voices in different projects. For example, several cultural values become salient throughout my research: *ukuhlonipha* (respect), reciprocity, *ubuntu* (humanness), and equality. Like many Indigenous languages, the subtleties that are lost in translation probably matter more to people in the culture, and this issue of when and how to translate is an ongoing topic of discussion among Indigenous scholars where there is currently no solution, outside of publishing in our own languages in the few journals that allow that. For my purposes here, I relate these Zulu words to their closest English equivalents (in parentheses), but since something is lost in the process, I will be more deliberate when I describe more abstractly the Zulu idea versus its English parallel concept.

Ukuhlonipha (respect) refers to a hierarchy-based respect, where one's societal responsibilities and social cues come from one's status relative to those with whom one is interacting. To a Zulu person, respect is mutual and must be reciprocated. The most salient regular demonstration of respect in the culture is greeting participants with their proper title, which attends to the hierarchical nature of Zulu culture by honoring one's age-set and status within the community. This example demonstrates a centering of Zulu cultural values in the research process and how a knowledge system is integrated as part of the process. By drawing from and through the use of local knowledge, this places emphasis on the idea of viewing the community as experts in knowledge construction. Important Zulu expressions that are meaningful to the community have also played a role in my interactions, including *kulahlwa kabili*, which roughly means 'kindness is reciprocated' (Nyembezi, 1954). This proverb was embodied in one study when I gave a child a lollipop and she ran off only to return with a piece of chocolate for me. Kindness must be reciprocated. As researchers we should always consider how our research benefits the communities being studied, and we should be conscientious about how participants are compensated. *Ubuntu* (humanness) refers to the connection all of humankind has to one another, and has been popularized as 'I am because we are,' denoting the African sense of self that is derived from community. Many of the communities I work with live in poverty, and by honoring important cultural values such as *ubuntu* I am able to rely on the community's understanding of fairness and equality.

As researchers, we should be mindful of not unintentionally creating more instability in a community. These are some of the few examples of how I have worked to center the community's values in my research, which leads to building trust and meaningful interactions. As an Indigenous scholar whose studies are often conducted in my own community, it becomes even more crucial to pay attention to these interactions because my relationships with these communities transcends the research process as a member of the community.

Longitudinal field research

If you conduct your research in a field site long-term, or when establishing a new research collaboration, you may visit a place or community several times, or even on a regular basis. But even when planning a short-term project in an established site, it can still be beneficial or necessary to spread your research activities over more than one visit. Revisiting a community offers important advantages when preparing for the field, and in some cases these advantages can outweigh the extra costs and time involved in traveling to a place multiple times. Here, we help readers think through some of these advantages and how to navigate a sustained research presence at a site, even when you are physically absent.

First of all, you can plan and prepare your research project and your collaboration with the community more thoroughly when revisiting a place. For example, you will have a better idea of what you need to bring along and what you can acquire locally when you return a second time. You also will have more time between visits to organize things you would like to contribute based on agreements with the community. Most importantly, conducting a research project through several visits gives you the possibility and time to rethink and adapt your research plan and design based on the things you learned during your past visit(s). This can be particularly useful and important if your research involves questions and methods that are new in the specific context and that you might want to discuss with local informants or try out in a pilot study first. For example, for most studies with children, it is advisable to conduct a small pilot study first in order to try out a procedure or to identify materials that are appropriate and intuitive for a particular age group or in a particular cultural setting. If your study involves a cross-cultural comparison, you may want to conduct a pilot in more than one site in order to find a method that is suitable and produces comparable results across sites and cultural contexts (e.g., Kanngiesser et al., 2022). In such cases, it can become necessary to plan for more than one visit to pilot and conduct a study in a particular site.

Second, not only can you as a researcher prepare better for the field, the community and people you work with have a better idea of what to expect from your presence, and can plan or (re) think how they would like to work with you the next time. Based on their experience during your past visit(s), they might be able to make concrete suggestions about when a good time would be for you to come back and how your research could be organized most efficiently, but also so that it fits in well with other community activities and their schedule. In the best case, you can plan consecutive visits together, either during your stay, or remotely by staying in touch while you are away.

Third, in some cases it can become important for your research to collect data at different points in time, especially if the availability of your participants or the phenomenon that you want to investigate could be influenced by seasonal activities and events or other changes in the community over time. For example, in some places your participant sample could be biased if recruitment takes place only during a particular time of year, e.g., if a certain age or gender group (or other sub-group of possible study participants) is involved in seasonal activities that prevent them from participating in your research. In other cases, the phenomenon or behavior you want to investigate may be affected by the specific timing of data collection more directly. For example, if you study children's social interactions (e.g., with adults and peers), your findings may be quite different if you collect data during the school term or holidays in some places. Thus, sometimes, you may even consider collecting your data during more than one visit in order to obtain more representative results.

While preparing for the field becomes easier when revisiting a place, it remains important that you cultivate your relationships and collaborations during your absence, and that you renew your agreements and consent with the community over iterative visits. This is particularly critical if your visits are irregular and involve longer absences of variable time (which is typical given the complexities of research work). Ideally, you can maintain connections while being away by staying in touch remotely with local colleagues, research assistants, and other community stakeholders. If your field site is in a remote place where people have little access or private means to contact you via phone or internet, you could develop specific strategies together with your local collaborators for staying in touch. For example, you could plan for mobile phones or phone credit in your research budget that can be used to contact you while you are away (see Section 5.3), or you could make a plan about who people should contact in order to get in touch with you. Even in places where communication via phone and internet is not feasible at all, you can usually find ways to stay in touch, for example, by collaborating with local institutions, organizations or other researchers in the area who may be able to transmit messages (or even deliver letters or small packages) from and to you.

If your visits to a community are irregular and with longer absences in between (and if communication during your absence is difficult), it becomes essential to invest time to re-establish relationships and reintroduce yourself and your research when you return the next time. But even if you visit a site on a regular basis, it benefits your research collaboration if you plan in some time for reconnecting and getting up to date at the beginning of each stay.

Finally, there is always the possibility that conditions and circumstances you expected to remain stable when planning your trip have changed while you were away, and you therefore have to adjust your current plans based on the latest developments. For example, collaborators or research assistants you planned to work with may no longer be available, or new people may be interested in working with you. Informants or participants you assumed to be there may have left the community, or others you did not expect may have moved in. Authorities or important gatekeepers may have changed positions, or collaborating institutions (e.g., schools) may have altered their organization and schedule in ways affecting your research plans. Or the community or participant group you planned to work with may have changed their attitude or expectations regarding your research based on experiences they had during your absence. Second, you may want to inform the community or people you work with about the progress of your research project(s) and, at the same time, give them a chance to raise questions and concerns, make suggestions regarding your current plans, or discuss possible changes regarding your work agreements. Most importantly, even if you continue a long-term project from previous visits, you should make sure to renew or (re) obtain the community's and participants' consent before restarting your activities.

5.3. Forms and resources

Permits & regulations

Understanding required research regulations and permits can be challenging, and local collaborators are crucial in such an endeavor. In the absence of such collaborators, talking to colleagues who have worked in the same places may also provide some insight, as noted above. In both cases, however, people in the past may not have followed all extant regulations and/or new regulations may have been put in place. It is therefore worthwhile to attempt web searches with keywords such as 'research regulation [COUNTRY NAME]' (in the appropriate country-specific languages) to check what may be present. It would be ideal to have a resource that links all the regulations relevant to research, research with children, or research with minorities, in the world, but to our knowledge, this does not yet exist.

The Language Acquisition Across Cultures team (LAAC), which includes one of us as a team leader (AC), recently reviewed regulation governing data protection specifically for several countries in Africa (Ghana, Malawi, Namibia, South Africa, Tanzania), Asia (China, India, Israel, South Korea, Vietnam), Europe (Denmark, Finland, France, Netherlands, Norway, Sweden, United Kingdom), Latin America (Argentina, Bolivia, Brazil, Costa Rica, Mexico, Uruguay), and Oceania (Australia, Papua New Guinea, Solomon Islands, Timor Leste, Vanuatu). Given that much research builds on the creation of datasets that contain potentially identifying data, and therefore personal data (according to most definitions), these reports may be useful to readers of this chapter. These reports were the fruit of internships or short contracts by non-specialists, so we recommend care when re-using them. On a more positive note, they are all publicly available (Léon & Cristia, 2024).

By and large, what the LAAC team found was that the extensiveness of data protection regulation varied across countries, with some having extremely detailed and extensive requirements (Uruguay) and others having nearly no requirements (Timor Leste), with the general trend being that regulation was most detailed in Europe and Latin America, less so in Asia and Africa, and least extensive in Oceania (with exceptions to these generalizations). Despite such variability, the LAAC team also found that, if one follows the most detailed regulation (e.g., Uruguay), one typically complies with all other regulations in broad terms. The most detailed regulation often has very simple and reasonable requirements (as summarized in Léon & Cristia, 2024), including ensuring and documenting informed consent, making data transfers secure, providing participants the right to withdraw their data, developing a data management plan which considers participant anonymity and privacy, and providing them with a way to contact researchers (which is a reason why ensuring multiple curators is essential when archiving—see Section 7.6).

Naturally, ensuring that participants can contact researchers may be difficult for remote populations, but this can be addressed by, for example, making sure that members of the community have the names, emails, and phone numbers of the principal investigators and those of trusted others, and asking them to pass on this information to anyone else who asks. This builds on best practices discussed above for building and maintaining good rapport with the community. For countries whose regulation does not require such specific actions, these can be viewed as best practices from an ethical standpoint. In addition, it is still worthwhile checking if a given country has a 'data protection agency' or something similar, which is typically a government agency that keeps track of all databases that include personal data from their citizens.

Note that the above-mentioned 'best individual data protection practices' are rights and not obligations, and also that they are not culturally neutral: participants who wish that their identifiable data be posted publicly can still ask for researchers to do so, and there are cases in which this appears like the best choice (e.g., to assure recognition of the holders of knowledge; see Box 5.1). One more issue that readers should bear in mind is potential commercial applications: some regulations rule out the use of research data for commercial applications (Namibia), because an entirely different procedure needs to be followed in the case of research with this potential. And yet, some communities may be interested in their data being licensed for commercial uses against the potential of economic gains (e.g., every time the dataset is downloaded, the community is paid; or if a product is developed based on it, then the community receives a portion of the profit). Therefore, rather than ruling out this possibility, we advise open conversations with the community as well as detailed perusal of extant regulation.

Local governments

Research involving Indigenous participants often requires authorization from local governments (e.g., city/village councils, public schools, educational districts). While we have emphasized the importance of working with communities, this aspiration can be complicated by tensions between Indigenous interests and those of the different layers of government that intersect their spaces and livelihoods.

In recent decades, a series of international instruments have been formulated to protect the rights of Indigenous peoples (United Nations, 2009), but these measures are still not implemented in many communities around the world. The absence of such instruments can be problematic in two ways. First, it may be a potential condition for the proliferation of research practices that do not ensure what is known as the 'four R's' (Louis, 2007): Relational Accountability, Respectful Representation, Reciprocal Appropriation, and Rights and Regulations during the research process. Second, it can be useful for certain local governments whose language and education policies are often at odds with decolonial research practices (Castro-Gómez & Grosfoguel, 2007; De Sousa Santos, 2009). This is because these types of research practices, based on sound ethical principles, tend to strengthen Indigenous knowledge and vernacular languages in the face of homogenization, monoculturalism, and monolingualism, which can run counter to state-building activities.

Within the so-called 'Global South', Latin America is a case in point. Although this region is an intercultural, multiethnic, and multilingual continent, the education policies of Latin American countries often ignore the numerous vernacular languages that have always circulated within contemporary national boundaries. In many Spanish-speaking countries, including Argentina, this disregard has its roots in the particular postcolonial history of linguistic homogeneity around Spanish as a national language (Vidal & Kuchenbrandt, 2015). One of us (AT) has worked as a researcher on the acquisition of the Indigenous language of the Chaco—Wichi lhomtes—and drew on an example of these epistemological and political tensions during an experience doing fieldwork in Indigenous schools in the Chaco Region, in line with other similar educational efforts in the region (e.g., Nercesian, 2014; Zidarich & colaboradores, 2006). This work led to the creation of mechanisms that allow Indigenous teachers to participate and drive an educational research agenda that meets the needs of their community (Taverna & Baiocchi, 2021). One example of this is the development of pedagogical and didactic resources (e.g., author-native children's books, literacy workshops in vernacular languages) that are culturally responsive to Wichi epistemologies and practices (Pérez et al., 2017a, 2017b, 2017c, 2017d, 2017e, 2021). The resources developed are based on two main premises, namely, that the understanding of the world is broader than the western understanding of the world and that diversity is infinite (De Sousa Santos, 2009). Thus, the content of these decolonial resources emphasizes alternative forms of thinking, representations of what we call 'nature' and the relationship between the human and non-human worlds.

The main obstacle is that a decolonial educational research agenda, such as the one in the above example, can come into conflict with the interests of local governments' educational policies, which may be in line with the hegemonic knowledge of western academia. This hegemony asserts, among other things, exchange value, individual ownership of land, and the primacy of the material over the spiritual, thereby blocking emancipatory knowledge and sacrificing alternatives from the perspective of Indigenous ways of knowing (De Sousa Santos, 2009).

Cross-fertilization between Indigenous community representatives, researchers, and local governments from the beginning of the research process is a *sine qua non* for the promotion of Indigenous initiatives in the mainstream, contributing to the emancipation of Indigenous knowledge and practices while creating opportunities for mutual openness between the academic field and the community (see also Box 5.1).

Institutional and Indigenous codes of ethics

It is common in many research settings that researchers working directly with people (i.e., human subjects) demonstrate that their intended research project has been reviewed by an outside—ideally impartial—body of experts to assure it is ethical in its design, methodologies, and aims. Here, we discuss common issues in proposing cross-cultural research with children to one type of ethical review body, often called an institutional review board. While the ethical review of research projects is certainly desirable, in practice new ethical dilemmas arise from attempting to navigate the realities of cross-cultural research with the requirements of top-down, institutionally mandated regulatory bureaucracy (Schrag, 2010), especially in light of some of the conflicts between Indigenous people and other governmental structures noted above. At the same time, some Indigenous peoples have created their own ethical guidelines for researchers to follow, which can perhaps be even more important for cross-cultural researchers.

Well before going to the field, research with human participants conducted by researchers affiliated with universities or other research institutions can require ethical approval by institutional review boards, or IRBs. These review boards often use ethical guidelines published by professional bodies (e.g., American Anthropological Association, American Psychological Association, British Psychological Association, or the Deutsche Gesellschaft für Psychologie) as the basis for their assessment. Such reviews can be meaningful in thinking through certain procedures, especially those around data privacy and consent, although recommendations from the IRB may not always reflect the practical realities on the ground. For instance, even if there are dedicated ethical review boards for social science research, they may have limited experience with cross-cultural or field-based research and may— as a default—expect written consent, which at times may not be feasible or advisable in some contexts, where verbal consent is more suitable (e.g., because of limited literacy skills) or better aligns with local norms. In the United States, the federal policy in place that mandates IRBs does allow for non-written consent, but the board may need to be made familiar with this (https:// americananthro.org/about/policies/statement-on-ethnography-and-institutional-review-boards/). Nonetheless, the researcher may feel that they are put into a situation of navigating between two sets of obligations—to their institution and to the communities with whom they work. This can be worse at institutions that do not have dedicated review boards for social science research (psychology, anthropology, etc.). These may require researchers to submit their studies for review to institution-wide ethics boards that were often set up to deal with medical or invasive research. As a consequence, reviewers and boards may be unfamiliar with study procedures and approaches in psychological, behavioral, or anthropological research, and can feel more like an impediment than a service (Schrag, 2010).

Moreover, multi-site studies often pose additional challenges as ethical review may need to be sought from various institutions (in different countries) that may differ in their ethical review procedures and requirements. For example, consent forms or procedures that are acceptable to one ethical review board may not be acceptable to another. Together, these challenges can potentially delay ethical approval substantively due to the need for detailed explanations and revisions to ethics applications and, at times, negotiations with ethical review boards about appropriate research procedures. It is sometimes possible to streamline the ethical review process and submit 'umbrella' applications to the lead investigator's institution that cover all data collection sites and, once the lead investigator has received ethical clearance, to submit this for expedited review at collaborators' institutions. One needs to be mindful, though, when working in diverse cultural contexts and/or across multiple sites, of so-called 'ethics dumping' (Schroeder et al., 2018). That is, of engaging in research that would be deemed unacceptable in one's own country because legal and ethical frameworks are more lax in other settings (usually resource-poor settings). It is paramount that the highest ethical standards are applied across sites, and it is up to the lead researcher(s) to ensure such is the case.

Indigenous scholars have also noted how little institutional review boards procedures tend to protect vulnerable, Indigenous, or otherwise historically marginalized communities (Fournier et al., 2023; Hayward et al., 2021; Hedgecoe, 2016; Schrag, 2010;

Stark, 2012). Specifically, they argue that the potential impact of the research on the participants and their community is only considered insofar as it could open institutions to liability. This is emblematic of western individualistic cultural values, which often fail to capture an interdependent worldview that would prioritize the community (Tauri, 2018). The research ethics system as it is currently set up is void of the relational importance that is crucial to the research process, particularly in Indigenous communities that value interconnectedness (see Box 5.1). While institutionalized ethical approval procedures serve a role in encouraging and/or enforcing ethical behavior, they are also subject to the critique that research conducted on Indigenous communities that employs ethical standards drawn from the values of the Global North continues the "disrespect and psychological harm to communities, societies, and nations to which research findings are generalized or extrapolated" (Chilisa, 2019, p. 84).

Thus, approval from one's institutions should not be the final say in maintaining an ethical research practice, especially with regard to vulnerable populations such as children and marginalized groups. If your institution requires you to obtain the approval of an ethics council to do your research, we recommend doing what you can to fulfill your obligations to your institution in an open dialogue (figuratively and literally) with the ethical demands of your field site. In recent years, some Indigenous ethics codes have been developed to address the ethical concerns of peoples that have been colonized and marginalized, and these might also inform your approach to ethical research policies no matter where you work.

The Indigenous perspective on research ethics is complicated, as illustrated by Māori scholar Linda Tuhiwai Smith (2022, p. 1), when she states that "The word itself, 'research', is probably one of the dirtiest words in the Indigenous world's vocabulary. When mentioned in many Indigenous contexts, it stirs up silence, it conjures up bad memories, it raises a smile that is knowing and distrustful." Indigenous research codes have now been developed by the Assembly of First Nations in Canada (Assembly of First

Nations, 2009), the Australian Institute of Aboriginal and Torres Strait Islander Studies (AIATSIS) (Australian Institute of Aboriginal and Torres Strait Islander Studies, 2020), the Pūtaiora Writing Group for Māori research ethics (Hudson et al., 2010), and the South African San Institute (South African San Institute, 2017). The opening paragraph to the AIATSIS Code of Ethics for Aboriginal and Torres Strait Islander Research (Australian Institute of Aboriginal and Torres Strait Islander Studies, 2020, p. 11), highlights why there is a need for Indigenous ethics codes above and beyond 'conventional' ethical frameworks (e.g., IRBs):

> This idea of ethical human engagement has interested philosophers and thinkers across all cultures for all time. However, our best selves do not always prevail. For Indigenous peoples, the ongoing experiences of colonisation, theft of lands and resources, disruption to societies and families, and suppression of culture and identity, is a denial of human dignity and respect. When done well, research can, and has, had positive impacts for Indigenous peoples, but research has not been immune to practices that are imbued with racism, exploitation and disrespect.

> While conventional ethics frameworks emerge from the obligation to respect individual human dignity and protect the vulnerable, the ethical principles underpinning this Code proceed from a presumption of Indigenous authority as self-determining peoples, and as rights holders, whose knowledge and contribution to research must be recognised, respected and valued. This does not mean that individual Indigenous people may not be vulnerable as a result of their personal circumstances, and indeed may be more vulnerable due to the impact of colonisation, racism and intergenerational trauma.

Researchers who work with communities and in sites where ethical codes of conduct do not (yet) exist, can familiarize themselves with the existing Indigenous codes of conduct as they will offer invaluable guidelines for how to engage communities in a respectful and ethical way. Research departments that engage with cross-cultural research may also consider drafting codes of conduct that provide detailed guidance on good and ethical practice (for a recent example, see Bruno et al., 2022 and Box 5.2).

Box 5.2 Experiences with international/multicultural teams

Cross-cultural research is best accomplished by combining multicultural skill sets and expertise. Teams may consist of scientists and students from diverse backgrounds as well as local research assistants and support staff, who may themselves come from several different cultural traditions. It is important to not only recognize the strengths of multicultural research teams, but also the challenges of working in a group where language, customs, taboos, even diets may vary considerably. This is especially pertinent when field conditions require team members to both live and work in close proximity for weeks or even months. Providing training and resources for all team members to minimize misunderstandings and interpersonal conflicts can be critical to the success of a field season.

Multicultural team leaders might consider:

- Providing incoming team members with an Orientation Document with information about the existing research site and team. This should include relevant information about the history, politics, and climate of the country/region, as well as an overview of the specific community, such as the names of community leaders, descriptions of customs and taboos, logistics resources such as a packing list, and a typical workday timeline.

- Implementing a Code of Conduct that covers the research team's general approach (e.g., make informed, locally appropriate decisions; engage with community subsections equally; treat others with respect) and makes explicit the team's policies on discrimination, bullying, fighting, theft, dishonesty, and harassment. It should also make clear any specific policies regarding interpersonal conflicts or romantic relationships within the team, or between the team and community members. It is important that it includes contact information for (ideally independent) people, in addition to the team leader, that can provide support, as well as ways in which conflicts of interest may be identified and addressed in conflict resolution. Finally, it should detail the team's policy on the acquisition and use of media collected during the research process with specific guidance on asking permission and obtaining consent for external use. This document should be agreed upon and signed by all team members, including the team leader.

- Regularly checking in with team members about their health (physical and mental), which will require learning the culturally appropriate way of doing so (e.g., Is this a private matter? Is physical health understood as reflecting mental health?).

- Coordinating recurrent team building and leisure activities throughout the research period (e.g., movie nights, card games, football games, or other appropriate activities).

- Organizing a debrief meeting at the end of the research period that can be used to recap what parts of the field season were difficult, fun, interesting, learning experiences, etc., and might be followed up with a more formal Debrief Document which could be used to inform the team leader about any potential conflicts and provide feedback for future seasons.

Leading or working in a multicultural team requires that each member is treated with respect, adequate resources are provided to prevent potential conflicts, and all issues are carefully considered through appropriate cultural lenses. When in doubt, talk to your team members!

Example Codes of Conduct:

https://www.povertyactionlab.org/page/
code-conduct-j-pal-community

https://www.hfedlab.com/opportunities

Designing a budget

Research project budgets are naturally highly specific to the needs of the work one is doing, and often constrained or guided by the policies of the institution funding the project (or that one hopes will fund the project). However, as the budget is the document that reflects the resources one is leveraging to conduct research, one cannot escape cultural and ethical considerations in designing how funds will be spent in the context of doing research with children and their families. Such considerations are most pronounced when the researcher works in relatively low-resource settings, or those with minimal integration in cash economies—settings where one's presence alone reveals the relatively significant resources that must have already been expended to bring the researcher to the community—but they are not restricted to such settings. How money is used in specific cultural contexts can have major implications for the researcher's scientific and relational aims. In particular, we will highlight two budgeting issues that require consideration of the particular cultural and geospatial contexts of the research setting: participant and community compensation and the health and safety of the research team.

Participant compensation is standard practice and should be budgeted for. However, in practice, it is not always straightforward to implement; for instance, if the study design involves a sampling technique that means only some people are eligible to participate.

This raises the question of whether only those people will be compensated. When working with small communities, this may create jealousy. One of us (AB) had such an experience doing doctoral work with hunter-gatherer and subsistence farmer children in the Congo Basin, where the sampling process meant 'working with' some children but not others. While only some children may have been the subject of the study, the actual methodology—observations of everyday life—meant time was spent with all of the children who were present in the social group of the 'subject.' From the children's perspective, they were all involved in the research, and indeed they were. Thus, ethnographic knowledge—not only the target sample size—must inform how much money is spent on compensation.

Additionally, in this same example, it was completely appropriate to give gifts—not cash—to the children directly as compensation. In the hunter-gatherer culture under investigation, children are given significant autonomy (e.g., Boyette, 2019; Boyette & Lew-Levy, 2021; Hewlett et al., 2011) and it would not make ethnographic sense to compensate the parents for their children's time (though parental consent was sought). In contrast, among the farming community, parents, especially fathers, decided how resources were to be distributed in the family, and it was most appropriate to provide compensation to the participating children's parents (Boyette & Lew-Levy, 2019). Moreover, through discussion with local interlocutors, it was decided that compensation for the participating farmer families was to be cash, and not gifts, as cash was more deeply integrated into their economy. While compensation was relatively equal, it was a challenge in this case to avoid jealousy within and between groups. Fortunately, the budget had been sufficiently flexible to accommodate these dynamics and to reduce jealousy. While this is a highly specific research context, it illustrates the ways in which ethnographic knowledge can inform budgeting, and, depending on whether participant compensation is in the form of gifts or cash, can facilitate planned expenses.

In later research in these and similar communities, the researchers elected to provide a larger gift to each household in recognition that, even if work was being done with children, the impact of the research was felt by the family and the community more widely. Such decisions were based on accumulated experience and continual discussion with local communities. Moreover, because this research program involved repeated visits, community compensation was also integrated into project budgets in order to compensate for the researchers' continued disruptions of community life—no matter how minor or how welcome. For some communities, this involved a 'right to research' fee, which was given publicly to the community leadership council, and for others, community projects were requested as compensation. Such expenses ought to be treated as programmatic necessities of the research project, based on a principle of generalized reciprocity.

While budgets typically include, at a minimum, line items for each of the scientific and logistical necessities of a research project, the researcher should also feel obliged to consider their own wellbeing and safety and that of their team during the project. Without researcher health, there is no research. Wellbeing and safety concerns certainly vary between research sites, and what are allowable expenses may depend on funding sources. However, preventive medicine (e.g., prophylaxis), emergency travel, and first-aid supplies are all reasonable and potentially critical line items to budget for during field research. Researchers working in contexts where health insurance is not socialized or mandatory should also consider whether their research assistants are insured against any injury or other harms that might result from their participation in research projects. Lastly, in fieldwork contexts, budgeting funds for communication with home—with families as well as home institutions—is more than reasonable and can be essential to wellbeing and safety.

Risk and safety

In the social sciences, there have been few attempts to systematize the issue of risk in fieldwork (e.g., Howell, 1990; Rudzki et al., 2022 for the sciences in general), although several well-known researchers have developed personal strategies from their own accumulated experiences across multiple jobs in high-risk contexts

(Goldstein, 2014; Ice et al., 2015; Jamieson, 2002; Martin-Ortega & Herman, 2009; Westmarland, 2002).

More recently, Boisen (2018) takes up two strategies—acceptance and the ethnographic approach (Goldstein, 2014)—as two methods for improving safety in fieldwork. As already discussed (see Section 5.2), building sufficient trust with the community through good rapport is critical to successfully conducting fieldwork and generating data (Taylor & Bogdan, 1996). However, as an acceptance-based security strategy, this rapport can also function as one of the researcher's most important security resources in complex environments (Boisen, 2018). Working on rapport in uncertain settings, however, is not without complications. Goldstein (2014) is highly successful in pointing out that rapport development is particularly difficult in contexts with high levels of violence. For this reason, it has been pointed out that in such contexts it is important to be extremely vigilant in identifying or creating the field role (Brown, 2009; Lee, 1995; Sluka, 1995). In this vein, Sluka (1995) emphasizes the importance of avoiding at all costs the assignment of a role that may be seen as a threat to those you work with, and actively seeking to fit into safer and more accepted roles in the community (as cited by Boisen, 2018).

Some authors refer to this method as a basic strategy to deal with an insecure environment. Goldstein (2014) calls this an ethnographic approach. This can also be understood as a strategy of imitation, adoption, or emulation, based on the researcher's ability to observe local behaviors and adopt them to reduce the risks they face. Similarly, based on his fieldwork with street children in Brazil, Kovats-Bernat (2002) emphasizes the need to develop what he calls localized ethics, which consists of following the advice and recommendations of local people (or your collaborators, if you are working with more experienced outsiders, see Section 5.2) regarding the issues one should be prudent not to discuss with others and, furthermore, adopting local behaviors to protect oneself and those around one in fieldwork.

The issue of risk in fieldwork concerns not only unsafe environments, but also the risks posed by the enormous inequalities and access issues facing researchers in the field. The recent scope of publications, news articles, and discussions about the widespread prevalence of inequities and safety risks in fieldwork suggests that there is a clear and urgent need for institutions to address how to make fieldwork safe, accessible, and welcoming for all (Demery & Pipkin, 2020; Jha, 2021; McGill et al., 2021; National Center for Science and Engineering Statistics, 2017; Olcott & Downen, 2020; Viglione, 2020). For researchers with marginalized identities, such as racial and ethnic minorities, researchers who are caregivers, researchers with disabilities, or those who identify as lesbian, gay, bisexual, transgender, queer, intersex, asexual, or with another sexual orientation or gender identity (LGBTQIA+), field experiences are more likely to be negative, hostile, or dangerous, and they may experience additional disadvantages due to intersecting identities (Clancy et al., 2017).

Boisen (2018) suggests incorporating risk analysis and assessment tools into the planning phase to enhance the ability to prevent and mitigate risk in fieldwork and provide elements to appropriately weigh acceptable levels of risk in projects. Incorporating these analysis and risk mitigation procedures in the planning phase and during fieldwork will help to improve the researcher's safety conditions and, consequently, the successful implementation of the research project.

References

Agar, M. (2008). *The professional stranger: An informal introduction to ethnography* (2nd ed.). Emerald.

Amir, D., & McAuliffe, K. (2020). Cross-cultural, developmental psychology: Integrating approaches and key insights. *Evolution and Human Behavior, 41*(5), 430–444. https://doi.org/10.1016/j.evolhumbehav.2020.06.006

Apicella, C., Norenzayan, A., & Henrich, J. (2020). Beyond WEIRD: A review of the last decade and a look ahead to the global laboratory of the future. *Evolution and Human Behavior, 41*(5), 319–329. https://doi.org/10.1016/j.evolhumbehav.2020.07.015

Assembly of First Nations. (2009). First Nations Ethics Guide on Research and Aboriginal Traditional Knowledge. https://arcticnet.ulaval.ca/wp-content/uploads/2022/04/

ASSEMBLY-OF-FIIRST-NATIONS_ethics-guide-on-research-and-AB-knowledge-1.pdf

Australian Institute of Aboriginal and Torres Strait Islander Studies. (2020). AIATSIS Code of Ethics for Aboriginal and Torres Strait Islander Research. *Australian Institute of Aboriginal and Torres Strait Islander Studies.* http://aiatsis.gov.au/ethics

Barrett, H. C. (2020). Deciding what to observe: Thoughts for a post-WEIRD generation. *Evolution and Human Behavior, 41*(5), 445–453. https://doi.org/10.1016/j.evolhumbehav.2020.05.006

Boisen, S. (2018). Evaluación y reducción del riesgo en el trabajo de campo. *Alteridades, 28*(56), 73–84. https://doi.org/10.24275/uam/izt/dcsh/alteridades/2018v28n56/Hjorth

Boyette, A. H. (2019). Autonomy, cognitive development, and the socialisation of cooperation in foragers: Aka children's views of sharing and caring. *Hunter Gatherer Research, 3*(3), 475–500. https://doi.org/10.3828/hgr.2017.23

Boyette, A. H., & Lew-Levy, S. (2019). Variation in cultural models of resource sharing between Congo Basin foragers and farmers: Implications for Learning to Share. In D. Friesem & N. Lavi (Eds). *Inter-Disciplinary Perspectives on Sharing among Hunter-Gatherers in the Past and Present.* The McDonald Institute.

Boyette, A. H., & Lew-Levy, S. (2021). Socialization, Autonomy, and Cooperation: Insights from Task Assignment Among the Egalitarian BaYaka. *Ethos*, etho.12284. https://doi.org/10.1111/etho.12284

Broesch, T., Crittenden, A. N., Beheim, B. A., Blackwell, A. D., Bunce, J. A., Colleran, H., Hagel, K., Kline, M., McElreath, R., Nelson, R. G., Pisor, A. C., Prall, S., Pretelli, I., Purzycki, B., Quinn, E. A., Ross, C., Scelza, B., Starkweather, K., Stieglitz, J., & Mulder, M. B. (2020). Navigating cross-cultural research: Methodological and ethical considerations. *Proceedings of the Royal Society B: Biological Sciences, 287*(1935), 20201245. https://doi.org/10.1098/rspb.2020.1245

Brown, S. (2009). Dilemmas of Self-representation and Conduct in the Field. In C. L. Sriram, J. C. King, J. A. Mertus, O. Martin-Ortega, & J. Herman (Eds). *Surviving Field Research. Working in Violent and Difficult Situations* (pp. 213–226). Routledge.

Bruno, D., Pope-Caldwell, S. M., Haberl, K., Hanus, D., Haun, D., Leisterer-Peoples, S., Mauritz, S., Neldner, K., Sibilsky, A., & Stengelin, R. (2022). Ethical guidelines for good practice in cross-cultural research. https://doi.org/10.17617/2.3391449

Castro-Gómez, S., & Grosfoguel, R. (2007). Prólogo. Giro decolonial, teoría crítica y pensamiento heterárquico. In S. Castro-Gómez & R. Grosfoguel (Eds). *El giro decolonial. Reflexiones para una diversidad epistémica más allá del capitalismo global* (pp. 9–23). Siglo del Hombre.

Chilisa, B. (2019). *Indigenous research methodologies* (2nd ed.). Sage.

Clancy, K. B. H., Lee, K. M. N., Rodgers, E. M., & Richey, C. (2017). Double jeopardy in astronomy and planetary science: Women of color face greater risks of gendered and racial harassment. *Journal of Geophysical Research: Planets, 122*(7), 1610–1623. https://doi.org/10.1002/2017JE005256

De Sousa Santos, B. (2009). A Non-Occidentalist West?: Learned Ignorance and Ecology of Knowledge. *Theory, Culture & Society, 26*(7–8), 103–125. https://doi.org/10.1177/0263276409348079

Demery, A.-J. C., & Pipkin, M. A. (2020). Safe fieldwork strategies for at-risk individuals, their supervisors and institutions. *Nature Ecology & Evolution, 5*(1), 5–9. https://doi.org/10.1038/s41559-020-01328-5

Fournier, C., Stewart, S., Adams, J., Shirt, C., & Mahabir, E. (2023). Systemic disruptions: Decolonizing indigenous research ethics using indigenous knowledges. *Research Ethics*, 17470161231169205. https://doi.org/10.1177/17470161231169205

Goldstein, D. M. (2014). Qualitative Research in Dangerous Places: Becoming an "Ethnographer" of Violence and Personal Safety (1; Drugs, Security and Democracy Program, Working Papers on Research Security). Social Science Research Council. http://webarchive.ssrc.org/working-papers/DSD_ResearchSecurity_01_Goldstein.pdf

Greenfield, P. M., Keller, H., Fuligni, A., & Maynard, A. (2003). Cultural Pathways Through Universal Development. *Annual Review of Psychology, 54*(1), 461–490. https://doi.org/10.1146/annurev.psych.54.101601.145221

Gurven, M. (2004a). Does market exposure affect economic behavior? The ultimatum game and public goods game among the Tsimane' of Bolivia. In J. Henrich, R. Boyd, S. Bowles, H. Gintis, E. Fehr, & C. Camerer (Eds). *Foundations of Human Sociality: Ethnography and Experiments in 15 Small-Scale Societies* (pp. 194–231). Oxford University Press

Gurven, M. (2004b). Economic Games Among the Amazonian Tsimane: Exploring the Roles of Market Access, Costs of Giving, and Cooperation on Pro-Social Game Behavior. *Experimental Economics, 7*(1), 5–24. https://doi.org/10.1023/A:1026256404208

Gurven, M. D. (2018). Broadening horizons: Sample diversity and socioecological theory are essential to the future of psychological science. *Proceedings of the National Academy of Sciences, 115*(45), 11420–11427. https://doi.org/10.1073/pnas.1720433115

Hayward, A., Sjoblom, E., Sinclair, S., & Cidro, J. (2021). A New Era of Indigenous Research: Community-based Indigenous Research Ethics Protocols in Canada. *Journal of Empirical Research on Human Research Ethics, 16*(4), 403–417. https://doi.org/10.1177/15562646211023705

Hedgecoe, A. (2016). Reputational Risk, Academic Freedom and Research Ethics Review. *Sociology, 50*(3), 486–501. https://doi.org/10.1177/0038038515590756

Hewlett, B. S., Fouts, H. N., Boyette, A. H., & Hewlett, B. L. (2011). Social learning among Congo Basin hunter-gatherers. *Philosophical Transactions of the Royal Society B, 366*, 1168–1178. https://doi.org/10.1098/rstb.2010.037

Howell, N. (1990). *Surviving fieldwork: A report of the Advisory Panel on Health and Safety in Fieldwork, American Anthropological Association.* American Anthropological Association.

Hudson, M., Milne, M., Reynolds, P., Russell, K., & Smith, B. (2010). Te Ara Tika: Guidelines for Māori research ethics: A framework for researchers and ethics committee members. https://www.hrc.govt.nz/resources/te-ara-tika-guidelines-maori-research-ethics-0

Ice, G. H., Dufour, D. L., & Stevens, N. J. (2015). *Disasters in field research: Preparing for and coping with unexpected events.* Rowman & Littlefield Publishing Group.

Jamieson, J. (2002). Negotiating Danger in Fieldwork on Crime: A Researcher's Tale. In G. Lee-Treweek & S. Linkogle (Eds). *Danger in the Field. Risk and Ethics in Social Research* (pp. 61–71). Routledge.

Jha, N. (2021). The Smithsonian's #MeToo Moment. *BuzzFeed News.*

Johnson, A. (1991). Regional Comparative Field Research. *Behavior Science Research, 25*(1–4), 3–22. https://doi.org/10.1177/106939719102500102

Kanngiesser, P., Schäfer, M., Herrmann, E., Zeidler, H., Haun, D., & Tomasello, M. (2022). Children across societies enforce conventional norms but in culturally variable ways. *Proceedings of the National Academy of Sciences, 119*(1), e2112521118. https://doi.org/10.1073/pnas.2112521118

Karasik, L. B., Tamis-LeMonda, C. S., Ossmy, O., & Adolph, K. E. (2018). The ties that bind: Cradling in Tajikistan. *PLoS ONE, 13*(10), e0204428. https://doi.org/10.1371/journal.pone.0204428

Kovats-Bernat, J. C. (2002). Negotiating Dangerous Fields: Pragmatic Strategies for Fieldwork Amid Violence and Terror. *American Anthropologist, 104*(1), 208–222. https://doi.org/10.1525/aa.2002.104.1.208

Krys, K., De Almeida, I., Wasiel, A., & Vignoles, V. L. (2024). WEIRD–Confucian comparisons: Ongoing cultural biases in psychology's evidence base and some recommendations for improving global representation. *American Psychologist.* https://doi.org/10.1037/amp0001298

LeCompte, M. D., & Schensul, J. J. (2015). *Ethics in ethnography: A mixed methods approach* (2nd ed.). AltaMira Press.

Lee, R. (1995). *Dangerous Fieldwork*. Sage. https://doi.org/10.4135/9781412983839

Léon, M., & Cristia, A. (2024). Data Protection Handbook for Long-Form Recording Research: Navigating Data Protection Laws across the Globe. https://doi.org/10.31219/osf.io/dy4wt

Leonard, W. R., Reyes-García, V., Tanner, S., Rosinger, A., Schultz, A., Vadez, V., Zhang, R., & Godoy, R. (2015). The Tsimane' Amazonian Panel Study (TAPS): Nine years (2002–2010) of annual data available to the public. *Economics & Human Biology, 19*, 51–61. https://doi.org/10.1016/j.ehb.2015.07.004

Louis, R. P. (2007). Can You Hear us Now? Voices from the Margin: Using Indigenous Methodologies in Geographic Research. *Geographical Research, 45*(2), 130–139. https://doi.org/10.1111/j.1745-5871.2007.00443.x

Martin-Ortega, O., & Herman, J. (2009). There and Back. Surviving Field Research in Violent and Difficult Situations. In C. L. Sriram, J. C. King, J. A. Mertus, O. Martin-Ortega, & J. Herman (Eds). *Surviving Field Research. Working in Violent and Difficult Situations* (pp. 227–241). Routledge.

McGill, B. M., Foster, M. J., Pruitt, A. N., Thomas, S. G., Arsenault, E. R., Hanschu, J., Wahwahsuck, K., Cortez, E., Zarek, K., Loecke, T. D., & Burgin, A. J. (2021). You are welcome here: A practical guide to diversity, equity, and inclusion for undergraduates embarking on an ecological research experience. *Ecology and Evolution, 11*(8), 3636–3645. https://doi.org/10.1002/ece3.7321

Morelli, C. (2012). Teaching in the rainforest: Exploring Matses children's affective engagement and multisensory experiences in the classroom environment. *Teaching Anthropology, 2*(2), 53–65. https://doi.org/10.22582/ta.v2i2.349

National Center for Science and Engineering Statistics. (2017). *Women, minorities, and persons with disabilities in science and engineering* (pp. 17–310). National Science Foundation.

Nercesian, V. (2014). *Manual teórico-práctico de gramática wichí.* Formosa: Editorial Universidad Nacional de Formosa.

Nosek, B. A., Ebersole, C. R., DeHaven, A. C., & Mellor, D. T. (2018). The preregistration revolution. Proceedings of the National Academy of Sciences of the United States of America, 115(11), 2600–2606. https://doi.org/10.1073/pnas.1708274114

Nyembezi, C. L. S. (1954). *Zulu Proverbs*. Witwatersrand University Press.

Olcott, A. N., & Downen, M. R. (2020). The challenges of fieldwork for LGBTQ+ geoscientists. *Eos, 101,* 22–24.

Pérez, A., Pérez, E., Taverna, A., & Baiocchi, M. (2017a). *Hal'o*. Formosa: EDUNaF.

Pérez, A., Pérez, E., Taverna, A., & Baiocchi, M. (2017b). *Laloy*. Formosa: EDUNaF.

Pérez, A., Pérez, E., Taverna, A., & Baiocchi, M. (2017c). *Tshotoy*. Formosa: EDUNaF.

Pérez, A., Pérez, E., Taverna, A., & Baiocchi, M. (2017d). *Tshotoy fwiy'ohen*. Formosa: EDUNaF.

Pérez, A., Pérez, E., Taverna, A., & Baiocchi, M. (2017e). *Tshotoy inhot lheley*. Formosa: EDUNaF.

Pérez, A., Pérez, E., Taverna, A., & Baiocchi, M. (2021). *Hunhat lheley (Habitantes de la Tierra)*. EDUViM-EDUNaF.

Rochat, P., Dias, M. D. G., Guo Liping, Broesch, T., Passos-Ferreira, C., Winning, A., & Berg, B. (2009). Fairness in Distributive Justice by 3- and 5-Year-Olds Across Seven Cultures. *Journal of Cross-Cultural Psychology, 40*(3), 416–442. https://doi.org/10.1177/0022022109332844

Rudzki, E. N., Kuebbing, S. E., Clark, D. R., Gharaibeh, B., Janecka, M. J., Kramp, R., Kohl, K. D., Mastalski, T., Ohmer, M. E. B., Turcotte, M. M., & Richards-Zawacki, C. L. (2022). A guide for developing a field research safety manual that explicitly considers risks for marginalized identities in the sciences. *Methods in Ecology and Evolution, 13*(11), 2318–2330. https://doi.org/10.1111/2041-210X.13970

Schrag, Z. (2010). *Ethical Imperialism*. Johns Hopkins University Press. https://doi.org/10.1353/book.471

Schroeder, D., Cook, J., Hirsch, F., Fenet, S., & Muthuswamy, V. (Eds). (2018). *Ethics Dumping: Case Studies from North-South Research Collaborations*. Springer. https://doi.org/10.1007/978-3-319-64731-9

Sluka, J. A. (1995). Reflections on Managing Danger in Fieldwork. In C. Nordstrom & A. C. G. Robben (Eds). *Fieldwork under Fire. Contemporary Studies of Violence and Survival* (pp. 276–294). University of California Press.

Smith, L. T. (2022). *Decolonizing methodologies: Research and indigenous peoples* (3rd ed.). Bloomsbury Academic.

South African San Institute. (2017). San Code of Research Ethics. https://www.khwattu.org/exhibitions/the-san-code-ethics/

Spradley, J. P. (1979). *The ethnographic interview*. Holt, Rinehart and Winston.

Stark, L. J. M. (2012). *Behind closed doors: IRBs and the making of ethical research*. The University of Chicago Press.

Tauri, J. M. (2018). Research ethics, informed consent and the disempowerment of First Nation peoples. *Research Ethics, 14*(3), 1–14. https://doi.org/10.1177/1747016117739935

Taverna, A. S., & Baiocchi, M. C. (2021). Elaboración de sistemas semióticos wichí con una metodología colaborativa: Libros infantiles ilustrados Hunhat lheley (Habitantes de la Tierra).

Taylor, S. J., & Bogdan, R. (1996). *Introducción a los métodos cualitativos de investigación: La búsqueda de significados*. Paidós.

Tuck, E. (2009). Suspending Damage: A Letter to Communities. *Harvard Educational Review, 79*(3), 409–428. https://doi.org/10.17763/haer.79.3.n0016675661t3n15

United Nations. (2009). Directrices sobre las cuestiones relativas a los pueblos indígenas. Grupo de las Naciones Unidas para el desarrollo. *United Nations*. https://www.acnur.org/fileadmin/Documentos/Publicaciones/2010/7374.pdf

Vidal, A., & Kuchenbrandt, I. (2015). Challenges of linguistic diversity in Formosa. In C. Stolz (Ed.). *Language Empires in Comparative Perspective* (pp. 89–112). DE GRUYTER. https://doi.org/10.1515/9783110408362.89

Viglione, G. (2020). Racism and harassment are common in field research—Scientists are speaking up. *Nature, 585*(7823), 15–16. https://doi.org/10.1038/d41586-020-02328-y

Weisman, K., & Luhrmann, T. M. (2020). What anthropologists can learn from psychologists, and the other way around. *Journal of the Royal Anthropological Institute, 26*(S1), 131–147. https://doi.org/10.1111/1467-9655.13245

Westmarland, L. (2002). Taking the Flak: Operational Policing, Fear and Violence. In G. Lee-Treweek & S. Linkogle (Eds). *Danger in the Field. Risk and Ethics in Social Research* (pp. 26–42). Routledge.

Zidarich, M., & colaboradores. (2006). Tsalanawu. Libro de lectura para la Alfabetización Inicial. In M. Zidarich & comunidades wichí del Bemerjo (Formosa) (Eds). *Auxiliares docentes de Sauzalito (Chaco)* (2nd ed.). Universidad de Buenos Aires.

6. Negotiating fieldwork challenges: Voices from the field

Coordinated by Jing Xu

Drawing from the main narrative device of personal storytelling, this chapter includes voices of researchers from different generations, cultural backgrounds, career stages and institutional settings. It summarizes what lessons researchers have learned, how they overcome challenges, and what strategies they have used to turn challenges into opportunities. Various personal narratives highlight the interactive nature, the polyvocal dimensions, and the intersubjective experience of fieldwork. Taken together, the core message of this chapter is that fieldwork is inherently an interpersonal process shaped by power structures, institutional constraints, social relationships, gender dynamics, ethical frameworks, emotional sensibilities, and historical contingencies. Therefore, as researchers we need to attune ourselves to all these aspects of fieldwork experience. We need to remind ourselves that our scientific conduct is intricately connected with moral responsibilities and political realities.

6.1. Why storytelling?

Jing Xu

What is fieldwork? For anthropologists, the very term 'fieldwork' carries a nearly sacred significance: fieldwork is not just a particular type of research or a particular mode of gathering data. It is how we get to know the world we are interested in. In the field, we immerse ourselves in the communities we study in order to

©2025 Jing Xu, et al., CC BY-NC 4.0

https://doi.org/10.11647/OBP.0440.06

understand people in their own contexts, and simultaneously, we get to better understand ourselves. We hear other people's stories, and we blend ourselves in. Therefore, we commit to a distinct epistemological orientation in the field, that is, no matter what concrete methods we employ, participant observation, interviews, experiments, questionnaire surveys, etc., our knowledge about human behavior and culture always emerges within social contexts and through social interactions and communication (Xu, 2024).

Due to its inter-subjective and often cross-cultural nature, fieldwork is inherently messy and unpredictable. Yet research publications tend to highlight the final product of fieldwork, e.g., the beautiful theories, the rigorous methods, the neat data which is so fruitful and orderly. Such final products tend to obscure the challenges and dilemmas of the fieldwork process, with some of those challenges unique to studying with children, and some of those dilemmas rooted in the researcher's identity and positionality. As our collective attempt to spotlight the fieldwork process itself, this chapter presents multiple voices of researchers from diverse backgrounds, working on various topics, and across different geographical regions, about how we negotiate challenges and find solutions. Some parts of this chapter (Sections 6.6 and 6.12) contain depiction and discussion of violent speech, sexual trauma, or trauma related to death and loss. Such content may be emotionally challenging for readers. Yet it is important to address such difficult issues in this chapter and honestly reflect on the complexity and precarity of fieldwork.

In what follows, Hewlett highlights the inherently polyvocal nature of fieldwork experience and the importance of respecting our research interlocutors' narratives of their own life stories. Drawing from large-scale cross-cultural research, Rawlings discusses the pitfalls and dilemmas of applying standardized experimental protocols across different cultural contexts and raises important questions for future research. Scaff details her experience of reassessing research plans in the field due to unexpected contingencies and disruptions. Gender is also an important factor shaping fieldwork experience: Abels reflects on how pregnancy and motherhood affects her fieldwork plans as well as how she coped with the challenges of raising children during fieldwork. An anonymous researcher bravely shares her experience as a victim of sexual harassment in the field and tells us how she survived that traumatic experience. Tian, Baldiani, Ndlovu, and Rosun share unique stories of how researchers' positionality affects their fieldwork and the kind of knowledge they develop. Their experiences and reflections together inspire us to transcend a simplistic, insider-outsider binary framework and work toward a more nuanced understanding of positionality. The final two sections offer conceptual resources and personal stories on fieldwork research ethics: Oppong provides a compelling argument against the current, western-centered framework of research ethics processes and prompts us to rethink the meaning of 'decolonization'; Hewlett advocates for 'compassionate research' as a basic guideline for fieldwork, through reflecting on traumatic experiences she and her research interlocutors encountered. "The field," as Hewlett (2019, p. 28) points out, "is a hard teacher, demanding that we as researchers question our personal morals, our professional ethics, and our responsibility to those who share their homes and lives so generously with us."

6.2. Many voices, many stories: The importance of polyvocality

Bonnie Hewlett

This story begins one hot afternoon with a knock on my door. Standing in my yard was a group of about eight Ngandu women and Adoxi, my Ngandu research assistant. "They want to talk to you," she said to me, "They want you to stop talking to the children and start talking to them." The women crowded around her, nodding in agreement. "They want you to hear about their lives. They want to tell you their stories." Not wanting to be left out, when Aka friends of mine heard about my work with the Ngandu women, they too wanted to work with me, to teach me. So I began listening as they told me what it means to be women of the forest and village, women of the Congo Basin.

I would have been happy to continue my research with the Central African 'teenagers' as it was amazingly interesting, very informative, and usually fun, but my study focus shifted abruptly with that knock on my door and I began talking in-depth with 16 women, eight from each community, and later included another 20 Aka and 20 Ngandu women to check the reliability and validity of the data. (The published monograph narrowed the focus to four women, two from each community [Hewlett, 2012].) This and other research continued over 12 years as I listened to the many stories of these women, their husbands, children, and friends. In multiple stories, we see the variety of ways individuals confront life's challenges, finding their own paths and ways of being.

Much of ethnographic research occurs as we sit 'around the fire', living with and listening to the life stories of people from around the world, but I know at times it was difficult for the many women I spoke to, who opened their homes, hearts, and lives, sharing their individual moments of everydayness with me, a very strange stranger (the anthropologist). But they did so because, they often told me, they wanted their stories heard, their lives known.

Nigerian novelist Chimamanda Adichie eloquently explains the importance of polyvocality:

> The single story creates stereotypes. And the problem with stereotypes is not that they are untrue, but that they are incomplete. They make one story become the only story. I've always felt that it is impossible to engage properly with a place or a person without engaging with all of the stories of that place and that person. The consequence of the single story is this: It robs people of dignity. It makes our recognition of our equal humanity difficult. It emphasizes how we are different rather than how we are similar (Adichie, 2010).

To understand these women's lives, as Adichie illustrates, multiple life stories have been the foundation of my research. I feel strongly that it is essential to pay attention to the multiple stories of everydayness, the life-stuff moments, for many reasons. Polyvocality, the stories and experiences shared by many voices, bring to light how ordinary life around the world extraordinarily unfolds in a way that a single story might not.

Polyvocality has been part of the methodological toolkit of ethnographic research for some time, particularly following the advent of post-modernism and post-feminist theory (see for example, Abu-Lughod, 1992; Wolf, 1992; Behar, 1993; Chapman Sanger, 2003; Connolly-Shaffer, 2012). Polyvocality is a narrative strategy encouraging transparency of methods and data, giving power and pre-eminence to multiple ways of knowing. Two examples from my research in Central Africa and Ethiopia come to mind.

Ngandu women recalling their childhood lessons:

> Our parents taught us that the husband and wife are not the same, they are not equal, because if you see a father and mother walking together, you do not know who is the father, who is the mother, who will do the work?

> When I was maybe 6 or 8 years old I began to work. If I was playing the dancing games with my friends, it was fun, but if my mother asked for help and I refused, my mother would hit me. My mother would take me from my friends to work in the fields and tell me, "You cannot play with your friends. Now you must work." I thought to myself, "This is bad to work in the fields."

> My grandmother taught me lessons of being a woman, but grandfather also taught me. They taught me that you work hard and show respect to people. The most important person in the house is the man, because the man commands. The women give all the care in the house, but men command, they give money for things like soap, clothes, medicine, and other things. I was taught that women are stupid if they try to command. It is the man who commands the house.

Aka women on being a child:

> When I became a little bigger I would watch my parents and I began to learn. My parents taught me that when you are a woman, that each day you decide what to do and together you do that with your husband. The work of males and females is not so different. If the woman is tired, the man will look for the wood and prepare the fire, get the water and cook the food.

> Mostly I played and played and did only a little work...

> My best memory when I was little was playing in the forest with my friends. I had so many friends and we loved each other. I remember

singing and dancing and swinging in the trees. Our parents would call for us, but we were playing so we did not come! This was our good fun.

The Aka and Ngandu live, and make a living from, a similar environment. They have a long-shared history. They have similar fertility and infant mortality rates. Yet they have adapted to their environment in very distinct and striking ways. They have very different kinship and political systems, modes of production, gender roles, husband-wife relations, and patterns of childcare. They each have differing stories to share.

I found much the same in Ethiopia where I have been conducting research for the past 12 years in an Ethiopian orphanage; that is, the human experience yields distinctive, and individual interpretations and understandings. In my study, I found that most of the children had either a mother or father, and/or an extended family. I spoke to those parents and families of the so-called 'relinquished' children and what follows are a few of their responses:

> When I gave my child away and I signed the papers, my hands were shaking and there were tears in my eyes. I feel sad. When we are together, at holiday ceremonies, eating together, my daughter asks me if he [his three-year-old son given to the orphanage] will be eating at a ceremony too. It is very hard to forget. —Birth father.

> Adoption means when you have a fatherless or motherless child, you give your child to another family to give good care. I gave my baby away because if she lives with me she may die. — Birth mother.

> It is best for your children to be adopted to America because if a child were to be adopted nearby by a family member or in another village your heart can't cool by seeing the child or by having the child nearby. By having a child sent away, your heart can cool and your child will have more and further distance means less worries. — Birth family.

> Babies are thrown away if they are too close to blood. Or relatives, like a grandmother will bring in her granddaughter because she can no longer protect her from rape. A mother or father may be dying of AIDS and will bring their child in, so they can have peace before they die, knowing their children will be taken care of. Or if they are too poor to grow their child they will bring them in. Sometimes an

older sibling will bring in younger siblings. There are also many unwed mothers who abandon their babies. Plus there are referrals from churches, district MOWA offices... — Orphanage owner.

The main reason for the increment of abandonment is the refus[al] of the government to legally receive children from the mothers who relinquish their child to the orphanage. Now the government or orphanages are refusing to take the child from the children's families, for that reason the people prefer to throw their children somewhere. The government refuses [and] discourages the adoption and by preferring the children being [...] with their relatives. — Social worker.

Many stories, many voices, woven together to present an intimate view of the infinitely complex world we live in, bringing to light our similarities, our differences, and perhaps ultimately bridging the gaps separating our understanding of one another. What might seem to be vast barriers stretching out between us, are often in fact partitions that are quite thin and permeable when sensitively approached, when gently challenged. And hopefully, as we listen to these stories, we come to have a deeper understanding of and appreciation for each individual.

As Adichie expresses, "Stories have been used to dispossess and to malign. But stories can also be used to empower, and to humanize. Stories can break the dignity of a people. But stories can also repair that broken dignity" (Adichie, 2010). So, let's come and sit awhile, listen to a few stories and begin that repair. Let's disrupt the silence, poke at the partition, and bridge the gap. Because these many stories matter, these many lives deserve to be known.

6.3. When standardized experiments travel across cultures

Bruce Rawlings

Over recent years, the pace and scope of cross-cultural research has rapidly expanded in the social sciences, in response to high-profile criticisms of an over-reliance on affluent and educated western populations (Broesch et al., 2020, 2022; Burger et al., 2022;

Henrich, 2020; Henrich et al., 2010; Nielsen et al., 2017; Sanches de Oliveira & Baggs, 2023). This expansion has diversified participant samples, bringing new and important insights into variation and consistency in human behavior across geographically and culturally diverse populations. In turn, however, it also brought to light new methodological challenges that we must face to ensure that the quality of our research and conclusions are optimal. In this section, I will use my own experiences to focus on some of the challenges we face when developing experimental protocols in cross-cultural research.

I was part of an ambitious, large-scale multi-population project investigating cognitive and social development in children across the globe. Our study communities spanned North and South America, Africa, Asia, and Oceania, those living in industrialized cities and those living in small-scale foraging communities. At the start of the project, my team and I spent hours, days, and weeks developing protocols to run cognitive experiments in our different populations. We scoured the literature, had multiple meetings, and lengthy discussions about whether we should use this task or that one, how experimenters should behave during experimental procedures, how long tasks should be, and so on and so forth.

These were not easy decisions, but eventually, we developed and refined our protocols and piloted our tasks on local (western) children. Much of this is part of a routine many laboratories go through when starting new projects. The key difference, of course, that we faced compared to many other labs is that we were going to run this battery of tasks on multiple populations of children. Anyway, after rigorous piloting, we were feeling fairly confident that we had designed a good set of protocols to run. Task materials were distributed to our research teams around the world, and we established detailed training programs for local researchers who would conduct the experiments.

However, we encountered some unexpected problems during the project. These varied in nature, but many of them related to our protocols. Some of our protocols were designed such that the experimenter should be completely neutral and not engage much with the child during testing (because, based on existing literature this was known to impact performance on the task). In some communities this is no problem, but in others, it is extremely strange (and even rude) to behave this way. In others, the materials and instructions we used—3D plastic shapes, pipe cleaners, pictures of animals, rule-following—which were all standard and widely used in western contexts, were completely unusual and occasionally even a little abnormal in some of our study populations outside of post-industrialized ones. Some words or phrases we initially used for protocol administration did not translate well to some languages and cultures.

More fundamentally, of course, the actual context of a child being alone with an (unfamiliar) adult, being observed and monitored, is much more familiar and comfortable to those who have grown up in formal schooling systems, where teachers frequently monitor academic progress and administer tests to do so, than to those who have not.

This dilemma produces a trade-off: should we aim for comparable cross-population protocols that may not capture exactly what we want (or think) in different societies but facilitate direct comparisons, or should we risk forgoing comparability and develop culturally grounded protocols which are likely to (and arguably should) vary from one cultural context to another? Should we have experimenters who are friendly, engaging and who build rapports with children in one population, but others who are neutral and disengaged in others? Should we run the same task with different materials across communities? Should we run different tasks completely? How does this impact behavior and our data?

Whether, and how well, protocols that are designed and validated in one cultural context transfer to others is a topic gaining increasing traction (Broesch et al., 2020, 2022; Burger et al., 2022; Hruschka et al., 2018; Kline et al., 2018). These are not easy decisions and researchers should carefully consider the cultural contexts they are studying when developing experimental protocols for administration across populations. Recent research has showed, for example, that careful engagement with local stakeholders and community members is a vital component of protocol development and avoids researchers bringing in any biases they may have inadvertently developed, and affords more accurate conclusions (Holding et al., 2018; Hruschka et al., 2018; Zuilkowski et al., 2016). It also contributes to equitable and participatory research practices, which should be a priority of any collaborative, cross-cultural project (Broesch et al., 2020; Urassa et al., 2021).

6.4. Reassessing your plans

Camila Scaff

My research project aims to describe children's vocal interactions and language development. I face unique challenges in the course of this work because of where I collect data: among the Tsimane people of the Bolivian Amazon.

I use highly specialized technology in my fieldwork. Among my tools are both budget-friendly and high-end recorders, with the latter requiring proprietary software for data extraction. To accommodate children of various ages, I use custom-sized t-shirts, specially designed to hold the recorders securely. I also rely on two laptops and a handful of tablets for data collection.

This collection of highly sensitive electronics provokes a fair amount of anxiety in me, because the Amazonian climate is famously known to be very humid and hostile to electronic devices. With no opportunity to test their performance beforehand, I could only hope that at least one recorder would withstand the challenging conditions.

For this project, I depended very strongly on my technical equipment. Without normal access to electricity, I had instead to rely on portable solar panels. Prior to departure, I researched the best portable solar panels available to power laptops in the field and tested them at my university. However, due to insufficient sunlight in the Parisian garden of my university, they failed to charge the computer. I crossed my fingers and did some kind of prayer that they would work better in Bolivia.

Before my first ever trip to a Tsimane community, I was also apprehensive about whether the locals would even accept my presence, let alone allow me to place the small recorders on their children. To my relief, the people were super welcoming, and the prospect of engaging in research activities particularly excited the young mothers. Even luckier, language research was especially appreciated; Tsimane are still mostly monolingual, and many worry about the loss of their language, as younger new generations increasingly learn Spanish in lieu of their mother tongue.

I was very lucky that the village chief, known as the Corregidor, suggested that his own children should be the first participants. This event kickstarted the entire study by setting a popular example in the community. All of a sudden, I found myself sitting down with pen and paper (along with my research assistant and different mothers in the local community), working up an appointment calendar for everyone's involvement in the study.

We thoughtfully administered both the affordable and high-end recorders, making sure to choose vests appropriate for 20-month-old and 36-month-old children. We immediately encountered an unforeseen challenge–the vests we brought were much too large for the Tsimane children. Rather than panic or attempt to ship new vests to Bolivia (which would likely take weeks to arrive, if ever), we adapted our plans, providing the 20-month-old with a 12-month-sized t-shirt and the 3-year-old with a 2-year-old-sized one. This seemingly trivial inconvenience, however, was consequential; it altered the sample age group distribution from what I had initially planned to observe. I couldn't record children younger than 6 months, because I didn't have the appropriate vest for them. However, I could instead record older children than I expected. This opened a new and interesting possibility.

The following day, I returned to the participants' homes to collect the data. The children didn't seem bothered by the recorders at all. Extracting data from the affordable recorder was simple and only took a few seconds. However, the high-end recorder posed a challenge, with a staggering 13-hour estimated extraction time. Daylight hours are fleeting without normal electricity, and my computer's battery doesn't last more than an hour or two. I swiftly set up the solar panels, and by a stroke of luck, they functioned properly! My jubilation was short-lived, though, as the blazing sun soon became too intense, causing the panels to overheat and stop working after just 30 minutes. Without stable electricity access, it was impossible to extract the data from the expensive recorders, so I could only use them once each before returning to town and having access to unlimited electricity again (notwithstanding rolling blackouts, which are frequent in the town).

These serious setbacks forced me to reassess my work plans. First, the age group of interest shifted towards children who were older than initially intended, and second, I was pushed to rely predominantly on budget-friendly recorders for the rest of the data collection period. These changes seemed trivial at first, but had far-reaching and interesting consequences for the aftermath of my trip to Bolivia.

By the end of the trip, the majority of data was collected using these low-budget recorders, rendering the algorithm that typically analyzes the data (normally collected by the more expensive devices) entirely unusable. Ultimately, though, it was a moot issue, because this algorithm was trained on western data, and designed mainly for identifying adult speech; it could not be simply adapted to meet our needs in this unique context.

We explored alternative methods to analyze the recordings, refusing to let setbacks hinder our progress, and the challenges we faced in the field spurred us to develop innovative solutions. The lab that originally sponsored this research project soon evolved into a pioneering hub for the democratization of this technology in child language studies worldwide.

Preliminary results from the recordings unveiled fascinating insights. As children age, their language input shifts, with older children becoming the primary source of language they hear. These findings opened up exciting new research paths, prompting us to delve deeper into the intricacies of language development in young minds.

My fieldwork experience, though arduous, presented a gateway to invaluable discoveries and broader applications. The uncontrolled setting of fieldwork proved to be a fertile ground for innovation to meet unusual and unexpected challenges, shaping not only the research but the technology itself. With ongoing research exploring the mysteries of language development beyond the lab, new insights will have untold impacts on global language studies.

6.5. Gender and precarity: Reflections on being a mother and fieldwork

Monika Abels

When I started planning to go to Tanzania to work with the Hadza, I had already been a researcher for many years with much fieldwork experience, particularly with families in rural India. While living in Germany and the US, I had worked in India nearly annually from the time I was a master's student until I finished a post-doc project. I had been through moments of cultural shock and had learned to navigate a multitude of social situations in the field and daily life in a radically different environment.

For my new research project with the Hadza, my life situation had changed, however. During the planning phase of the project, I became pregnant. I was still determined to do the data collection during the second trimester, having read that was usually a good time of the pregnancy for most women. While it later turned out that my employer did not have sufficient financial resources to fund my project, the company doctor also informed me that I would not be able to conduct the data collection for safety reasons. My potential research assistant from Germany, who had lived in Tanzania before, also felt it was a crazy risk to travel during the pregnancy.

Nevertheless, I was determined to make the project happen, so I acquired funding to do it and was ready to travel approximately three years later, when I was the mother of two who were supposed to accompany me, along with my husband and my stepson, a young adult, who was supposed to babysit. Again, there was backlash, this time from my extended family, questioning my decision to bring the children to the field.

Of course, I knew that there were others who had been to the field with their children (e.g., Cassell, 1987; Gottlieb & Graham, 1994). However, I was not sure how we would handle the complexity of the situation. I want to focus on my children's experiences interacting with the different social contexts they encountered.

One of my children, I will call them Koda here, is very social and sees opportunities in life's changes. When confronted with the prospect of moving to a new country, they commented "great, a chance to make some new friends." The other child, I will call them Moss here, is somewhat shy and dislikes changes. Now that Moss is older, they claim that they need to know others for extended periods of time to become friends with them. While they enjoy being admired, at the same time they do not really like being the center of attention.

Although this was not the plan, we spent a good amount of time in Dar es Salaam, the biggest city in Tanzania, getting the paperwork and equipment for the research project ready. During this time, we stayed in a hotel in a simple neighborhood. The hotel was surrounded by flat buildings with corrugated metal roofs inhabited by families living their life in plain view and running tiny businesses selling homemade snacks or daily goods. Our family was always met with curiosity in the neighborhood, with many adults asking us questions and children trying to get in contact with our children, presumably the first white children they had seen in the neighborhood.

Koda enjoyed the attention and receiving an occasional small present, often something edible, like a banana. They made friends with the local children, playing and eating the candy the local children generously shared with them. Moss, on the other hand, felt overwhelmed by the many children who wanted to touch them and interact with them. They did not want to leave the compound of the hotel and asked to be picked up and carried when we went out. I was somewhat concerned about the imminent fieldwork with the Hadza.

When arriving in the first Hadza camp, my children had brought some of their toys, which I suppose must have been novel and attractive to the Hadza children. My children found a place to sit and play and the Hadza children sat a few meters away. This was a very comfortable distance for Moss who did not feel threatened. Over the course of the morning, the Hadza children slowly edged closer and finally ended up interacting with our children. Instead of feeling overwhelmed and threatened by the Hadza children, Moss actually felt eager to spend time with them, inquiring each morning "are we going back to the children today?" Koda also had a good time and learned greeting people in several new languages, but Moss flourished, even taking an occasional leadership role, initiating games with the Hadza children.

Hadza adults seemed very calm and considerate with both my children and me. With both the Hadza and the neighbors in Dar es Salaam, Koda was less willing to share than culturally expected. I found this embarrassing, but I did not feel that the Hadza blamed my parenting. Some Hadza were critical of my attempts to potty train one of my children. They felt that I was overburdening the child who was not ready for it.

While my children gained valuable experiences, for example they also developed their fine motor skills by picking up seed beads and stringing them, I am certain that I would have objected had my children wanted to try smoking or drinking alcohol as the Hadza children do.

6.6. The other side: Sexual harassment in the field

Anonymous

It was the last week of the trip, and I was already exhausted from fieldwork: changing environments, temperamental equipment, and ensuring high-fidelity data collection, all on a constantly shifting schedule. I had already achieved my core research objectives, so I had time to collect supplemental data for a side project that I was working on with collaborators. I was also simply enjoying some time with the locals, just visiting people and hanging out.

Since most of our work was already completed, many of my research team had already left. Remaining were my two female research assistants, the little five-year-old niece of one research assistant, and me. Even though we had been an established presence in the community for several weeks, this shift in our research team composition had a palpable impact on the atmosphere of our living- and work-space. Typically, we would find a host family who would allow us to pitch our tents near their homes. When we first arrived, I pitched my tent in a cluster with the male research assistant and the two project supervisors, and the rest of the team preferred the vacant empty house right next to us.

After they had left, my tent was out in the open, isolated and exposed. I had the option to move my tent inside the vacant house that had been lent to us, where my two female research assistants had pitched their tents, but the space inside was cramped, hot, and noisy. For the sake of privacy for both myself and my research assistants, as well as considering general comfort, it seemed reasonable to keep my tent where it was, absent any other considerations.

On our last Sunday in the community, on the eve of a national holiday, my colleagues and I were conducting an experiment for the side project on our porch. I had planned it out such that people could hang out on the porch together while waiting for their turn, socializing with one of my research assistants and drinking and eating some juice and snacks that I had provided.

Previously, I had almost exclusively interacted with women and children, so this experiment was the first time I interacted closely with men during fieldwork. We had a good turnout for this experiment and high community engagement, so our research activities were proceeding smoothly and according to plan. Most of the men I met were as pleasant and welcoming as their wives, and similarly curious about our work.

But it was in this context that a particular man arrived, accompanied by a friend and his friend's wife. They all wanted to participate as well. I had never seen him before, and the trio told me that they crossed the river specifically to participate in our study.

This man caught my attention immediately. He wasn't shy or hesitant; he wasn't even patient or polite, as most people in this community are when you meet them for the first time. Instead, he was aggressive, and demanded his turn as immediately as possible, with no regard for our protocol, nor for the sizable congregation of his own neighbors, who had all been waiting patiently on our porch before he had even arrived. Accommodating as most people in this community are, everyone actually agreed to allow this man to go before them, so I restructured my planned work to sit this group of visitors after I finished the group I had already prepped for the experiment. I figured that it would be best to work with this new group and dismiss them as quickly as possible, lest they further disrupt the smooth flow of work I had established with all the other community members.

As I finished my work with the group I was working with, I noticed that this man pointed in the direction of my tent. More alarming was that both of my research assistants, who are usually extremely friendly and chatty, were answering his inquiries in one-word utterances. Having worked closely with my assistants, I could recognize that the atmosphere was starting to turn bleak. All my internal alarms started to ring as if I were in acute danger. Yet, still focused on my research work, I couldn't quite understand why.

After finishing with the group I was with, I started to work with the trio from across the river, including this unknown, aggressive man. During the experiment, he was unusually uncooperative compared to everyone else I had worked with. Despite our instructions to pay attention to the stimuli and the experimental task, he relentlessly joked and commented with his friend, including ignoring things I said to him directly. Instead of answering me, he responded by asking me personal questions. Was I the only foreigner around? What happened to the rest? When was I leaving? He asked me those questions directly in a language I could understand, but once we finished the experiment, he started to ask more questions of myself and my research assistants in the local language, leaving me out of the conversation.

It started to get dark, and people started to go home for the night. The trio from across the river prepared to leave as well but told us that they would come back to visit us again later in the week before we left the community.

In our first moment alone together, my research assistants immediately instructed, not suggested, that I move my tent inside of the room with them. I asked them what had happened, but they didn't want to elaborate; they just said that it wasn't nice and that the rude visitor from across the river was a "bad man."

I felt the weight of those words, and I believed them, but I simply could not move on until I knew exactly what he had said to them. They outright refused. I had to get pushy and even a bit angry for them to finally share the dirty details. It wasn't comfortable to do that, but I felt that it was important information to have.

They told me that he had identified my tent and asked if it was mine, and that he was going to come back at night. He had asked if I was married, or if I had ever had a baby. He said to them that I wasn't going to leave the community without him putting a baby in my belly.

At this point, I was overwhelmed by alarm, dread, and of course, that unique kind of fear that only women seem to understand when they are put in this kind of situation. I stormed out of the house hoping to find cellphone service and some aid or support. One of my supervisors was still in the territory but in a different city. I wasn't sure of the protocol for responding to things like this, or what the best practice was for how to resolve such situations. I managed to eke out just a couple of texts.

The replies took a long time to arrive. The message was clear: if I don't feel safe, I should leave.

So, I instructed my research assistants to pack the essentials right away, and that we would return another day to pick up the rest of the camp. But, as we prepared to leave, we also saw the night sky turn grayer and grayer as the night wore on. Rain began to fall. In another context, rain is hardly more than an inconvenience, but when dirt roads and trails are the only way to get from town to town, rain is nature's way of immediately stopping everything we have planned. No cars come to the village, the road washes away, and getting stuck somewhere is all but assured.

So, we had to stay in that same exact place, across the river from that man. Not a single vehicle came through town the following day. Nor the day after, or the day after that...

I was trapped. Alone.

With my two young female research assistants, a 5-year-old, and the fear.

In the days following that man's visit, we were immobilized by the rain, but restless in alarm. We had packed up everything we had, ready to leave the community for the season at the first opportunity, but still, we had to wait. I tried to function. Keeping busy helped keep my mind occupied.

I did some more experiments, and we visited some of the families that I enjoyed spending time with the most. But it was passing time through the night that was the problem. I was terrified of falling asleep, I wanted to be prepared if he was coming. Prepared for what though? Would I stand a chance?

Even the slightest rustle in the grass outside would bolt me awake, so I would wake every five minutes. The field is not silent at night.

During that time, I also started to hear the stories. I think word spread among the women of the community about my encounter with that man. Each day, more and more women would come to our porch to hang out. In the beginning, I thought they were routine visits, but the women seemed to linger for longer than usual. There was some confusion, and some women thought that we had had problems with drunken neighbors. I said no, no problems so far.

Finally, one of the women who had been my neighbor for the past several weeks opened up to me. She told me that it was good that I moved my tent, and she started to share some of her own personal stories. No details were explicitly specified, but I understood immediately what she meant. One of my research assistants responded by sharing stories about her own ex. I began to understand what the local women meant when they simply referred to certain people as being 'a bad man'.

During the day, I started to feel protected by these women, who spontaneously and independently decided to spend their time with me for the sake of my own safety. We would chat, and they would tell some of their stories about 'bad men'. They all had one. But they also told me about motherhood, about what it is like not to have children in their community, and how they all had children. We talked about hobbies and laughed about flirting. We discussed the pill and abortion.

I felt strangely included, part of this local group of women in a small-town community. As we chatted, one woman would braid my hair, and I would braid the hair of the little five-year-old in turn.

I felt like they saw what I was. Another victim, another simple woman. And I felt like they were trying to protect me.

I felt like I wouldn't have had those intimate moments with the women or felt that closeness and comradery if it wasn't for the incident. But I only managed to come to that realization years later.

I couldn't really sleep again until we finally managed to leave and return to the big town with the hotel and the locked doors.

I had PTSD when I came back home after this happened. I took a long time to recover. It affected my personal life and relationships. It made me angry, and I felt so small. I couldn't understand how this man's words were so powerful, that he could inflict so much fear and pain. I didn't understand how this could have been allowed to happen.

How many times had this happened before and no one knew about it? I know it happened, and I know it is real from the stories I heard. Those women understood what I was going through, extremely well. They understood it so well that it still breaks my heart to think about it.

I seriously considered quitting academia and not finishing my PhD. Ultimately, I decided to continue; I graduated, found a fellowship, and continued my career. I like what I do. The thrill of research excites the mind in a way normal life rarely does.

But I don't think that it is fair that this continues to happen. It can be avoided. It should be avoided.

No one should be alone in the field.

6.7. Positioning the researcher in the local social context: Adults studying children

Xiaojie Tian

Anthropologists typically engage in long-term fieldwork within unfamiliar communities. Building good relationships with local people is the crucial first step that every researcher practices in the field. Although it may sound simple, establishing a strong rapport in a foreign society requires flexibility and a willingness to adapt one's position according to the interactions with local individuals at various stages of the fieldwork process. This process begins from the moment the researcher arrives as a stranger or foreign visitor in the community. As the fieldwork progresses, the researcher may gain a certain social status based on age, gender, and other factors. They might even receive a local name in the community's language. Indeed, such positioning is intricately linked to local norms and institutional roles, which can, at times, constrain the researcher's observations and his/her interactions with individuals of different social titles within the community. This is particularly true when studying children in communities where labor divisions and age systems are well-established. Below, I draw from my own fieldwork experience in the pastoralist Maasai society to elucidate this issue.

My research focuses on the cultural learning and transmission of pastoralist Maasai children in Southern Kenya, with long-term ethnographic fieldwork as the main research method. Similar to many other pastoralist groups in East Africa, the Maasai have an age system, whereby men pass through three age stages from boys to youths to elders, and women pass through two stages from unmarried girls to married women (Spencer, 1993). Labor divisions in Maasai society are closely tied to this age system, with local people, including children, assuming different labor roles in daily subsistence activities (Tian, 2016). Existing literature has focused on this age system and children's participation in subsistence-based labor tasks, with very limited information about their play. In the first two fieldwork trips, I had reaffirmed children's active involvement in subsistence tasks, but rarely observed their play.

As such, my initial findings, like many earlier studies, highlighted the active roles of children in local subsistence activities and their learning experiences, yet depicted a limited image of play in the lives of pastoralist children.

During my third fieldwork trip, I consulted with Maasai adults about their childhood play experiences. Some of them were skeptical about documenting childhood play, questioning if it was an important academic task assigned by the university, and whether it could contribute to my graduation. Some male elders even mentioned that they never played during their childhood, because they were fully engaged in tending livestock, which they were proud of. While conversing with adults, the children surrounding us laughed and later took me to their playground, a reserved open space for tending juvenile livestock that surrounded the homestead. From then, I got a chance to observe and participate in their play. It was interesting that Maasai children actually play a lot during the breaks in their subsistence tasks. When they were playing, adults kept their distance and refrained from participating or closely observing children's play, sometimes even intentionally avoiding eye contact with the children. According to local adults, play was considered the domain of children, and therefore, it was culturally inappropriate for adults to take part in or direct children's play. One girl explained that they did not invite me to join their play, because I am an adult, who should not participate in children's play. From this experience, I noted how different the roles of adults in and local attitude towards play is from my own.

By sharing this experience, I wish to highlight two key points concerning the researcher's positioning within the local community during fieldwork. Firstly, establishing a sustainable relationship with the local community requires the researcher to align themselves with the local age system or other relevant social institutions. Secondly, while this positioning allows for social acceptance by the local community, it may also impose certain limitations on the researcher's communication with participants. In the case of the Maasai, being perceived as an adult limited my opportunities to observe and join children's play. Fortunately, the children understood my purposes and cooperated with my work, allowing me to gain a different understanding of their lives and learning. To briefly conclude, effectively engaging with various members of the community—including children—and gaining comprehensive insights into their lives and experiences requires sensitivity and adaptability from the researcher, to navigate the complexities of one's positioning in the field. Improper positioning can lead to communication gaps, negatively impacting data collection effectiveness and potentially resulting in misunderstandings and misinterpretations of the needs and perspectives of the children.

6.8. Seeing self in others' stories: Parenting values in India

Feryl Badiani

I grew up in a Gujarati family, an Indian linguistic community, where the core value involves being able to make money through enterprise. For most Gujaratis, this often comes at the cost of pursuing higher education, since children are always encouraged to take over or join the family business as soon as they can.

Despite being a Gujarati, I was born and raised in Mumbai, a multicultural city, in the state of Maharashtra. Maharashtra is the state of the Marathi, another Indian lingual community. This community is starkly different to the Gujarati community in how they understand success and economic norms. For the Maharashtrians, education is the key to success, hence children are pushed towards achieving better grades and pursuing higher education. This community is also generally risk averse and prefers holding salaried positions that offer a safety net, over a more risk-taking enterprise driven field. A lot of Gujarati parents find themselves in Maharashtra since Mumbai, the financial capital of the country, is also the capital of this state.

I also went to an international school. As such, prestige, and aspiration for me were conflated with the idea of being able to speak English fluently, having at least a postgraduate degree, and a well-paying salaried job. My parents supported my education but were disappointed when I chose a salaried position over the family business that they developed over the years from scratch. My mother's disdain went as far as to compare having a salaried position to being enslaved by someone else. Clearly then, in my upbringing, there was a strong juxtaposition between traditional communal values, and other standards of success, morality, and values.

I saw a very similar pattern repeat itself amongst other Indian parents whom I interviewed as a part of my salaried job as a research associate for a market research company. I interviewed Gujarati and Maharashtrian parents as a part of a brief, where the client owned a school. They wanted to understand parental attitudes towards education, and different educational programs that they could launch. During these interviews, parents from both communities seemed to be navigating and negotiating a space between their own norms and others' norms.

Gujarati parents living in Maharashtra found themselves at a crossroads between preserving their traditional values and adopting external values of the state they were living in, and the rising global standards of success. Marathi parents, on the other hand, also face a similar confusion between navigating traditional values of focusing on education and a more global perspective of child-rearing that posits a balance between education and hobbies as the best form of child-rearing.

Maharashtrian parents expected the schools to provide more room during the school day for children to pursue their hobbies, so that children could then attend tuition classes (i.e., tutoring) after school to ensure academic excellence. That way, education remained a key priority. Gujarati parents, on the other hand, started supporting their children's educational pursuits a lot more. They often found a balance by nudging them towards studying business abroad to acquire the fame and prestige required to eventually come back and take over the family business.

Moreover, since Gujarati families are traditional business owners, it was the norm only to let the boys of the family take over the business, while the girl child was sidelined to be married off. However, Maharashtrians enable a lot more gender equality in education and employment. This influence was also visible among Gujarati parents who would boast about the fact that they were proud of their daughters and wanted their daughters also, if not to take over their business, to have a career of their own.

This suggests that child-rearing is a constant process of negotiation between traditional norms and outside norms that are becoming more prevalent in all communities due to multi-culturalism and globalization.

6.9. Walking the tightrope: Navigating the ethics of insider research in fieldwork

Nokwanda Ndlovu

As a scholar, I am cognizant of my unique positionality as a member of an Indigenous African group that historically has been the object of study rather than the author. My research has been predominantly with communities that I consider to be home to me. As a cultural insider to the amaZulu and amaXhosa communities of South Africa, I am able to offer a unique perspective on the challenges and opportunities of conducting research in these communities. Due to the fluid nature of identity, cultural insiders find themselves in a dynamic insider/outsider role that can evolve throughout the study (Cui, 2015; Kanuha, 2000; Kwame, 2017; Mandiyanike, 2009; Zhao, 2017), so there is a heightened need for reflexivity and systematic questioning of positionality, on top of added considerations for interacting with a vulnerable population (Kwame, 2017; Liamputtong, 2007; Schmid, 2019). There are many benefits to conducting insider research (i.e., quicker access to participants leading to faster rapport-building, a unique perspective for interpretation, an equal relationship between participant and researcher); however, these advantages are not without their own challenges, hence the heightened need for reflexivity (Chavez, 2008). One strength of emic research from which I have benefited is the potential to create an inquiry that is informed by local customs, norms, and the socio-historical context of the community.

In the process of conducting research in my home and neighboring communities, there were times where it became challenging to tease apart the different identities I hold: that of a child of the community and that of a researcher. One of the hurdles that I have faced is how I honor my cultural identity— where my sense of self has been shaped through belonging to these communities—while navigating the responsibilities I have as a researcher that call for me, from time to time, to step back from my community membership and keenly observe my community with impartiality. Much of this challenge comes from the relational nature of Zulu culture that underscores all interpersonal interactions, where we believe we derive our self through our ties to others. The community is central to Zulu culture, which is evident through the proverbial conception of the Zulu ethical principle of *ubuntu*: 'I am because we are' or 'a human becomes a human through others.' These values have molded and guided me to become the person that I am, and I try to reflect these values in my research and interactions with community members (see also Box 5.1). Examining how cultural values permeate my interactions is one way I have stayed true to my cultural values. Indigenous research has the mandate of regular self-reflection and critiquing of one's own positionality and perspective, which must apply to both cultural insiders and outsiders (Ali, 2015; Chilisa, 2020; Kwame, 2017).

While important to any cultural context, reflexivity and self-reflection is particularly essential in Indigenous studies, which promotes "research by and for Indigenous peoples that reflects Indigenous knowledge, cultures, values, and beliefs" (Ryen, 2019, p. 2). Indigenous methods are part of broader movements by Indigenous scholars that work to emphasize decolonization and self-determination through the promotion of Indigenous histories, languages, worldviews, knowledge, value systems, and broader Indigenous experiences in a post-colonial lived experience (Chilisa, 2020; Ryen, 2019). Other essential components that are critical in Indigenous research approaches include having an open and nuanced discussion of the positionality and reflexivity of the researcher (Chilisa, 2020; Cui, 2015; Denzin, 2017). In this essay, I will discuss some of the key considerations for researchers who are working with historically marginalized groups, and share some of my own experiences as a researcher working in my home communities.

The fluidity of my identity helps shape many of my reflections and interactions throughout the research process. For instance, there are times I need to think as a researcher, but I also benefit from knowing how an Indigenous participant might be misunderstood or misinterpreted without contextualization and insider knowledge. These observations became apparent to me in a study where I inquired how Zulu parenting values are transmitted through child-rearing practices and how these practices may have evolved over time. During the interview process, my identity was further challenged by the mismatch between the researcher/participant and child/elder dynamics, given my age and status difference within the culture in interviews with mothers and elders. Zulu culture is very hierarchical and so much of how we operate in Zulu society, especially our interactions, is informed by our age, status, and general standing within our communities. For example, there are cultural expectations about how I should dress (related to age, gender, and marital status) with some Zulu participants that would potentially create otherness in certain contexts (i.e., urban vs. rural environments) for me. Particularly, many of the interactions with parents in the culture placed me in a 'child' role, which flipped the researcher vs. participant dynamic on its head and created unique hurdles to my research that would not exist for a cultural outsider.

One topic that needs more consideration by scholars is the complexity of access, and what blind spots may stem from one's relationship to a site (see also Section 1.6). Cultural outsiders are aware of many challenges to access, namely physical remoteness and hurdles in rapport-building due to language differences, but this is just the tip of the iceberg. One of the challenges that I encountered in my study about parenting values among the Zulus came from the issue of sampling. While sampling during the parenting study described above, I ran into an impasse where urban mothers became inaccessible because many of these parents worked long hours during the week and had to take care of household responsibilities at the weekends. Realizing this made me appreciate my insider knowledge even more, as this could have been an area of potential bias in my sample that may have been a possible misstep if I were approaching this research inquiry from outside this community. The participants to whom I had access through local leaders (gatekeepers) and on a normal schedule (daylight hours) was not a sample that would do the study justice by helping to paint a complete picture of what was truly happening. To capture a representative sample of township mothers, I had to work on their schedule, which was both inconvenient and potentially unsafe. I had to stay late at night, meet on weekends around their social schedule (e.g., church). It was significantly more work to capture this particular sample, but I knew that this phenomenon needed to be captured and I needed to have these parents' voices and experiences represented. This sampling issue highlights bigger systematic challenges and a lived reality faced by the working poor mothers, in which they had to work away from their families and entrust the care of their children to grandparents during the day, while undeniably still playing a large role in rearing their children. Without this prior cultural knowledge, I could have mistakenly excluded these mothers, rather only recruiting the participants who were readily accessible. To address potential blind spots like this, researchers need awareness of how those to whom they have access might create a biased or limited sample because of specific restraints.

To that end, I am particularly aware of the privileged access I have as an insider to marginalized communities in accessing knowledge that might be considered sacred and closed off from those who do not belong to these communities. Access to a community must be a major source of reflection along all cultural lines. In my own emic research, I actively consider how access and consent are interrelated concepts. Gaining access to historically marginalized communities—and the knowledge within—requires scholars to make concerted efforts to respect cultural norms, expectations, and behaviors. This may include conducting research in the local language, and adhering to local norms about greeting, respect, and reciprocity. Community collaboration should also meaningfully involve local stakeholders in the research as co-creators throughout the research process. My insider membership also comes with tremendous responsibilities to the communities, particularly how I share and portray the knowledge gained with those outside of our community. Consequently, I make a conscious effort to move away from stories that perpetuate harm and that may reinforce negative images about our communities. This includes making efforts to have community members be part of the research process, which is crucially important in my representation of the community.

6.10. Outside insider: Towards a multi-dimensional view of positionality

Nachita Rosun

Positionality and the issues around being insiders and outsiders as researchers have been extensively discussed across a variety of social sciences (Adu-Ampong & Adams, 2019; Aiello & Nero, 2019; Mwangi, 2019). Scientists have moved towards more elaborate discussions of researcher positionality as layered and dynamically evolving (Narayen, 1993). However, the implications of the different ways in which we attempt to include individuals from diverse cultures have largely not been addressed. My experience with inclusivity involved moving to and being assimilated into a WEIRD (Western, Educated, Industrialized, Rich, and Democratic) institution: my research career only really started with migrating to the UK to join a graduate program.

During this period as an early career researcher, I established a field site in Mauritius, the country in which I grew up. Doing research in my birthplace has always been discussed as a positive thing in terms of expanding the inclusivity of samples and of researchers—an insider doing research within their community is seen as a mark of the diversification of science. Between the concept of a Mauritian identity being poorly defined, the culture changing at a very fast pace, and the country not being my home anymore, my being an insider really comes from growing up on the island, and, by extension, the other skills that contribute to this insider status: fluency in Mauritian Creole, established relationships within the community, and an understanding of cultural cues across a range of settings. Nonetheless, across my field trips, I find that the community's expectations associated with my insider status are balanced against the growing cultural distance that both the community and I perceive.

While the familiarity makes navigating fieldwork easier for me in some ways compared to non-native researchers, the insider status means that there are explanations with which I am not provided, and questions that I cannot ask, as I am expected simply to know. Being accompanied by outsider collaborators during my field trips has made space for observations about the type of information we are offered. In various settings, the community tends to look to me as somewhat of a tour guide, while my collaborators are given elaborate descriptions of cultural norms and ritual practices: for Eid celebrations, a family hosts us and walks my collaborators through the ins-and-outs of how and why animal sacrifices are made, looking to me for help with translations and to confirm some aspects of the explanation. Throughout the celebration, our presence is introduced to other guests in terms of the outsiders' interest in the event. While I inadvertently blend in, further explanations and details about the ritual that I am not aware of are provided to my collaborators by other guests.

Irrespective of my familiarity with Mauritian culture, becoming embedded into western society and its research institutions has shifted the perception of my position from insider to outside insider: this is reflected in conversations with locals about cultural loss, my new status, and informants' expectations attached to relational information-sharing. At the same Eid celebration, it was suggested that migration implies the loss of cultural values, and a lack of care for the community. An informant introduced me to their mother-in-law as "my friend, she's a doctor," intending for the title to be a demonstration of her having friends in high places. Another informant thanked me for listening and said goodbye with "I hope you do great things for women in Mauritius," adding a layer of expectations to our talk about how motherhood and childcare have been changing.

Whilst perceived shifts in position have been discussed by scholars, we address any cultural mismatch that results from being assimilated into outside research cultures less frequently. Similar to how migrants acculturate to their new society, researchers adopt philosophies and practices from western research institutes when being trained and working within them. Despite my Mauritian upbringing, the lens through which I conduct research is intrinsically westernized, influencing my research designs, fieldwork, and broader access to resources. Differences in my approach compared with my Mauritian colleagues are subtly striking through casual suggestions from local academics, such as questioning the legitimacy of Creole survey measures, because Creole, though widely spoken, is believed to be too informal for academic research. The advantages that come with being from an outside institution have been more openly discussed: the policing of research topics by local organizations will not be something that I am affected by, and local universities often do not have infrastructures in places that support applications to funding that I have access to. Although not comparable, these trade-offs suggest important dimensions to consider in the conversation around inclusivity.

As we move towards less polarized views of insider and outsider positionality, in order to reach a more multidimensional view it is important to engage with what it means to be either, or both, and what this implies for how we approach inclusivity. Is insider status based on cultural knowledge and community access, and how does one's research philosophies feed into the insider standpoint?

6.11. Decolonizing ethical processes in cross-cultural developmental research

Seth Oppong

Why the ethics process?

The ethics process, or the process of obtaining ethics approval to conduct fieldwork, is an essential first step to implement a sound study protocol (see also Section 5.3). This is done for several reasons, including ensuring that the rights and welfare of the research participants are protected, as well as conducting the research in a responsible manner (Society for Research in Child Development [SRCD], 2021). What is the typical ethics process? Often, a researcher or team of researchers affiliated with a particular university or research institution prepares the research proposal, completes all the necessary documentation, and submits the required documents to the ethics committee or institutional review board of the university for consideration (see Oppong, 2018; Thutoemang & Oppong, 2021). However, variations of this process do exist. For instance, in some countries, they have multiple ethics committees, or at some universities, there exist multiple ethics committees including at the departmental levels. To document Indigenous knowledge about child-rearing practices, for instance, we have obtained ethics approval in Zambia at a university and in Malawi from the National Committee on Research in the Social Sciences and Humanities at Malawi's National Commission for Science and Technology.[1] Regardless of how the ethics committee is structured or governed in a particular country, the process will usually culminate in some feedback to improve the research protocols and subsequently an approval subject to renewal after a year.

Problematizing the typical ethics process as a western practice

The formalization of the ethics process and ceding of authority to a committee of professionals (such as academics and ethicists) is a part of western science, and science in the US in particular (Chaurey, 2020; Iaccarino, 2001). Therefore, the formal process of obtaining ethics approval prior to conducting fieldwork is one that has been globalized as part of the globalizing tendencies of science (Ake, 2012; Oppong, 2023, 2019b, 2015, 2013). This is not to say that there never previously existed formal means of obtaining

---

1   This is a study Seth Oppong is conducting with colleagues in Ghana and Botswana, with support from a colleague at the University of Zambia.

permission. Outside of western societies, there exist elaborate systems of rituals for seeking permission to enter a community for any kind of work, including research. Of course, these are a type of a formal process, but these processes have not ceded the moral authority to professionals. For instance, among the Ewes and Akans of Ghana, a researcher, accompanied by some influential members of the community, will have to go the chief's palace with a bottle of schnapps (or Kola nuts in Northern Ghana) and other items for the elders of the community to make libation to pave way for the researchers to be welcomed into the community (Appiah, 2021, 2020; Gavi et al., 2022). The acceptance of the items and the invocation of the blessings of the community (both the living and the ancestors) through the chief is the granting of ethics approval to proceed. We shall refer to this process of community entry and subsequent granting of approval as a community ethics process. Thus, it is fair to say that the contemporary ethics process in the Majority World is an imported product, though it has been heavily influenced by local cultural practices. Whether or not institutional ethics approval is granted, the community ethics process is the one that determines whether any study will take place in the community. Therefore, it will make more sense to consider both the institutional ethics process and community ethics process as equals in the grand scheme of things.

In addition to the problematic nature of the formal ethics process, the ethical principles themselves have been criticized (Oppong, 2019a). For instance, Oppong (2019a) demonstrates that differences exist when ethical decision-making is viewed through a social justice perspective as opposed to an African philosophical perspective, the Wireduian Principle of Sympathetic Impartiality. Of greater concern when conducting child research (research involving studying the children themselves as opposed to studying children through their parents) is the issue of the principle of autonomy or respect for the rights and dignity of research participants. The current practice is to seek the informed consent of the parents or legal guardian and assent from the children (Ebrahim, 2010). However, in many African societies, for example, African personhood or becoming a person is a gradual social process negotiated through actions that consider other people's needs (Gyekye, 2010; Oppong, 2023). For instance, a funeral rite as a celebration of the life of a person upon passing away is not held for children, adolescents or adults who die without children while children are not expected to be able to make independent moral decisions (Gyekye, 2010; Oppong, 2023). As a result, children's assent may not be viewed by the community as being of the same import as the legal guardian or parent or caregiver (see also Section 5.2). This understanding is needed as the consent of a parent may appear to coerce children into participating in research of which they do not want to be part. However, within the first 1,000 days of the child's life, both western ethics and Majority World ethics would agree that parents are expected to make moral decisions for and on behalf of the child. The form that the consent takes (written or oral) is also problematic. Usually, written consent is required as part of the western ethical practice, while in many settings outside of it, the community members prefer verbal consent (Adu-Gyamfi, 2015; Chaurey, 2020). Thus, verbal consent should be treated as being of equal status to written consent, except that researchers should find ways to document such verbal consent. It is also important to realize that the community ethics process also produces verbal ethics approval as well. Variations on the process for documenting community ethics approval can be adapted to document the verbal consent as well. For community ethics approval, in the context of publication, the researchers should mention the name and contact address or cellphone number (with permission) of the community leader to provide assurance that it can be cross-checked. This should be kept in the journal database without making this information public.

Related to apparent conflict between parental consent and children's assent is an implicit assumption that seems to accompany the assumed superiority of the university-based or institutional ethics process. This assumption relates to the view that the community members are naïve and need to be protected by ethicists located far away from the communities in mostly wealthy countries or in urban centers in the same country. This assumption does not show respect for the rights and dignity of research participants, the right to self-determination and to be seen as a moral being capable of making moral decisions about their own condition if they are given all the necessary information. As much as this is a show of disrespect, one cannot also forget about the possibility of the research teams willfully withholding vital information from the community to induce participation. There have been countless examples in history as well as in contemporary times (McDermott & Hatemi, 2020). Therefore, funders, governments, universities, and journal editors should demand evidence of both institutional and community ethics processes as part of a sound ethical research process. Beyond this, there is also perhaps a need to consider other ethical principles that exist outside of western philosophy. For instance, Gyekye (2010) outlines the nature of African ethics, and this outline can form the basis of an alternative ethics system to expand the existing western ethics that guide the research process. According to Gyekye (2010), the African humanitarian ethics emphasizes social ethics (as opposed to individualistic ethics), the ethics of the common good (as opposed to the ethics of the individual interest), and the ethics of duty (as opposed to ethics of right). Of particular interest is the ethics of duty, as it imposes a moral duty on a person to demonstrate concern for the interests of others and is given expression through ethical values such as compassion, solidarity, reciprocity, cooperation, interdependence, and social well-being. The notion of ethics of duty elevates the morality of duty to the same status as that given to the ethics of rights in western ethics. By implication, the researcher operating from an African humanitarian ethical perspective is duty-bound to show concern for the interests of the research participants and their community, not because failing do so violates the research participants' rights, but because the researcher has a duty to the community that s/he decides to study; we can, therefore, talk about the violation of the duty of the researcher rather than the violation of the rights of the research participants. One's moral personhood is bolstered by avoiding the violation of duty. Western ethics codes are often written from the rights perspective (to protect the rights of the research participants) as opposed to the duty perspective (to impose a moral duty on the researcher to promote the welfare of the research participants). Much of the unethical research conducted in recent history might have been avoided if the researchers felt a moral duty to do right by the research participants, rather than acting in ways so as not to violate their rights. Thus, we must not only decolonize the ethics process, but we must also decolonize the ethical principles that undergird the process as well. This implies that the search for alternative ethical principles is long overdue in the process of decolonization. A major starting point for decolonizing ethics will be Gyekye (2010) and Oppong (2019a). Another useful framing might be the work by Sempere et al. (2022) that sought to decenter the west in the research process in the context of international development programs, though it focused more on incremental changes required in current research practice as opposed to a focus on creating new or expanded ethical principles.

6.12. When quitting is okay: Our responsibility in fieldwork and compassionate research

Bonnie Hewlett

Having a house full of my own teenagers at home and noticing a void in ethnographic work on adolescents from small-scale cultures, I began my research by working with Central African youth among Aka foragers and their horticulturalist neighbors, the Ngandu. They readily shared their experiences of life in and at the edge of the forest, detailing family and friend relations, issues of gender, and mate attraction. Working with the adolescents, I noticed how very often they spoke of the frequent deaths of their parents, relatives, siblings, and friends.

My next field project arose from these tragic accounts of loss, and I began a comparative research study examining responses to death and loss among these two culturally distinct adolescent groups. Overall, 40 Aka and Ngandu adolescents remembered the loss of 953 individuals, or an average of 24 individuals per adolescent. In looking at grief in these two small-scale cultures the human universals of loss and grief emerged, but demographic and cultural contexts contributed dramatically, not only to diversity in the experience of loss and grief but how healing occurs.

While conducting this research on death and loss, I interviewed one young adolescent who listed 52 deaths in his relatively short life. Recounting the loss of both his father and mother within a short period of time, the young boy ended the interview crying and saying his maternal uncle, "... looks after me like a father, but no one is like a mother to me. I miss my mother." This was the last interview I conducted on the topic of loss. I am a mother who just happens to be an anthropologist and the deaths, the losses, and the tragedies these children were sharing with me became emotionally overwhelming. While the Aka and Ngandu profoundly deepened my academic and personal understanding of the nature of loss, grief, and eventually, healing, I was devastated and saddened because questions often prompted tears. That year I learned that adapting in the field can mean stopping what you are doing, moving on, and that at times this is necessary and okay (see Hewlett, 2019 for more details).

Another more recent example, in an Ethiopian orphanage where I have been conducting research for the past 12 years, I found that most of the children had either a mother or father, and/or an extended family. They were 'social orphans'. Many of these parents expressed their extreme sadness in having felt that the best choice they could make for their child's survival was to give them away.

One young 16-year-old unwed mother saved enough money each month for a bus ride into town to visit her young baby girl whom she had relinquished to the orphanage. The social worker of the orphanage informed me, "This girl was raped," he explained, "when she went to get medicine for her sick father. Her family told her when she became pregnant she would have to give the baby to the orphanage as she was unwed and they could not afford to take care of her and her baby." I met the young mother at the orphanage, where she confidently told me, "I am certain my baby will someday return to visit me." Baby brokers, adoption agencies and/or owners of the orphanages often made many hollow promises to the parents, reassuring the mothers and fathers of a better life abroad for their relinquished child and guaranteeing the parents they would be able to see and hear from their children. They also often told the impoverished families they would be given money to provide a better life, and survival, for their remaining children.

Should I have told the young mother that the chances of reconnecting with her child were not very high? Many of the parents I spoke to believed they were giving their children to a family which they, as the child's biological parents, would remain a part of forever. The grief they experienced was raw and hard as time passed, and they discovered the reality that the ties to their children were forever severed. This young woman, and many other parents, asked if I could find information about their children, or asked if I knew how to get in touch with the adoptive parents, or if I could somehow even just get a photo. The best I could do was try to work with the social worker of the orphanage to see if it would be possible to make a connection. Other babies were abandoned, some killed; do I also speak to these mothers and fathers? Do I interview adoptive parents and agencies making promises that aren't kept? I learned to be very careful about the questions I asked about these sensitive topics, careful in how deeply into these personal, and often tragic, experiences I probed. I was also given the opportunity to interview people known to be involved in child trafficking. I started to look into this topic but over time it became clear that it was physically dangerous to me, so I terminated this study.

As field researchers it is not uncommon to encounter many such grave ethical concerns and moral dilemmas. I have learned it is important to question and understand what our impact is and what our role as individuals are toward those with whom we share this world.

Had I pursued either line of research—whether speaking further with grief-stricken Central African adolescents or young Ethiopian women—my research would have no doubt been fuller, richer. But I learned that in both instances, and several others, it is essential to be flexible, honest, respectful, and to choose my battles. I think it is important to know what you can and cannot do, to know your own limits, to understand that sometimes saying no, terminating a line of questioning or research, is okay when it feels inappropriate or unkind. Ruth Benedict once said that anthropologists can "... make the world a better place, a safer place for all." (Haviland et al., 2008, p. 402). It is up to each of us to pursue that opportunity and perhaps in knowing our boundaries, choosing our battles, conducting research with compassion, we can also make the world a kinder place.

Finally, as an anthropologist, I've found that many researchers have learned enduring lessons from conducting research 'in the field'. The field teaches us to be patient, to observe, to learn how to fail and get up again. The field teaches us how to handle ourselves in diverse and sometimes dangerous situations, and also when it is time to just quit and go home. The field teaches us to understand, accept, and value that there are other ways of knowing and being. The field teaches us to question our work, the questions we ask, the methods we use, the permissions we ask to be granted, the ways in which we live and interact with research participants, the cost to them, and ourselves, of our presence in their homes and communities. The field is a hard teacher, demanding that we as researchers question our personal morals, our professional ethics, and our responsibility to those who share their homes and lives so generously with us (Hewlett, 2019). It is important to question and understand what our impact and role as individuals are toward those with whom we share this world. There is indeed a responsibility in scholarship, and it should be based upon a foundation not only of scientific rigor, but compassionate research.

References

Adu-Ampong, E. A., & Adams, E. A. (2019). "But You Are Also Ghanaian, You Should Know": Negotiating the Insider–Outsider Research Positionality in the Fieldwork Encounter. *Qualitative Inquiry, 26*(6), 583–592. https://doi.org/10.1177/1077800419846532

Aiello, J., & Nero, S. J. (2019). Discursive Dances: Narratives of Insider/Outsider Researcher Tensions. *Journal of Language, Identity & Education, 18*(4), 251–265. https://doi.org/10.1080/15348458.2019.1623035

Abu-Lughod, L. (1992). *Writing Women's Worlds: Bedouin Stories.* University of California Press. https://doi.org/10.1525/9780520934979

Adichie, C. (2010). *The danger of a single story.* [Video]. TED Conferences. http://www.ted.com/talks/chimamanda_adichie_the_danger_of_a_single_story.html

Adu-Gyamfi, J. (2015). Ethical challenges in cross-cultural field research: A comparative study of UK and Ghana. *African Social Science Review, 7*(1), Article 3. http://digitalscholarship.tsu.edu/assr/vol7/iss1/3

Ake, C. (2012). Social Science as Imperialism. In H. Lauer and K. Anyidoho (Eds). *Reclaiming the Human Sciences and Humanities through African Perspectives* (pp. 1–30). Sub-Saharan Publishers.

Ali, R. (2015). Rethinking representation: negotiating positionality, power and space in the field. *Gender, Place & Culture, 22*(6), 783–800. https://doi.org/10.1080/0966369X.2014.917278

Appiah, R. (2020). Community-based participatory research in rural African contexts: Ethico-cultural considerations and lessons from Ghana. *Public Health Reviews, 41*, 27. https://doi.org/10.1186/s40985-020-00145-2

Appiah, R. (2021). Gurus and Griots: Revisiting the research informed consent process in rural African contexts. *BMC Medical Ethics, 22*, 98. https://doi.org/10.1186/s12910-021-00659-7

Behar, Ruth. (1993). *Translated Woman: Crossing the Border with Esperanza's Story.* Beacon Press.

Broesch, T., Crittenden, A. N., Beheim, B. A., Blackwell, A. D., Bunce, J. A., Colleran, H., Hagel, K., Kline, M., McElreath, R., Nelson, R. G., Pisor, A. C., Prall, S., Pretelli, I., Purzycki, B., Quinn, E. A., Ross, C., Scelza, B., Starkweather, K., Stieglitz, J., & Mulder, M. B. (2020). Navigating cross-cultural research: methodological and ethical considerations. *Proceedings of the Royal Society B: Biological Sciences, 287*(1935), 20201245. https://doi.org/10.1098/rspb.2020.1245

Broesch, T., Lew-Levy, S., Kärtner, J., Kanngiesser, P., & Kline, M. (2022). A roadmap to doing culturally grounded developmental science. *Review of Philosophy and Psychology.* https://doi.org/10.1007/s13164-022-00636-y

Burger, O., Chen, L., Erut, A., Fong, F. T. K., Rawlings, B., & Legare, C. H. (2022). Developing Cross-Cultural Data Infrastructures (CCDIs) for Research in Cognitive and Behavioral Sciences. *Review of Philosophy and Psychology.* https://doi.org/10.1007/s13164-022-00635-z

Cassell, J. (1987). *Children in the field.* Temple University Press.

Chapman Sanger, P. (2003). Living and Writing Feminist Ethnographies: Threads in a Quilt Stitched From the Heart. In R. P. Clair (Ed.). *Expressions of Ethnography: Novel Approaches to Qualitative Methods* (pp. 29–44). State University of New York Press. https://doi.org/10.1515/9780791486320-004

Chaurey, K. (2020). Decolonising ethics frameworks for research in Africa. https://blogs.lse.ac.uk/africaatlse/2020/01/08/decolonising-ethics-frameworks-research-africa/

Chavez, C. (2015). Conceptualizing from the Inside: Advantages, Complications, and Demands on Insider Positionality. *The Qualitative Report*. https://doi.org/10.46743/2160-3715/2008.1589

Chilisa, B. (2019). *Indigenous research methodologies* (2nd ed.). Sage.

Connolly-Shaffer, P.K. (2012). *Staging Cross-Border (Reading) Alliances: Feminist Polyvocal Testimonials at Work* [Doctoral dissertation, University of Minnesota]. http://conservancy.umn.edu/bitstream/handle/11299/141437/ConnollyShaffer_umn_0130E_13269.pdf?sequence=1&isAllowed=y

Cui, K. (2015). The insider–outsider role of a Chinese researcher doing fieldwork in China: The implications of cultural context. *Qualitative Social Work, 14*(3), 356–369. https://doi.org/10.1177/1473325014545412

Denzin, N. K. (2017). Critical Qualitative Inquiry. *Qualitative Inquiry*, 23(1), 8–16. https://doi.org/10.1177/1077800416681864

Ebrahim, H. B. (2010). Situated ethics: possibilities for young children as research participants in the South African context. *Early Child Development and Care, 180*(3), 289-298. https://doi.org/10.1080/03004430701822958

Gavi, J. K., Akotia, C. S., Osafo, J., Gyasi-Gyamerah, A. A., Andoh-Arthur, J., &. Asafo, S. M. (2022). Conceptions of personhood in Ghana: An emic perspective. *Ghana Social Science Journal, 19*(1), 16–31. https://journals.ug.edu.gh/index.php/gssj/article/view/1905/1094

Gottlieb, A., & Graham, P. (1994). *Parallel worlds: An anthropologist and a writer encounter Africa*. University of Chicago Press.

Gyekye, K. (2010). African Ethics. In E. N. Zalta (Ed.). *The Stanford Encyclopedia of Philosophy* (Fall 2011 ed.). https://plato.stanford.edu/archives/fall2011/entries/african-ethics/

Haviland, W.A., Prins, H. E. L., Walrath, D., & McBride, B. (2008). *Cultural Anthropology: The Human Challenge* (15th ed.). Wadsworth.

Henrich, J. (2020). *The WEIRDest People in the World: How the West Became Psychologically Peculiar and Particularly Prosperous*. Farrar, Straus and Giroux.

Henrich, J., Heine, S. J., & Norenzayan, A. (2010). The weirdest people in the world? *Behavioral and Brain Sciences, 33*(2–3), 61–83. https://doi.org/10.1017/S0140525X0999152X

Hewlett, B. L. (2012). *Listen, Here is a Story: Ethnographic Life Narratives from Aka and Ngandu Women of the Congo Basin.* Oxford University Press.

Hewlett, B. L. (2019). Introduction. In B. L. Hewlett (Ed.). *The Secret Lives of Anthropologists: Lessons from the Field* (pp. 1– 20). Routledge. https://doi.org/10.4324/9781315144580

Holding, P., Anum, A., van de Vijver, F. J. R., Vokhiwa, M., Bugase, N., Hossen, T., Makasi, C., Baiden, F., Kimbute, O., Bangre, O., Hasan, R., Nanga, K., Sefenu, R. P. S., A-Hayat, N., Khan, N., Oduro, A., Rashid, R., Samad, R., Singlovic, J., Faiz, A., & Gomes, M. (2018). Can we measure cognitive constructs consistently within and across cultures? Evidence from a test battery in Bangladesh, Ghana, and Tanzania. *Applied Neuropsychology: Child, 7*(1), 1–13. https://doi.org/10.1080/2162 2965.2016.1206823

Hruschka, D. J., Munira, S., Jesmin, K., Hackman, J., & Tiokhin, L. (2018). Learning from failures of protocol in cross-cultural research. *Proceedings of the National Academy of Sciences of the United States of America, 115*(45), 11428–11434. https://doi.org/10.1073/pnas.1721166115

Iaccarino, M. (2001). Science and ethics. As research and technology are changing society and the way we live, scientists can no longer claim that science is neutral but must consider the ethical and social aspects of their work. *EMBO reports, 2*(9), 747–750. https://doi.org/10.1093/embo-reports/kve191

Kanuha, V. K. (2000). "Being" Native versus "Going Native": Conducting Social Work Research as an Insider. *Social Work, 45*(5), 439–447. https://doi.org/10.1093/sw/45.5.439

Kline, M. A., Shamsudheen, R., & Broesch, T. (2018). Variation is the universal: making cultural evolution work in developmental psychology. *Philosophical Transactions of the Royal Society B: Biological Sciences, 373*(1743), 20170059. https://doi.org/10.1098/rstb.2017.0059

Kwame, A. (2017). Reflexivity and the insider/outsider discourse in Indigenous research: my personal experiences. *AlterNative: An International Journal of Indigenous Peoples, 13*(4), 218–225. https://doi.org/10.1177/1177180117729851

Liamputtong, P. (2007). Researching the Vulnerable. Sage. https://doi.org/10.4135/9781849209861

Mandiyanike, D. (2009). The dilemma of conducting research back in your own country as a returning student – reflections of research fieldwork in Zimbabwe. *Area, 41*(1), 64–71. https://doi.org/10.1111/j.1475-4762.2008.00843.x

McDermott, R., & Hatemi, P. K. (2020). Ethics in field experimentation: A call to establish new standards to protect the public from unwanted manipulation and real harms. *Proceedings of the National Academy of Sciences of the United States of America, 117(*48), 30014–30021. https://doi.org/10.1073/pnas.2012021117

Mwangi, N. (2019). 'Good That You Are One of Us': Positionality and Reciprocity in Conducting Fieldwork in Kenya's Flower Industry. *The Politics of Conducting Research in Africa*, 13–33. https://doi.org/10.1007/978-3-319-95531-5_2

Narayan, K. (1993). How Native Is a "Native" Anthropologist? *American Anthropologist, 95*(3), 671–686. https://doi.org/10.1525/AA.1993.95.3.02A00070

Nielsen, M., Haun, D., Kärtner, J., & Legare, C. H. (2017). The persistent sampling bias in developmental psychology: A call to action. *Journal of Experimental Child Psychology, 162*. https://doi.org/10.1016/j.jecp.2017.04.017

Oppong, S. (2013). Indigenizing knowledge for development: Epistemological and pedagogical approaches. *Africanus, 4*(2), 34–50. https://doi.org/10.25159/0304-615X/2300

Oppong, S. (2015). A critique of early childhood development research and practice in Africa. *Africanus, 45*(1), 23–41. https://doi.org/10.25159/0304-615X/252.

Oppong, S. (2018). Investigating comprehension of road hazard communication designs and safety climate as correlates of risk perception and road traffic accident using mixed methods design. In *Sage Research Methods Cases Part 2*. Sage. https://dx.doi.org/10.4135/9781526439079

Oppong, S. (2019a). When the ethical is unethical and the unethical is ethical: Cultural Relativism in Ethical Decision-Making. *Polish Psychological Bulletin, 50*(1), 18–28. https://doi.org/10.24425/ppb.2019.126014

Oppong, S. (2019b). Overcoming obstacles to a truly global psychological theory, research and praxis in Africa. *Journal of Psychology in Africa, 29*(4), 292–300. https://doi.org/10.1080/14330237.2019.1647497

Oppong, S. (2023). An indigenous representation of personhood for citizenship behaviours. In J. Osafo & C. S. Akotia (Eds). *Personhood, Community and the Human Condition: Reflections and Applications in the African Experience* (pp. 27–47). Ayebia Clarke Publishing Limited.

Ryen, A. (2020). Indigenous Methods. In P. Atkinson, S. Delamont, J. W. Sakshaug, & R. A. Williams (Eds). *SAGE Research Methods Foundations*. Sage. https://doi.org/10.4135/9781526421036854700

Sanches de Oliveira, G., & Baggs, E. (2023). *Psychology's WEIRD Problems*. Cambridge University Press. https://doi.org/10.1017/9781009303538

Schmid, J. (2019). Autoethnography: Locating the self as standpoint in post-apartheid South Africa. In S. Laher, A. Fynn, & S. Kramer (Eds). *Transforming Research Methods in the Social Sciences* (pp. 265–279). Wits University Press. https://doi.org/10.18772/22019032750.22

Sempere, M.J. C., Aliyu, T., & Bollaert, C. (2022). Towards Decolonising Research Ethics: From One-off Review Boards to Decentralised North–South Partnerships in an International Development Programme. *Education Sciences, 12,* 236. https://doi.org/10.3390/educsci12040236

Society for Research in Child Development. (2021, March). *Ethical Principles and Standards for Developmental Scientists*. https://www.srcd.org/about-us/ethical-principles-and-standards-developmental-scientists

Spencer, P. (1993). Being Maasai, being in time. In *Being Maasai* (pp. 140–156). James Currey.

Tian, X. (2016). Day-to-day accumulation of Indigenous Ecological Knowledge: a case study of pastoral Maasai children in southern Kenya. *African Study Monographs*, *37*(2), 75–102. https://doi.org/10.14989/215710

Thutoemang, T., & Oppong, S. (2021). Utilizing cross-sectional study design, multi-site sampling, and multiple data collection platforms to investigate the influence of paternal involvement on female reproductive strategies. In *Sage Research Methods Cases Part 1*. Sage. https://dx.doi.org/10.4135/9781529761429

Urassa, M., Lawson, D. W., Wamoyi, J., Gurmu, E., Gibson, M. A., Madhivanan, P., & Placek, C. (2021). Cross-cultural research must prioritize equitable collaboration. In *Nature Human Behaviour* (pp. 1–4). Nature Research. https://doi.org/10.1038/s41562-021-01076-x

Wolf, M. (1992). *A Thrice-Told Tale: Feminism, Postmodernism, and Ethnographic Responsibility*. Stanford University Press. https://doi.org/10.1515/9780804788243

Xu, J. (2024). *"Unruly" Children: Historical Fieldnotes and Learning Morality in a Taiwan Village*. Cambridge University Press. https://doi.org/10.1017/9781009416269

Zhao, Y. (2017). Doing fieldwork the Chinese way: a returning researcher's insider/outsider status in her home town. *Area*, *49*(2), 185–191. https://doi.org/10.1111/area.12314

Zuilkowski, S. S., McCoy, D. C., Serpell, R., Matafwali, B., & Fink, G. (2016). Dimensionality and the Development of Cognitive Assessments for Children in Sub-Saharan Africa. *Journal of Cross-Cultural Psychology*, *47*(3), 341–354. https://doi.org/10.1177/0022022115624155

7. Sharing your research

Coordinated by Tanya MacGillivray

This chapter outlines the various ethical and practical issues that arise regarding the dissemination of research data and findings. Our aim is to outline best practices for sharing research on childhood learning in an ethical and impactful way. We break the chapter into five sections: (1) best practices for involving communities in the sharing process, (2) achieving community-engaged research, (3) considerations for communicating with academic audiences, (4) communicating with the public sector, and (5) how and why to conduct research within an open science framework. We describe the ethical and practical issues pertaining to each section and recommend ways to achieve best practices for each. Front and center of this chapter is the critical importance of taking an Indigenous and community perspective when deciding how to share research on childhood learning.

7.1. Ownership and accountability

Tanya MacGillivray

When embarking on a research project involving children, families, and culture, there is necessarily a built-in level of accountability to the communities themselves, the stakeholders in the research process, alongside the funders, colleagues, and interested parties in the topic itself. That is a lot of responsibility. How does one share the ideas, process, findings, in a way that satisfies all parties and respectfully communicates the project in its entirety to the members, or interested individuals, or groups? To begin to address

©2025 Tanya MacGillivray, et al., CC BY-NC 4.0   https://doi.org/10.11647/OBP.0440.07

the enormity of this issue, we do what a good academic does: we break it down into manageable pieces.

First, we start by emphasizing that sharing research starts before the research has even begun. Specifically, Tian and Wang provide a historical and cross-disciplinary account of why and how to involve community members in research. They outline traditional methods of community involvement and explain how community-engaged research (CER) can break down the researcher-researched dichotomy, dispelling misconceptions about children's lives across cultures in the process. MacGillivray, Wang and Duggirala provide a strong argument for conducting CER from the outset. They claim that CER is a worldview and can be put into practice by engaging in a dynamic approach that can involve communities in the research process at various stages and is critical to achieving high quality, ethical science with children in different settings, including western settings. The next issue we address is how to make decisions about sharing research with an academic audience to ensure that knowledge translation goals are met. Cristia, Dutra, and Tian address publishing, identifying outlets for research, timing, and which language to publish in. Next, Milks, Amir, and Hodson provide an overview of the issues that can arise when communicating research with the public. They begin by describing the various sub-levels of private and public considerations and provide a strong argument for careful planning to ensure responsible use and interpretation of the data. They also describe the considerations that arise in the field of childhood learning and culture. Lastly, Dutra, Cristia, and Pope-Caldwell argue for an early start and a broad lens when deciding how to share data. They show that it is critical to have communities at the forefront when deciding how, with whom, and for how long the research should be shared. Together, these contributions outline best practices for sharing research with communities, the public, and academic audiences, and provide some guidance for doing community-engaged research as well as considering an open science framework.

7.2. Perspectives on community involvement

Xiaojie Tian & Yitong Wang

In cultural anthropological studies, the issue of how to involve community members in research has been widely discussed (e.g., James, 2007). Anthropologists focus on the lived experiences of people within diverse socio-cultural, economic, and political contexts. In contrast, psychologists may not always have similar training. To understand the socio-cultural features of human groups—or the behaviors and ways of life of individuals—two approaches, the emic and etic perspectives, are commonly applied. An emic perspective adopts an insider's view to understand the values, beliefs, and interpretations of community members. In contrast, an etic perspective reflects an outsider's view, typically used to test scientific theories or frameworks. These concepts were first introduced by linguist Kenneth L. Pike in the 1940s to study the significance of verbal communication in human languages and were later expanded to include nonverbal behaviors (Pike, 1967; Harris, 1976). Researchers' involvement of community members in their studies often depends on the balance between these two approaches.

When studying the lives of specific communities, ethnographers often emphasize the emic perspective. For example, researchers may develop questions that explore local concepts and attitudes toward particular behaviors or cultural systems. Long-term ethnographic fieldwork, including participant observation, is often considered the most effective method in this context. This approach allows researchers to develop communication skills and social ties with the target population. By living among community members, researchers can empirically and emotionally learn the local language, behaviors, and customs. Consequently, ethnographic data is viewed as representing the 'reality' of local life. An emic approach inherently involves engaging with the people and communities being studied, interpreting and justifying individual behaviors through careful contextualization within local socioeconomic systems, worldviews, and cosmologies.

We argue that this practice should be embraced across all behavioral sciences, particularly when studying children. Many anthropologists have worked both directly and indirectly with children to understand their social roles, daily lives, and concerns. For instance, studies have explored pastoralist perceptions of children's roles in daily subsistence (Galaty, 1989; Krätli, 2006), examining their work, play, companions, and the cultural values assigned to these activities by the children, their families, and their communities (Dyson, 2014; Tian, 2018, 2019). Such research critiques misinterpretations of pastoralist livelihoods (e.g., poverty, child labor), and highlights the nuanced realities of pastoralist children's development and learning in the international sphere.

The etic approach, on the other hand, often relies on interdisciplinary collaboration to conduct cross-cultural comparisons. Researchers applying an etic perspective frequently draw upon emic findings to design their studies. Since the 1980s, cross-cultural comparisons of children and childhood have challenged the generalizability of western notions of child development and child-rearing practices to other cultural settings. For instance, by analyzing ethnographic data from diverse small-scale societies, Lancy (2017) demonstrated that teaching plays a less central role, and play has a more central role, to children's learning. Findings from etic research can thus illuminate the lived experiences of the global majority for policymakers and practitioners, whose decisions directly impact local communities and their well-being (Dyer, 2014; James, 2007; see also Chapter 9).

An increasing amount of research is now conducted in international and intercultural settings. However, academic and community collaborations are often shaped by power hierarchies and influenced by the privilege associated with identity—both within societal norms and within the specific dynamics of community–academic relationships. Disparities between the cultural context in which the researcher is working and the researcher's own cultural identity can result in misguided assumptions and misinterpretations. These incongruences shape methodological, epistemological, and ethical decisions at every stage of the research process (Muhammad et al., 2015). When conducting research with communities with which one is less familiar or not deeply embedded, a primary goal is to dissolve the boundaries between academic researchers and community participants. Given the complexity of these dynamics, community engagement is critical for fostering co-learning and building collaborative relationships between researchers and communities.

Here, and throughout, we argue that community-engaged research (CER) is a powerful tool for providing an inclusive framework that equitably involves community members throughout the research process. CER emphasizes building collaborative and reciprocal partnerships among community members, researchers, and stakeholders, while acknowledging and leveraging community strengths. A researcher's identity in CER encompasses societal status and specific relationships with community members, mediated by factors such as ethnicity, education level, life experiences, shared values, and research motivations. It is therefore essential to recognize the researcher's identity and consider how it interacts with the community's culture and power dynamics. This interplay shapes the research process and outcomes. Power imbalances and conflicting assumptions or perceptions between researchers and community partners pose significant challenges to fostering mutual respect and equitable collaboration (Mikesell et al., 2013). For instance, when researchers unfamiliar with cultural practices interpret empirical findings without input from cultural insiders, they risk adopting a deficit perspective (Lansford et al., 2019). Recognizing and addressing these challenges is vital to producing meaningful, respectful, and impactful research.

7.3. Community-engaged research

Tanya MacGillivray, Yitong Wang, and Srujana Duggirala

Cooperation is essential to achieving high-quality ethical science when working with human participants in the social sciences. One must keep communities, participants, and partners front and center from the outset, especially when working with populations and communities unfamiliar to the researcher (Broesch, Crittenden et al., 2021). This is especially important for communicating and sharing research accurately, sensitively, and ethically with communities. To achieve this, there are various approaches and strategies that can be implemented. In this section, we discuss community engagement as fundamental to achieving and sharing accurate and informed science on child learning in diverse contexts. First, let us begin by identifying key questions regarding community-engaged research which will guide our section below. What is community engagement? How can it be achieved while conducting research on childhood learning in diverse cultural contexts? What are the barriers to achieving engaged research? Are there different levels and ways to involve communities? Community-engaged research has been used in the field of international and economic development for over half a century. In fact, community-engaged research began long before it was referred to as 'community-engaged' and there have been several iterations and labels, as well as many lessons learned from this body of work.

Defining community-engaged research (CER)

Here, we define community-engaged research (CER) as the process of involving community members with the goal of enhancing research, fostering communication with communities, and adhering to the principles of participation, cooperation, collaboration, knowledge translation, and empowerment (McKenna & Main, 2013; Mathie & Cunningham, 2003). As evident from this definition, CER is fundamentally focused on community communication and engagement. Recently, Lepore, Hall, and Tandon (2023) summarized CER succinctly, describing it as a perspective, a worldview, and an approach to science in their book *Bridging Knowledge Cultures*. To successfully implement CER, researchers must carefully consider their mindset, goals, and assumptions about their scientific endeavors, particularly when working with children.

Considerations and mindset: Two-eyed seeing

Two persistent problems in research with human participants often undermine a community-engaged approach: (i) the extent to which the research framework and mindset are extractive, and (ii) the degree to which participants are viewed as collaborators with meaningful contributions and insights. To shift from an extractive research objective toward a cooperative partnership, researchers might ask, "How can our objectives work together?" rather than, "How can I achieve my research objective while including community perspectives?"

We suggest that researchers prioritize shared goals and keep this focus at the forefront of their work. Achieving this requires collaboration with participants, partners, and community members to identify mutual interests and objectives. While this may sound simple at first glance—and the message is indeed straightforward—it hinges on a fundamental shift in mindset. By adopting this perspective from the outset, CER becomes both achievable and less complex. Consider the contrast between the two research objectives mentioned earlier: Starting with shared objectives allows for the co-creation of the research program. In contrast, beginning with a hierarchical model of objectives embeds that hierarchy into the research from the beginning, ensuring that an extractive approach permeates all aspects of the research program. This is especially challenging when conducting research with children. The contributions of children, their perspectives, and their potential benefit from the co-creation of knowledge should not be overlooked. Children have unique perspectives on the world and we can gain a lot from engaging in dialogue with children (Rogoff et al., 2018). In fact, prominent developmental psychologists have argued that developmental science must shift to documenting children's lived experience instead of the scientists' interpretation of their behavior and experience (Rogoff et al., 2018).

If the mindset is one of co-creation of knowledge and bridging long-held knowledge gaps, there must also be recognition of the different goals, perspectives, relationships, and histories of the stakeholders involved in the research. Researchers can begin to understand the complexity by explicitly articulating who the research is for, by, who benefits, and how. By explicitly asking and reflecting on these questions, and including the answers in the research design, process, and outputs, we can begin to move toward a CER approach that is more balanced and equitable in the benefits of the research.

Another assumption that works against CER is that science can only be defined by scientists, and that community members cannot be scientists. This is a flaw in the scientific community and will take enormous effort to overcome. An alternative approach known as 'two-eyed seeing' was introduced by Mi'kmaq Elders, Albert D. Marshall and Mudena Marshall, as a way to recognize the unique and equally valid contributions of academic scientific and Indigenous knowledge (Wright et al., 2019). This approach is summarized by Elder Albert D. Marshall in the following way: "Two-Eyed Seeing refers to the mindful effort of learning to see from our one eye with the strengths of the Indigenous knowledges and ways of knowing while also learning to see from other eye using the strengths of Western (or mainstream, or Eurocentric, or conventional) scientific knowledges and ways of knowing..." (Bartlett, 2006, p. 4). This approach has been widely adopted in Canada by several universities, government policies, and funding institutions. With a mindset committed to learning 'two-eyed seeing' to achieve community-engaged research, the implementation process will incorporate both approaches and therefore achieve a more equitable research product (Bartlett et al., 2012).

Dynamic and continuous process

To fully achieve a community-engaged approach, which in turn moves us toward a decolonial science, we suggest developing a check-in plan or process throughout the project to ensure that researchers don't fall back on western ways of engaging in science. The CER approach should be developed at the outset, and flexibly continued throughout the research process. Lastly, great efforts should go into ensuring that the research product is of interest, use, and accessible to community members. This includes publishing in open science venues and continually reflecting upon the publishing process.

7.4. Communicating with academic audiences

Alejandrina Cristia, Natália Dutra, and Xiaojie Tian

When it comes to academic audiences, there are a number of questions to ask oneself: who would benefit most from reading about this work? Which theories can be informed by it? Which bodies of data can it be integrated with? What applications may it be relevant to? The answers to these questions can help identify the specific subset of the academic population that makes up the ideal audience, and, as a result, which are the best means to communicate about the work so that it reaches this ideal audience. In an interdisciplinary, cross-cultural domain such as the topic of this book, the answers may not be easy, and your ideal audience may best be served by considering whether to communicate about the work through several means.

To make this more concrete, imagine that you believe the ideal audience is very wide, including anthropologists, linguists, and developmental psychologists. Today, there is no single journal that is read by these three types of academics, except if we consider highly interdisciplinary venues like *Science*, which is less than ideal because it has acceptance rates in the single digits and a unique, overly short format. Being pragmatic, one can choose based on the venue that is most likely to reach much of your ideal audience as well as result in a communication that happens in a reasonable timeframe. In the example just mentioned, one could choose to write up an article for a linguistic anthropology journal and present this work in a developmental psychology conference, in addition to publicizing the work through social media.

By and large, there are the following potential venues: blog entry, preprint, conference presentation (with or without proceedings), book chapter or book, journal publication without peer review, journal publication with peer review. These venues vary in the number of people that are likely to be reached, the diversity of the audience, the amount of work that will be requested before the piece is accepted, and the prestige associated with the actual output. The best choice may depend on the specific work and the potential effects on the writers; for instance, a blog entry may be ideal for a small piece of work produced by someone who is in a tenured position where they are not typically evaluated; a journal publication with peer review may be ideal for someone who will soon be on the job market.

Often, work is collaborative, in which case one needs to reflect on how to optimize across the collaborating team, considering typical publication schedules. For example, a typical response rate from a developmental psychology journal is one month for eligibility (when the action editor decides whether the manuscript is appropriate to the journal and either issues a 'desk rejection', or sends it out for review), three months until the first round of reviews is back, three months given to authors to respond, with two rounds of review being almost the norm before acceptance, leading to a timeline of one month for a desk rejection and a year for an acceptance. In contrast, leading economics journals have a much faster desk rejection response (often less than one week), but authors targeting papers to economic audiences tend to submit to the same journals sequentially, leading to overall potentially slower publication times.

Many readers may ask: should I publish in English or a local language? Our view is: why 'or'? Undoubtedly, if our ideal audience contains both people who only read in English (many scientists) and people who cannot read English (also many scientists), then we should optimize our publication strategy so that information present in our work reaches both. One way in which we can do this is by parceling results such that an aspect of the results is reported in an English-written venue and the others in a local-language venue. Alternatively, we can write a single main paper to be submitted to e.g., a journal, then automatically translate it (e.g., with a free translation tool) and post the other-language version of the paper as a preprint. In both cases, we can communicate about the paper in less scientific terms through social media to maximize the availability of the information.

7.5. Communicating with the public

Annemieke Milks, Dorsa Amir, and Claire Hodson

While researchers bear a significant responsibility to communicate their scientific work effectively to the public, they often lack formal training in media communication and may have limited understanding of the challenges they might encounter in this undertaking. When done properly, scientific outreach can bridge the gap between researchers and the public, helping foster a greater appreciation for science and empowering a new generation of thinkers. As a researcher, your primary role is to synthesize large and often inaccessible bodies of knowledge into a clear, accessible format, and disseminate that information broadly. In this section, we will provide a brief overview of best practices for scientific outreach. Additionally, we will address the unique challenges faced by cross-cultural researchers when communicating their work to the public, offering practical tips on how to overcome these obstacles.

Let's start with the content itself, be it a popular press piece or a social media post. The first tip, in essentially any communicative act with the public, is to use clear and accessible language. Avoid jargon, unless necessary, using plain language that can be easily understood by listeners of all backgrounds. This is an important first step toward increasing the accessibility of science and lowering the barriers that traditionally keep people out. To maximize engagement, it's also often helpful to tell a compelling story. This is where communication between scientists diverges sharply from communication to the public. Scientific writing, for instance, is essentially a record of research, and it serves distinct functions, such as ensuring reproducibility and transparency. Popular writing, on the other hand, is very different. While it is important to preserve the scientific foundations of the work, the goal of popular writing is largely to engage and explain. This is where storytelling plays a vital role. Ask yourself: what is the story behind the research question? What did researchers think was happening before this finding? Why does it matter to the average person? Are there vivid anecdotes or illustrative examples that you can tie in to engage the reader's attention? When delving into complex phenomena—e.g., the determinants of human behavior—it's also important to be both transparent and honest about the limitations of the work, the complexities of the research, and the nuance in our interpretations of findings.

How does this content then make its way out into the world? In certain media (e.g., a blog or social media post), you as the author will have control. In other circumstances, however, you will not. When writing for magazines or newspapers, for instance, you will usually be paired with an editor and sometimes an independent fact-checker who will help you fine-tune the content for the medium's specific audience. A lesser-known part of this process is that editors have independent control over the title and subtitle of the piece, and you will often not know what those are until it is published. If it is extremely important to get the language right, you can consider asking the editor to run it by you beforehand, if possible. You will also rarely have control over the outlet's social media posts, how they choose to promote the piece, or where the piece will be promoted.

When communicating about cross-societal research, there are also a handful of special considerations to keep in mind. The first of these concerns the way in which cultural variation is addressed, keeping in mind common and pernicious tropes that plague the popular understanding of cultural diversity, such as a perceived spectrum of 'primitive' to 'civilized' cultures. These are especially critical when communicating about work with marginalized or minoritized communities. All of our scientific outreach should maintain respect and sensitivity toward different ways of life, making sure to avoid ethnocentrism of one's own culture or the exoticization of others. It's also important to respect privacy and confidentiality when discussing the cultural practices of specific communities and when including potentially identifying information, such as photographs. Be aware that your work and the coverage of that work can be skewed to support incorrect or harmful stereotypes about vulnerable groups and take care to clearly communicate those dangers in the piece itself, if possible.

When our research finds its way into the media and is reported by science journalists, or we are asked to comment on others' research to the press, there are further considerations. In such instances, the title, subtitle and content are even more out of our control than when writing a public-facing piece for the media ourselves. We can sometimes communicate concerns around language and image choice to the journalists and media outlets, but with no guarantee that those used will reflect our values. Most universities have a media team whose role it is to support researchers to write press releases, and it is good to engage with the team early on in the process to guide communication. When asked to provide comment on others' research, consider how any given statement may be taken out of context. You may prefer to provide such comments in writing rather than over the phone, and in many cases 'less is more'. Also consider the track record of the media outlets or journalists, and whether you are comfortable working with them. When invited to give a live interview, consider these few tips: have water with you, imagine you are speaking to a non-academic friend, consider the key messages that you want communicated, and keep language simple. Ask yourself "so what?" beforehand and be ready to answer that.

Visual material is a powerful tool for communication, and far from being a passive tool it can be an exciting way to engage readers. When taking, storing, and sharing images of children, we should always consider how images can be reproduced and shared out of context, or intentionally or unintentionally misinterpreted. Photographs and videos of children from any society must be used with caution, as there can be concerns around child protection and safeguarding. When sharing image content online, whether it is in a journal format or in the media, these images can be downloaded, shared without attribution or context, and/or screenshotted. Similarly, we should consider, when sharing images, whether the publisher or platform technically owns the rights to that image once shared. Ethics applications usually have special sections around consent to take photographic and videographic content of children. Think about who is giving this consent on behalf of children, and whether that consent accounts for children's rights to their image being shared in that way, potentially in perpetuity. Although consent usually includes the right to withdraw consent, in reality, removing images from the internet can prove very challenging. When taking all these issues together, it may well be that the sharing of images of children is unnecessary to communicating the research.

Alternatives to photographic and videographic media can include creative approaches such as drawings, paintings, sculptures, and other forms of digital images including those generated by Artificial Intelligence. Archaeological research on children in the past frequently uses such images to visually humanize the past. Such artistic reconstructions could also be a reasonable solution to the sharing of images with journals and the media, and artists' fees can be built into grant applications. Pitfalls to consider include reproducing and reinforcing stereotypes, including particularly in relation to both the perceived passivity of children, and of gender roles; the exoticizing of cultures; and producing images through a colonial lens.

To ensure the effective dissemination of research data in a way that is appreciated, applicable, and sensitive to various audiences, it is essential to have considered the technologies and approaches available. However, recognition of these mechanisms and modes of delivery are not the only aspect required; awareness of the composition of the audience itself is essential. It would be careless of us to assume that all audiences engage, comprehend, and experience in an identical way the various ways in which we present often highly technical and/or specialized research. Indeed, as with any topic, not all of us will have the same interest level, willingness to engage, or comfort with participation regarding certain topics. Similarly, our own cultural, social, and/or religious backgrounds, our own knowledge base and experiences, and even our perceptions, including political ideologies, can influence how we interpret information delivered to us. This ubiquity of individuality is not in itself a concern for the dissemination of research; rather, it is part of the importance of knowledge exchange between researchers and more general audiences. However, anticipating and considering the various ways our research might be understood, perceived, and reflected in ways beyond our control is necessary.

One fundamental aspect of audience composition that is sometimes overlooked is age. This seems particularly pertinent given the remit of this book; how do we communicate this research back to our primary dataset—relaying information about children to children? Children are often viewed as products of their surroundings, innocent templates on which we imbue our thoughts, opinions, beliefs, likes, and dislikes, amongst other things. Yet, the characteristic naivety and passivity with which childhood has historically been idealized and perceived is now widely challenged, with recognition of both the agency and autonomy of the child. Consequently, disseminating research with children is important, often for broadening their awareness and appreciation regarding a range of subjects, but also for us as researchers, to be able to explain all the intricacies of our work with clarity, in an engaging and informative way. As such, how to communicate our research with children requires thoughtful consideration.

Additionally, children can often be my (CH) harshest critics as well as pose some of the more left-field and challenging questions I have had to answer. Yet, watching inquisitive minds explore a new concept or use a new technology with only a fuzzy idea of what should happen, or how they should be behaving, can be so starkly different from comparable interactions with adults using the same materials and concepts. Thus, the impact of age, and the perspectives we develop as we age, can dramatically alter how an individual engages with information, and even their willingness to do so. Consequently, we should never underestimate the importance of communicating and engaging with children, regardless of the complexity of the ideas and topics we are exploring, as so often these early interactions with new concepts are fundamental in shaping how children grow up to consider these things as adults.

7.6. Data sharing—open and reproducible science(s)?

Natália Dutra, Alejandrina Cristia, and Sarah Pope-Caldwell

Many people believe that data sharing is equivalent to posting things on the web so that they are accessible to anyone without any restriction. In 2025, options for archiving are a great deal more nuanced and intelligent than the 'private/public' dichotomy. At heart, the importance of sharing intermediate research products (i.e., stimuli, code, notes, data) comes from imagining that the people we are today will not be the only individuals in the universe and in the history of personkind for whom those products are valuable. For instance, they could be valuable to:

- us in the future, after 10 years have elapsed and we have forgotten everything we did, and have had several computers and hard drives die on us;

- participants and participants' descendants, as well as other individuals with legal and/or ethical claims on those products;

- collaborators, collaborators of our collaborators, and researchers at large.

When viewed from this lens, we begin to understand why it is important to consider sharing even as we organize our intermediate research products. Given the complexity of the topic, and the many ways in which those products could be valuable, we cannot cover all best practices here, but as much as possible point to other documents that explain this in more detail. Specifically, an introduction to four key principles that should be considered regarding data and resource sharing (that they are Findable, Accessible, Interoperable, and Re-usable–FAIR) can be found in Wilkinson et al. (2016). The intersection of FAIR with the interests of Aboriginal and Indigenous peoples has led to the development of a second set of principles, called CARE (Collective Benefit, Authority to Control, Responsibility, and Ethics), a discussion of which can be found in Carroll et al. (2020). For a focused guide adapted to anthropology, see the volume edited by Femenías (2016).

It is helpful to think about what archiving options are available for a specific project's intermediate products. The precise identity may not matter, but the Open Science Framework (OSF; https://osf.io) is a good option because it is general and can accommodate any type of data or intermediate research products. There are many archiving options such as:

- Databrary (https://databrary.org)

- tDAR (https://core.tdar.org/)

- OpenICPSR (https://www.openicpsr.org/openicpsr/)

Most of them will provide at least three levels of sharing. The first two correspond to the above-mentioned dichotomy: *Anyone in the world* (i.e., public), *Nobody* (i.e., private). Even if we do not share with anybody, it is nonetheless interesting to archive our intermediate products because it helps us organize the materials and prepare them for future use, for instance, by ourselves in the future, or by members of the population we have been working with and who want to gain access to these materials five, 10, or 20 years from now. Ideally, however, we will not be the only people with access to these materials, because when we retire or die, then they are locked from everyone, including people with ethical and legal claims over them. Here is where the third level of sharing present in most modern archives becomes crucial: *Other designated archive members.* Thanks to this level, we can make sure someone else can take over, thus ensuring access after we are no longer capable. For instance, in OSF, we may keep our project private (i.e., invisible to the world) but accessible to us, trusted collaborators, and trusted members of the population we are working with.

In the same way that we recommend thinking about archiving from the beginning, we believe consultation with the community with whom we are collaborating in a study will be crucial. Most one-shot consent procedures, in which we ask participants and their community about data archiving and sharing, will be inappropriate, as some potential uses—and the resulting positive and negative consequences—of data sharing only become apparent later. For example, the researchers who collected and openly shared HeLa cells could not have foreseen the extent of the benefits their use would generate, which profoundly improved lives but did not directly benefit Henrietta Lacks or her family (Skloot, 2010). Financially, companies have earned millions by selling HeLa cells for research purposes, yet Lacks' descendants lived in poverty for decades. Health-wise, despite the pivotal role HeLa cells played in advancing cancer treatments, Henrietta Lacks' family faced barriers to accessing medical care, including cancer screenings and treatments, that HeLa cells helped to improve. This is, of course, simplifying a very complicated and well-studied case, but the point is to keep in mind that, at least for some kinds of data, it is important to make sure that the community keeps some degree of control, particularly for applications (as reflected in the above-mentioned CARE principles).

Similarly, the San people of southern Africa have developed a code of ethics to ensure that research involving their communities is conducted in a way that is transparent, respectful, and beneficial. This was born out of past experiences where researchers violated trust by misrepresenting the purpose of their research, publishing biased results, or failing to share findings with the community before publication (South African San Institute, 2017). To address these issues, the San code requires researchers to align their work with local needs, ensure continuous communication, and guarantee that tangible benefits—such as co-research opportunities, skill-sharing, and employment for translators or research assistants—return to the community. An illustrative case is the Hoodia plant, traditionally used by the San as an appetite suppressant. Researchers and pharmaceutical companies extracted knowledge about the plant without prior consultation or agreements with the San. Although the resulting product, a diet supplement, generated significant commercial interest, the San initially received no share of the benefits. Following advocacy and legal negotiations, a benefit-sharing agreement was reached, entitling the San to a portion of future royalties.

Researchers can avoid such conflict by accompanying shared data with licenses that allow commercial or social applications only if part of the benefits are redirected to the community, and also enabling the community to participate in the development (or even reclaim it; South African San Institute, 2017; see also Assembly of First Nations, 2009; Hudson, 2010). This can be aided by legislation on benefit-sharing (e.g., the Namibian 2017 Regulations Under Access to Biological and Genetic Resources and Associated Traditional Knowledge Act; but see Nakanyete, Matengo, & Diez, 2024). Such license decisions are independent of how openly the data is archived: something can be accessible to anyone but still off-limits for certain uses, such as the Disney trademark. This allows individuals and groups to post their data publicly while maintaining legal grounds to contest unwanted applications.

One of the most important considerations when communicating your research will be how you describe the participating communities. Your participant description may be the readers' only experience with the communities involved, especially for those from more remote or small-scale societies (Clifford, 1983). Providing thoughtful and accurate context to your data is not only critical for careful interpretation of results, but an ethical imperative. Prior to dissemination of results, participant communities should be engaged by the research team to advise on (i) how they wish to be portrayed to larger audiences, (ii) what, if anything, should be omitted from descriptions (e.g., if hunting is illegal, then hunting activities should not be reported), and (iii) whenever possible, how they interpret the results of the study—a point to which we return below.

One final consideration is how to communicate research with participant communities themselves. Sharing the products of their efforts, the outcome of your shared collaboration in bringing the research project to fruition, can help build an engaged and sustainable relationship with your participant base. Note, if a separate trip would be required to communicate results after a planned study, consider including it in the grant budget. The types of dissemination materials used in a given community should reflect the participants' own interests, which should be a part of the CER approach (see Section 7.3). When appropriate, and where participant privacy is maintained, it can be worth the extra effort to customize dissemination materials to match the interests of the participants. If you are unsure which aspects of the research may be of interest to the participant communities, one approach is to propose or create dissemination materials on a number of levels. Dissemination materials might consist of printed or recounted summaries, written in lay terms for a broad, non-scientific audience and translated into participant communities' most accessible language(s). Another option is to communicate results using posters or other graphic representations, which can be engaging alternatives to text. Keep in mind that interest may extend beyond the results that made it into the final paper. For example, in a recent study exploring children's attitudes towards other animals, one of us (SPC) asked children which animals they thought were the smartest, most beautiful, etc. When disseminating these results, we could share which animals were most often considered beautiful and how this differed across communities where the study was conducted. Disseminating research back to the participant communities may not only be valuable for building a long-term relationship with participants; it can also provide a fruitful insight into participants' interpretations of their own results, as it spurs further conversations around the topic. If the partnership is truly engaged, this step becomes less of a 'reveal' and more of a continuation of the project dialogue. This engaged dialogue is critical throughout all stages of the research and informs interpretation as well as guiding decisions about methods and processes throughout.

7.7. Discussion and conclusion

In this chapter, we outlined considerations for sharing social science developmental cross-cultural research. We discussed the historical and contemporary motivations for why and how to involve community members in research. We outlined problems as well as solutions and recommended a strong shift in the mindset of this scientific endeavor to one of co-creation of knowledge. To achieve this, we argued that a community-engaged approach is required as well as a recognition that not only 'scientific' methods count as evidence, data, and knowledge. Furthermore, we argued that one must carefully consider who owns and has rights to the knowledge/ data/findings of a research program or project. While recognizing the complexity of this issue, we provided suggestions for sharing research findings with communities in a meaningful way. Ultimately, this rests on dialogue with community partners to determine how data should be shared. Community members must be at the forefront of this decision-making to determine how, with whom and for how long research should be shared. Together, these contributions outline best practices for sharing research with communities, the public, and academic audiences, and provide some recommendations for co-constructing knowledge with communities.

References

Assembly of First Nations. (2009). First nations ethics guide on research and aboriginal knowl- edge. https://achh.ca/wp-content/uploads/2018/07/Guide_Ethics_AFN.pdf

Bartlett, C. (2005, November). Knowledge inclusivity:"Two-Eyed Seeing" for science for the 21st Century. In *Proceedings of the Workshop on Learning Communities as a Tool for Resource Management* (pp. 4-5).

Bartlett, C., Marshall, M., & Marshall, A. (2012). Two-Eyed Seeing and other lessons learned within a co-learning journey of bringing together indigenous and mainstream knowledges and ways of knowing. *J Environ Stud Sci, 2*, 331–340. https://doi.org/10.1007/s13412-012-0086-8

Broesch, T., Crittenden, A. N., Beheim, B., Blackwell, A. D., Bunce, J., Colleran, H., Hagel, K., Kline, M., McElreath, R., Nelson, R. G., Pisor, A. C., Prall, S., Pretelli, I., Purzycki, B., Quinn, E. A., Ross, C.; Scelza, B., Starkweather, K., Stieglitz, J., & Borgerhoff Mulder, M. (2020). Navigating cross-cultural research: methodological and ethical considerations. *Proceedings of the Royal Society B, 287*(1935), 20201245. https://doi:10.1098/rspb.2020.1245

Carpendale, J. I., Atwood, S., & Kettner, V. (2014). Meaning and mind from the perspective of dualist versus relational worldviews: Implications for the development of pointing gestures. *Human Development, 56*(6), 381-400. https://doi.org/10.1159/000357235

Carroll, S. R., Garba, I., Figueroa-Rodríguez, O. L., Holbrook, J., Lovett, R., Materechera, S., Parsons, M., Raseroka, K., Rodriguez-Lonebear, D., Rowe, R., Sara, R., Walker, J. D., Anderson, J., & Hudson, M. (2020). The CARE principles for indigenous data governance. *Data Science Journal, 19*, 43–43.https://doi.org/10.5334/dsj-2020-043

Clifford, J. (1983). On Ethnographic Authority. *Representations, 2*, 118–146. https://doi.org/10.2307/2928386

Dyer, C. (2014). *Livelihoods and learning: Education for all and the marginalisation of mobile pastoralists.* Routledge.

Dyson, J. (2014). *Working childhoods: Youth, agency and the environment in India.* Cambridge University Press.

Femenías, B. (2016). *Bringing Digital Data Management Training into Methods Courses for Anthropology.* American Anthropological Association.

Galaty, J. G. (1989). Cattle and cognition: Aspects of Maasai practical reasoning. In J. Clutton-Brock (Ed.). *The walking larder: Patterns of domestication, pastoralism, and predation* (1st ed., pp. 215–230). Routledge.

Harris, M. (1976). History and significance of the emic/etic distinction. *Annual Review of Anthropology, 5*, 329–350. https://www.jstor.org/stable/2949316

Holmes, A. G. D. (2020). Researcher Positionality--A Consideration of Its Influence and Place in Qualitative Research--A New Researcher Guide. *Shanlax International Journal of Education, 8*(4), 1–10.

Hudson, M., Milne, M., Reynolds, P., Russell, K., & Smith, B. (2010). *Te ara tika : guidelines for Māori research ethics : a framework for researchers and ethics committee members.* Health Research Council of New Zealand on behalf of the Pūtaiora Writing Group.

James, A. (2007). Giving voice to children's voices: Practices and problems, pitfalls and potentials. *American Anthropologist, 109*(2), 201–272.

Krätli, S. (2006). Culture roots of poverty? Education and pastoral livelihood in Turkana and Karamoja. In C. Dyer (Ed.). *The education of nomadic peoples: Current issues, future prospects.* Berghahn Books.

Lancy, D. (2017). *Anthropological Perspectives on Children as Helpers, Workers, Artisans, and Laborers.* https://doi.org/10.1057/978-1-137-53351-7

Lansford, J. E., Gauvain, M., Koller, S. H., Daiute, C., Hyson, M., Motti-Stefanidi, F., Smith, O., Verma, S., & Zhou, N. (2019). The importance of international collaborative research for advancing understanding of child and youth development. *International Perspectives in Psychology, 8*(1), 1–13. https://doi.org/10.1037/ipp0000102

Lepore, W., Hall, B. L., & Tandon, R. (2023). *Bridging Knowledge Cultures: Rebalancing power in the co-construction of knowledge.* Brill. https://doi.org/10.1163/9789004687769

Mathie, A., & Cunningham, G. (2003). From clients to citizens: Asset-based community development as a strategy for community-driven development. *Development in practice, 13*(5), 474–486.

McKenna, S. A., & Main, D. S. (2013). The role and influence of key informants in community-engaged research: A critical perspective. *Action Research, 11*(2), 113–124. https://doi.org/10.1177/1476750312473342

Mikesell, L., Bromley, E., & Khodyakov, D. (2013). Ethical community-engaged research: a literature review. *American journal of public health, 103*(12), e7–e14. https://doi.org/10.2105/AJPH.2013.301605

Muhammad, M., Wallerstein, N., Sussman, A. L., Avila, M., Belone, L., & Duran, B. (2015). Reflections on Researcher Identity and Power: The Impact of Positionality on Community Based Participatory Research (CBPR) Processes and Outcomes. *Critical Sociology, 41*(7-8), 1045–1063. https://doi.org/10.1177/0896920513516025

Nakanyete, N. F., Matengu, K. K., & Diez, J. R. (2024). Rich resources from poor communities: An analysis of Namibia's access and benefit-sharing legislation. *Environmental Development, 49*, 100943. https://doi.org/10.1016/j.envdev.2023.100943

Pike, K. L. (1967). *Language in relation to a unified theory of the structure of human behavior* (2nd ed.). Mouton.

Rogoff, B., Dahl, A., & Callanan, M. (2018). The importance of understanding children's lived experience. *Developmental Review, 50*, 5–15. https://doi.org/10.1016/j.dr.2018.05.006

Skloot, R. (2010). *The immortal life of Henrietta Lacks*. Crown Publishers

South African San Institute (2017) San code of research ethics. Available at: https://www.globalcodeofconduct.org/wp-content/uploads/2018/04/San-Code-of-RESEARCH-Ethics-Booklet_English.pdf

Tian, X. (2018). Generating pastoral skills through work and play in the daily life of Maasai children in Kenya. *Journal of ethnobiology, 38*(2), 170–186. https://doi.org/10.2993/0278-0771-38.2.170

Tian, X. (2019). The role of social norms and interactions in the process of learning-by-doing: From the ethnography of daily work, play, and school participation of children in contemporary pastoralist Maasai Society in Southern Kenya. *African Study Monographs, 40*(2–3), 77–92. https://doi.org/10.14989/244851

Wilkinson, M. D., Dumontier, M., Aalbersberg, I. J., Appleton, G., Axton, M., Baak, A., Blomberg, N., Boiten, J. W., da Silva Santos, L. B., Bourne, P. E., Bouwman, J., Brookes, A. J., Clark, T., Crosas, M., Dillo, I., Dumon, O., Edmunds, S., Evelo, C. T., Finkers, R., Gonzalez-Beltran, A., ... Mons, B. (2016). The FAIR Guiding Principles for scientific data management and stewardship. *Scientific data, 3*, 160018. https://doi.org/10.1038/sdata.2016.18

Wright, A. L., Gabel, C., Ballantyne, M., Jack, S. M., & Wahoush, O. (2019). Using Two-Eyed Seeing in Research With Indigenous People: An Integrative Review. *International Journal of Qualitative Methods, 18*. https://doi.org/10.1177/1609406919869695

8. Learning to navigate change: Case studies in education across cultural boundaries

Coordinated by Dustin Eirdosh

This chapter explores the complex cultural dynamics of schooling and social learning traditions across diverse communities, shedding light on the potential conflicts and opportunities found at the intersection of globalized educational models and local community values. The concept of ethno-diverse theories of schooling is introduced as a general frame to reflect on the cultural-cognitive models influencing individual, community, and even expert perceptions of educational policies and practices. A series of case studies from researchers and practitioners across globally diverse communities reveals systemic challenges and opportunities in the adaptation of local contexts to global educational change. These cases vary widely in terms of author foci and community demographics, yet some connective themes become clear. Conclusions highlight two key implications for globalizing educational policies, drawn from across these diverse communities. Ultimately, educational policy must better account for local cultural context, while also more proactively driving participatory means of valued school improvement.

8.1. Introduction

Dustin Eirdosh & Susan Hanisch

Humans and our ancestors have been engaged in cultural learning to survive, adapt, and (sometimes) thrive in ever changing

©2025 Dustin Eirdosh, et al., CC BY-NC 4.0

https://doi.org/10.11647/OBP.0440.08

environments, likely for thousands of years into our deep history (Csibra & Gergely, 2011; Sterelny, 2012; van Schaik et al., 2019). The emergence and global spread of more formal institutions of learning, particularly in the form of public schooling, represents a relatively recent yet drastic change in the structure of social learning, from the scale of small groups and communities in day-to-day life, up to the more long-term cultural evolutionary dynamics of the global collective knowledge of humanity. What is more, the models of schooling that continue to be globally predominant today have been shaped largely by 19th-century WEIRD (Western, Educated, Industrialized, Rich, and Democratic; Henrich et al., 2010) societal values, beliefs, and needs. As a report by the OECD (2019, p. 9) states: "Most 21st-century students are still being taught by teachers using 20th-century pedagogical practices in 19th-century school organizations." A mismatch and conflicts are emerging between the values and ideas that have shaped school systems in a top-down manner, and the values and ideas of school communities about what schooling should be like, not only in western societies but also across global cultural diversity.

This chapter curates a very diverse collection of case studies from communities and researchers around the world, looking at the interface of changing social-economic landscapes, the emergence of formal schooling, and the cultural values of marginalized communities. While the researchers and communities profiled in these case studies are each very different from the other, a few overlapping themes are important to note across them. In most of the cases presented, you will find the stories of both researchers and communities working to navigate the complex social conflicts between community and school values, and conceptual differences that emerge when global models of schooling encounter, or are forced upon, otherwise autonomous cultures with their own long histories of social learning and norms related to childhood and the relationships between generations.

We begin by briefly framing the concept of ethno-diverse theories of schooling, that is, the cultural-cognitive models of individuals and communities related to schooling. All humans who grow up in or near communities that have schools are likely to develop a range of concepts, attitudes, values, and beliefs related to the nature, purpose, and function of schooling in their own lives, in their communities, and in the world at large. Here, we call these theories of schooling (ToS), which are hypothesized to integrate a range of other ethnotheories, including those related to human development, parenting, learning, intelligence, and the larger society (Eirdosh & Hanisch, 2023; see also Keller et al., 2006; Leseman, 2020). An increasing percentage of those humans with some (intuitive, developing) ToS will actually go on to attend a school. Some of those will go on to complete secondary school. Some of these individuals may pursue higher levels of education, while a greater percentage overall will likely pursue other jobs, and ultimately have children that will again attend the next generation of schooling. An incredibly small percentage of overall humanity will gain enough education and political power to influence and implement educational policies that deeply structure social learning dynamics from local to national and global scales. From this view, it can be easy to see how conflict could emerge between top-down globalized ToS, and more bottom-up local or regional ToS (and learning). The case studies below certainly represent the potential for that broadly framed conflict; however, they also provide a qualitative reflection on the incredible complexities that we find at this cultural interface.

Greenfield provides an overview of 42 years of fieldwork studying weaving apprenticeships in a Maya community, in relation to the rise of schooling within the culture. Schooling has impacted the fabric of social learning in this community, including the practices, norms, and values of weaving traditions. Hermida addresses education and child cognitive development under poverty, and highlights the differences between rural and urban poverty, challenging us to think more deeply about our theories of schooling in relation to economic equity and global development.

Next, Simatende provides a comparative analysis of the concepts of intelligence that inform schooling in Zambia, compared with the (ethno-)concepts of intelligence found across this country. This view offers challenging questions about the most basic framing of the high-level organizing concepts that underpin the theories, assessment tools, and overall design of schooling in this context. Following this, Prasetijo and Aprilia looks at the social identity dynamics of the Orang Rimba communities, as related to government schooling policies and the government recognition of ethnic identities. The description of a program for hunter-gatherer children from these communities highlights the ongoing need and complexity of embracing comprehensive educational reform in cooperation with the marginalized communities themselves.

Two cases then look at marginalized Adivasi peoples within India. Lavi, Kakkoth, and Chellan take a critical view on the long-term impacts of boarding schools for the Adivasi peoples. Highlighting some successful cases, this contribution adds to the call for comprehensive and community-based reforms that better align government-created theories of schooling with the values and understandings of local communities. Sarala Nanu focuses on education in Adivasi communities during the COVID-19 pandemic, highlighting how technology, power, and culture interact to create unique challenges in navigating adaptations during the global health crisis.

The last three case studies in this chapter take on a more directly applied, interventionist approach. Rothstein-Fisch and Trumbull look at the *Bridging Cultures* project to explore strategies for cultural adaptation of the standard curriculum for Latino students. Among other facets, this work highlights the potential to leverage students' shared community values to shift pedagogical approaches from individual to collective learning strategies. Guerrero-Meyer offers a unique perspective from a practitioner with a background in cross-cultural developmental psychology, reflecting on the experience of becoming a teacher in Los Angeles working with students of Mexican heritage. Here we see the challenges of navigating personal and professional knowledge with the theories of schooling that are required by a state-mandated curriculum. In the only case study from a European context, Eirdosh and Hanisch summarize a community science project that challenges students, teachers, and school administrators to make their implicit theories of schooling explicit, and to critically evaluate claims about the nature of human learning (across cultures) and the relative role of student autonomy and curriculum structure in adaptive learning strategies.

8.2. A 42-year history of weaving apprenticeship in a Maya community

Patricia M. Greenfield

I start this case history of three generations of learning to weave in a Zinacantec Maya community with a quote from our 1980 article, an account of weaving apprenticeship in the first generation, observed in 1970:

> Blanco and Chodorow (1964), studying children's work and obedience in Zinacantan, found that most chores were done on command, although older girls tended to do chores more autonomously. Another pertinent finding was that almost all commands are obeyed; yet almost no discernible reinforcement takes place[...]. In learning to do chores, the children are acquiring the skills of their parents. Mead (1943) contrasts the intergenerational continuity promoted by this process with modern education, which promotes discontinuities between parents and children (Childs & Greenfield, 1980, p. 270).

Learning to weave on a backstrap loom is the most complex contribution to household subsistence carried out in the highland Maya communities of Chiapas, Mexico. Blanco and Chodorow's characterization fits what we found in our video study of girls learning to weave in 1970 in the hamlet of Nabenchauk. At that time, not one of the skilled teenage weavers had any experience with formal schooling (Childs & Greenfield, 1980). Schooling for girls was starting, and a few girls between the ages of eight and 10 had some school experience (Greenfield & Childs, 1977). "One reason given for not sending girls to school is so that they should learn to cook and weave at home" (Childs & Greenfield, 1977, p. 271). At the time, we did not think this reason was valid. However, it turned out to be very prophetic!

The learning process

In 1970,

> Zinacanteco girls weaving their very first article looked amazingly expert in comparison with a beginners' class of adult American women observed in Cambridge, Massachusetts. It seemed likely

> that they gained this proficiency by watching older girls and women weave. Our video records indicate that, on the average, one girl under six was visible near each weaver. These incidental data indicate that young girls have plentiful opportunity to observe (Childs & Greenfield, 1980, p. 302).

Microanalysis of our video records indicated that observation occupied more than 50% of the time when learners were attempting their first weaving. The percentage of time steadily declined as learners acquired increasing levels of weaving experience and expertise. Expert weavers never observed someone else weave while they were weaving a piece. Inversely, the percentage of time spent participating in the weaving process increased steadily as girls became more experienced weavers. Visual attentiveness to the task at hand was amazing: Even first-time learners spent only eight percent of their time visually distracted from their loom; by the time learners were on their third weaving, visual distraction had completely disappeared. We concluded that:

> learners will display a high degree of attentiveness when they are learning a skill that is crucial for their group. The large proportion of time spent observing among beginning weavers actually has a second significance: if the learner is watching the teacher, then the teacher is actually doing weaving; this [is] one form of [task] simplification or scaffolding. But there is a second, lesser degree of teacher intervention: the teacher may do the weaving cooperatively with the weaver (Childs & Greenfield, 1980, pp.302-303).

Our thesis was that scaffolding—that is, teacher help—would be developmentally sensitive and that scaffolding would decline as learners became more expert weavers. This is exactly what occurred: as learners became more experienced (measured by how many weavings they had ever completed), there was a decline in the teacher taking over the loom and the weaving process; instead, cooperative weaving (that is, the teacher helping the weaving learner) increased. Participation had two different forms: cooperative work with the teacher and independent weaving. Independent weaving (with no teacher help) also increased steadily with experience—from seven percent of the time for first-time weavers to 100% of the time for expert weavers.

Teaching techniques were correlated with skill level rather than with age. This pattern indicated a good 'match' between learner characteristics and teacher input. In this sense, contrary to some claims in anthropology that learners learn subsistence skills by themselves in village or nomadic settings, we found that the subsistence skill of weaving elicited developmentally sensitive teaching. In terms of the role of verbal instruction, again, the techniques were sensitive to the developmental stage of weaving expertise. For first-time weavers, teachers provided the most verbal structure: 91% of verbalizations were directives or commands. Teacher statements and questions increased as weaving learners gained more experience. Explanations and reinforcement (praise or criticism) were almost completely absent, but criticism was more frequent than praise.

Social change

As the community's economy shifted from subsistence and agriculture to money and commerce (from more Gemeinschaft [community] to more Gesellschaft [society], to use German sociologist Tönnies' terms), the 1990s generation of weaving learners (all descendants of first-generation learners in our earlier study) became more independent in the way they learned to weave; that is, they received less help from a teacher (Greenfield, 2004; Greenfield, Maynard, & Childs, 2003). Part of the reason for this shift was that many mothers, the most usual teachers, were away selling at markets, leaving learners at home with siblings and cousins. Under these conditions, not only did the learners become generally more independent of a teacher, but they also relied more on their peer generation to help them, and less on the older generation.

Although schooling was more frequent in the second generation of weaving learners than in the first generation, most girls left elementary school after a few years. However, by the time we studied weaving apprenticeship in the third generation (2012), commercial activity had developed much further and completing elementary school had become normative for girls (Figure 8.1). For the first time in three generations, some mothers—many of whom would have studied as weaving learners in the prior generation—had attended school (Maynard et al., 2023).

At this point, we found that the fears expressed in 1970 were now historical fact: girls with more schooling had less weaving expertise, and, overall, weaving expertise had declined since the prior generation, as school education had increased (Maynard et al., 2023). At the same time, teacher praise, so valued in our individualistic culture, had increased, as had the ratio of praise to criticism. Perhaps most interesting, as mothers began to attend school, they began, for the first time, to use verbal explanation, a behavior of schoolteachers, to help the next generation learn to weave.

Fig. 8.1 Three Nabenchauk girls work independently at the school blackboard, Nabenchauk, 1991. ©Lauren Greenfield/Institute. All rights reserved.

8.3. Poverty and schooling outcomes in Argentina

Maria Julia Hermida

Among the factors affecting education that are addressed in this chapter, economic differences deserve special mention. Most non-WEIRD countries share one characteristic: they are poor. Poverty is one of the main factors affecting child cognitive development (Farah et al., 2006) and educational opportunities (UNESCO, 2020). Several decades of research conducted by developmental psychologists have shown how living in a low-socioeconomic-status home is associated with lower levels of intelligence, executive functioning, and other cognitive functions (Farah et al., 2006) as well as lower school achievement (Bradley & Corwyn, 2002). Further recent research has also shown differences in brain structure according to income (Noble et al., 2015).

Among the multiple factors moderating this relationship, language (associated with parental educational level) and stress have been considered as the main home factors. Unfortunately, in most cases, education is not sufficient to reduce the gap between the poor and the non-poor children. Educational opportunities are significantly lower for poorer children: financial costs of schooling are higher for poorer families; poor schools have lower financial incentives and, thus, the most educated teachers usually prefer to teach in richer schools; poor children have less access to educational materials (such as textbooks); and the list goes on (UNESCO, 2020). As a result, poor children experience fewer opportunities from the beginning and education has failed to close that gap.

Furthermore, science analyzing the association between socioeconomic status and child cognitive development or education has been mainly driven by studies conducted in WEIRD countries. The lack of diversity in child development research is a central concern in the field (Moriguchi, 2022; Nielsen et al., 2017), with specific calls to increase child cognitive research in non-WEIRD samples (Miller-Cotto et al., 2022; Rowley & Camacho, 2015), including in Latin America (Alves et al., 2022). In particular, current knowledge about poverty is based mostly on American children living in low-socioeconomic-status homes; however, American poverty might not reflect the kind of poverty present in the majority of the world.

In fact, life in poverty varies significantly according to the region. For example, being extremely poor in East Asia, the Pacific, Middle East, and North Africa means lack of access to sanitation; in Europe and Central Asia it is associated with no schooling enrollment; in South Asia and Latin America it implies lack of adequate sanitation or electricity; and in Sub-Saharan Africa, extreme poverty involves a combined lack of access to sanitation, electricity, and schooling

(World Bank, 2018). As such, we should expect that different types of poverty might differently impact child cognitive development, and thus, might prepare children in different ways for school.

Data from a study conducted in Argentina (Hermida et al., 2019) has shed light on this issue. The study investigated how children living in the same country, sharing the same general values, attending public schools with similar curricula, and considered poor, but living in rural and urban contexts had different cognitive performance. Executive functions and non-verbal intelligence performance, as well as individual and environmental information, were obtained from 131 five-year-old children living in Argentinean low-socioeconomic-status rural and urban contexts. Additionally, some contextual and individual variables that are typically associated with child cognitive development (i.e., parental education and occupation, school assistance, family size, and other socioeconomic information related to the families), were measured. The results showed that, among children living in poor homes, rural children had significantly lower scores in all cognitive tasks. Also, rural children have significantly lower access to preschool education than their urban counterparts, and their fathers (usually in charge of family income) have lower education and occupational levels than urban fathers. These variables explained the urban–rural gap.

These results suggest that poverty measures (usually generated in urban contexts) are not sensitive enough to describe the scarcity of rural contexts. In other words, the classic classifications of 'low' and 'middle' socioeconomic status are not sufficiently nuanced to describe different types of poverty. Even in the same country, and the same culture, children who are considered poor can have very different opportunities and risks for development. Also, since different types of poverty (within the same country and culture) have differential effects on child cognition, we can expect that the effects of poverty in the non-WEIRD world will be different from those in the WEIRD (and well-studied) world. Thus, it is important to extend research to low socioeconomic samples from non-WEIRD countries and avoid generalizations based only on WEIRD data.

8.4. Ethno-concepts of intelligence in Zambia

Barnabas Simatende

Psychometric measures of intelligence (popularly known as the IQ test) have widely been exported around the world. These tests bring with them both ostensible utility and hidden implications that may or may not be valuable to the society into which they are imported. As noted by Ball & Pence (2000), one of the main avenues for subjugating Indigenous peoples to colonial culture and governance has been the imposition of childcare and education that has denied the legitimacy of thought, lifestyles, religions, and languages of First Nations people. Furthermore, Vernon (1967) and Durojaiye (1984) argued that politicians and other representatives of the African people had deliberately, and wisely, opted for a western-style education as an instrument of national modernization, through which the human capital of the economy would be transformed to address the challenges of the modern state. Yet there is increasing evidence that there exists ethnocentric error in the development, administration, and interpretation of tests. Zambia is no exception as she, like several African countries, adopted and used western assessments of intelligence to classify, sort, and rank children and candidates in relation to opportunities in life.

Psychometric theorists hence define intelligence as an intellectual trait or a set of traits that differ among people and so characterize some people to a greater extent than others (Shaffer & Kipp 2007). In Africa, communities have well-developed and culturally embedded motivational and cognitive assessment systems of intelligence that integrate skill and knowledge about all aspects of life, which are traditionally implemented in the child's daily routine as a preparation for successful life in community (Nsamenang, 2006; Akinsola, 2011). Research by Simatende among the Lozi people of Western Zambia, and that by Serpell among the Chewa of Eastern Zambia, indicates that, "the concepts of intelligence are highly characterized by social responsibility" (Serpell 1993, p. 16). A study by Sternberg and others further affirms that a person who is cognitively quick but lacks social responsibility is generally not regarded as intelligent (Sternberg, Conway, Ketron, & Bernstein, 1981). This points to a hypothetical understanding that African language groups not only possess some common concepts of intelligence and how it is assessed, but further possess common social cultural practices that are key to the socialization of neophytes or children into the local culture.

Qualitative research that explored the embedded, traditional, cultural, motivational, and cognitive assessment practices through which child intelligence is assessed among the seven major language groups of Zambia—Lozi, Tonga, Chewa, Luvale, Kaonde, Bemba and Lunda—was conducted. Research revealed that across these seven major language groups, there exist common themes that characterize intelligence and criteria to identify it. Verifiable categories that were identified reveal a common hierarchy of assessment criteria. Social responsibility is ranked as the highest level of intelligence, followed by industriousness and/ or ingenuity. Respect and obedience are collectively third on the hierarchy, followed by cognitive ability, honesty, trustworthiness, and initiative. This implies that intelligence is characterized by these social and cultural developmental values that form a child's developmental niche. Furthermore, these findings indicate that there is an established local cultural (Indigenous) education system and assessment criteria that aims to aid children to develop into productive and responsible adults; there is learning that takes place in a local cultural setting that is centered on both the individual and the well-being of the local community, village, and society at large; and there are various subject materials that a developing child is expected to learn, assigned to them by gender and age.

These research findings present an ongoing need to explore contextual concepts of intelligence that should guide education systems of different cultures and peoples. Intelligence, understood as socio-culturally influenced, challenges the idea that general universal education systems and universal assessment procedures are viable means of assessing education and educational achievements. It is therefore arguable that the process of institutionalizing intelligence testing in Africa threatens to distort important aspects of education in dysfunctional ways, rather than enhancing its precision and efficiency, because how individual children's progress is appraised varies according to parental goals and aspirations, cultural norms, and social organization.

8.5. The Orang Rimba's struggle for public acceptance of education in Indonesia

Adi Prasetijo & Cika Aprilia

Six hundred and thirty-three ethnic groups live in Indonesia (Central Statistics Agency, 2015); each has its own language, religion, customs, traditions, conventions, and work ethic. Sectoral, ministerial, and regional legislation promote customary communities; the Indonesian constitution acknowledges them. Special education for rural or impoverished regions and isolated Indigenous populations is required under the National Education System Law. Due to geography, external cultures, and the availability of education, providing special education programs for Indigenous tribes is difficult. Yet, according to the Research and Development Agency of the Ministry of Education and Culture, local customs, traditional activities, and Indonesian national ideals should complement each other (Pusat Penelitian Kebijakan Pendidikan dan Kebudayaan, 2016). Here, we focus on the case of a special education program for the Orang Rimba.

Indonesia's Orang Rimba are a hunter-gatherer group living in Jambi, Sumatra Island, Indonesia. According to a 2008 KKI Warsi bioregion survey, there were 3,650 Orang Rimba in Jambi. Each Orang Rimba group exhibits unique ecological traits and lifestyles shaped by the specific characteristics of their respective regions (Prasetijo, 2021, p. 236) (Figure 8.2).

In the early 1980s, large-scale infrastructure, settlement, and oil palm plantation development projects changed the Sumatran landscape (Prasetijo, 2021). These projects replaced forest habitats, depleted forest resources, and thus, food options for forest dwellers. Further, forest conversion practices have impoverished Orang Rimba hunting and gathering. Despite these obstacles, Orang Rimba children, who were displaced by post-1970s forestry and plantation growth, want numerous types of careers. An organization called KKI Warsi supports the rights to education of Orang Rimba people.

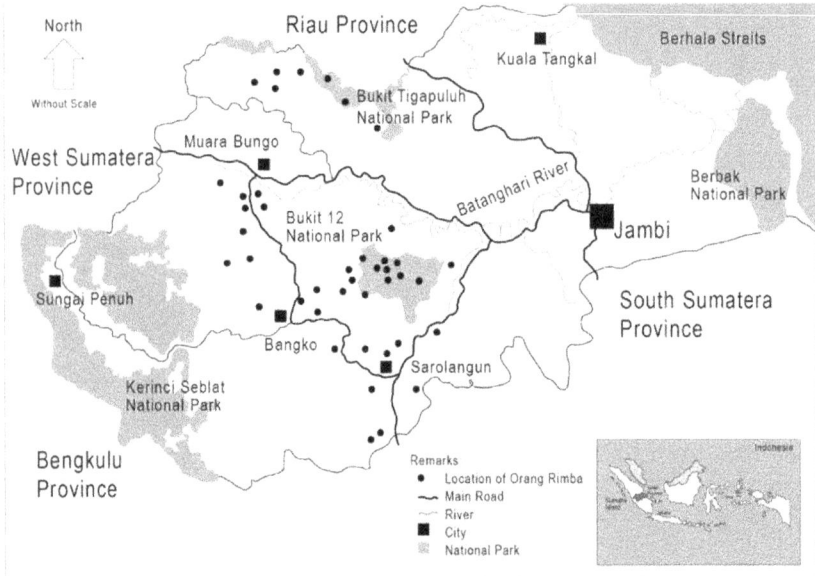

Fig. 8.2 Map of The Orang Rimba's habitation area in the Jambi Province.
©KKI Warsi. All rights reserved.

Advocacy and education

KKI Warsi is a non-profit organization that carries out community assistance activities in and around the forest. KKI Warsi acts as an advocate and companion for the Orang Rimba, who are marginalized by government development. Their area of activity includes Sumatra, Kalimantan, and Papua. KKI Warsi tackles politics, education, health, and administration. KKI Warsi's work on sustainable livelihoods has made forest protection essential (Warsi, 2011: xi). For example, through participatory mapping, KKI Warsi recommended the expansion of the Bukit Duabelas Biosphere Reserve, which is the only remaining area of lowland natural forest accessible for Orang Rimba in the center of Jambi Province.

KKI Warsi is also working with Yusak Adrian Hutapea to provide alternative education to the Orang Rimba. This step has been taken to eradicate illiteracy and increase the Orang Rimba's understanding of the outside world. The special education program is developed in accordance with the customs and culture of the Orang Rimba, using the read, write, and count pattern method

(Warsi, 2011). Education cadres or trained individuals from among the Orang Rimba are also involved in providing education, so that it is more easily accepted by group members. In this way, KKI Warsi supports the Orang Rimba community in their right to culturally relevant education.

Between formal and informal education

Table 8.1. Orang Rimba participation in alternative education. Data obtained from Warsi (2011)

No	Category	Can read, write, & calculate	Package A (Elementary equivalent)	Package B (Junior High equivalent)	Formal Senior High School
1.	Orang Rimba who live in Bukit 12 National Park	345	19	4	1
2.	Orang Rimba people in the southern part of the province of Jambi, along the highway route	19			

Orang Rimba people follow ancestral practices, notably *cempalo*—a set of taboos and protective boundaries used to maintain their cultural identity and limit outside influences. Orang Rimba religious life acknowledges the interdependence of *halom* (custom) and *halam* (nature). Violating *halom* implies breaking customs. Education is considered alien, leading Orang Rimba to be *orang terang* (enlightened), and thus, to lose their forest and culture. Awareness of the cultural background of the Orang Rimba is an important first step in designing appropriate education. Recognition of their specificity must be reflected in specialized treatment from educational actors. A friendly and sustainable approach to education is one that is co-constructed with the Orang

Rimba community, involving the joint study of their problems, the search for alternative solutions, and the implementation of real actions together. KKI Warsi wants a community-built inclusive education system for Orang Rimba. By 2011, a total of 345 students living in Bukit Duabelas National Park received alternative education under two program streams, called 'packages' (Table 8.1; see also Warsi, 2011, pp. xix, xi–xiii). Package A is equivalent to elementary school. Package B is equivalent to junior high school.

Table 8.2. Challenges and strategic approaches in the Orang Rimba education program

No	Education program of the Orang Rimba	Recommended Approach
1	Education relevant to the background of the Orang Rimba	Governments must modify the curriculum or education policy to encourage education. This will allow Indigenous Indonesians to access equal opportunities and connect with the public without abandoning their traditional identity
2	External support for Orang Rimba education	Outside parties help the Orang Rimba education program understand the adaptation to mainstream society by providing educational opportunities that facilitate social integration
3	Reading and writing skills are developed via participation in the Orang Rimba community development program	Educational programs raise Orang Rimba awareness of equal opportunities
4	The education level required to complete formal education is equivalent to packages A, B, and high school	This program supports Orang Rimba's adaptations to life in general society, which they could not adapt to previously. Education is a path to social integration

The settlements near Bukit Duabelas National Park enrolled 19 Orang Rimba children in schools in early 2009. This initial cohort had just seven students who finished elementary school. By 2020, about 350 Orang Rimba youngsters attended kindergarten to high school, with some pursuing military careers. Although children have the option to attend formal schooling, it is not compulsory so the decision to attend formal education is determined by the respective families. Thus, improved regulations and institutional support are urgently needed to provide wider and appropriate access for Indigenous communities (Chamim, 2020: 261-263). Yet, challenges persist. Because their forest homes have been turned into plantations, Orang Rimba are forced to live on the road and struggle to find permanent homes (Warsi, 2011, pp. 99–100). The Orang Rimba's nomadic lifestyle and displacement have contributed to public misconceptions and stigma. Further, environmental changes that affect hunting and gathering require the development of new skills that can be difficult to acquire. Education can help Orang Rimba fight stigma, advocate for their own rights, and develop necessary skills. Table 8.2 shows the challenges identified by KKI Warsi, and their recommended approach to tackling these challenges.

Conclusion

The Orang Rimba, a hunter-gatherer group in Indonesia, confronts challenges related to social isolation and environmental displacement. Government institutions must focus on Indigenous educational services. Despite challenges, Orang Rimba children now benefit from the education provided by KKI Warsi, which has supported them in claiming their rights. Ensuring formal education for all Orang Rimba children will require continued support from both governmental and non-governmental institutions.

8.6. Boarding schools for extremely marginalized Adivasi (Indigenous) people in India

Noa Lavi, Seetha Kakkoth, and Vinod Chellan

The Kattunayaka and Cholanaickan are two small Indigenous (also referred locally as Adivasi) communities living on the forested slopes of the Western Ghats mountain ridge in south India, on the border between the states of Kerala and Tamil Nadu. These communities are recognized under India's Scheduled Tribes (STs), a term that clusters various historically disadvantaged groups and entitles them to government protection and support (Constitution of India, Article 342). They are also included under Particularly Vulnerable Tribal Groups (PVTGs), an official classification that singles out certain ST groups based on criteria such as stagnant or dwindling population size, and what is considered to be pre-agricultural level of technology, as well as extremely low social, economic, and educational backgrounds.

Historically classified as hunter-gatherers, both communities used to be semi-nomadic and relied on forest produce as well as the trading of Non-Wood Forest Produce (NWFP). Their life, culture, child-rearing practices, and learning systems were intimately tied to the surrounding ecology. However, in recent decades, processes of deforestation, resettlement, and sedentarization have led to increased interaction with mainstream society and fewer opportunities to rely on the forest for their livelihood. Labelled under ST and PVTGs, both of the communities are targeted for aid and development initiatives aimed at promoting socio-economic change, including formal education which is considered to be a key policy for social 'upliftment'.

While day schools are available for some ST communities across both states, Cholanaickan and Kattunayaka children are often taken to boarding schools, also known as Residential or Ashram schools. These schools have been set up since the 1990s specifically for children belonging to the PVTGs. Run by the Scheduled Tribes Development Department (STDD), residential schools aim to provide free education and hostel lodging to support children's assimilation into the mainstream school system. However, despite substantial investments, educational outcomes like literacy remain low. Dropout rates are very high, especially in the transition from primary to secondary levels (Rajam & Malarvizhi, 2011).

Today, both communities are under intense pressure to send children to residential schools run by the state and staffed predominantly by members of more dominant social groups, whose understanding of childhood and learning is very different from that of the children's families. Prioritizing residential schools over day schools is a decision rooted in a common belief among school and government officials that in those communities, the family poses a central obstacle to children's education (Kakkoth, 2014a; Pandita, 2015; Sujatha, 2002). Parents have been described by many officials as uncompetitive, lacking aspiration and knowledge of outside habits and norms and careless towards their children's education, future, and wellbeing (Kakkoth, 2014a, b; Lavi 2018). In this short section, we argue that this discourse not only reflects social stigma about Cholanaickan and Kattunakas; it also works to reproduce this stigma. Doing so, it undermines the significant challenges faced by families in their engagement with school institutions and works to delegitimize community lifeways and perspectives about their own children. Moreover, we will show that this approach has devastating long-term implications on communities and children, and it has not been proven to result in better school achievements. Examining the situation through the perspectives of the Kattunayaka and Cholanaikan parents and children sheds light on the experience and impacts of residential schools and reveals a complex negotiation between hope and concern.

Many Kattunayaka and Cholanaickan parents and children express interest in schools and perceive the future benefits that formal education has to offer, particularly for the children's future relations with neighboring communities. A Kattunayaka elder told Lavi that "children should know how to speak Tamil and Malayalam so they can get along with people in town" and understand how to properly behave in their presence to gain their respect. Parents also mentioned the hope that if their children attend school, the community will no longer be easily cheated by employers, shopkeepers, and officials (Lavi, 2018). In the case of Cholanaickan, parents also showed enthusiasm in sending their children to school with the hope that they will improve their opportunities in life (Kakkoth, 2014a, b). Yet, concrete experiences quickly lead to disillusionment.

One of the key constraints is the poor-quality teaching and the attitude towards the children demonstrated by the teachers at these schools. They are frequently absent from class and show little commitment to students. Belonging to more dominant social groups, teachers lack knowledge of the children's culture and often perceive students as socially inferior, 'slow learners', which leads to discrimination and verbal abuse (Kakkoth, 2014a; Lavi, 2022a). In many schools, harassment and punishments like beatings, ear pinching, and ridicule create an unsafe environment which discourages many students and leads them to drop out (Kakkoth, 2014a, b). Today, the stigma is enhanced by the problem of alcoholism in many villages. Rather than supporting parents in this challenge, many teachers minimize their interactions with parents and opt to separate children from their communities as a solution.

Formal schooling also brings with it a profound clash of cultures. Differences between home and school child-rearing practices and values pose profound challenges for the children. For the teachers, this justifies their perspective of parental carelessness and incapacity, as they see the children who arrive at school at the age of five or six unequipped with the skills required for school learning (Kakkoth, 2014a). However, we argue that Cholanaickan and Kattunayaka parents are not careless. In fact, there are many elaborate parenting strategies that they use to direct their children through their learning journey (e.g., Lavi, 2022b; Naveh, 2016). Yet the core values and child-rearing practices fostered by the community differ significantly from those highlighted by the school, and reflect a very different understanding of childhood.

Cholanaickan and Kattunayaka children are brought up with ample autonomy from infancy. Autonomy and social skills are core values, considered by parents as vital to child development and markers of personhood. Adults intentionally refrain from direct top-down verbal teaching and coercion, instead striving to provide opportunities for self-directed learning and access to materials, tools, and activities. Learning is done mainly through observation, participation, and trial and error, and adults' guidance is subtle and allows room for the child's autonomous choices (Bird-David, 1999; Lavi, 2022a, b; Naveh, 2016). In residential schools, top-down adult-led teaching methodology provides stark contrasts to these local learning systems. Formal rote learning clashes with the local preference for learning through lived experiences. Alien school knowledge ignores and undermines communities' ecological expertise, impressing a mainstream perspective and identity on the children. Children are compelled to obey strict rules and schedules that they have not set and cannot change. The conflict between ideas of autonomy and obedience and the regimented nature of boarding schools creates frustration among the children and represents a prison-like environment for many of them (Kakkoth, 2014a, b). Likewise, while maintaining relations is a core value among both communities, Kakkoth (2014a) showed that teachers were using harsh corporal punishment to break students' social bonds, which they view as conflicting with the obedience they expect from the children.

There are many stories documented of Kattunayaka and Cholanaickan children who escaped school and never returned after a holiday, unable to bear the alienating prison-like atmosphere (Kakkoth, 2014a, b; Lavi, 2022a). Autonomy plays a part here as well. As, in these communities, children choose their learning path, parents are often reluctant to force school attendance, instead expressing sympathy for children's dissatisfaction. They will encourage children, but will refrain, for example, from sending back children who choose to drop out (Lavi, 2022a). Children have the right to exert their customary independence. The decision to attend school regularly lies in the hands of the individual child. "Our children withdrawn from education primarily centered around dissatisfaction. We refrain from pressuring them as we acknowledge the sincerity of their feelings and concerns," testified a parent. As parents and children are both quickly disillusioned by the current experience of formal education, dropout rates remain high.

It is important to note, however, that despite the common official resentment towards community parenting practices, parents do not perceive themselves as hindering their children's prospects. Lavi (2022b) showed that Kattunayaka parents foster autonomy and social skills as they consider those traits to be vital not only within the community but in other contexts throughout a child's life. These skills are valued as a precondition of any learning, including academic or practical learning. Parents consider willingness to explore and experiment, and the ability to create and maintain contacts, as valuable and required for learning in all social contexts, including in the classroom.

Three decades following the inception of residential schools for the Cholanaickan and Kattunayaka children, it is vital to examine the long-term impact on these communities. While seeking to empower, schooling often exacerbates Indigenous groups' vulnerability (Ninkova et al., 2024). Formal education profoundly impacts identity, socialization, knowledge, and worldviews. In South India, a primary consequence is the systematic delegitimization of communities' lifeways. Schools construct home-school relations hierarchically, positioning themselves as the professional authority and measuring parental practices against school values (Dale, 1996). Cultural differences are labelled by school officials as deficiencies rather than diversity. This delegitimizes long-standing parental perceptions and practices. Children experience this criticism from the moment they arrive at school. They are discouraged from using their mother tongues and are often encouraged by teachers "not to be like their parents" (Lavi, 2018).

Coping with endemic discrimination and verbal abuse creates lasting trauma and social rupture. The regimented nature of schooling also impacts the children's personality and socialization, and gradually diminishes their autonomy and transforms learner-led and cooperative community dynamics. Indeed, those children who chose to remain in school are forced to submit to its hierarchical social order, authoritarian control, and fixed schedules dictating their entire day. Absorbing new behavioral norms, they begin to imitate teachers and attempt to order and coerce other children. They also become more compliant to instructions, surrendering the autonomy valued in their communities. In this, rigid school discipline aimed at obedience directly suppresses the autonomy considered critical for maturity, thus eroding local egalitarian dynamics and dramatically changing social relations (Lavi, 2022a).

Elders painfully observe the consequent rupture: "These children, they are Malayali now. They do not care for their *sonta* [relatives], never want to be with us... They are no longer

Nayaka." (Lavi, 2018). Another Kattunayaka mother complained, "In the Ashram school they are living in a cage from 5 years to 15 years. They do not have any love towards their parents also. In the Ashram school they live like orphans" (Kakkoth, 2014a). Vinod Chellan, the Cholanaickan scholar who co-authored this section, observed: "Within our community, we have a unique system of community education which focuses on practical teachings about life encompassing economic principles, social duties, customs, values, rights, and future prospects. But unfortunately, the present school education system fails to recognize this social learning, contributing to the erosion of the community's cultural heritage."

As learning occurs in the community through observing and participating in adult activities, ruptured intergenerational bonds diminish children's learning opportunities. This leads to their de-skilling and greater dependence on state support. With low-quality schooling rarely improving economic mobility, losing local knowledge and skills increases poverty and desperation. Vinod Chellan added: "Children who return from school seem to struggle to adapt here and appear unfit for both the forest and the external world." Unable to rely on their community's traditional knowledge, yet excluded from professional employment, they fall between two worlds. Ultimately, the promise of advancement through education rings hollow when structural barriers persist. The benefits of schooling fail to materialize, while loss of traditional knowledge and ties is certain.

However, taking himself as an example, Vinod Chellan, who pursues higher education in a University in Kerala, argues that children's struggles can be significantly eased with the support of caring and dedicated teachers. Reflecting on his own education journey he recollects:

> Yes, I also struggled a lot like others during my school days. But somehow or other I could get along with the system with the help of very few teachers. The positive relationships I've cultivated with [a few of my teachers] have not only enhanced my academic performance but also nurtured my skills in sports and the arts. Teachers have been instrumental in recognizing and fostering these talents, contributing significantly to my overall development.

He adds: "These teachers could understand my cultural background and gave me ample time for my overall development. Yes, we need someone to walk with us as a facilitator."

Today, there are a few Cholanaickan (the first-generation learners who joined the Ashram School in late 1990s) who, like Vinod, could pursue their education at secondary level and had secured jobs in the Forest Department as forest guard, forest watcher, beat forest officer, etc. They are now keen on sending their own children to schools. This has created a positive wave in society to send more children to school. However, it is important to note that, despite this enthusiasm, they too have adopted a non-coercive approach and refrain from pressuring their children to go back to school, if they happen to face circumstances leading them to drop out.

While these few success stories offer a glimpse of hope, it is crucial to recognize that the vast majority of the Cholanaickan and Kattunayakan children still face significant challenges. To truly create an inclusive education system and support these children's journeys in school, we argue that a fundamental transformation in educational systems is essential. The attitude, understanding and commitment of teachers is the first key condition to create positive changes in the system. Another condition is a deep understanding and respect for communities' values and practices. As argued by Serpell (1994; 2011), for any program or policy to receive recognition as a source of guidance for families, it must not only meet the criteria of a community of scholarship but must also resonate with community understanding. Legitimizing local notions of childhood and learning methods (including child-led ones), perceiving parents as partners in supporting children's learning rather than impeding it, and integrating the cultural dimensions of these communities into the curriculum, can ease children's experience in school and reduce intergenerational rupture and distress. These steps are necessary to improve both communal wellbeing and children's academic attainments.

8.7. Educational programs for Adivasi and Adivasi Gothrabandhu during the COVID-19 pandemic in Kerala

Athul Sarala Nanu

The Adivasi (Indigenous) peoples in Kerala were one of the most affected communities during the COVID-19 pandemic. The normalized underlying disparities were exacerbated by the crisis that arose with the onset of the pandemic, which exposed the social inequalities that affect marginalized groups including the Adivasi peoples. The state's programs and projects relating to Adivasi education exposes policies that are counterproductive to their stated aims.

Kerala state managed to curb the pandemic situation relatively more quickly than the other states in India. However, the experiences of the Adivasi peoples were much worse than those of the dominant populations in Kerala. The real impact of the pandemic for the Adivasi peoples of Kerala is yet to be discovered. Yet, we now know that lockdown, for example, had drastic effects on the education sector as most of the institutions and schools in Kerala were completely shut from the onset of the virus in March 2020.

In 2020, in response to the long lockdown, the state initiated the online education program called the 'First bell' which was the first among such initiatives in the whole of India. 'First bell' is a project launched by the Department of Public Education to provide education to school students online (https://firstbell.kite. kerala.gov.in/). The program telecast episodes of teaching modules on television ('Kite-victers channel'), online, and on social media in Malayalam. The episodes are universal, and the local teachers acted as additional mentors to make the process more fruitful by providing additional attention to individual students.

Online classes were launched despite the state's knowledge that many children, particularly those belonging to Adivasi communities, had no access to the new platform. Even today in Kerala, many of the Adivasi families have no access to the internet, smartphones, or even a television. There are also Adivasi hamlets in remote areas where there is no road, electricity, or mobile network. Particularly in Adivasi-dominated regions, the classes started before these children knew anything about them. The approach projected by the state towards these marginalized communities points to a more critical problem beyond the lack of access and infrastructure: it reflects the continuum of historical injustice towards the Adivasi and Dalit communities and society's systemic expulsion of the downtrodden.

The new circumstances of the pandemic and the shift to online education has completely or partially disabled Adivasi children from continuing their education in many of the hamlets, particularly those still living in remote areas in Attappady-Palakkad district and Wayanad district. Beyond the problem of the lack of access and infrastructure, the Adivasi children in these hamlets faced new challenges which the other children did not face. As previously mentioned (see also Section 8.6), the Adivasi communities have distinct languages and ways of living that are different from those of other marginalized communities who are more dispersed culturally. The homogenous nature of the online classes was even more challenging for the Adivasi children in primary school, as these classes were not recorded in their mother tongue. Without the mediator teachers to ease the transition from their mother tongue to Malayalam (the main language spoken in Kerala), the Adivasi children were completely lost in the process. Even the few children who did have access to a television and other devices faced challenges as they were not able to follow or understand the telecasted episodes, which were shot in the Malayalam language.

The offline mode of teaching they used to receive in their local public schools prior to the pandemic was at least comprehensible to these children, as the teachers were local and in some cases there were Adivasi Gothrabandhu teachers present in the school. This was vital in keeping the children in school, as the dropout rates in these hilly districts are very high.

At a much later point in the pandemic, after many voices were raised against this discriminatory policy, the state had to introduce a new set of episodes that were translated from Malayalam into a number of Adivasi languages. The program was named 'Mazhavil poovu' (The rainbow flower) and telecasted episodes in the Paniya, Kuruma, Kattunayaka, Adiya, Uraali, Kurichya, and Mannan languages. The telecast was not shown on the television as the audience was a micro minority. So, the mentor teachers and the other teachers had to make it available to the Adivasi children at their houses. For this purpose, temporary arrangements called 'Samoohya padanamuri' (local learning centers) were established near to the settlements. However, the newly designed episodes were direct translations of the episodes that were previously made in the Malayalam language, which raises several concerns regarding the design of these episodes, though the program 'Mazhavil poovu' managed to appease the criticisms temporarily.

The challenge of language reflects a much bigger and overarching obstacle faced by the Adivasi children. In many studies conducted among these communities, even before the pandemic, the language problem was reported to be one of the main contributory factors towards the increase in the dropout rate. To tackle this, in 2020 the Scheduled Tribes Development Department (STDD) introduced a scheme called Gothrabandhu, primarily to address the issue of dropouts and ensure student enrolment. The project aimed to support the 2016 educational improvement provisions of students from the Adivasi communities, namely Adiya, Paniya, Kattunayka, and Oorali. Initially, the government had issued an order to appoint 241 mentor teachers from the different Adivasi communities in the government primary schools in Wayanad district.

In practice, however, this initiative had several notable downfalls. First, the Gothrabandhu project devised only a vague set of criteria for the selection of the candidates, stating, "The dexterity of the candidate in Adivasi artforms, culture, and Tribal languages could be considered as an extra merit for the candidates." Another criterion was that the candidate should be selected from the Adivasi communities present in the area of the school. In theory, the Gothrabandhu teachers were meant to act as a bridge for the Adivasi children from their communities to enter the alien Malayalam school. In practice, however, these Gothrabandhu teachers were temporary teachers who were appointed by the state as teachers coming from other, more dominant communities, and they often failed to understand the cultural nuances of the children's communities; they were also unable to communicate with the Adivasi children effectively. The Gothrabandhu teachers were indeed members of an Adivasi community, but they often came from the more privileged communities among the Adivasi fold rather than the children's own communities. As there are significant differences, as well as clear power relations between the different Adivasi communities, this made the relationship between the children and the Gothrabandhu teachers less easy. Before the pandemic, Gothrabandhu teachers were appointed in their respective schools. During the pandemic, these teachers were the only support for the Adivasi children. In most cases, these teachers had to communicate with children from three or four communities as most of the schools were composed of Adivasi students from multiple communities. The children therefore spoke different languages and the teachers, belonging to a different community, often found themselves unable to communicate with students properly and thus reproducing language difficulties. In sum, these Adivasi educational programs are primarily designed to appease criticism; they represent tokenistic gestures with minimal meaningful impact on the Adivasi children in Kerala.

8.8. Re-interpreting a standard classroom practice for immigrant Latinx students

Carrie Rothstein-Fisch & Elise Trumbull

The early childhood instructional example detailed here occurred within the context of the Bridging Cultures Project.TM The Bridging Cultures Project™ began as a collaboration among four researchers to explore if and how the cultural values framework of individualism and collectivism might be useful for teachers serving large numbers of immigrant Latinx students. Individualism is the culture of schools (and the dominant value framework in US society as a whole), whereas these children from immigrant Latinx homes had been socialized into a more collectivistic set of values and practices.

Seven Spanish/English bilingual teachers participated in an initial training of three days over a four-month period. All seven teachers reported numerous changes in their pedagogy and expressed a desire to continue meeting. At that point, they became teacher-researchers, documenting their own practice and its impact on students and parents (Trumbull et al., 2001). The project continued with meetings of the seven teachers and four researchers every three to four months for more than five years. During that time, teachers shared innovative ideas with the group, provided insights through individual interviews, and were observed in their classrooms at least twice.

One example of using an understanding of a collectivistic perspective to bridge home and school ways of learning was observed by the first author in Mrs. Pérez's third-grade classroom, with children from Oxnard, California, a large agricultural area home to many farmworker families. These children were among the most recent immigrants to the US from Mexico, and their families were highly collectivistic.

Thus, it was very surprising to see a 'star chart' in the classroom. A star chart is typically used to motivate the performance of children as individuals. The chart displays each child's name along the Y or vertical axis of the chart, and cells for stars along the X or horizontal axis, to record mastery of specific skills. In this case, the skill was mastery of timed recitation of multiplication tables. The chart seemed to the observing researcher (the first author) to be a very individualistic and competitive strategy, incongruous with the collectivistic practices the teacher had cultivated to be in harmony with her students.

During the debriefing session conducted by the researcher immediately after the classroom visit, Mrs. Pérez was asked about the use of the start chart. She explained that she had used it without success during her early years of teaching and had consequently put it away in the closet. "It had not worked well" she said. However, through participation in the Bridging Cultures Project, she "learned about the success of groups collectively." During a class meeting,

Mrs. Pérez showed the children the star chart. She said, "We have a problem," remarking on how few stars had been added to the chart. She asked the children for their suggestions about what to do. The children immediately said, "Wouldn't it be so neat if it was a solid block of stars, and the whole chart was filled in?"

In this case, the children did not see the chart as an opportunity to compete with each other. In fact, they didn't focus at all on the question of which child had earned more stars than another. From their collectivistic perspective, they saw only that the chart needed more stars. When Mrs. Pérez asked how they wanted to achieve a "solid block of stars," the children immediately suggested that they wanted math buddies to help them. In that way, the cultural values of helping others, prominent in their home cultures, would be invoked in service of the group goal of having all the students succeed in mastering multiplication facts (Rothstein-Fisch et al., 2003). These students knew what would motivate them (a group goal) and how to achieve it (helping others), and Mrs. Pérez allowed them to act on these collectivistic cultural values to use the star chart in a culturally congruent manner.

The buddies worked together, but when it was time for each child to be tested by the teacher, the buddies wanted to participate too. Mrs. Pérez reminded the buddies that they could not help their partners when she was testing them. The children accepted this rule but insisted that they wanted to be present at the testing to support their buddy. If a child was successful, then the success was shared and celebrated throughout the class. The student rang a bell, signaling that another star was being added to "their" chart. The children stopped their work and clapped. The child who passed knew the accomplishment was appreciated. If the student being tested was unsuccessful, the buddy could observe the challenging factors and knew immediately what timed math facts to focus on. In the end, every child passed. According to Mrs. Pérez, "In third grade, the goal was to reach timed multiplication facts up to the 5s, but every child knew their timed facts up to the 6s, and some went as far as the 12s!"

This example demonstrates the value of leveraging students' home values regarding learning in service to school success.

Progress toward solving a problem began when the teacher used the collective pronoun 'we' to identify the problem. The children did not construe the problem as the failings of individual students but as a classroom challenge. In turn, Mrs. Pérez encouraged students' own approach to learning. It was clear that the children themselves knew what would motivate them and how they could achieve the objective of everyone's mastering multiplication facts. They wanted a "solid block of stars," where the goal was the success of the group (the collective) versus the success of the individual. They also knew that the use of buddies would benefit everyone in striving for the group goal. To her credit, Mrs. Pérez had the wisdom to ask the children how they wanted to learn and how they wanted to be assessed. It seems that even third-graders can take an active role in identifying instructional and assessment strategies that will help them learn.

8.9. Cultural negation in the classroom

Blanca Guerrero-Meyer

I was one of the originators of the Bridging Cultures project, as I found myself in the right place at the right time, facing the conflicts of culture in my own life as a college student at UCLA and an immigrant mother from a rural province in Mexico. The project was inspired by my personal experiences and, after graduating from UCLA, I experienced the same cultural shock I had encountered as a mother and student—but now from the perspective of a teacher. I became a kindergarten teacher in a bilingual classroom with 33 Spanish-speaking students from new immigrant families. I was hired as a teacher with an emergency teaching permit in the Los Angeles School District. I had no teacher training and was placed in a bilingual classroom almost immediately after I applied.

I came to the classroom with knowledge of my own culture and language only, plus what I had learned from developmental psychology during college. I drew on what I knew from my own experience as a student in Mexico. I received no training in classroom management or the enculturation of schooling in the

US. This freed me to practice the only culture I knew, the one I shared with my students. The collectivistic culture from which we came guided our behaviors with no disruptions, as we were unaware of other expectations. I did not give much thought to classroom management. My students were used to knowing their roles and to acting as a group already from their family's culture. Little did I know that this harmony of values and expectations would cause me so many problems with my supervisors and ultimately cause me to abandon my vocation as a teacher. There were three main sources of cultural conflicts reflected in my classroom management: the values of private property, personal accountability, and independence.

I received all the toys and materials for the classroom and organized everything by categories (e.g., organizing crayons by colors), and we all shared them. I did not assign rules on the use of toys; it was understood that we all helped clean up, and when everyone was finished, a few students always helped. During activities, students moved freely to help other students who were struggling in the classroom without being asked to do that. As far as I was concerned, I had the perfect classroom. The students seemed at ease and for the most part had found a role they liked. The few students who did not follow these implicit arrangements were pushed by the other children, thanks to their modeling and sometimes their open requests to follow these norms. When I received my first evaluation after the vice-principal came to observe my class, I was very surprised and confused. I had received a very negative review because my practices were not teaching the values of private property. According to the vice-principal: (1) The crayons and materials should have been distributed as individual property to each child so they could learn to be responsible for their own property; (2) The children should have all cleaned up after themselves and nobody should clean up for others, as this is not fair; (3) Children should be responsible for finishing their own work and not be helped by others, as that is cheating.

I still think of how happy those children seemed when we were following our own culture and how foreign all these rules seemed when I tried to implement them. They eventually learned the new rules, but I have to say that the feeling of being part of a group who helped each other, who valued the different skill sets of different children, and who knew how to develop socially responsible behavior by sharing common property and responsibilities was a great loss, not only to the classroom culture, but to the sense of belonging of the students. It is sad to think that this is the kind of loss many other cultures must go through to become successful as students in a US school. This was not the kind of teacher I wanted to be.

8.10. A school fit for humans? A conversation starter for eliciting and discussing theories of schooling

Dustin Eirdosh & Susan Hanisch

How do students and teachers reason about the role of autonomy and structure in relation to the design of their school, to their understanding of human diversity, and to their understanding of our changing global society? This ambitious question helped frame the aims of the Evolving Schools Project, an effort from our community science lab model (Eirdosh & Hanisch, 2023) to engage students in exploring more specific conceptual issues at the center of school design and educational innovation.

The project began in 2019 as a means of developing strategies to engage students in critically reflecting on the bio-anthropological claims of education researcher and critic Peter Gray. Gray has argued and built a self-directed education (SDE) model on a theory of humans as social learners, drawing on the anthropological record (especially from hunter-gatherer societies) to argue that the human drive even of young children, under the proper conditions, can provide an environment where students can be free to learn on the basis of their own passions and interests (Gray, 201, 2013, 2017). Our interest was to develop conversation-starters to engage students and teachers in critically analyzing the scientific merit of Gray's claims in relation to their own understanding of human motivations and capacities for learning in the 'modern' world.

The approach has taken a few forms through a variety of simple survey instruments as well as an interview protocol. In all cases a sufficiently detailed but still concise overview of Peter Gray's claims was offered to the participants. Concrete school design elements of the SDE model that were presented included no homework; no exams; no required curriculum; students learn in mixed-age groups; adults only teach when students ask; and students have a vote in all school decisions. Participants' opinions and attitudes about the scientific merit and personal or societal desirability of Gray's model are then elicited with multiple choice and open response questions. In classroom contexts this can be followed up with a variety of possibilities to link to school improvement efforts.

In the city of Leipzig, we engaged in iterative design explorations across the survey and interview tools, concluding in a Creativity, Activity, Service project from a local secondary school student and a master's thesis from the University of Leipzig (Hammel, 2022) analyzing interviews with students, teachers, and a school administrator. The qualitative analysis of these interviews suggests some pedagogically and cross-culturally interesting spaces for further investigation. In this urban private school environment, upper-grade secondary school students, teachers, and one administrator tended to be quite skeptical of Gray's claims on the whole, and yet there was a kind of universal valuing of individual autonomy. Virtually all participants expressed in some way that student autonomy should be optimized and yet almost all of them suggested a need for some supportive or even coercive structures for the good of the student or society. Interestingly, the exact nature of what should be required in this otherwise minimal curriculum was highly variable, that is, there was a very high level of individual variation across the small sample of this thesis, which has been congruent with continued informal replications in classroom settings since.

We also engaged participants (n=64) from the US, Canada, Ireland, UK, and Germany, who were recruited during an online event and within a university class, via an online survey. Participants included school students, university students, teachers, parents, education researchers/teacher educators, and other education stakeholders. Overall, participants rated their own school experience to be quite different from the SDE model, with a tendency for the elements "no homework" and "students have a vote in all school decisions" to be more prevalent in people's own school experience. When asked to what degree people think that students and teachers would like to be learning and teaching in a school that adopted this kind of SDE model, some interesting patterns emerged across stakeholders. Overall, school and university students, as well as parents, were of the opinion that students would only somewhat enjoy learning in this kind of school, whereas parents and education researchers predicted that students would very much like to be learning in this way. Similarly, school and university students predicted that teachers would only somewhat or not much like to be teaching in this kind of school, while teachers and education researchers thought that teachers would like to work in such schools. When asked to what degree participants think the SDE model is a "good fit for human nature" across a number of statements, answers were very variable. For example, there was relatively high agreement with the statements "Exams and grades destroy motivation and curiosity" and "All humans are born with natural curiosity to learn what they need in life." There was less agreement with the statement "SDE schools are better suited for human nature than most other schools are." While these survey results are by no means representative and do not have strong statistical power, they point to the potential and need to engage the diversity of school stakeholders in deeper discussions about their values and beliefs around schooling, as a foundation for a participatory, reflective, and bottom-up approach to school design.

Overall we continue to find a deep appreciation among students, teachers, parents, and even school administrators in engaging the school community in such critical conceptual reflections on the design of schools. Stakeholders at all levels of a school community often have strong intuitive and implicit theories about these dynamics in their own education and that of others. Engaging in such discussions across stakeholders and communities with differing theories of schooling (ToS), including experiences with different school models, has the potential to surface and confront the actual variation in ToS that exists, as a foundation to develop school models in the future that are more in line with local values. By developing empowering participatory processes to help elicit, document, reflect, share, compare, refine, and democratically apply the everyday theories that drive the ultimate design and efficacy of our schools, cross-cultural and developmental researchers can collaborate with schools in a uniquely authentic space of interest.

8.11. Discussion and conclusion

Dustin Eirdosh & Susan Hanisch

In the last ~200 years, the global population has inverted the ratio of humans that will attend school in their lifetime, from less than 20% in the 1820s to more than 80% (Our World in Data, 2024). This represents perhaps one of the most rapid and dramatic shifts in the social learning patterns of humans in our entire evolutionary history. In this context, it is not surprising that conflict and complexity dominate the narratives of communities working to adapt to these changes. The cases above are highly diverse in terms of focal topics, communities, and researcher perspectives, and yet, there are also deep thematic similarities that point to a range of critical needs for understanding the role of schooling in our globalizing world. Most notably, the cases presented here point to the real difficulties that many communities around the world will continue to face in this context. However, these cases also point to some hopeful strategies. We highlight here just two broad implications for educational policy emergent from across this work.

Global educational policy may be able to better account for cross-cultural development by:

- Understanding the contextual factors that influence the functions of schooling systems across diverse communities. Every community highlighted across the case studies in this chapter represents a unique historical tapestry of influence from individuals and other communities, past, and present. Adaptive theories of schooling need to more deeply account for the historical, current, and possible future contexts of individual communities in order to empower all learners towards more valued life outcomes.

- Working towards the participatory improvement and integration of governmental theories of schooling (e.g., curriculum requirements) with the evolving ethnotheories of schooling developed by individual stakeholders, as reflected in local values, concepts, norms, and traditions of social learning. All of the schools and communities highlighted across the case studies in this chapter exist within some governmental policy context. Equally, all of these schools and communities reflect ongoing needs (and widely varying levels of capacity) for the active participation of students, parents, and teachers in the design of their school. Adaptive theories of schooling must more actively promote collaborative processes to align values, concepts, norms, and practices across local, regional, and global scales.

Together, these cases emphasize and clarify the vital importance of adopting a cross-cultural perspective on childhood learning in considering the challenges and opportunities presented by the rising global mandates for formal education, as well as the need to innovate education systems to meet the demands of the 21st century. By recognizing cultural diversity, engaging experts and communities in productive collaboration, elevating shared values, reflecting on the nuances of conceptual understanding, and engaging insights from educational research on the merits of diverse educational practices, school communities may be able to learn to navigate this change with a greater sense of purpose, history, and vision.

References

Akinsola, E. F. (2011). Relationships between parenting style, family type, personality disposition and academic achievement of young people in Nigeria. *Ife PsychologIA, 19*, 246–267. https://hdl.handle.net/10520/EJC38880

Alves, M. V., Ekuni, R., Hermida, M. J., & Valle-Lisboa, J. (2022). *Cognitive sciences and education in non-weird populations: A Latin American perspective.* Springer International Publishing. https://doi.org/10.1007/978-3-031-06908-6

Arnett, J. (2008). The neglected 95%: Why American psychology needs to become less American. *American Psychologist, 63*(7), 602–614. https://doi.org/10.1037/0003-066X.63.7.602

Ball, J., & Pence, A. (2000). A Post-Modernist Approach to Culturally Grounded Training In Early Childhood Care and Development. *Australian Journal of Early Childhood.* https://doi.org/10.1177/183693910002500106

Bird-David, N. (1999). 'Animism' Revisited: Personhood, Environment, and Relational Epistemology. *Current Anthropology 40*(S1), S67–91. https://doi.org/10.1086/200061

Bradley, R. H., & Corwyn, R. F. (2002). Socioeconomic status and child development. *Annual Review of Psychology, 53*(1), 371–399. https://doi.org/10.1146/annurev.psych.53.100901.135233.

Cabrera, N. L., & Cabrera, G. A. (2008). Counterbalance assessment: The chorizo test. *Phi Delta Kappan, 89*(9), 677. https://www.jstor.org/stable/20442604

Central Statistics Agency. (2015). Mengulik Data Suku di Indonesia. https://www.bps.go.id/id/news/2015/11/18/127

Chamim, M. (2020). *Menjaga Rimba Terakhir.* Warsi.

Csibra, G., & Gergely, G. (2011). Natural pedagogy as evolutionary adaptation. *Philosophical Transactions of the Royal Society B: Biological Sciences, 366*(1567), 1149–1157. https://doi.org/10.1098/rstb.2010.0319

Dale, N. (1996). *Working with Families of Children with Special Educational Needs: Partnership and Practice.* Routledge.

Eirdosh, D., & Hanisch, S. (2023). A Community Science Model for Interdisciplinary Evolution Education and School Improvement. In A. du Crest, M. Valković, A. Ariew, H. Desmond, P. Huneman, & T. A. C. Reydon (Eds). *Evolutionary Thinking Across Disciplines: Problems and Perspectives in Generalized Darwinism* (pp. 125–146). Springer. https://doi.org/10.1007/978-3-031-33358-3_7

Farah, M. J., Shera, D. M., Savage, J. H., Betancourt, L., Giannetta, J. M., Brodsky, N. L., Malmud, E. K., & Hurt, H. (2006). Childhood poverty: Specific associations with neurocognitive development. *Brain Research, 1110*(1), 166–174. https://psycnet.apa.org/doi/10.1016/j.brainres.2006.06.072

Gray, P. (2011). The Evolutionary Biology of Education: How Our Hunter-Gatherer Educative Instincts Could Form the Basis for Education Today. *Evolution: Education and Outreach, 4*(1), 28–40. https://doi.org/10.1007/s12052-010-0306-1

Gray, P. (2013). *Free to Learn: Why Unleashing the Instinct to Play Will Make Our Children Happier, More Self-Reliant, and Better Students for Life*. Basic Books.

Gray, P. (2017). Self-Directed Education—Unschooling and Democratic Schooling. In *Oxford Research Encyclopedia of Education*. https://doi.org/10.1093/acrefore/9780190264093.013.80

Henrich, J., Heine, S. J., & Norenzayan, A. (2010). *The weirdest people in the world? Behavioral and Brain Sciences, 33*(2–3), 61–83. https://doi.org/10.1017/S0140525X0999152X

Hermida, M. J., Shalom, D. E., Segretin, M. S., Goldin, A. P., Abril, M. C., Lipina, S. J., & Sigman, M. (2019). Risks for Child Cognitive Development in Rural Contexts. *Frontiers in Psychology, 9*. https://doi.org/10.3389/fpsyg.2018.02735

Hewlett, B. S. (2016). Social Learning and Innovation in Hunter-Gatherers. In H. Terashima & B. S. Hewlett (Eds). *Social Learning and Innovation in Contemporary Hunter-Gatherers. Replacement of Neanderthals by Modern Humans Series*. Springer. https://doi.org/10.1007/978-4-431-55997-9_1

Kakkoth, S. (2014a). Square pegs in round holes: perceptions of hunter-gatherer school dropouts of Kerala, South India. *Eastern Anthropologist, 67*, 433–450.

Kakkoth, S. (2014b). Go up in smoke: Hunter-Gatherer children's Encounter with Ashram School Education. *Proceedings of the National Conference on 'Education for Human Resource Development and Management (EHRDM-2014), Department of Education, Mother Teresa Women's University, Kodaikanal*.

Keller, H., Lamm, B., Abels, M., Yovsi, R., Borke, J., Jensen, H., Papaligoura, Z., Holub, C., Lo, W., Tomiyama, A. J., Su, Y., Wang, Y., & Chaudhary, N. (2006). Cultural models, socialization goals, and parenting ethnotheories: A multicultural analysis. *Journal of Cross-Cultural Psychology, 37*(2), 155–172. https://doi.org/10.1177/0022022105284494

Lavi, N. (2018). "'Developing relations': rethinking the experience of aid and development interventions, a case study from the Nayaka of South India." PhD thesis, University of Haifa. https://www.proquest.com/dissertations-theses/developing-relations-rethinking-experience-aid/docview/2585369566/se-2?accountid=104801

Lavi, N. (2022a). The Freedom to Stop Being Free: Rethinking School Education and Personal Autonomy among Nayaka Children in South India. *Hunter-Gatherer Research, 5*(1), 39–66. https://doi.org/10.3828/hgr.2019.3

Lavi, N. (2022b). 'We only teach them how to be together': parenting, child development, and engagement with formal education among the Nayaka in south India. *Anthropology & Education Quarterly, 53*(1), 84–102. https://doi.org/10.1111/aeq.12406

Leseman, P. P. M. (2020). The Power of Ethnotheories in Changing Societies: Commentary on Cross-Cultural Research on Parents: Applications to the Care and Education of Children. *New Directions for Child and Adolescent Development, 2020*(170), 195–200. https://doi.org/10.1002/cad.20342

Moriguchi, Y. (2022). Beyond bias to western participants, authors, and editors in developmental science. *Infant and Child Development, 31*(1), Article e2256. https://doi.org/10.1002/icd.2256

Nielsen, M., Haun, D., Kärtner, J., & Legare, C. H. (2017). The persistent sampling bias in developmental psychology: A call to action. *Journal of Experimental Child Psychology, 162*, 31–38. https://doi.org/10.1016/j.jecp.2017.04.017

Ninkova, V. Hays, J., Lavi, N., Ali, A., Lopes da Silva Macedo, S., Davis, H. E., & Lew-Levy, S. (2022). Hunter-Gatherer Children at School: A View from the Global South. *Review of Educational Research*, 00346543241255614. https://doi.org/10.3102/00346543241255614

Nsamenang, A. B. (2006). Human ontogenesis: An indigenous African view on development and intelligence. *International Journal of Psychology, 41*(4), 293–297. https://doi.org/10.1080/00207590544000077

Our World in Data. (2024). Graph: Share of the world's population with formal basic education. Based on Wittgenstein Center (2023); World Bank (2023); van Zanden, J. et al. (2014) – with major processing by Our World in Data. "No formal education" [dataset]. Wittgenstein Center, "Wittgenstein Center Population and Human Capital Projections 2023-05-10"; World Bank, "World Bank Education Statistics (EdStats) 2023"; van Zanden, J. et al., "How Was Life? Global Well-being since 1820 - Education 2014" [original data]. https://ourworldindata.org/grapher/share-of-the-world-population-with-at-least-basic-education

Pandita, R. (2015). Dropout percentage of Scheduled Caste and Scheduled Tribe children in India: a decadal analysis up to secondary level. *Journal of Indian Education, XXXXI*, 97–117.

Prasetijo, A. (2021). Displacement as Experienced by the Orang Rimba Hunter-gatherers. *Senri Ethnological Studies, 106*, 235–252. https://doi.org/10.15021/00009710

Pusat Penelitian Kebijakan Pendidikan dan Kebudayaan. (2016). Pelayanan pendidikan bagi komunitas adat (p. 80). Kementerian Pendidikan dan Kebudayaan. Retrieved from https://litbang.kemdikbud.go.id

Rowley, S. J., & Camacho, T. C. (2015). Increasing diversity in cognitive developmental research: Issues and solutions. *Journal of Cognition and Development, 16*(5), 683–692. https://doi.org/10.1080/15248372.2014.976224

Rothstein-Fisch, C., Trumbull, E., Isaac, A., Daley, C., & Pérez, A. I. (2003). When helping someone else is the right answer: Bridging Cultures in Assessment. *Journal of Latinos and Education, 2*(3). 123–140. https://doi.org/10.1207/S1532771XJLE0203_01

Schaik, C. P. van, Pradhan, G. R., & Tennie, C. (2019). Teaching and curiosity: Sequential drivers of cumulative cultural evolution in the hominin lineage. *Behavioral Ecology and Sociobiology, 73*(1), 2. https://doi.org/10.1007/s00265-018-2610-7

Serpell, R. (1993). *The significance of schooling: Life journeys in an African Society*. Cambridge University Press.

Serpell, R. (1994). The cultural construction of intelligence. In W. L. Lonner & R. S. Malpass (Eds). *Psychology and culture* (pp. 157–163). Allyn Bacon.

Serpell, R. (2011). Social Responsibility as a Dimension of Intelligence, and as an Educational Goal: Insights from Programmatic Research in an African Society. *Child Development Perspectives, 5*(2), 126–33. https://doi.org/10.1111/j.1750-8606.2011.00167.x

Shaffer, D. R., & Kipp C. (2007). *Developmental Psychology, Childhood & Adolescence* (7th ed.). Thomson Wadsworth.

Sternberg, R. J., Conway, B. E., Ketron, J. L., & Bernstein, M. (1981). People's conceptions of intelligence. *Journal of Personality and Social Psychology, 41*(1), 37–55. https://doi.org/10.1037/0022-3514.41.1.37

Sterelny, K. (2012). *The Evolved Apprentice. How Evolution made Humans Unique*. MIT Press.

Sujatha, K. (2002). Education among Scheduled Tribes. In R. Govinda (Ed.). *India education report: a profile of basic education* (pp. 87–94). Oxford University Press.

Trumbull, E., Rothstein-Fisch, C., Greenfield, P. M., & Quiroz, B. (2001). *Bridging cultures between home and school: A guide for teachers.* Lawrence Erlbaum. https://doi.org/10.4324/9781410604958

UNESCO. (2020). Informe de Seguimiento de la Educación en el Mundo 2020: Inclusión y educación: Todos y todas sin excepción. *UNESCO.* https://unesdoc.unesco.org/ark:/48223/pf0000374817

Vernon, P. E. (1969). *Intelligence and Cultural Environment.* Butler & Tanner. https://doi.org/10.4324/9781315879949

Warsi (2011). *Meretas Aksara di Belantara.* PT Elex Media Komputindo.

World Bank (2018). Poverty and shared prosperity: Piecing together the poverty puzzle. *World Bank.* https://www.worldbank.org/en/publication/poverty-and-shared-prosperity-2018

9. Policy: A brief guide to understanding and influencing real-world decision making

Coordinated by Ilaria Pretelli

This chapter focuses on one often overlooked outcome of behavioral research: its potential to guide policymakers and local actors in designing projects with real-world impact. Research impact is not only of interest to funding agencies and university hiring committees. It is also a sincere concern for many researchers, but we often lack the tools to effectively interact with policymakers. In this chapter we provide researchers with a general understanding of the policy world, provide examples of real-world interventions, and outline pathways by which researchers working in education, psychology, and anthropology can influence real-world outcomes. Much charitable action focuses on children, and research on children's learning across cultures can provide important avenues to make this action more culturally appropriate, effective, and ultimately beneficial to children across the globe.

9.1. A toolkit for researcher-policy interactions

Ilaria Pretelli

This chapter is an attempt to bridge the gap between the basic research most often carried out in universities and research centers all around the globe, and the people who end up making policy decisions in the real world. As politicians, practitioners, and aid workers could all benefit from getting a better understanding

©2025 Ilaria Pretelli, et al., CC BY-NC 4.0

https://doi.org/10.11647/OBP.0440.09

of the behavioral sciences, researchers in these disciplines face the challenge of facilitating the flow of information from the academic world into the hands of those who make practical decisions. This chapter provides tools to empower researchers aiming to contribute to the policy world.

This chapter's first goal is to understand the complex world of policy. To do so, Pretelli illustrates how decision-making processes happen within governmental and non-governmental organizations. The focus is on when and how scientific findings are taken into consideration, as the policy world itself strives to promote evidence-based action. Pretelli also highlights how policy interventions should consider cross-cultural variation, a task for which the readers of this book are particularly suited. Asatsa, Pretelli and Puschkarsky then provide examples of cases of policy interventions that included the collaboration of researchers. Finally, Pretelli outlines the main pathways researchers can follow to bring change in the real world through policy, including practical considerations and potential pitfalls.

The chapter aims to allow researchers to better understand the mechanisms guiding decision making in the real world, as those in policy environments follow rules very different from the rules of academia. Armed with this understanding, we hope researchers can develop constructive interactions with policymakers, provide helpful tools to aid workers, and spread the valuable knowledge acquired during years of academic training to the general public, whose opinion is the motor of change.

9.2. Why think about policy?

Ilaria Pretelli

Researchers working with children in cross-cultural settings have a privileged eye on diverse cultural practices related to parenting, education, and learning more generally. This diverse perspective can promote a desire for action, either because of the recognition of novel behavioral patterns in the studied population that could potentially benefit the wider community, or, more commonly, in the hope to improve the lives of marginalized communities that researchers collaborate with. As scientists studying children, we also find ourselves in a privileged position in which we interact with the different actors involved in making decisions about children's lives. By working closely with communities, we are in a position to integrate these communities' needs and requests into designing research studies that can inform global or local policymakers in ways that are congruent with the local communities. Indeed, many researchers have highlighted that traditional ecological knowledge or parenting practices are not considered by political or charitable agencies, sometimes disrupting centuries-long ecological or social equilibria, and researchers can thus attempt to bring the communities' perspectives back into the discussions (Berkes, Colding, & Folke, 2000; Michelitch, 2018; Morelli et al., 2018; Oppong, 2020).

Sometimes it even becomes apparent that schools, promoted parenting practices, or governmental programs interact with children's lives in ways that are in contradiction with our scientific results. One example, clearly outlined by Morelli and colleagues (2018), shows how 'positive parenting practices' based on western-centric attachment theory, but promoted as universal standards of good care, can be in clear contradiction to established cultural practices in many parts of the world. For researchers armed with the tools of cross-cultural comparisons and an appreciation for diversity, it becomes a preeminent goal to develop science that has real-world impact and can improve the lives of children in the researched communities or worldwide. However, the implementation of such a goal often is complicated by structural and cultural factors: funds for research are limited, career goals might not align with the timelines and necessities of intervention programs, information flow between research and policymakers is often stunted, especially when research comes from areas such as anthropology or psychology.

The flow from scientific results to policy is impaired even though political actors (politicians, big and small non-governmental organizations [NGOs]) have an interest in defining policies that are scientifically driven and evidence-based, often due to the fact that they tend not have the time to keep in touch with the most recent scientific reports. It is then the responsibility of the researchers (or of some specialized NGOs, as we will see later) to make scientific results available and digestible for policymakers.

Additional motivations for participating in policymaking might come from novel incentive structures within academia. While traditional evaluation often does not consider contributions to intervention programs and policymaking, more attention has been paid in recent years to how scientists' research programs impact real-world issues. For example, the British Research Excellence Framework (REF) considers 'impact' as one of the metrics by which researchers are evaluated, with impact defined as "an effect on, change or benefit to the economy, society, culture, public policy or services, health, the environment or quality of life, beyond academia." Even though defining impact can be overly complicated (Hopkins, Oliver, Boaz, Guillot-Wright, & Cairney, 2021), a larger number of hiring committees value commitment to social and world issues, and are likely to positively evaluate efforts spent on policy-related research.

While researchers are pushed to interact with the policymaking world for a variety of reasons, they often lack the tools to understand the mechanisms governing such a world, or encounter difficulties in being heard by policymakers. This chapter aims on the one hand to help researchers understand the policy world through a brief summary of the main concepts and theories within policymaking, and, on the other hand, to suggest pathways and offer guidelines on how to make researcher's voices heard in the policymaking community.

9.3. How does the policy world work?

Ilaria Pretelli

What is policy?

"Policy is a deliberate system of guidelines to guide decisions and achieve rational outcomes. A policy is a statement of intent and is implemented as a procedure or protocol," states the page on policy in Wikipedia (Wikipedia contributors, 2023). Unfortunately, this definition lacks specificity. In fact, defining policy in more concrete terms might be difficult. The concept of policy can range from the actions of governments and political decisions on the implementation of programs (Birkland, 2011), or what is normally called public policy, to very locally relevant rules, for example those that govern the management of a shared kitchen in an academic department. For the purpose of this chapter, we focus on the sets of rules and indications concerning children's welfare and education, thus ignoring company policies, foreign policies, and many others. Still, policy, as intended in the present discussion, encompasses very broad fields, including, for example, processes that fall into health, social, and educational policies. Educational policies can take many different forms, for example, local governments can allocate funds to build schools, national governments define school programs, large NGOs such as UNICEF promote programs for girls' participation in education, and small NGOs can address local problems by helping teachers develop new methodologies. While covering in detail all these different aspects of policy is neither possible nor useful, we present general information that can help researchers navigate the (often unknown) world of policy.

Interested parties (stakeholders)

The range of actors involved in educational- and child-related policies is incredibly vast, with national and local governments, large and small NGOs, actors on the ground (such as teachers or parents), and, finally, researchers acting at different levels. Despite justified concerns about the colonial implications of the word (Sharfstein, 2016), these actors are commonly defined as stakeholders, i.e., persons or entities that have interest, economic or not, in the success of a specific project. Despite generally being interested in the success of a project, these actors are motivated by very different incentive structures, which influence not only their priorities and objectives, but also their timelines and commitment. Understanding how the motivations of stakeholders influence and determine the policymaking process is fundamental, and the field of political science, as well as that of management, has developed procedures for this, generally defined as 'stakeholder analysis' (Brugha & Varvasovszky, 2000), which aim to help policymakers plan and deploy successful interventions by accounting for the needs and interests of the stakeholders. In lay terms, when approaching policy issues, it is important to consider the actors involved: who is financing the project? Who is implementing it on the ground? Who is (supposedly) benefitting from the project? The priorities and beliefs of these actors shape the planning and development of policy implementations: for example, politicians might be interested in promoting a project if it can increase their chances at the next elections, so they might be more invested in short-term, visible projects and may shy away from long-lasting but complicated interventions. Intergovernmental Organizations (IGOs) such as the World Bank can promote policies that they believe will improve the standing of member nations and provide funding and support for deploying a certain project. NGOs are limited by resources and human power, their objectives are often defined by their funder, and they usually aim to act on specific projects on pre-defined timelines. A key consideration is that stakeholders differ in their relative power, so that if a funder refuses to finance a project that they don't believe would be viable, the project will likely be canceled, while if recipients of the project don't think it would be helpful for them, they might still be the unwilling recipients of the project's results.

In recent decades, more importance has been given to the benefiting communities, as they represent a key agent in policymaking (Michelitch, 2018). As a result, community-based programs have been on the rise since the 1990s. The role played by communities within community-based programs can vary widely, as they are not only called to play a role as the location or setting of the program, but they can, and should, also be engaged in the different phases of projects (McLeroy, Norton, Kegler, Burdine, & Sumaya, 2003). Sometimes communities are the target of the action, and the goal of a project is to impact some community-level feature or resource. More often, communities' contribution is key during planning, as advisory committees or associations of community members can help tailor projects to the specifics of a certain community and facilitate the enactment of the project. Communities should also be seen as a resource, in terms of knowledge and human capital, and programs should aim to incorporate the potential of communities to foster their deployment. Finally, communities can be seen also as active actors in a project's deployment, and may actually carry out sections of the project itself. However, communities' involvement has to be planned carefully: especially in low- and middle-income countries, power and knowledge differentials between community members and elites or foreign actors can complicate interactions between communities and other stakeholders (Edwards, 2019).

How policy works: A sketch

The mechanisms that tick within the policy process have been dissected and analyzed in numerous ways, but given the complexity of the processes at hand, most descriptions have been found wanting, one way or another. One commonly used theorization of the policy process is Anderson's description of the policy cycle in his 1975 *Public Policymaking* (now in its 9th edition, Anderson, Moyer, & Chichirau, 2022). This sees the processes concerning policymaking as following a cyclical structure that begins by identifying the problem, continues by defining possible plans of action, deciding which plan to follow, putting that plan into practice, and concludes by evaluating the effectiveness of the adopted measures. At this point, according to the policy cycle, new problems are identified, and the cycle begins anew (Figure 9.1).

Many other versions of policy cycles exist; however, cyclical approaches have been contested as not being accurate or helpful (Sabatier, 1991), and can only retain some usefulness as abstract descriptions of the policymaking process (Howard, 2005). Policymaking is also described as a network, as every step can communicate directly with the others. For example, in order to decide what to do, a smaller policy cycle can be formed separately, as the policymaker wants to know, and appropriately evaluates, whether a certain intervention can indeed achieve the desired result. Moreover, a complete closure of the policy cycle can be wishful thinking, in the sense that all policies are financially constrained, and one might secure enough funding to test an intervention, but then have none to implement it over a larger section of the population.

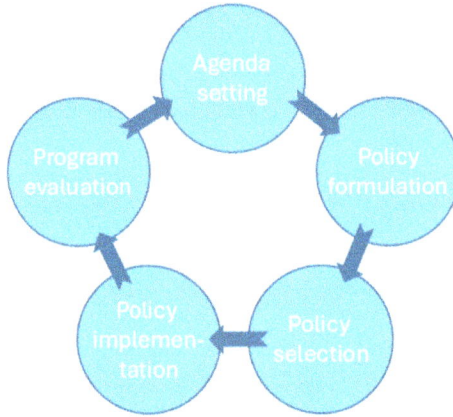

Fig. 9.1 Schematic example of a policy cycle. Redrawn from McNutt & Hoefer (2021, p. 134).

One fundamental aspect of policymaking is its constrained nature. Policies have to be effective, but they also have to require a certain amount of money and take a certain amount of time. Estimating the time and money required to implement an intervention is a key component of a project, and projects are routinely evaluated, keeping into account their cost effectiveness and expected timelines.

Evidence-based policy

How are policy decisions made? In far too many cases, especially in small venues such as universities' faculty meetings, policies are defined based on the common sense and past experiences of, in best-case scenarios, informed, smart and well-meaning individuals. It is only rarely that problem-specific, quantitative data are used to define policies relative to university management, and most often such decisions are taken without running an experiment on students first. On the contrary, during the last decades, the policy world recognized that the competence and intuition of decision-makers might not be enough to devise the optimal policy in most situations, and that better kinds of data are often necessary: data that can inform decision-makers on whether a measure will work, to what extent, and which kind of investment is needed.

Evidence based medicine opened the path for a more applied use of scientific knowledge to guide policy decisions. Between the 1980s and 1990s, a good understanding of the pathophysiological process appeared to be insufficient to select a treatment. It became clear that a quantitative analysis of the outcomes of that treatment was necessary to evaluate its effectiveness and decide whether to administer it to a patient (Sackett & Rosenberg, 1995). The key intuition is that randomized control trials can prove that a treatment works better than a placebo under control conditions, and that summaries of such studies, such as reviews and meta-analyses, are necessary to evaluate the effects of a treatment.

The social sciences swiftly followed. In the early 2000s, social scientists involved in policymaking were considering how to improve their contributions to rigorous, quantitative work to define the effectiveness of interventions (Young, Ashby, Boaz, & Grayson, 2002). A premium was placed on careful and well-justified systematic reviews that do not arbitrarily select results favorable to one specific intervention, but rather clearly define the search and selection processes by which the corpus of relevant work was identified. Summaries (or summaries of summaries, namely targeted reports) are then produced and used to inform policymaking.

Policymakers receive access to evidence through several different avenues, including government finance analyses, experiments, and long-term research that target specific outcomes of interest, or open-ended studies that can improve their ability to produce effective policies. IGOs such as the World Bank produce a monthly series of notes called 'Evidence for Policy' that summarizes the work done by the Strategic Impact Evaluation Fund. This section of the World Bank "supports scientifically rigorous research that measures the impact of programs and policies to improve education, health, access to quality water and sanitation, and early childhood development in low- and middle-income countries" (*The*

Strategic Impact Evaluation Fund (SIEF), World Bank, SIEF website, 2023). More interestingly, several non-profit research centers are committed to improving policymakers' access to scientific evidence. An early example is the Cochrane Collaboration (https://www.cochrane.org/). Founded in 1993, Cochrane produces systematic reviews of available evidence in medical fields for the usage of health practitioners, thus enabling a better flow of information from medical research into practice. Other large research centers with different foci emerged in the following decades, for example J-PAL (Abdul Latif Jameel Poverty Action Lab, https://www.povertyactionlab.org/) and IPA (Innovation for Poverty Action, https://poverty-action.org/), which both have sections dedicated to education, or EGAP (Evidence in Governance and Policy, https://egap.org/). These share the goal to reduce poverty worldwide by improving policymakers' access to relevant research. They produce usable summaries, novel research, and actively engage with governmental officials across the globe.

Thanks to these resources, a flow between policymaking and research is now constant, though not without problems. Governments and governmental institutions fund and request research to put potential interventions to the test; think tanks and research institutes produce large amounts of reports and relevant research. However, behavioral sciences that could inform policymaking are very diverse, and thus important evidence is fragmented between disciplines, published in non-specialistic journals, and, in general, remains underutilized. Additional complications arise because often these disciplines use non-overlapping jargon and only rarely coordinate their scientific efforts. This makes it very difficult for results developed by certain fields of research to reach policymakers. There are, however, advancements in improving the flow of information from the behavioral sciences to policymakers. Specifically, NGOs such as UNICEF and Save the Children inaugurated specialized teams to integrate results from the behavioral sciences, widely defined. For example, they are starting to employ psychologists and anthropologists in these teams, thus bringing diverse perspectives on child-related policies.

Causal inference and policymaking

The gold standard for evidence-based policy has been the use of Random Control Trials, or RCTs. RCTs are an experimental technique that involve applying a treatment to a part of a sample, while the other part of the sample becomes a control. RCTs assume that (i) probabilistic dependence implies causal explanation, or that the fact that some outcome is more probable in one setting implies that there is a causal explanation for this outcome; (ii) experimental design ensures randomness between the samples assigned to the treatment and control conditions, i.e., the samples do not differ in any trait that can have consequences for the outcome apart from their assignment to treatment or control; (iii) if the outcome is more probable in the treatment than in the control group, the only possible explanation is that the outcome has been caused by the treatment (Cartwright, 2011).

If there is a significant change in the section of the sample exposed to the treatment, the treatment is considered to be effective. In medical sciences, treatment is often a medicine, with an active ingredient, while the control group receives a placebo, often an identical pill without the active ingredient. In the social sciences, the concept of a 'control' is more complicated. For example, recent work in economics evaluated whether administering training in mental imagery, or the ability to picture the development of possible scenarios and consequences to possible or past actions, can improve labor outcomes, and used different types of controls (Delfino et al., n.d.). In one case, a selection of refugees in Addis Ababa received four hours of training, while another selection received no training at all. This could create confusion, as the effect of the training might be due to the attention received by the trainees, rather than as a specific effect of the mental imagery training, i.e., any other training, or even just psychological support might have reached the same or a better outcome. In a different iteration of the same study, small entrepreneurs in Bogota, Colombia, received either training in mental imagery, traditional business training, or no training at all. There the effect of mental imagery training could be contrasted to that of traditional business training, which provided a more reliable control (Delfino et al., n.d.). In general, provided that appropriate controls are defined, RCTs are considered to be a reliable technique that allows researchers to isolate the effect of a specific treatment in a population.

One additional benefit of RCTs is their ability to quantify the effects of intervention. As outlined in previous sections, policymakers are heavily limited in their range of action by time and money, so they are very interested in understanding how much an intervention will cost, or what results can be obtained with a certain amount of money, and how long it will take to be implemented. Thus, estimating such aspects of an intervention in an RCT or with another approach can be an important element that makes a study relevant to policymakers.

However, RCTs have several limitations that complicate their employment in a variety of conditions. It's highly unethical to assign individuals to treatments that have a high chance of negative outcomes (e.g., smoking, car accident). It's sometimes unethical to randomly assign individuals at risk to potentially positive treatment, if the control group doesn't receive access to potentially life-saving treatment. Hence other non-experimental techniques can be used, such as case-control studies (Breslow, 1996). These kinds of studies rely on the presence of groups in the population that happened to be differently exposed to certain treatments or interventions, leveraging differences in outcomes between these groups while accounting, or attempting to account for, other differences between these groups (e.g., Bhuiyan, Zaman, & Ahmed, 2013). In case-control studies, selecting an appropriate control group is even more important, as they forego the randomization step. More generally, what RCT and case-control studies, and other similar experimental or pseudo experimental techniques are aiming for is causal inference, or the ability to state that a certain intervention will produce a specific result.

However, running RCTs, or other experimental approaches, concerning children's learning in cross-cultural settings can be very complicated, or highly unethical. Luckily, some approaches have been developed that allow behavioral social scientists to make causal inferences from observational data. The core concept is to consider counterfactual situations, i.e., what would have happened under different conditions (Glymour & Spiegelman, 2017). Being able to evaluate this change can explain the causal effect of predictors of interest. In order to calculate counterfactuals, some approaches rely on characteristics of the specific dataset to study sources of variation, such as discontinuity analysis that quantifies the difference in the outcome variable before and after a specific moment in time when the 'intervention' (or some sort of change in the conditions) happened (Thistlethwaite & Campbell, 1960). A more principled approach is do-calculus (Pearl, 2009), which builds on probability theory to provide an accessible tool that facilitates the identification of causal effects in non-parametric models, or models where the causal effect cannot be interpreted directly from parameter values (see Section 4.3 on quantitative causal analysis). Integrating more clearly causal considerations in research on children learning across cultures can be a great way to facilitate the use of the research for policy purposes. For example, Weissman (2021), states that:

> Sound educational policy recommendations require valid estimates of causal effects, but observational studies in […] education research sometimes have loosely specified causal hypotheses. The connections between the observational data and the explicit or implicit causal conclusions are sometimes misstated. The link between the causal conclusions reached and the policy recommendations made is also sometimes loose.

Generalizability and policymaking

Finally, and most relevantly for those who study cross-cultural variation, policymaking is becoming very sensitive to issues related to generalizability. Generalizability, transportability, or more generally external validity, address the question of whether findings relative to one context can be generalized to a larger context or exported to a different one. This requires considering which aspects of the original setting were relevant for the specific results obtained, how they influenced the results and how differences in a new setting can be addressed by changing aspects of the intervention. Here, again, causal approaches can play a leading role, as it is necessary to understand causally why a certain intervention worked in a certain place (Cartwright & Hardie, 2012; Deffner, Rohrer, & McElreath, 2022). Accurate planning for addressing the generalizability of projects should include evaluating how the samples drawn for the original study relate to the new target population and how populations differ, as well as considerations about time and modes of intervention (Findley, Kikuta, & Denly, 2021).

A very important aspect of generalizability is the need to develop interventions that are culturally appropriate for target populations. A common complaint of behavioral scientists is that interventions planned and carried out by big international organizations are based on scientific results relative to western populations and fail to be culturally respectful or inclusive (Morelli et al., 2018). It is true that 'evidence-based' policies drawing from the behavioral sciences have failed to address generalizability issues, and that often they have been drawn from frameworks, such as attachment theory, deeply rooted in western cultural practices. In this sense, culturally appropriate work from cross-cultural behavioral scientists can provide the information needed to opportunely modify target goals and methods to the needs of the communities.

In what follows, we present a few projects involving children and education that illustrate the actors involved, the limits to action, and possible avenues for intervention.

9.4. Indonesia cocoa farming and children's safety

Ilaria Pretelli

- Goal: Reduce children and teenagers' participation in hazardous tasks in cocoa farms in Indonesia by increasing knowledge and awareness of the laws concerning underage labor, and the risks associated with certain tasks.

- Stakeholders: A large international chocolate company (funder); an international NGO (including their branches in Indonesia, the US, and the unit specializing in behavioral sciences), a local behavioral scientist, an international academic (psychologist), and a local implementation and data collection firm (who implement the intervention); cocoa farmers, their families, and the families of children employed in the industry (recipients).

- Project: Fieldwork, including semi-structured interviews, focus groups, and behavioral observations, to understand the causes and beliefs concerning underage labor and plan possible avenues to reduce risks (phase 1) and behavioral intervention aimed at changing these beliefs among cocoa farmers via exposure to purposefully made videos, plus evaluation of the intervention through a Randomized Control Trial (RCT) with pre- and post-video surveys (phase 2).

- Researcher contributions: These were made through scientific papers on behavioral interventions, which inform the choices of NGO actors; and information on the risks associated with children's labor, which influences the desire of the funder to pursue the goal, and informs the team developing the methods. Moreover, researchers, both the locally hired behavioral scientist and the international academic, worked directly with the NGO developing and deploying the intervention.

For our first case study, we will travel to the Indonesian island of Sulawesi and explore the world of underage labor in cocoa farms. Indonesia is the third largest producer of cocoa in the world, with a sector largely dominated by small producers (around 90% of the production). Children and teenagers of various ages engage in different phases of the cocoa production, either by contributing to the family cultivation, or as hired workers on someone else's farm. In both cases, minors end up being exposed to risks such as pesticides or physical injuries (e.g., suffering cuts with machetes while opening the cocoa husks). Indonesian legislation is very clear on which types of tasks are acceptable at different ages, however, law enforcement and understanding of regulations is very spotty, and a proportion of minors encounter consequential accidents.

A large international chocolate company decided to invest in reducing children's engagement in hazardous tasks in cocoa farms in South Sulawesi Province, where they source their cocoa. The goal is hence directly set by the funder, and the other stakeholders are involved as either enablers, executors, or recipients of the project, i.e., they are supposed to benefit from the project. The chocolate company organized a bid where different organizations competed for the chance to develop the project on the ground. A large international NGO won the bid by proposing a diverse set of approaches that targeted the issue from a variety of angles. Here we shall focus on the project carried out by the unit that specializes in behavioral-science-based interventions.

Their first move was to hire a local behavioral scientist with an understanding of the problem. The local behavioral scientist, a PhD candidate from Lee Kuan Yew School of Public Policy in Singapore, and the NGO's local and behavioral branches laid out a first phase with the goal of better framing the problem in the specific context (i.e., what are the main pathways that lead to children getting injured; why do caregivers allow children to engage in dangerous labor; what are the local beliefs concerning child labor etc.) and developed the understanding necessary to plan the intervention (which tools could be used in order to reduce risk of harm for underage laborers). The result of this seven-month phase of the project was an 86-page report that summarizes the main findings and lays out possible interventions.

Findings reveal that there are two types of child laborers: children who are employed in paid labor instead of attending school because adverse conditions make it impossible for their families to subsist in any other way, and children laboring in their family farms who take pride in participating in the family economy and usually do so outside of school hours. The danger of various activities tends to be underestimated not only by children, but also by the adults supervising them, due to a combination of lack of understanding (e.g., the effects of pesticide exposure) and a belief that adult or parental supervision will reduce the risks. The team believed that raising knowledge and awareness of the effective dangers of these activities, as well as providing guidelines on safe activities by age, would reduce the negative impact on children's lives of laboring in cocoa farms. But how to raise knowledge and awareness among parents and employers? The team proposed different options, and, after multiple rounds of brainstorming, group activities, and research, including an evaluation of the concept by the funder, they settled on producing a short documentary about the potential dangers and permitted activities for underage laborers as a means to reach the relevant people and raise knowledge and awareness in the involved communities.

Phase two of the project, then, aimed to produce such a short documentary, organized projections to show the documentary to the communities, and evaluated the change in knowledge, intentions, and behaviors about child labor as a result of watching the documentary. This 12-month phase, developed and carried out at breakneck speed with a reduced budget, involved not only the work of the behavioral and the local Indonesian team, but also a content producer (who developed the video), a psychologist from the Lenoir-Rhyne University in the US, a local Indonesian firm specializing in implementation and data collection, and a variety of actors involved in the documentary production, project deployment, and evaluation. Once the video became available, cocoa farmers were reached by representatives of the Indonesian firm, and those who showed interest and availability were invited to attend a documentary projection session within the following week, and asked to fill in a brief survey concerning their knowledge, intentions, and behavior regarding child labor. Half of these cocoa farmers were randomly assigned to watch the documentary produced by the team, and the other half watched a generic video on cocoa farming practices. All participants were then interviewed again after watching the documentaries to evaluate any change in knowledge, intentions, and behavior about the role children can play in cocoa farms. Results indicated that watching the child-labor-focused documentary changed perceptions about what are acceptable activities for children in cocoa farms, as well as cocoa farmers' intentions to assign children to hazardous tasks, hopefully leading to safer practices and less danger for children.

9.5. Mental health in Kenyan schools: Integrating theory, practice and research

Stephen Asatsa

- Goal: Improve the mental health of high school students from disadvantaged neighborhoods in Nairobi and provide opportunities for training to psychology students.

- Stakeholders: Department of Psychology at the Catholic University of Eastern Africa (who designed and deployed the project); psychology trainees and high school students (who benefitted). The project worked together with other collaborating NGOs: Healthy Thinking International, Uzima Psychosocial Support Initiative, and BeautifulMind Consultants who provided support in terms of publicity literature and pamphlets on relevant topics, and supervision staff who helped to check the quality of services delivered by the trainee psychologists.

- Project: Need and opportunity for the project was identified drawing from the personal experiences of researchers involved in the project. After a survey to identify mental health issues for the communities in slum areas in Nairobi, psychology trainees were deployed to offer mental health counseling to students and personnel in disadvantaged areas of the Kenyan capital. The effectiveness of the program, in terms of mental health evaluation and the satisfaction of the stakeholders were reviewed at regular intervals.

- Researcher contributions: The project was initiated and developed by researchers at the Catholic University of Eastern Africa, in particular by Dr. Stephen Asatsa, who is Head of the Department of Psychology and author of this section.

This project was part of the service-based teaching model that is under implementation in the Department of Psychology at the Catholic University of Eastern Africa. It emerged as an opportunity to combine the needs of two different groups of young Kenyans: high school students, especially in slum areas, who are plagued by a huge mental health burden, which extends to the whole education sector in Kenya; and the trainees in Counseling Psychology, who struggle to practice the theories they learn and face a shortage of counseling practice laboratories in universities. The personal experiences of Dr. Asatsa, who worked as a high school teacher for 15 years and is now leading a university-level psychology department, were key, as he was aware of the relevant needs for psychological support in schools and of the lack of sufficient counseling laboratories in universities. He could thus develop a project to address them both, creating a symbiotic relationship between the psychology department and the community.

Counseling psychology students are required to be deployed to the community (a component of training known as 'clinical attachment') and offer supervised mental health services to community members. Clinical attachment enables trainees to be placed in a facility where they can interact with populations in need of psychosocial support. Trainees are required to complete a certain number of internship hours, which are not paid. Most training institutions lack enough places to send their trainees to practice their counseling skills. At the same time, there is little mental health support available in Kenyan schools. In principle, every school is supposed to employ a psychologist to support the mental wellness of students. However, this is often not the case, and most schools are only able to offer counseling teachers, who are not specially trained to offer mental health services. The counseling teacher is drawn from the regular school staff, and is called to combine teaching and counseling services, against the ethical guidelines of psychological counseling. In most cases, these teachers offer counseling as a secondary service since their core business is teaching. School children from slum areas have an even higher than average need for mental healthcare, as they grow up in a very challenging environment, characterized by high crime rates, poor sanitation, high rate of diseases, and lack of trained teachers. This project was designed to bridge these two different problems by matching the need for training in clinical psychology in one community, and the need for psychological support in the other.

The first step was to conduct a needs assessment exercise in the communities where the schools are located, with the goal to identify the pressing mental health needs of the schools. This was run as a survey commissioned by the Department of Psychology and conducted by students taking classes in Research Methods. These students thus had the opportunity to apply the knowledge acquired in class in a real research scenario. Various schools were chosen for this program, after which the department negotiated memoranda of understanding (MOUs) with each school, which defined the modalities by which counselors (trainees) could offer free services to the learners and teachers there. An MOU is a document prepared by two or more collaborating organizations outlining the role of each partner and the terms of engagement. Meanwhile, the psychology students preparing for their internship received the list of available schools and applied for specific slots. The project received overwhelming acceptance by the students and the schools.

The department deployed over 30 students in 15 schools at the onset of the program. They were to operate in the schools daily, offering mental health services, and the time spent there was used to count their required internship hours. The interns met weekly with an assigned clinical supervisor from the Department of Psychology to discuss the cases encountered in the schools. The supervisors were thus able to monitor the quality of the service offered and the skills development of the students. Within one year since the onset of this program, the project has grown tremendously, with over 20 schools involved and more than 100 psychology trainees.

Regular evaluation surveys are conducted both in the schools and among our psychology students for assessment of the success of the program and possible areas for improvement. Data from these surveys is very helpful for the university to evaluate the impact of the training programs. Schools, on the other hand, are encouraged to conduct continuous assessment of the program and report to the Department of Psychology. Moreover, the evaluations involve monitoring changes in the number of indiscipline cases reported in the schools, reports of parents on general conduct of the learners while at home, and short surveys given to learners and teachers on their mental health status. So far, stakeholders are reporting great improvement in the discipline, performance, and general mental wellbeing of students and teachers.

This project's funding needs were addressed by initiating a collaboration with multiple interested stakeholders and the community. Different needs that would have otherwise required large sums of money were provided in kind as a result of these partnerships. Thanks to this project, the need for mental health services in schools and the lack of internship opportunities for the psychology trainees have been jointly addressed and the program continues to expand for generalization in other areas.

9.6. Mother-tongue educational materials and human rights in the Central African Republic

Tatjana Puschkarsky

- Goal: Develop educational materials for Indigenous communities in the Central African Republic (CAR) in their mother tongue.

- Stakeholders: Local BaAka and Sangha-Sangha school children, teachers and families; Ndima-Kali (a local youth association), OrigiNations (an international NGO), regional educational authorities.

- Project: School materials (booklets and classroom posters) in Indigenous languages and representing locally relevant themes were developed and deployed to improve school attendance and results. These were printed in large numbers and distributed to local schools and educational offices.

- Researcher contributions: The finding that educational programs delivered in the students' mother tongue have much higher success than non-native language programs was leveraged to promote the development of new educational materials.

It is a well-known conclusion of educational research that mother-tongue education is essential for the learning success of children at school (see for example Skutnabb-Kangas, 2014). However, this has rarely been integrated into policy or applied by institutions responsible for Indigenous students, who are often a minority in their schools. Hunter-gatherer students, in particular, tend to be represented in small numbers and are thus regularly overlooked by decision-makers or actively bypassed by relevant laws and provisions. In the protected area of Dzanga-Sangha, the homeland of BaAka hunter-gatherer and Sangha-Sangha fishing communities in the Central African Republic, this has been addressed by a local youth association, Ndima-Kali, whose members belong to both communities, with the support of OrigiNations, an international NGO that focuses on Indigenous education.

Until a few years ago, school materials in the area were either in French (the colonial language) or in Sangho (the national language), so that BaAka children raised in Aka, their mother tongue, experienced difficulties in learning how to read and write and to follow classes. Moreover, the official school materials depicted French landmarks such as the Eiffel Tower or unfamiliar objects such as apples. By developing new materials in their mother tongues and introducing elements of the local culture, Ndima-Kali aimed to help students acquire new knowledge in connection to known elements, while acknowledging their life-worlds in a context of utter discrimination, marginalization, and neglect. They were supported in this project by OrigiNations, whose role was to provide information on research findings relative to mother-tongue education, to facilitate contacts with other external organizations and educational authorities, and to finance the printing of the materials, while the core of the contribution rested in the hands of Ndima-Kali. Dissatisfied with the alienating character of their education, Ndima-Kali created the learning booklets and classroom posters featuring elements of their own Indigenous cultures and daily lives (Figures 9.2 and 9.3). The classroom materials were shared with the educational authorities of the region, who were supportive of the initiative and accompanied Ndima-Kali to the schools in order to distribute the materials to students and teachers. This initiative by a local civil society organization was highly appreciated and well received by the population, students, teachers, parents, and regional authorities. Furthermore, the experience was very empowering for Ndima-Kali's young members who belong to a people which is heavily discriminated against in school and everyday life. This effort will hopefully promote mother-tongue education and influence regional school policies in a significant way.

Outside actors, such as researchers or NGOs, can support communities not only in influencing policy but also in enforcing existing policy which is favorable to them, bringing to their attention national or international legal frameworks not being implemented by local authorities. Just becoming acquainted with such a legal instrument can spark local action. An example is the International Labor Organization (ILO) 169 Convention, which contains important provisions for Indigenous rights and self-determination, including in education. The Central African Republic is the only African country to have signed it. However, its enforcement is cursory and sporadic. OrigiNations pointed to concrete examples of how the convention's provisions can positively impact communities. As a consequence, Ndima-Kali set out to promote the implementation of ILO 169 in its region in a momentous way. They conceptualized and helped establish a Human Rights Centre which today supports the BaAka population in gaining access to justice and furthers the protection of their rights. This new institution monitors violations at the community level and accompanies victims to the police and to the courts. Since its inception in 2016, Ndima-Kali has cooperated with the Human Rights Centre by carrying out awareness-raising campaigns to educate the population about their rights through interventions in schools, radio programs, films, theatre performances, and sports events. Ndima-Kali's members in the different settlements of the region act as eyes and ears for the Centre, monitoring the situation in the villages and reporting abuses.

For more information about Ndima-Kali and their initiatives regarding education and human rights, visit their website: www. ndimakali.org and www.origi-nations.org/.

Fig. 9.2 Learning to use modern technologies for the purpose of documenting their own culture ©Ndima-Kali (http://www.ndimakali.org/). All rights reserved.

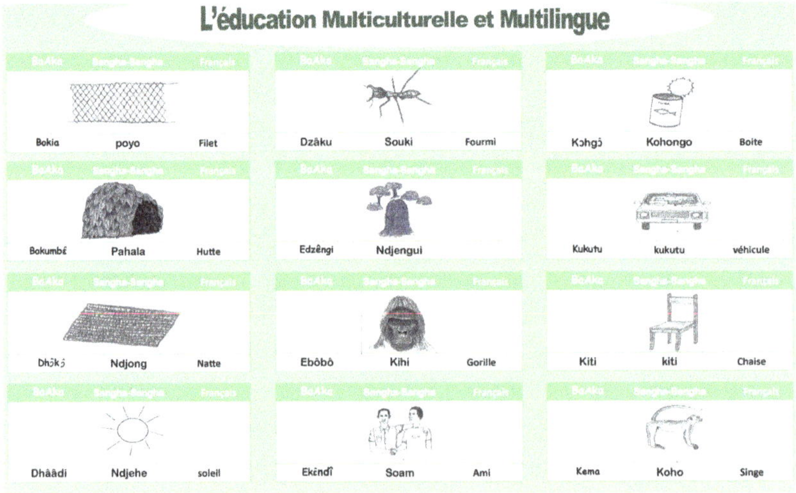

Fig. 9.3 Example of didactic poster in Aka, Sangha-Sangha and French, for schools in the Dzanga-Sangha protected area, as produced by the local youth association Ndima-Kali. ©Ndima-Kali (http://www.ndimakali.org/). All rights reserved.

9.7. How to influence policy

Ilaria Pretelli

Now that we have a better understanding of how policy works and have seen a couple of examples of interactions between researchers and policy interventions, we can take a step back and ask ourselves how a researcher, who has mostly been navigating the halls of universities, can have an actual impact on what is going on out there, in the real world. Many behavioral sciences have large untapped potential to contribute new perspectives to the policy world (see Gibson & Lawson, 2014; Schimmelpfennig & Muthukrishna, 2023). We will review four main pathways, highlighting the potential for impact and outlining some considerations to improve impact.

Be your own promoter

One of the main reasons why we might want to intervene in the real world is because we are concerned for the people we work with, especially if we engage in substantial participative fieldwork in a setting much poorer than our usual home. Facing poverty, disease, lack of opportunities, and often a lack of support for the local/Indigenous population by governments can be extremely disconcerting, and we can feel the need to intervene somehow. On the one hand, we must be extremely careful not to impose our views of what is ideal on the people with whom we are visiting and collaborating, remembering that we are first and foremost visitors with a very limited understanding of the needs of the communities we frequent for a relatively short period of time (falling victim to the white savior complex is always a risk). However, it is also true that, as individuals often living on the border between developed societies and Indigenous/traditional communities, researchers can also act as spokespeople for the latter or have access to resources that are often beyond the reach of many of our partners. One way to move forward is to collaborate with NGOs acting in the area. One relevant example is the One Pencil Project (https://www.onepencilproject.org/), which collaborates with local and Indigenous peoples in Namibia, in the Kunene region, and in

Bolivia, specifically with the Tsimane, to enable school attendance and successful education for students of these marginalized communities. In taking this path, it is worth noting how important it is to include the communities themselves in the design and organization of the NGO. Community members can participate as members of the NGO's board, as employees, as consultants, or the NGO can regularly interact with local councils, or any combination of these. Adopting such an approach can be incredibly time consuming, but it might be the most effective way to enact change in a respectful and culturally appropriate way.

The example of Dr. Asatsa's project in Kenya (Section 9.5) illustrates another pathway to intervention, that of local action. By coordinating the needs of different institutions, such as the schools and university in Nairobi, the project was able to provide benefits to all the parties involved without investing in the creation and maintenance of an NGO or additional organization. Such a system can have a high success rate and be self-sustainable, as all parties involved are able to reach their goals and obtain economic benefits.

More generally, outside actors such as researchers or NGOs can help facilitate the exchange of information between communities, research, and policy. As we have seen in the example of Ndima-Kali (Section 9.6), they can share research findings relevant to communities' lives or introduce them to national and international policy that can improve their circumstances. At the same time, collaborative research with the local population can help highlight a region's challenges as well as its potential, bringing these to the attention of policymakers and authorities, who might more readily read a scientific report than interact with communities directly. Unfortunately, in many places, knowledge stemming from (western) universities still receives more attention from policymakers than knowledge generated locally, especially when it comes to hunter-gatherers.

Researchers can thus serve as communication vehicles for communities' concerns. They can also bring to the fore important knowledge possessed by Indigenous peoples and local communities. By acting in a facilitating, supportive role, taking care not to impose their own solutions but rather engaging in the respectful exchange of knowledge and timely sharing of information and resources, outside actors can contribute to the communities' process of self-empowerment and their efforts to enhance their agency and strengthen their capacity to effect change.

Collaborate directly with policymakers

The world of policymakers is very wide and moves fast. They often have little time to invest in developing a deep understanding of the problems they are called to solve, so they like to rely on scientists to help them devise solutions. From the perspective of the average researcher, the idea that researchers have time is nonsensical, but the truth is that each of us invests much more time and energy in a specific problem, place, and/or method, which makes us extremely competent on a small range of subjects. In particular, researchers investing in long-term field sites develop interpersonal relationships with local communities and, thus, can help mediate across cultures. This is fundamental to the realization of policy projects, but basically impossible to develop for NGOs and politicians, who work on shorter timescales. In short, policymakers need our competence and often search for it. Scientists are regularly called to provide reports to large IGOs such as the World Bank, and are consulted by smaller NGOs as part of their projects.

For example, we saw that in the case of the Indonesian cocoa farms (Section 9.4) a local PhD student was involved from the beginning in the development of the project, and a researcher from a university in the US collaborated in another specific phase. Sometimes researchers can collaborate as consultants, and even be paid for their services, or they can integrate the project itself into their scientific goals, thus producing papers and other academic outcomes based on their results. However, it is fairly uncommon for behavioral scientists to act in these roles (possibly because of the tighter connections between the economic and political science fields and the policy world). Several NGOs are interested in changing this status quo. For example, both UNICEF and Save the Children opened branches that specialize in implementing methods from the behavioral sciences in their projects, and they aim to integrate more behavioral scientists too. CUBIC, the behavioral science unit of Save the Children, is working on putting together a database of scientists that could be contacted for specific projects, organizing them by geographical and scientific area.

While these systems are put in place, however, being contacted by policymakers to contribute to a relevant project still relies on mechanisms such as word of mouth or online searches of institutional websites. For example, Prof. Charles Efferson and Sonja Vogt were contacted by UNICEF Switzerland to contribute with their expertise on mechanisms of cultural change to projects related to female genital mutilation in Sudan and on sex-specific abortion in Armenia. This led to them leading extensive projects in both countries and to the production of several scientific papers (Efferson, Vogt, Elhadi, Ahmed, & Fehr, 2015; Schief, Efferson, & Vogt, 2021; Vogt, Mohmmed Zaid, El Fadil Ahmed, Fehr, & Efferson, 2016 etc.). For most behavioral scientists, being contacted by policymakers remains mostly subject to luck, but there are a few ways to improve the chances, such as contacting NGOs that work in the same geographical area, or having clear and accessible personal pages, either on university or personal websites, that include messages for policymakers—for example, stating areas of expertise and interest in collaboration with NGOs and policymakers. Moreover, an additional option to increase points of contact with the policy world is to consider inviting policymakers to conferences, as speakers or audience. They are often interested in developing contacts with researchers in relevant areas and can bring interesting perspectives to academic environments, so that their participation at conferences can bring multiple benefits for all of those involved.

Produce influential work

An alternative way to contribute to the discussion on policymaking is to produce science that is directly relevant to it. Behavioral scientists regularly produce results that have policy implications, but only rarely do our results feed into policy practices and goals.

This can be due to limited information flow between disciplines, and to the fact that the policy world has been historically much more connected to fields such as economics than, say, psychology. This creates both a thematic and a linguistic barrier, as orienting oneself in an unknown literature is often perplexing and uncomfortable, making papers targeted to a psychology audience unlikely to be read by an economics-trained policymaker.

Certain characteristics make research more likely to be picked up and integrated into the world of policymaking. We can think of scientific process as moving from (i) exploration of possible mechanisms, (ii) development of theory, (iii) production of evidence close to theory, (iv) definition of application in the real world, and (v) testing of these applications within real implementation scenarios. Policymakers, as well as researchers working in close contact with policymakers, can pick up on any of these kinds of research from other fields, especially if certain aspects are considered. Phases i–iii are the most commonly pursued within fundamental, non-applied research. While they are obviously, by definition, fundamental steps of the scientific process, they are less likely to be relevant to policymakers, because a key tenet of evidence-based policy is that policies should be based on careful tests of the intervention, possibly in the context in which the intervention will be enacted.

However, research produced by phases i–iii can become the subject of further investigation by economists or political scientists, who can then develop phases iv and v. This uptake is more likely if the specific research points to clear policy implications (such as "based on our results, we believe children could achieve better scholastic results if they were allowed to speak their native tongue at school" rather than "our results have implications for educational policies") and if these results and indications were to be presented in an accessible format (report, infographic, lay summary) in easy-to-reach venues (social media, personal websites, popular science news). Summaries, such as reviews and meta-analyses, are also particularly sought-after as material of interest, so investing in these kinds of policy-oriented outputs can yield real-world effects. But if a researcher wants to produce results that are directly relevant for policymakers, they should consider which characteristics policymakers value in the scientific results they consider. While they tend not to be interested in results that present generic associations between variables, policymakers look for clear quantification of explicitly causal mechanisms, which are normally associated to RCTs (but also to other methodologies, see the discussion of causality in Section 9.3). A researcher whose goal is to produce scientific results that are relevant to policy should consider constructing a study that uses explicit experimental set-ups to test the outcome of potential policy interventions in a specific population.

For example, a lab that believes they have the expertise to integrate Indigenous knowledge practices in school programs for Indigenous children could design a school program, implement it in half of the classes in their community, run evaluations of the children's results and carefully report improvements in school attendance or scholastic attainment. Interestingly, there are specific sources of funding for running such experimental designs, as well as more qualitative approaches that can have relevance for policymaking, provided by charitable organizations and NGOs, of which behavioral scientists are often not aware. Structural Transformation and Economic Growth (https://steg.cepr.org/funding/open-upcoming-funding-calls) is an initiative that promotes growth in developing countries by funding research, similarly to the International Growth Center (https://www.theigc.org/researchers/funding), and many others. Most of these are economy-focused, but it can be worth investigating the possibility of funding policy-oriented research projects through these pathways. As interdisciplinarity is fundamental to achieving broader impact, collaborating and publishing across disciplines, especially in those that are most likely to be read by policymakers (namely, public policy, but also economics or political science), can help overcome the impasse, even though this can be complicated (learning new discipline-specific jargon and culture is costly, timelines of publication and collaboration habits can substantially differ, etc.).

One additional consideration is that policymakers only rarely have time to read full papers and prefer to read reports and summaries. In order to facilitate their job and to produce reports and meta-analyses that are easily accessible to policymakers, a few associations have been developed since the early 1990s (see the discussion of evidence-based policy in Section 9.3). Getting in touch with the relevant branches of these associations (for example the sector of J-PAL that deals with education https://www.povertyactionlab.org/sector/education), to obtain help to run appropriate studies or to point out a result we believe they should cover in their report could be a way to promote the utilization of our research in policy. It is also possible to self-nominate to become an affiliate researcher of J-PAL, so that one can apply for funding from J-PAL or work with a J-PAL regional office to implement their evaluation (https://www.povertyactionlab.org/invited-researchers). Policymakers do use scientific results in their decision-making processes, and behavioral scientists have multiple avenues to increase the likelihood that this includes their results.

Reach out

One last, rarely considered, path to influence policy is outreach. We have seen in the Indonesian cocoa farm example (Section 9.4) that the goal of the intervention (to reduce child labor and make it safer) was set at the outset of the project by the funder, i.e., the large international chocolate company. Politicians carefully choose to promote projects that can boost their approval and most NGO goals are tied to funding from large companies or charitable organizations whose interests align with public opinion. A multinational food company might want to promote a certain program for education because it benefits their image, and the extent to which their image would benefit from implementing the program depends on how much the public values the program. Similarly, charitable organizations decide which programs to fund depending on what specific individuals or public opinion find to be a good thing. For example, there is a widespread opinion that child marriage (defined as marriage before the age of 18 years) is a bad thing, whereas there are reports that, in certain cases and situations, girls can benefit from marrying during late adolescence

(Schaffnit, Wamoyi, Urassa, Dardoumpa, & Lawson, 2021). Thus, policy interventions that act to disincentivize adolescent marriage are likely to be funded by well-meaning benefactors, even though in some contexts such disincentives can actually reduce girls' wellbeing. In such cases, producing outreach that can educate the general public (among which are founders and counselors of big charitable organizations, employees of the World Bank, other relevant actors and, in general, public opinion) on cultural diversity and the needs of minorities can be a very effective way to direct policy interventions in relevant directions. This kind of outreach can span from publishing popular science books, to much less time-consuming activities such as editing or creating Wikipedia pages on relevant subjects, or putting effort into publicizing scientific results in popular science venues.

References

Anderson, J. E., Moyer, J., & Chichirau, G. (2022). *Public policymaking*. Wadsworth.

Berkes, F., Colding, J., & Folke, C. (2000). Rediscovery of Traditional Ecological Knowledge as Adaptive Management. *Ecological Applications, 10*(5), 1251–1262. https://doi.org/10.1890/1051-0761(2000)010[1251:ROTEKA]2.0.CO;2

Bhuiyan, M. U., Zaman, S., & Ahmed, T. (2013). Risk factors associated with overweight and obesity among urban school children and adolescents in Bangladesh: A case–control study. *BMC Pediatrics, 13*(1), 72. https://doi.org/10.1186/1471-2431-13-72

Birkland, T. A. (2011). *An introduction to the policy process: Theories, concepts, and models of public policy making* (3rd ed.). M.E. Sharpe.

Breslow, N. E. (1996). Statistics in Epidemiology: The Case-Control Study. *Journal of the American Statistical Association, 91*(433), 14–28. https://doi.org/10.1080/01621459.1996.10476660

Brugha, R., & Varvasovszky, Z. (2000). Stakeholder analysis: A review. *Health Policy and Planning, 15*(3), 239–246. https://doi.org/10.1093/heapol/15.3.239

Cartwright, N. (2011). A philosopher's view of the long road from RCTs to effectiveness. *The Lancet, 377*(9775), 1400–1401. https://doi.org/10.1016/S0140-6736(11)60563-1

Cartwright, N., & Hardie, J. (2012). *Evidence-based policy: A practical guide to doing it better*. Oxford University Press.

Deffner, D., Rohrer, J. M., & McElreath, R. (2022). A Causal Framework for Cross-Cultural Generalizability. *Advances in Methods and Practices in Psychological Science, 5*(3), 25152459221106370. https://doi.org/10.1177/25152459221106366

Delfino, A., Ashraf, N., Bryan, G., Holmes, E., Iacovone, L., Meyer, C., & Pople, A. (n.d.). *Learning to See the World's Opportunities: Memory, Mental Experiencing and the Economic Lives of the Vulnerable* with N. Ashraf (LSE), G. Bryan (LSE), E. Holmes (Karolinska Institutet), L. Iacovone (WB), C. Meyer (Oxford) and A. Pople (WB).

Edwards, D. B. (2019). Shifting the perspective on community-based management of education: From systems theory to social capital and community empowerment. *International Journal of Educational Development, 64*, 17–26. https://doi.org/10.1016/j.ijedudev.2018.11.004

Efferson, C., Vogt, S., Elhadi, A., Ahmed, H. E. F., & Fehr, E. (2015). Female genital cutting is not a social coordination norm. *Science, 349*(6255), 1446–1447. https://doi.org/10.1126/science.aaa7978

Findley, M. G., Kikuta, K., & Denly, M. (2021). External Validity. *Annual Review of Political Science, 24*(1), 365–393. https://doi.org/10.1146/annurev-polisci-041719-102556

Gibson, M. A., & Lawson, D. W. (2014). *Applied Evolutionary Anthropology: Darwinian Approaches to Contemporary World Issues*. Springer. https://doi.org/10.1007/978-1-4939-0280-4

Glymour, M. M., & Spiegelman, D. (2017). Evaluating Public Health Interventions: 5. Causal Inference in Public Health Research-Do Sex, Race, and Biological Factors Cause Health Outcomes? *American Journal of Public Health, 107*(1), 81–85. https://doi.org/10.2105/AJPH.2016.303539

Hopkins, A., Oliver, K., Boaz, A., Guillot-Wright, S., & Cairney, P. (2021). Are research-policy engagement activities informed by policy theory and evidence? 7 challenges to the UK impact agenda. *Policy Design and Practice, 4*(3), 341–356. https://doi.org/10.1080/25741292.2021.1921373

Howard, C. (2005). The Policy Cycle: A Model of Post-Machiavellian Policy Making? *Australian Journal of Public Administration, 64*(3), 3–13. https://doi.org/10.1111/j.1467-8500.2005.00447.x

McLeroy, K. R., Norton, B. L., Kegler, M. C., Burdine, J. N., & Sumaya, C. V. (2003). Community-Based Interventions. *American Journal of Public Health, 93*(4), 529–533. https://doi.org/10.2105/AJPH.93.4.529

McNutt, & Hoefer, R. (2021). *Social welfare policy: Responding to a changing world* (2nd ed.). Oxford University Press.

Michelitch, K. (2018). Whose Research Is It? Political Scientists Discuss Whether, How, and Why We Should Involve the Communities We Study. *PS: Political Science & Politics, 51*(3), 543–545. https://doi.org/10.1017/S1049096518000422

Morelli, G., Quinn, N., Chaudhary, N., Vicedo, M., Rosabal-Coto, M., Keller, H., Murray, M., Gottlieb, A., Scheidecker, G., & Takada, A. (2018). Ethical Challenges of Parenting Interventions in Low- to Middle-Income Countries. *Journal of Cross-Cultural Psychology, 49*(1), 5–24. https://doi.org/10.1177/0022022117746241

Oppong, S. (2020). Towards a Model of Valued Human Cognitive Abilities: An African Perspective Based on a Systematic Review. *Frontiers in Psychology, 11*, 538072. https://doi.org/10.3389/fpsyg.2020.538072

Pearl, J. (2009). *Causality* (2nd ed.). Cambridge: Cambridge University Press. https://doi.org/10.1017/CBO9780511803161

Sabatier, P. A. (1991). Toward Better Theories of the Policy Process. *PS: Political Science and Politics, 24*(2), 147–156. https://doi.org/10.2307/419923

Sackett, D. L., & Rosenberg, W. M. C. (1995). On the need for evidence-based medicine. *Journal of Public Health, 17*(3), 330–334. https://doi.org/10.1093/oxfordjournals.pubmed.a043127

Schaffnit, S. B., Wamoyi, J., Urassa, M., Dardoumpa, M., & Lawson, D. W. (2021). When marriage is the best available option: Perceptions of opportunity and risk in female adolescence in Tanzania. *Global Public Health, 16*(12), 1820–1833. https://doi.org/10.1080/17441692.2020.1837911

Schief, M., Efferson, C., & Vogt, S. (2021). Investigating the Structure of Son Bias in Armenia With Novel Measures of Individual Preferences. *Demography, 58*(5), 1737–1764. https://doi.org/10.1215/00703370-9429479

Schimmelpfennig, R., & Muthukrishna, M. (2023). Cultural evolutionary behavioural science in public policy. *Behavioural Public Policy*, 1–31. https://doi.org/10.1017/bpp.2022.40

Sharfstein, J. M. (2016). Banishing "stakeholders". *The Milbank Quarterly, 94*(3), 476. https://doi.org/10.1111/1468-0009.12208

Skutnabb-Kangas, T. (2014). The Role of Mother Tongues in the Education of Indigenous, Tribal. Minority and Minoritized Children: What can be done to Avoid Crimes Against Humanity? In P. Orelus (Ed.). *Affirming Language Diversity in Schools and Society.*

Beyond Linguistic Apartheid. (pp. 215–249). Routledge. https://doi.org/10.13140/2.1.3350.9764

The Strategic Impact Evaluation Fund (SIEF) [Text/HTML]. (n.d.). *World Bank.* https://www.worldbank.org/en/programs/sief-trust-fund

Thistlethwaite, D. L., & Campbell, D. T. (1960). Regression-discontinuity analysis: An alternative to the ex post facto experiment. *Journal of Educational Psychology, 51*(6), 309–317. https://doi.org/10.1037/h0044319

Vogt, S., Mohmmed Zaid, N. A., El Fadil Ahmed, H., Fehr, E., & Efferson, C. (2016). Changing cultural attitudes towards female genital cutting. *Nature, 538*(7626), 506–509. https://doi.org/10.1038/nature20100

Weissman, M. B. (2021). Policy recommendations from causal inference in physics education research. *Physical Review Physics Education Research, 17*(2), 020118. https://doi.org/10.1103/PhysRevPhysEducRes.17.020118

Wikipedia contributors. (2023, September 29). Policy. *Wikipedia.* https://en.wikipedia.org/wiki/Policy

Young, K., Ashby, D., Boaz, A., & Grayson, L. (2002). Social Science and the Evidence-based Policy Movement. *Social Policy and Society, 1*(3), 215–224. https://doi.org/10.1017/S1474746402003068

10. Looking forward, looking back

In this final chapter, we offer emerging scholars in cross-cultural childhood learning research the advice we wish we had received at the start of our careers.

In this book, we have aimed to take you through the entire life cycle of cross-cultural research on childhood learning. We started in Chapter 1 by asking: What is childhood? What is culture? What is learning? And most importantly: Why should you study childhood learning across cultures? We made the case that research on this topic should be ethical, respectful, and holistic—themes that we revisited throughout the book.

In Chapter 2, we reviewed the history of research on cross-cultural childhood learning through an overview of methods and theory from the disciplines of developmental psychology, anthropology, and philosophy from across Africa, China, and Japan. Chapter 3 expanded on universalist and culturalist approaches, ultimately arguing that, to truly understand child development, we must draw on the best of both approaches. Chapter 4 brought together diverse methodologies, and explored their theoretical, ethical, and practical implications.

In Chapter 5, we discussed the practicalities of preparing for 'the field', from building trustful relationships with communities and stakeholders, to staying safe and planning a budget. Chapter 6 provides personal narratives ripe with honest descriptions of challenges encountered, and lessons learned by scholars working near and far from home.

Chapter 7 considered research sharing, from design to publication. Chapter 8 provided a series of case studies on global education, demonstrating that educational policy can better account for local cultural contexts through direct participation

©2025 S. Lew-Levy, S. Asatsa, et al. CC BY-NC 4.0 https://doi.org/10.11647/OBP.0440.10

of communities. Finally, Chapter 9 tells us about the policy cycle, offering practical advice about how to engage policymakers, so that our research ultimately benefits children from around the world.

This volume represents the book we wish we had had when we started studying children's learning across cultures. And while, normally, books like these end by telling you, the reader, what we hope the field will look like in the future, ultimately, if you're reading this book, you are the future of our field. Thus, rather than tell you what we think, we want to end by providing you with advice we wish we had had at the start of our research journeys. We hope the advice below, and the book more generally, helps you on your path.

"Two bits of advice given to me by mentors early in my career continue to resonate. First, it's better to come home with no data and good relations, than the reverse. And second, it's OK to come home early from fieldwork if you need to." –Sheina Lew-Levy

"Everything will take much longer than you think. And you will find out much more than you were trying to learn. Expand your timelines, expectations—and supply of digestive aids." –Ivan Kroupin

"Life is larger than work." –Jing Xu

"Things take time, things go well, and things go badly. That's completely normal. Try your hardest to learn as much from what goes wrong as you do from what goes right." –Bruce Rawlings

"Expect the unexpected—always. Expect things to break you never thought would break. Your health is more important than data. Have a good supply of comfort food."—Patricia Kanngiesser

"You've probably heard the expression that 'anything worth doing isn't worth doing perfectly'. That's even more true if you have dengue fever. Also, if you don't frequently push yourself outside your comfort zone, you won't learn as much as you could, nor will others learn as much about you." –Michael Gurven

"The core ingredients of good science are curiosity, serendipity, and respect. Respect for the knowledge and perspectives of your colleagues, coworkers and informants—they are all co-creators of whatever final results you end up with." –Felix Riede

"Do not follow best career options when you are not passionate about the topic. Develop awareness about your own biases. Question taken-for-granted assumptions. Be courageous and enjoy what you are doing." –Heidi Keller

"If you are planning ethnographic fieldwork, you should know that you will have plenty of idle time in the field! Don't try to optimize everything or always obtain useful information—it's impossible. Instead, prioritize fitting into the local routine and building good relationships with people. 'Dead time' is absolutely part of an ethnographer's work. And a very practical piece of advice: if your field site is far from where you live, plan your fieldwork in stages, if possible. Spend a few months in the field, then some time back at the university, and afterward, return to the field. The time back at the university is very useful for processing your material, realizing what is missing, and better preparing for your final stay." –Chantal Medaets

"Learn to live with pending tasks without getting stressed out: that's the life of a researcher. And don't forget to have fun and make friends along the way." –Julia Hermida

"I found that at the start of my fieldwork in Yasawa, I recognized many familiar things: families living together, feeding their kids, looking after their elders, doing daily chores. It all felt quite 'normal' to me, despite being far from my culture of origin. The longer I spent living in the villages there, the more I found deeper ways in which day-to-day experience, meaning-making, and relationships varied from what I was used to. I suppose the takeaway is to remain humble, and spend a lot of time just living where you study and trying to understand how others are living in a qualitative way, even if your research demands quantitative outputs." –Michelle Kline

"It is helpful to be prepared, but many plans will not work out, and that's okay. Don't be too sad about everything; awe and bewilderment can co-exist." –Gairan Pamei

"This career will test your patience, confidence, and drive. Fieldwork will be unpredictable, papers will get rejected, and feedback will feel brutal. But resilience isn't just pushing through—it's adapting. Be open to shifting your research questions, methods, and perspectives. Growth comes from flexibility, not perfection. Keep learning, keep adjusting, and trust that setbacks are just part of the process." –Nicole Wen

"Is there anyone among this set of authors from around the globe who would not tell a younger self to be more fearless in pursuing his or her passion? Yet, of course, others will have self-guidance that reflects their unique geographies, histories, and personalities. In my case, I would advise Elise to take herself both more and less seriously: Have the confidence to pursue burning questions and act on her deepest values, but accept falling short of her ideals with more equanimity and less self-criticism. I would urge her to be a more assiduous scholar of languages and linguistics—her greatest intellectual passions and the source of much of whatever insight she has been able to bring to research on educational reform, particularly in the arena of student assessment. Finally, I would bolster her belief in collaboration—a natural proclivity of hers and a major reason for her best accomplishments. She would be very fortunate in finding strong, devoted, brilliant, and intellectually generous colleagues, who would also become friends." –Elise Trumbull

"I try, I fall, I try again, I fall better." –Barnabas Simatende

"Embrace intellectual curiosity. Some of the most meaningful insights will come from unexpected places. Trust your instincts when a topic or question sparks your interest, even if it doesn't fit neatly into existing frameworks. Your work will help you understand the power of listening and deep human connection. The most rewarding moments won't come from publications or accolades, but from the people you meet—colleagues, students, research participants, and friends. Balancing marriage, children, and an academic career won't be easy. But don't feel guilty for wanting both or at times investing in one more than the other. Academia, or your own guilt, can make you feel like you must choose, but personal experiences will enrich your work and your work will enrich your personal life in ways you never imagined. Finally, be patient with yourself. Your career will evolve in ways you can't foresee. There will be detours, frustrations, and moments of self-doubt. But trust that you're building something meaningful—one conversation, one field season, one page at a time." –Bonnie Hewlett

"Always back up your data and store the two extra copies at different locations." –Katja Liebal

"Things will nearly always somehow go 'wrong' in research, and that's ok. You'll always have something to build on, even if it didn't turn out exactly (or even a little bit!) the way you'd imagined or planned for. Be easy on yourself, be respectful of your colleagues, and don't forget to have fun!" –Annemieke Milks

"Fieldwork is unique among research methods as it's built on genuine interactions with people and their environment. During fieldwork, living alongside children and their families allows you to see the world through their eyes and understand different ways of relating to others and nature. While not always smooth, the process is grounded in everyday moments. You may begin by feeling the breeze, the rain, or the heat of the sun, watching birds fly and clouds drift, hearing children play and laughter, or joining in adults' gossip." –Xiaojie Tian

"That working in the field allows you to immerse yourself in the wisdom of the people, in the simple environment and the depth and spirituality that guides them." –Andrea Taverna

"Be open to learning from others and be ready to learn a lot about yourself. Take breaks and pause from time to time to take in and enjoy the moment—some of the most interesting insights come not from studying but from experiencing what is around you." –Marie Schäfer

"Remember that this book is written by 'survivors': Fieldwork is not for everyone, and it does not mean someone is weaker if they decide to leave early or not to go back. Even those who go back several times may eventually accumulate difficult (perhaps even traumatic) experiences that make their everyday life harder, and perhaps feel ashamed to share their struggles. So be particularly careful and gentle with your students." –Anonymous

"Relax and enjoy the process. Try not to lose sight of the beauty and awe of exploring another culture or region of the world for your data-driven and time-sensitive (and career dependent) research goals. Stop, step back, and watch everything. Sit, sit, and sit some more. Make time to do nothing with people. You'll learn more than you can imagine by just hanging out. Recognize your bias and be explicit about it. You may arrive ready to explore a question in one way but if you open your eyes and ears, you will likely discover there's much more to the question than you thought. Be prepared to discard your old ideas and follow new leads. And, have fun!" –Tanya MacGillivray

"Look for networks where your work resonates and where you can engage in meaningful dialogue in the field and out. These connections can be a source of strength and encouragement, providing feedback and support every step of the way. Local researchers, community leaders, and other stakeholders can provide invaluable support and insights during your fieldwork. You'll show up with big plans, and many of them will be wrong. Learn from the people around you; ask for their input and guidance. Regarding the dissemination of your work: focus on sharing your work with the networks you've developed, share widely, and be transparent. Also remember that no one knows how hard you worked to do your research, so it's important to remember that the value of your research is not diminished by a lack of immediate recognition. Do good work, stay committed to your vision, and continue to share your findings confidently." –Helen Elizabeth Davis

"Always run pilots. Lots of them. Keep a research journal, write about anything that comes to mind. Ask for help. Sometimes, your supervisors are wrong. Good research projects take time. A lot of what you do and feel proud of will probably never be in a scientific paper. Learn what and who is worth your time and energy (I am still learning that one). You are more than your research." –Natália Dutra

"There will never be perfect advice to guide you through the many difficult, exciting, annoying, and consequential decisions you will make during fieldwork (and life for that matter!). Be okay with failing. Be proud of succeeding. Be kind and open to experience. Be willing to learn. And if you accidentally buy 10 cartons of coffee instead of 10 cans, roll with it." –Sarah Pope-Caldwell

"Be ready to accept that plan A, B, or C might not work and that is ok! Take time to rest and be in your best health, you will need it. Be humble and enjoy the unique experience you are having! And take the time to watch, learn, share, and admire the amazing people you are about to meet." –Camila Scaff

"You are going to hit obstacle after obstacle. Just keep going. Those you think should help you, won't. So don't expect help—you're in charge. You'll be told your ideas aren't worthy. They are. And it will seem like the thing you really want to do won't happen. But it will. If you persevere. So, keep your head down and bite off more than you can chew ... then chew really bloody hard." –Mark Nielsen

"I wish I had learned the importance of patience (or perhaps I should have listened to those advising me to do just that!) and the value of maintaining curiosity, especially outside the study setting. The most essential aspect of field research in psychology is understanding people, which comes not only from running studies but from spending time with them, appreciating their perspectives, listening to stories, and never missing a football match (/huru bolsa)." –Roman Stengelin

"In my research journey, I have learned that the true experts are the community members—most of whom are typically seen as uneducated—rather than the professors and PhD scholars, whom we often regard as highly educated and who usually design and conduct the research. The final resting place for research findings should be the community and NOT the library." –Stephen Asatsa

Plates

1. Julia Hermida on fieldwork in rural northern Argentina

2. Andrea Taverna doing fieldwork with Wichi children in Formosa, Argentina

3. Ilaria Pretelli on fieldwork on Pemba Island

4. A group of BaAka sharing songs and stories around the fire in a forest camp ©OrigiNations

5. Play in multi-aged child groups is also an important arena for socialisation in post hunter-gatherer societies (Botswana, 2000) ©Akira Takada

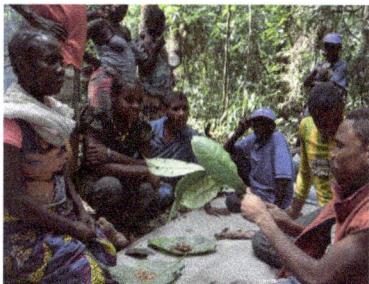

6. Intergenerational sharing of BaAka knowledge of medicinal plants ©OrigiNations

7. Learning to be a father through talking with the child (US, 2011) ©Akira Takada

8. Hut and sky in the Kalahari. The Kalahari sunsets are as beautiful as ever, although the San's huts in the settlement have become larger, like those of the agro-pastoralists (Botswana, 2015) ©Akira Takada

9. Vidrige Kandza on fieldwork in a BaYaka camp.

10. Stephen Asatsa and his research team join a night vigil at a funeral.

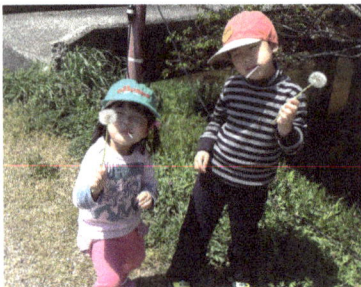

11. Sibling learn from each other in language socialisation (Japan, 2014) ©Akira Takada

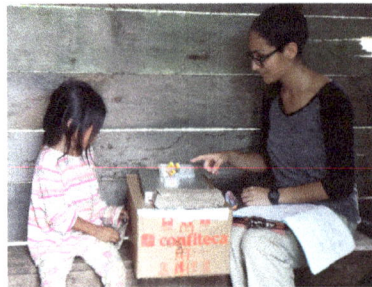

12. Dorsa Amir conducting experimental studies on preferences in Ecuador, 2015.

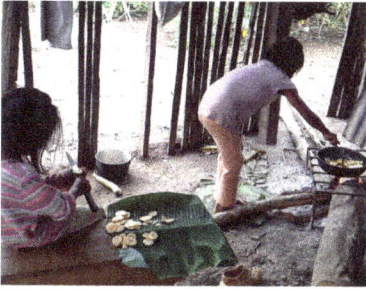

13. Shuar girls frying chifles on the fire, Ecuador, 2016.

14. Arthur Wolf's teenage research assistant, MC (Ms. Chen) playing with research participants. MC was popular, and children called her "Older Sister Chen." Photo taken by Arthur Wolf during his fieldwork in a Taiwanese village (1958-1960). Photo shared with permission from Dr. Hill Gates, the holder of the Arthur Wolf archive.

15. Children walking to school in Manipur, photo by Gairan Pamei.

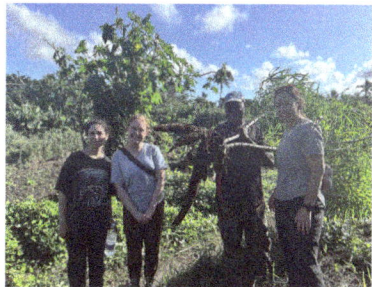

16. Tanya MacGillivray and her students learning local farming practices at the Simon Fraser University Field School in Vanuatu (2023).

17. Seetha Kakkoth and Vinod Chellan enjoying school vacation with Cholanaickan and Kattunayakan children.

18. Menencia Xulubte', age seven, daughter of Petul Xulubte', tries to help her niece Rosy make a heddle out of a piece of red threat. Rosy participates by holding the stick that will be used to attach the thread. Nabenchauk, 1991. ©Lauren Greenfield/Institute.

Index

About the Team

Alessandra Tosi was the managing editor for this book.

Annie Hine and Lucy Barnes were in charge of proofreading; Lucy indexed this manuscript.

Jeevanjot Kaur Nagpal designed the cover. The cover was produced in InDesign using the Fontin font.

Cameron Craig typeset the book in InDesign and produced the paperback and hardback editions. The main text font is Tex Gyre Pagella and the heading font is Californian FB. Cameron also produced the PDF and EPUB editions.

The conversion to the HTML edition was performed with epublius, an open-source software which is freely available on our GitHub page at https://github.com/OpenBookPublishers.

Jeremy Bowman created the EPUB edition.

This book was peer-reviewed by two referees. Experts in their field, our readers give their time freely to help ensure the academic rigour of our books. We are grateful for their generous and invaluable contribution

This book need not end here...

Share

All our books — including the one you have just read — are free to access online so that students, researchers and members of the public who can't afford a printed edition will have access to the same ideas. This title will be accessed online by hundreds of readers each month across the globe: why not share the link so that someone you know is one of them?

This book and additional content is available at:
https://doi.org/10.11647/OBP.0440

Donate

Open Book Publishers is an award-winning, scholar-led, not-for-profit press making knowledge freely available one book at a time. We don't charge authors to publish with us: instead, our work is supported by our library members and by donations from people who believe that research shouldn't be locked behind paywalls.

Why not join them in freeing knowledge by supporting us:
https://www.openbookpublishers.com/support-us

We invite you to connect with us on our socials!

BLUESKY
@openbookpublish
.bsky.social

MASTODON
@OpenBookPublish
@hcommons.social

LINKEDIN
open-book-publisher

Read more at the Open Book Publishers Blog
https://blogs.openbookpublishers.com

You may also be interested in:

Learning, Marginalization, and Improving the Quality of Education in Low-income Countries

Daniel A. Wagner, Nathan M. Castillo and Suzanne Grant Lewis (Eds)

https://doi.org/10.11647/obp.0256

(An)Archive
Childhood, Memory, and the Cold War

Mnemo ZIN, Zsuzsanna Millei, Nelli Piattoeva and Iveta Silova (Eds)

https://doi.org/10.11647/obp.0383

Play in a Covid Frame
Everyday Pandemic Creativity in a Time of Isolation

Anna Beresin and Julia Bishop (Eds)

https://doi.org/10.11647/obp.0326

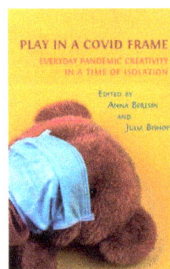

www.ingramcontent.com/pod-product-compliance
Lightning Source LLC
Chambersburg PA
CBHW051441270326
41932CB00025B/3392

* 9 7 8 1 8 0 5 1 1 4 6 6 6 *